ALACHUA COUNTY

BLACK BOOK

ACCOUNTS OF ENSLAVED PEOPLE DISCOVERED IN ANCIENT RECORDS

Coleen DeGroff

Alachua County Black Book
Accounts of Enslaved People Discovered in Ancient Records
by Coleen DeGroff

1. HIS036120 **HISTORY**/United States/State & Local/South
(AL, AR, FL, GA, KY, LA, MS, NC, SC, TN, VA, WV)
2. SOC054000 **SOCIAL SCIENCE**/Slavery
3. HIS056000 **HISTORY**/African American & Black

ISBN (hardcover): 979-8-88636-063-9
ISBN (paperback): 979-8-88636-055-4
ISBN (ebook): 979-8-88636-056-1

Library of Congress Control Number: 2025914336

Cover design by Lewis Agrell
Author headshot photography by Adrienne Fletcher

Printed in the United States of America

Authority Publishing
13389 Folsom Blvd #300-256
Folsom, CA 95630
800-877-1097
www.AuthorityPublishing.com

Dedicated to Curt,
For always believing in me

ABOUT THIS BOOK

Buried deep in public records, people enslaved in Alachua County Florida through the end of the Civil War appear in legal documents such as bills of sale, wills, mortgages, and more. Because they were considered personal property, enslaved people appear in these records along with other personal property such as cattle, horses, and pigs.

The names of the enslaved who were bought, sold, willed, and used as collateral for loans by planters and other enslavers appear in the vast majority of these documents. Their monetary value is often mentioned. Many of the enslaved were children. Some were as young as infants. With very few exceptions none of the enslaved people in these records appear with last names.

Alachua County Florida was home to dozens of plantations, many of which produced Sea Island cotton. A valuable cash crop which powered the Southern economy, Sea Island cotton was very labor intensive.

Many planters from South Carolina and Georgia uprooted their families to move to the area to establish plantations, bringing the people they enslaved along with them.[1]

"In East Florida, most slaves lived in Alachua and Marion counties, where plantations also produced significant cotton crops. The number of slaves on plantations varied from small plantations (less than 500 acres and fewer than 20 slaves to large plantations that ranged in slave populations from 20 to over 200."[2]

The earliest document I discovered about slavery in Alachua County in these ancient public records dates to 1815 when Florida was still under Spanish rule. Don Francisco Roman Sanchez petitioned the Governor of East Florida for a 4,000-acre tract of land by the Santa Fe River that he could settle on with his family and the people he enslaved to raise cattle and pursue other farming interests. His petition was granted (Alachua County Ancient Records, Deed Book B page 312).

The last document I found that mentions slavery in Alachua County was an April 11, 1865 foreclosure on a mortgage where an enslaved man named John was used as collateral for a loan. The loan was not paid back. As a result, John was to be seized and sold at auction so that the money could be paid back (Johanna Burgheim vs Abraham and C. Fredenburg, Alachua County Ancient Records, Chancery Order Book A pages 186-187).

Decades ago, Alachua County Florida made a concerted effort to digitize their ancient public records, with dozens of volunteers stepping up through the years to transcribe these handwritten documents to make them more readable. Both the transcriptions and images of the original documents can be viewed online and searched by keyword.

Unless you are a historian or an academician or an avid genealogist there's a really good chance you wouldn't even know these records existed.

I am not a historian, or an academician, or an avid genealogist. I am a writer and a retired real estate agent who lives in a leafy subdivision built upon the grounds of an old cotton plantation on the outskirts of a Southern college town. During the summer of the George Floyd protests, there was an effort to get "Plantation" dropped from the name of the neighborhood because of the history of the land. Efforts to change the name failed. But they did lead me to want to learn more about where I live.

I became a volunteer docent at one of the last antebellum homes in the area built by enslaved craftsmen. The home and its surrounding 1500 acres was once the site of a Sea Island cotton plantation worked by dozens of enslaved laborers -- lands that are now the site of the neighborhood where I live. During a conversation with local historian Karen Kirkman I learned about Alachua County's public records that dated back centuries and that the names of enslaved people appear in many of these documents. That started my mission to wade through these records to learn more.

Alachua County Black Book is a compilation of the accounts of enslaved people as well as their enslavers as told through excerpts of ancient public documents dating from 1815-1865. Notations at the end of each entry direct readers where they can access the full records, including images of the handwritten originals. A book index containing names of the enslaved, their enslavers, and other parties mentioned in these documents is also provided to make the information more accessible.

This book is not an official record. It is a compilation of ancient public documents about the half century of slavery in Alachua County that I uncovered during my search. There may very well be more. Any errors or omissions are unintentional.

Alachua County Black Book is written in honor of the enslaved people who lived and toiled and helped to build our country before their names and stories are lost to time and memory. You are not forgotten.

DISCLAIMER: In order to preserve the authenticity of the time period in which they were written, the document excerpts appearing in this book contain the odd spellings, missing punctuation, and random capitalizations from the original documents as they appear in the transcriptions. For ease of reading, line breaks have been added to break up the text.

1810's

Don Francisco Roman Sanchez petitions the Governor to grant him 4,000 acres of vacant land (Translation): "To the Governor: Don Francisco Roman Sanchez native and inhabitant of this Province with close respect to your Lordship, says, that on the South part of the River known by the name of Santafe, about Ten miles to the westward of the Alachua Road to St. Marys, there is a great quantity of vacant Land, adapted for cultivation and raising of stock to which he intends dedicating himself for the purpose of increasing the same, and as the petitioner has not obtained any concession of Land, on which he can establish himself as he wishes, with all his family and slaves, he therefore prays your Lordship will be pleased grant him four thousand Acres of Land at said place, bounded on the North by said River Santafe, and on the other sides by Vacant Lands, which quantity of Land are necessary not only on account of the number of Negroes he owns, but also for the raising of stock, and many other purposes useful to a planter - A favour which he hopes to merit from the goodness of your Lordship

St. Augustine Florida Dec'r 18th 1815 - Francis R. Sanchez

St. Augustine

In consideration of the Urgent necessity there is of fomenting in this Province, by all possible means the raising black cattle, on account of the great scarcity thereof, which is already noted, let it be granted to the Petitioner the four thousand Acres of Land in the place solicited by him, without injury to a third person, and for his security, let a certified copy of this Petition and decree be issued to him by the Secretarys office"

December 18, 1815
St. Augustine, FL
Recorded in Archives of East Florida March 23, 1836
Recorded in Alachua County April 4, 1840
From Alachua County Ancient Records
Deed Book B page 312

Don Jose Simion Sanchez petitions the Governor to grant him 2,000 acres of vacant land for a plantation (Translation): "His Excellency the Governor - Don Jose Simion Sanchez a native and inhabitant of this province to your Excellency respectfully showeth, that he wishes to employ himself and slaves in Agriculture forming a plantation, and as for this object he needs a grant of Land of good quality to which he considers himself intitled in virtue of the merits and services he has performed in the year 1812 against the disloyal inhabitants of the Province, and in 1817 Against those who took possession of Amelia Island, the particulars of which he does not state they being well known to the Government - Therefore he prays that your Excellency will be pleased to grant him Two thousand Acres of Land, on Santafe River, bounded on the West by Lands of Don Francisco Roman Sanchez and on the other side by said River, which number of Acres are to him absolutely necessary not only for the establishment of a good plantation, but for raising of stock, to which he intends dedicating himself, which gifts he hopes to merit from the goodness of your Excellency - St Augustine January 7th 1818

St Augustine January 12th 1818 - Grant to the Petitioner the Two thousand Acres of Land, which he selects, without injury to a third person, as it is well known to the Government, the services which he says he has rendered, and for his security let there be given him, from the Secretarys Office a certified copy of this memorial and decree in the usual form"

Recorded April 4, 1840
City of St. Augustine, Territory of Florida
From Alachua County Ancient Records
Deed Book B pages 315-316

1820's

Joseph Chaldeas to Gad Humphreys for $300: "Know all men by these presents that I Joseph Chaldeas of Florida have sold for the consideration of three Hundred dollars this day in hand received to Gad Humphreys of said Territory **a Negro Woman Slave named Phillis & her issue** now or late in the Creek Nation of Indians to have and to hold to the said Humphreys for his use and behoof the said property hereby warranting the full right and title to the same against all claims whatsoever."

June 26, 1828
Territory of Florida, Alachua County
From Alachua County Ancient Records
Deed Book B page 078

John M. Hanson to Gad Humphreys for $200: "Know all men by these presents that I John M. Hanson have this day bargained, sold and delivered to Gad Humphreys **a Negro Woman Slave named Pamella** now in the Seminole Nation of Indians for and in consideration of Two Hundred dollars to me in hand paid by said Humphreys."

May 28, 1828
Territory of Florida, St. Johns County
From Alachua County Ancient Records
Deed Book B page 077

Joseph Hernandez to Co'l Gad Humphreys for $325: "Know all men by these presents that I Joseph Hernandez of the County aforesaid for and in consideration of the Sum of Three hundred & Twenty five dollars money of the United States of America to me in hand paid the receipt whereof I do hereby acknowledge. Have granted bargained and sold, and by these presents do grant bargain & sell and deliver unto Co'l Gad Humphreys now in the Territory of Florida aforesaid his heirs and assigns a certain **Negro Boy named Toney about fourteen years of age**. A native of the City of St Augustine Territory aforesaid To have & to hold the said bargained property to him the said Gad Humphreys his heirs & assigns forever"

December 28, 1829
Territory of Florida, St Johns County
From Alachua County Ancient Records
Deed Book B page 135

John A. Kennedy to marry Charlotte Rochell recognizing the property she owns coming into the marriage: "This Indenture made this the fifth of February one thousand eight hundred and twenty four between John A. Kennedy of the Town of Camden in the District of Kershaw and State aforesaid of the one part, and Thomas Starke of the District and State aforesaid Trustee of Charlotte Rochells, of the other part; Witnesseth that whereas a marriage is shortly to be had and solemnized between the said John A. Kennedy and Charlotte Rochell of Fairfield District; And whereas the said Charlotte Rochells is seized and possessed of the following negroes and other property hereafter mentioned and specified that is to say, **Gabriel, a Negro man, Pratilda, Nelly, Serena, and Stephen, the**

two last being children of the said Nelly, which said property the said John A. Kennedy is anxious to settle on the said Charlotte Rochell his said intended wife and the heirs of her body forever is the said marriage should be and made solemnized as aforesaid. It is therefore covenanted and agreed by these presents between the said John A. Kennedy and the said Thomas Starke Trustee of the said Charlotte Rochell in manner following that is to say, that said John A. Kennedy for himself, his heirs, Executors, and Administrators have & do hereby covenant & agree with the said Thomas Starke as the Trustee of the said Charlotte Rochell that in case the said marriage should be had and solemnized as aforesaid that he the said John A. Kennedy will by good & sufficient conveyance or conveyances in law settle the whole of the property above mentioned upon the said Charlotte Rochell in manner following, that is to say, first upon himself and the said Charlotte Rochell during the time of their natural lives and if the said John A. Kennedy should die first, then upon the said Charlotte during her natural life and after her death upon heirs of her body lawfully begotten and if she should die without issue, as aforesaid then upon the next of Kin and heirs at law of the said Charlotte Rochell & I do hereby bind myself my heirs, Executors and administrators in case the said marriage should be had & solemnized to make and execute this said marrige settlement and settle the whole of the property above mentioned upon the said Charlotte Rochell in manner and form above mentioned and it is the express agreement and understanding of the parties aforesaid that no part of the above mentioned property shall at any time be subject to His debts, contracts, or encumbrances of the said John A. Kennedy the aforesaid marriage about to be had and solemnized to the cautionary not with standing"

February 5, 1824
South Carolina, Fairfax District
From Alachua County Ancient Records
Deed Record A pages 057-058

Moses Elias Levy to Joseph Delevante as collateral for a loan of 2,110 pounds Sterling: "This Agreement made the fifteenth day of March in the year one thousand eight hundred and twenty seven, Between Moses Elias Of Alachua, east Florida, Planter now residing at No 1 Row Knights Bridge in the County of Middlesix England of the one part and Joseph Delevante of No 3 Kimbolton Place Bromton in the County of Middlesix England of the other part. Whereas the said Moses Elias Levy is possesed of or entitled unto nineteen thousand two hundred acres of land being part and parcel of a certain tract of land, situate and being in the County formerly called Saint Johns now called Alachua in East Florida aforesaid and herein after more particular discribed & also the said Moses Elias Levy is possessed of or entitled unto other nineteen thousand Two hundred acres of land and also to nineteenth part of a tract of land containing fourteen thousand five hundred five hundred acres situate and being on the west side of the St. Johns river in E Florida aforesaid. Under and by virtue of a certain contract or agreement. But the conveyance thereof have not been made and executed the whole of which amounting to about fifty one thousand five hundred fifty acres subject nevertheless to the charge and condition hereinafter mentioned in common with the premises herein after discribed and the said Moses Elias Levy is also possessed of or entitled unto one undivided moity of and in twenty thousand acres of land part and parcel of a certain tract or parcil of land containing twenty five thousand acres in the Teritory of E Florida aforesaid and herein after more particular discribed subject nevertheless to the charge herein after mentioned - In common with the premises herein after discribed and the Moses Elias Levy is also possessed of or entitled unto one undivided moiety or half [unreadable] of and in several tract or parcels of ground in E. Florida aforesaid containing together about forty nine thousand eight hundred acres and herein after more particularly discribed, the whole of which property is subject to two different liens or Mortgages (that is to say) the undivided moiety of the twenty thousand acres and the and the forty nine thousand eight hundred acres last mentioned are subject to a certain lien or Mortgage thereon for the sum of about ten thousand dollars but of which said sum the said Moses Elias Levy is chargable with and liable to payment of above three thousand five hundred dollars after which the one undivided moiety of the twenty thousand acres and the forty nine thousand Eight hundred acres last mentioned together with the first mentioned three parcils of land amounting to about fifty one thousand four hundred and fifty acres are subject to an additional lien or Mortgage under certain conditions for the additional sum of fifty thousand pounds Sterling english money will more fully appear by the mortgage deed executed in Paris, the capital of France on the the tenth day of January in the year one thousand eight hundred and twenty six by the said Moses Elias Levy in favor of Serephina Chauveteau a widow and whereas the said Moses Elias Levy being indebted to the said Joseph Delevante for the sum of two thousand one hundred and ten pounds Sterling proposes to secure the said debt with the payment of the anual interest of five per Ct. Per Annum and to which the said Joseph Delevante consents in the manner herein after contained

Now this agreement witnesseth that for and in consideration of the sum of two thousand one hundred and pounds Sterling to him the said Moses Elias Levy well and truly paid the Receipt whereof the said Moses Elias Levy doth hereby acknowledge and thereof and there from the same and every part thereof doth acquit release and discharge the said Moses Elias Levy hath granted bargained, sold and aliened released and confirmed and by these presents doth grant bargain, sell alien release and confirm unto the said Joseph Delevante his heirs and assigns forever, all those nineteen thousand two hundred acres of land being part and parcil of a certain tract of land situate and being in the County formally of St. Johns in East Florida afore aid in that part of this County Known as and now called the Alachua County which said tract of land was by grant bearing date the twenty second day of December One thousand eight hundred & seventeen granted by the Spanish Government to Fernando dela Maza Arredondo son and Joseph Arredondo by the name and discription of Fernando Dela Maza Arredondo and Son, and by them granted and conveyed to the said Moses Elias Levy in and by a certain Instrument bearing date the thirteenth day of July One thousand eight hundred

& twenty four. And all those other nineteen thousand two hundred acres of land and nineteenth part of and in a tract of land containing about fourteen thousand five hundred acres situate and being on the west side of the St. Johns River in East Florida aforesaid and to which the said Moses Elias Levy is entitled under and by virtue of a certain contract of agreement entered into with the said Fernando Dela Maza Arredondo, But the conveyance hath not yet been made and executed, and also an undivided moiety of and in twenty thousand acres of land part and parcil of a certain parcil of land consisting of twenty five thousand acres which were originally granted to Philip R. Young by concession or grant bearing date the eleventh day of February One thousand eight hundred & seventeen and which were confirmed to the said Philip R. Young by a Royal title or grant in absolute property bearing date the twenty second day of February One thousand eight hundred and seventeen which said concession and Royal title were made under the Authority of the King of Spain by Don Jose Coppinger then Governor of East Florida eight thousand acres thereof being situate on the west side of a place called long pond about forty miles south of lake Young on the west side of the River St. Johns aforesaid. And twelve thousand acres residue thereof being situate on the Lake named second and on the west side of said Lake in East Florida aforesaid and which said twenty thousand acres of land was sold and transferred to the said Philip R. Young to Mr William Travers. Conveyed to the said Moses Elias Levy by indenture bearing date sixth day of August one thousand eight hundred and twenty four. Subject nevertheless in common with the premises herein after discribed to the lean or charge before mentioned and also undivided moiety of and in the following certain tract or parcil of land (that is to say) of and in ten thousand four hundred acres of land being part and parcil of a tract containing of fifteen thousand acres of land situate and being on the River Saint Johns about twelve miles south of Lake George in East Florida aforesaid which said tract of land was originally granted to Don Antoinia Huesta in absolute property by concession bearing date on or about the the about the fifteenth day of September One thousand eight hundred and seventeen by the said Don Jose Coppinger and which was afterward sold transferred and conveyed by the said Antonia Huesta to Juan De Entralgo, and also of in one other tract or parcil of land containing four thousand acres situate and being on Black Creek in East Florida aforesaid which said tract or parcil of land was originally granted to Fernando de la Maza Arredondo Jun'r by a grant or concession bearing date the twentieth day of March one thousand eight hundred and seventeen by the said Don Jose Coppinger and afterwards confirmed to the said Don Jose Coppinger and afterwards confirmed to the said Fernandes de la Maza Arredondo Jun'r by a Royal title or grant in absolute property bearing date - ninth day of August one thousand eight hundred and twenty two Also made by the said Don Jose Coppinger which said last mentioned tract or parcil of land was sold and conveyed by the said Fernandes de la Maza Arredondo Jun'r to the said Juan de Entralgo, and also of and in twenty thousand acres of land, part and parcil of a certain tract or parcil of land consisting of twenty two thousand acres of land situate and being in Alachua County, at a place called Cuscowella and Cochala in East Florida aforesaid which said tract of land last mentioned was granted to George F. Clark by a Concession and grant in absolute property bearing date on or about the seventeenth day of December one thousand eight hundred & seventeen made the said Don Jose Coppinger and which last mentioned tract or parcil of land was transferred and conveyed to the said Juan de Entralgo by the said George F. Clarke and also of and in one other tract or parcil of land containing one thousand acres situate and being at a place called the Waterpen in East Florida aforesaid which said last mentioned tract of land was granted to the said Juan de Entralgo in absolute property by Royal title or absolute grant bearing date on or about the fifteenth day of November one thousand eight hundred and seventeen by the said Don Jose Coppinger and also of and in one other tract or parcil of land containing two thousand acres situate in a place called Seder Swamp in East Florida aforesaid which said last mentioned tract of land was granted to the said Juan de Entralgo in absolute property by a Royal Title or absolute grant bearing date fifteenth day of November one thousand eight hundred and seventeen made by the said Don Jose Coppinger, and also of and in four thousand acres of land situate and being about five miles of Spring Garden in east Florida aforesaid

11

which said four thousand acres of land together with four thousand acres of land before mentioned are part and parcel consisting of ten thousand acres granted to Fernando de la Maza Arredondo , by concession or grant bearing date the twentieth day of March one thousand eight hundred and seventeen and were sold and conveyed by the said Fernando de la Maza Arredondo to the said Don Juan de Entralgo to the said Moses Elias Levy by and Indenture bearing date the sixth day of August one thousand eight hundred and twenty four together with all the crops and produce of the said several tracts or parcels of land and all the slaves and personal property thereon and all houses out houses Edifices Buildings trees, woods underwoods commons ways paths passages, waters, water courses, profities commodities advantages privaleges heredetriments Rights members and appurtenances and the revision and revisions Remainder and Remainders Rents issues and profit

And also of an in four thousand acres of land situate on the River Saint Johns at a place called the English big Spring at about twenty five miles south of Saint Georges Lake in East Florida aforesaid, and one of a tract or parcel of land granted to Don Pedro Miranda by a concession *** bearing date on or about the sixteenth day of September one thousand eight hundred and seventeen made by the said Don Jose Coppinger and which were confirmed to the said Don Pedro Miranda by royal title of absolute grant bearing date on or about the eleventh day of April One thousand eight hundred and twenty one made also by the said Don Jose Coppinger which said four thousand acres of land were sold and transferred by the said Pedro Miranda to the said Juan de Entralgo. And of and in three thousand four hundred acres of land situated or near the place called the English Big Spring in about twenty five miles south from St. Georges Lake on the River St. Johns in E. Florida aforesaid which said three thousand four hundred acres are part and parcil of land granted to the aforesaid Don Pedro Merranda by the concession and Royal title made to the said Don Pedro Merranda as herein last before mentioned and which were sold and transferred by the said Pedro Merranda to the said Juan de Entralgo. And also of an in one other tract or Parcil of land containing one thousand acres situate on the E. Side of the St. Johns River in East Florida aforesaid at a place called Rolls Town which said last mentioned Tract was granted to the said Juan D. Entralgo by a concession bearing date on or about the seventeenth day of December One thousand eight hundred and sixteen by the said Don Jose Coppinger (which are referance to the said several concessions or grants in the Office of the public Archives of East Florida aforesaid now in the City of St. Augustine will more fully and at large appear. And which said several tract or parcils of land containing in the whole forty nine thousand eight hundred acres were with the Appurtenances there unto belonging sold and conveyed by the said Don Juan de Entralgo to the said Moses Elias Levy by an Indenture bearing date the sixth day of August one thousand eight hundred and twenty four Together with all the crops and produce of the said several tracts or parcils of land **and all of the slaves and personal property thereon**. And all houses and out houses Edifices Buildings trees woods, underwoods commons ways, paths, passages waters watercourses, profits commodities advantages preveleges hereditriments Rights members and appurtenances, whatever to the aforesaid several tract pieces and parcels of land belonging or in any wise appurtening and the revision and revisions, remainder and remainders, Rents issues and profits thereof and of every kind of him the said Moses Elias Levy of in and to the said tracts parcils of land and premises herein beforementioned and intended to be hereby granted and released and every of them and every part thereof. To have and to hold the said several tract and parcels of land and undivided moieties of tracts and parcil of land and premises herein before mentioned and intended to be hereby granted and released with their and every of their appurtenances unto the said Joseph Delevante his heirs and assigns forever subject nevertheless to the charge or incumberance herein before mentioned and also to the provisions conditions for the redemption of the said premises as herein after contained, provided allways and these presents are upon this condition and it is the true intent and meaning hereof and of the parties hereto that if the said Moses Elias Levy his heirs Executors and Administrators or assigns, do and shall from time to time on the fifteenth day of September and on the fifteenth day of March in each and every year during the space of six years from the day of the date hereof well and truly pay or cause to be paid to the said Joseph Delevante his heirs executors administrators or assigns at London in the County of Middlesix aforesaid without any deduction defalcation or abatement whatsoever interest on the said sum of two thousand one hundred and ten pounds Sterling at and after the rate of five per cent per annum and also shall and will on or before the fifteenth day of March which will be in the year one thousand eight hundred and thirty three well and truly pay or cause to be paid the full and whole sum of two thousand one hundred and ten pounds Sterling without and deduction or abatement whatsoever as before mentioned there and in such case the said Joseph Delevante his heirs Executors Administrators and assigns shall and will at any time or times after such payment being made as aforesaid at the request cost and charges of the said Moses Elias Levy his heirs Executors administrators or assigns, re conveyed and re assume all and singular the tracts of land hereditrements and premises hereby granted and released or intended so to be with all and every their appurtenances, unto the said Moses Elias Levy his heirs and assigns forever as he or they shall by writing under his or their hands and seals direct and appoint free from all incumberances whatsoever to be made done or committed by the said Joseph Delevante his heirs executors administrators or assigns or any other person or persons whomsoever claiming or to claim under him or them or any of them so as for the making or doing thereof the said Joseph Delevante his heirs executors administrators or assigns be not compeled or compelable to go or travel from his or their place or places of abode. And the said Moses Elias Levy for himself his heirs executors and administrators and for every one of them, doth covenant promise grant and agree to and with the said Joseph Delevante his executors administrators and assigns in manner following (that is to say) that he the said Moses Elias Levy his heirs executors or administrators or someone of them shall and will well and truly pay or cause to be paid unto the said Joseph Delevante his heirs executors administrators or assigns the interest on the said sum of two thousand one hundred and ten pounds Sterling at the rate of five per cent per annum, and the days and times and places before mentioned and also the said full and whole sum of two thousand one hundred and ten pounds Sterling on the said fifteenth day of March one thousand eight hundred and thirty three without any deduction or abatement as foresaid according to the true intent and meaning of these presents. And also that he the said Moses Elias Levy now is lawfully absolutely possessed of or intitled unto the tract and parcels of land herein before mentioned and intended to be hereby granted and released (subject as aforesaid) and now hath in him good rights full power and lawful and absolute authority to grant release and convey the same in manner and form aforesaid and according to the true intent and meaning of these presents and further that it shall and may be law full to and for the said Joseph Delevante his heirs executors and assigns from and after default shall be made in payment of the sum of two thousand one hundred and ten pounds Sterling and interest at the rate and times aforesaid, Contrary to the form and effect of the aforesaid proviso and covenant for payment of the same peaceably and quietly to enter in or to have hold ocupy or possess and enjoy all and singular the tracts and parcils of land hereby intended to be released and conveyed with appurtenances and all and singular the slaves crops produce and property thereon found and take the Rents issues and profits thereof and of every part thereof to and for him and their own use and benefit. And also in case default shall be made or happen to be made in two half yearly payments of Interest at the rate time and places aforesaid it shall and may be lawful for the said Joseph Delevante his heirs executors administrators and assigns immediately to demand payment of the said sum of two thousand one hundred and ten pounds Sterling and also interest then due thereon notwithstanding the term of six years for which the said sum of money is hereby intended to be advanced shall not be there expended or near expiring and in case of the non payment thereof to enter and take possession of the said tracts or parcils of land and premises in manner and form herein before mentioned and further that the said Moses Elias Levy his heirs and assigns and all every other person or persons having or claiming any estate right title or interest on to or out of the said tracts of land and premises hereby intended to be granted and released shall and will from time to time after default shall happen to be made in payment of the said sum of two thousand one hundred and ten pound Sterling and interest aforesaid Contrary to the true intent and meaning of these presents at the request costs and charges of the said Joseph Delevante his heirs executors administrators or assigns make do and execute or cause and procure to be made done and executed all and every such further and Other acts deeds conveyances and assurances in law whatsoever for the further better more perfect and more absolute granting conveying assuring and confirming the said tract and parcils of land and promise with appurtenances unto and to the use and behoof of the said Joseph Delevante his heirs and assigns as he or they or her or their Council in Law shall be lawfully advised devised or required And it is also declared and agreed by and between the said parties of presents that untill default shall happen to be made in payment of the sum of two thousand one hundred and ten pounds Sterling and interest or some part thereof contrary to the intent and meaning of the aforesaid proviso and covenant for payment thereof it shall and may be lawfull for the said Moses Elias Levy his heirs and assigns peaceably and quietly to hold occupy possess and enjoy the same tract of land and premises and every part and parcil thereof and to Receive the Rents and issues thereof and profits for his and their own use and benefit without any let or denial whatsoever of him the said Joseph Delevante his heir or assigns or any other person or persons whatsoever And further it is hereby also agreed and declared by and Between the said parties that whereas one of the considerations of the mortgage granted by the said Moses Elias Levy to Seraphina Cheauveteau as aforesaid for the sum of fifty thousand francs as appears by the Indenture dated as aforesaid the thirteenth day of January one thousand eight hundred and twenty six is that at it shall and may be lawful for the said Moses Elias Levy to borrow and take up at interest any sum or sums of money not exceeding in the whole the sum of one hundred thousand in addition to the one borrowed of fifty thousand francs as aforesaid on the security of the said tracts of land and premises hereby intended to be released and conveyed which securities or sureties when so executed shall rank with and be considered equal to the on granted as foresaid in favor of the said Seraphina Chauventeau which shall enjoy no preferance or priority whatsoever over those which may thereafter be executed as foresaid

It is therefore Covenanted and agreed, Between the present and Contracting parties Moses Elias Levy aforesaid on the one part and Joseph Delevante aforesaid on the other, that the said sum of two thousand one hundred and ten pounds Sterling secured by this agreement as aforesaid shall rank with and enjoy to all intents and purposes the same priority as the one granted to Seraphina Chaventeau as aforesaid and which in no wise shall claim any preference or priority whatever and as it is further agreed and covenanted that the said Moses Elias Levy shall not grant any other mortgage upon the land aforesaid with the same priority now granted to the said Joseph Delevante for the sum of two thousand one hundred and ten pounds Sterling as aforesaid. Without the full consent and permission of the said Joseph Delevante, well understood that this restriction is merely Confined to the land herein intended to be released and conveyed and not the personal property, Negroes and cattle which at any time may be found on the lands and premises aforesaid"

March 15, 1827
From Alachua County Ancient Records
Deed Book A pages 023-039
See also Deed Book A pages 001-015
See also Deed Book B pages 140-153

Moses Elias Levy in East Florida, planter, now residing in County of Middlesex England to Joseph Delevante in County of Middlesex England as collateral for a loan of 2,110 pounds sterling with interest: "This Indenture made the fifteenth day of March in the year one thousand eight hundred and twenty seven. Between Moses Elias Levy of Alachua in East Florida planter, now residing at No 1

Park Row Knights Bridge in the County of Middlesex England, of the one part, and Joseph Delevante of No 3 Kimboton Place Brompton in the said County of Middlesex England of the other part, Whereas the said Moses Elias Levy is possessed of or entitled unto nineteen thousand two hundred acres of land being part and parcel of a certain tract of land situate and being in the County formerly called St Johns, now called Alachua in East Florida aforesaid, and herein after more particularly described and also the said Moses Elias Levy is possessed of or entitled to other nineteen thousand two hundred acres of land, and also to nine tenth parts of and in a tract of land containing fourteen thousand five hundred acres Situated and being on the West side of Saint Johns River in East Florida aforesaid under and by virtue of certain contracts or agreements, but the conveyance thereof have not yet been made and executed, the whole of which amounting to about fifty one thousand four hundred and fifty acres subject nevertheless to the charge and condition herein after mentioned in common with the premises hereinafter described, and the said Moses Elias Levy is also possessed of or entitled unto one undivided moiety of and in twenty thousand acres of land part and parcel of a certain tract or parcel of land containing twenty five thousand acres in the Territory of East Florida aforesaid and hereinafter more particularly described, Subject nevertheless to the charge hereinafter mentioned, in common with the premises hereinafter described, and the said Moses Elias Levy is also possessed of or entitled unto one undivided moiety or half part of and in several tracts or parcels of ground in East Florida aforesaid, containing together about forty nine thousand eight hundred acres, and hereinafter more particularly described, the whole of which property is subject to two different liens or mortgages (that is to say,) the undivided Moieties of the twenty thousand acres and the forty nine thousand eight hundred acres last mentioned are subject to a certain lien or mortgage thereon, for the sum of about ten thousand dollars, but of which said Sum the said Moses Elias Levy is charged with, and liable to the payment of about three thousand five hundred dollars, after which the one undivided moiety of the twenty thousand acres, and forty nine thousand eight hundred acres last mentioned, together with the first mentioned three parcels of land amounting to about fifty one thousand four hundred and fifty are subject to an additional lien or mortgage under certain conditions for the additional sum of fifty thousand francs money of France, or about two thousand pounds Sterling, English money as will fully appear by the mortgage Deed executed in Paris the capital of France on the thirtieth day of January in the year one thousand eight hundred and twenty six, by the said Moses Elias Levy in favor of Seraphina Chauvetau Widow, and whereas the said Moses Elias Levy being indebted to the said Joseph Delevante for the sum of Two thousand one hundred and ten pounds Sterling, proposes to secure the said debt with the payment of the annual interest of five per cent per annum, and to which the said Joseph Delevante consents in the manner hereinafter contained,

Now this agreement Witnesseth that for and in consideration of the sum of two thousand one hundred and ten pounds Sterling, to him the said Moses Elias Levy well and truly paid the receipt whereof the said Moses Elias Levy doth hereby acknowledge and thereof and therefrom the same and every part thereof doth aquit, release, and discharge the said Joseph Delevante his heirs, Executors and administrators, and every one of them by these presents the said Moses Elias Levy hath granted, bargained, Sold, aliened, released, and confirmed, and by these presents doth grant, bargain, sell, alien, release and confirm unto the said Joseph Delevante his heirs and assigns forever, all those nineteen thousand two hundred acres of land being part and parcel of that certain tract of land situate and being in the County formerly of Saint John in East Florida aforesaid, and in that part of the said County known as and usually now called the Alachua County, which tract of land was by grant bearing date the twenty second day of December one thousand eight hundred and seventeen granted by the Spanish Government to Fernando Dela Maza Arredondo Senior and Joseph Arredondo by the name and description of Fernando dela Maza Arredondo and Son, and by them granted and conveyed to the said Moses Elias Levy in and by a certain Indenture bearing date the thirteenth day of July one thousand eight hundred and twenty four, and these other nineteen thousand two hundred acres of land, and nine tenth parts of and in a tract of land containing about fourteen thousand five hundred acres, situate and being on the west side of Saint John's River in East Florida aforesaid, and to which the said Moses Elias Levy is entitled under and by virtue of a certain contract of agreements entered into with the said Fernando dela Maza Arredondo, but the conveyances of which have not yet been made and executed, and also an undivided moiety of and in twenty thousand acres of land part and parcel of a certain parcel of land consisting of twenty five thousand acres which were originally grant Philip R. Young by a concession or grant bearing date the eleventh day of February one thousand eight hundred and seventeen, and which were confirmed to the said Philip R. Young by a Royal title or grant in absolute property bearing date the twenty second day of February, one thousand eight hundred and seventeen, which concession and royal title were made under the authority of the King of Spain by Don Jose Coppinger then Governor of East Florida, eight thousand acres thereof being situate on the west side of a place called Long pond about forty miles south of Lake George, on the west side of the River Saint John aforesaid, and twelve thousand acres residue being situated on the Lake named Second and on the west side of the said Lake in East Florida aforesaid, and which said twenty thousand acres of land were Sold and transferred by the said Philip R. Young to Mr. William Travers, and by the said William Travers conveyed to the said Moses Elias Levy by Indenture bearing date the Sixth day of August one thousand eight hundred and twenty four (Subject nevertheless in common with the premises hereinafter described to the lien or charge before mentioned) and also an undivided moiety of and in the following certain tracts or parcels of land (that is to say) of and in ten thousand four hundred acres of land being part and parcel of a tract consisting of fifteen thousand acres of land situate and being on the River Saint John about twelve miles south of the Lake George in East Florida aforesaid, which said tract of land was originally granted to Don Antonia Huertas in absolute property by a concession bearing date on or about the fifteenth day of September one thousand eight hundred and seventeen by the said Don Jose Coppinger and which was afterwards sold transfered and conveyed by the said Antonia Huertas to Don Juan de Entralgo and also of and in one other tract or parcel of land containing four thousand acres situated and being on Black Creek in East Florida aforesaid, which said tract or parcel of land was originally granted to Fernando dela Maza Arredondo Junior by a grant or concession bearing date the twentieth day of March one thousand eight hundred and seventeen, by the said Don Jose Coppinger, and afterwards confirmed to the said Fernando dela Maza Arredondo Junior by Royal title or as grant in absolute property bearing date the ninth day of August one thousand eight hundred and twenty two also made by the said Jose Coppinger which said last mentioned tract or parcel of land was sold and conveyed by Fernando dela Maza Arredondo to the said Juan de Entralgo, and also of and in twenty thousand acres of land part and parcel of a certain tract of land consisting of twenty two thousand acres of land situate and being in Alachua County at places called Cascowilla and Chachala in East Florida aforesaid which said tracts of of land last mentioned was granted to George I.F. Clark by a concession and grant in absolute property bearing date on or about the seventeenth day of December one thousand eight hundred and seventeen made by the said Don Jose Coppinger, and which last mentioned tract or parcel of land was transfered and convey to the said Juan de Entralgo by the said George F. Clark, and also of and in one other tract or parcel of land containing one thousand acres situate and being at a place called Water Penn in East Florida aforesaid, which said last mentioned tract of land was granted to the said Juan de Entralgo in absolute property by Royal title or absolute grant, bearing date on or about the fifteenth day of November one thousand eight hundred and seventeen, by the said Don Jose Coppinger, and also of and in one other tract or parcel of land containing two thousand acres situate in place called Cedar Swamp in East Florida aforesaid, which said last mentioned tract of land was granted to Juan de Entralgo in absolute property by a Royal title, or absolute grant, bearing date the fifteenth day of November one thousand eight hundred and seventeen, made by the aforesaid Don Jose Coppinger, and also of and in four thousand acres of land Situate and being about five miles from Spring Garden in East Florida aforesaid, which said four thousand acres of land together with four thousand acres of land before mentioned are part and parcel of a tract or parcel consisting of ten thousand acres granted to Fernando de la Maza Arredondo by concession or grant bearing date the twentieth day of March one thousand eight hundred and Seventeen, and were sold and conveyed by the said Fernando de la Maza Arredondo to the said Don Juan de Entralgo, and also of and in four thousand acres of land situate on the River Saint John at a place called the English Big Spring at about twenty five miles south from Saint Georges Lake in East Florida aforesaid, and are part of a tract or parcel of land granted to Don Pedro Miranda by a concession or grant bearing date on or about the Sixteenth day of September one thousand eight hundred and seventeen, made by the said Don Jose Coppinger, and which were confirmed to the said Don Pedro Miranda by Royal title or absolute grant bearing date on or about the eleventh day of April one thousand eight hundred and twenty one, made also by the said Don Jose Coppinger, which said four thousand acres of land were sold and transfered by the said Pedro Miranda to the said Juan de Entralgo, and of and in three thousand four hundred acres of land situate at or near a place called the English Big Spring, about twenty five miles south from Saint Georges Lake on the River Saint John in East Florida aforesaid which said three thousand four hundred acres of land are part and parcel of land granted to the aforesaid Don Pedro Miranda by the concession and Royal title made to the said Don Pedro Miranda as is herein before last mentioned, and were sold and transfered by the said Pedro Miranda to the said Juan de Entralgo, and also of and in one other tract or parcel of land containing one thousand acres Situate on the East side of Saint Johns River in East Florida aforesaid, at a place called Rolls town which said last mentioned tract was granted to the said Juan de Entraglo by a concession bearing date on or about the seventeenth day of December one thousand eight and sixteen by the said Don Jose Coppinger (which on reference to the said several Concessions or grants in the office of the Public Archives of East Florida aforesaid now in the city of Saint Augustine, will more fully and at large appear) and which said Several tracts or parcels of land containing the whole forty nine thousand eight hundred acres were with the appurtenances thereto belonging Sold and conveyed by the said Don Juan de Entralgo to the said Moses Elias Levy by an Indenture bearing date the sixth day of August one thousand eight hundred and twenty four. Together with all the crops and produce of the several tracts or parcels of land, **and all the slaves and personal property thereon**, and all houses out houses, Edifices, buildings, trees, woods, underwoods, commons, ways, paths, passages, water courses, profits, commodities, advantages, priveledges, hereditamemts, Rights, members, and appurtenances whatever to the aforesaid several tracts pieces and parcels land belonging or in anywise appertaining, and the reversion and reversions, remainder and remainders, Rents, Issues, and profits thereof and every kind of him the said Moses Elias Levy, of in and to the said tracts, parcels of land and premises herein before mentioned, and intended to be hereby granted and released, and every of them, and every part thereof to have and to hold the said several tracts and parcels of land, and undivided moieties of tracts and parcels of land premises herein before mentioned and intended to be hereby granted and released with their and every of their appurtenances unto the said Joseph Delevante, his heirs and assigns for ever, Subject never the less to the charges or encumbrances hereinbefore mentioned, and also to the proviso or condition for the redemption of the said premises as herein after contained provided always, and these presents are upon this condition, and it is the true intent and meaning hereof and of the parties hereto that if the said Moses Elias Levy, his heirs Executors, Administrators, or assigns do and shall from time to time on the fifteenth day of September and on the fifteenth of March in each and every year, during the space of of six years from the day of the date hereof, well and truly pay or cause to be paid to the said Joseph Delevante, heirs, Executors, Administrators, or assigns at London in the County of Middesex aforesaid in without any deduction, defaloution or abatement whatsoever, interest on the said sum of two thousand one hundred and ten pounds Sterling at and after the rate of five per cent per annum, and shall and will on or before the fifteenth day of March which will be in the year one thousand eight hundred and thirty three well and truly pay or cause to be paid the full and whole sum of two thousand one hundred and two pounds Sterling, without any deduction or abatement whatsoever as before mentioned then and in such case the said Joseph Delevante, his heirs, Executers, Administraters and assigns, shall and will at any time, or times after such pay being made as afore said at the request costs and charges of the said Moses Elias Levy, his heirs Executors, Adminisraters, or assigns, reconvey and reassure and in Singular the Tracts of land, herediaments and premises hereby granted and released or intended so to be with all and every the appurtenances unto the said Moses Elias Levy his heirs and assigns for ever, As he or they shall by writing under his or their hand and seal direct and appoint free from all encumbrances whatsoever to be made, done or committed by the said Joseph Delevante his heirs, executors, or Adminisraters, or any other persons whatsoever claiming or to claim under him or them or any of them so as for the making or doing thereof, the said Joseph Delevante his heirs, Executors administrators or assigns be not compelled or compellable to go or travel from his or their places of places of abode, and the said Moses Elias Levy for himself, his heirs Executors and administrators and for every one of them doth covenant, premise grant, and agree to and with the said Joseph Delevante his Executors, administrators and assigns in manner following (that is to say) that he the said Moses Elias Levy, his heirs, Executors or administrators or some or one of them, shall and well and truly pay or cause to be paid unto the said Joseph Delevante, his Executors, administrators or assigns, the interest on the said sum of two thousand one hundred and ten pounds Sterling at the rate of five per cent per annum at the day and times and place before mentioned, and also the said full and whole sum of two thousand one hundred and ten pounds sterling on the said fifteenth day of March one thousand eight hundred and thirty three, without any deduction or abatement as aforesaid according to the true intent an meaning of these presents, and also that he the said Moses Elias Levy now is lawfully and absolutely possessed of or entitled unto the tracts and parcels of land herein before mentioned and intended so to be hereby granted and released, (subject as aforesaid) and now hath in him good right full power and lawful and absolute authority to grant, release and convey the same in manner and form aforesaid and according to the true intent and meaning of these presents, and further that it shall be, and may be lawful to, and for the said Joseph Delevante, his heirs, Executors and assigns from and after default shall be made in payment of the said sum two thousand one hundred and ten pounds sterling and interest at the rate and times aforesaid contrary to the form and effect of the aforesaid proviso and covenant for payment of the same, peaceably and quietly to enter in, or to have hold, occupy, possess and enjoy all and singular the tracts and parcels of land hereby intended to be released and conveyed with the appurtenances and all and singular the slaves crops, produce and property thereon found and take the rents, issues and profits thereof, and of every part thereof to and for him and their own use and benefit, and also in case default shall happen to be made in two half yearly payments of interest at the rate times and places aforesaid, it shall and may be for the said Joseph Delevante, his heirs Executors, administrators and assigns immediately to demand payment of the said sum of two thousand one hundred and ten pounds sterling, and all interest then due thereon, notwithstanding the term of six years for which the said sum of money is hereby is intended to be advanced shall not be then expired or near expiring and in case of the non payments thereof, to enter and take possession of the said tracts or parcels of land and premises in manner herein before mentioned and further, that the said Moses Elias Levy, his heirs, and assigns, and all and every other person or persons having or claiming any Estate right, title, or interest into or out of the said tracts of land and premises hereby intended to be granted and released shall and will from time to time after default shall happen to be made in payment of the said sum of two thousand one hundred and ten pounds sterling, and interest as aforesaid containing the true intent and meaning of these presents, at the request costs and charges of the said Joesph Delevante, his heirs Executors administrators or assigns make do and execute or cause and procure to be made, done and executed all and every such further and other acts, deeds, conveyances and assurances in the law whatsoever for the further better more perfect and absolute granting, conveying, assuring and confirming the said tracts and parcels of land, and premises with the appurtenances unto, and to the use and behoof of the said Joseph Delevante his heirs and assigns as he or they, or his or their counsel in the law shall be lawfully advised, devised, or required, and it is also declared and agreed by and between the said parties to these presents, that until default shall happen to be made in payment of the said sum of two thousand one hundred and ten pounds sterling and interest, or some part thereof contrary to the intent and meaning of the aforesaid previso and covenant for payment thereof, it shall and may be lawful for the said Moses Elias Levy his heirs and assigns peaceably and quietly to hold, occupy, possess and enjoy the same tracts of land and premises, and every part and parcel thereof, and to receive the rents and issues and profits thereof for his and their own use and benefit without any let or denial whatsoever of him the said Joseph Delevante, his heirs or assigns, or any other person or persons whomsoever, and further it is hereby also agreed, and declared by and between the said parties, that whereas one of the conditions of the mortgage granted by the said Moses Elias Levy to Seraphina Chauveteau as aforesaid for the sum of fifteen thousand francs as appears by the Indenture dated as aforesaid the thirtieth day of January one thousand eight hundred twenty six, is that it shall and may be lawful for the said Moses Elias Levy to borrow and take up at interest any sum or sums of money not exceeding in the whole the sum of one hundred thousand francs in addition to the one borrowed of fifty thousand francs as aforesaid on the security of the said tracts of land and premises hereby intended to be released and conveyed, which security or sureties where so executed shall rank with and be considered equal to the one granted as aforesaid in favor of the said Seraphina Chauveteau which shall enjoy no preference or priority whatever over those which may thereafter be executed as aforesaid. It is therefore covenanted and agreed between the present contracting parties Moses Elias Levy aforesaid on the one part, and Joseph Delevante aforesaid on the other, that the said sum of two thousand one hundred and ten pounds sterling secured by this agreement as aforesaid shall rank with and enjoy to all intents and purposes the same priority as the one granted to Seraphina Chauveteau as aforesaid, and which in no wise shall claim any preference or priority whatever, and it is further agreed and covenanted that the said Moses Elias Levy shall not grant any other mortgage upon the lands aforesaid with the same priority now granted to the said Joseph Delevante for the sum of two thousand one hundred and ten pounds sterling as aforesaid without the full consent and permission of the said Joseph Delevante, well understood that this restriction is merely confined to the land herein intended to be released and conveyed and not to personal property negroes and cattle which at any time may be found on the lands or premises aforesaid. In witness whereof the said parties have hereunto set their hands and seals the day and year first above written

Consulate of the United States of America
London

I Thomas Aspinwall Consul of the United States of America for London and the dependences thereof, do hereby make known and certify to all whom it may concern, that on the day and date hereafter expressed, personally appeared and came before me Moses Elias Levy and Joseph Delevante, who Signed and Sealed the foregoing instrument, and in my presence acknowledged the Same to be their voluntary act and deed, and I do further certify that Julius LeSouef and James McCurley did in my presence Sign and then and there attest to the Same Signatures and execution as aforesaid, In testimony whereof I have hereunto set my hand and affixed the Seal of the Said consulate in London aforesaid thirtieth day of March in the year of our Lord one thousand eight hundred and twenty seven, and in the fifty first year of the Independence of the said United States

Thos Aspinwall
United States of America
State of New York

on the eleventh day of May in the year one thousand eight hundred and twenty Seven, personally before me appeared Jonathan Thomson Collector of the part of New York, who being by me duly Sworn, deposed and gave evidence Satisfactorily proving to me that the above Signature of Thomas Aspinwall consul of the United States of America for London and that the seal affixed to the above certificate is the consulor Seal of office of the said consul all which I certify.

Sam R. Betts Judge of the United States for the Southern District of New York

Territory of Florida
County of Alachua

The within instrument of writing and certificates thereto annexed are recorded in my office in Book A page 27, at the request of Davis Floyd Esqr

Witness my name
Bennett M. Dell Clk

London the twenty fourth day of May one thousand eight hundred and fifty four, whereas by a Deed of Mortgage annexed bearing date the fifteenth of March one thousand eight hundred & twenty seven, granted by Moses Elias Levy Esquire, then residing in Park Row Knights Bridge, in the County of Middlesex England, planter and land holder in Alachua East Florida, United States, unto Joseph Delevante Kimbolton Place Brompton in the County of Middlesex, Merchant, and certain landed Estates in Alachua East Florida, unto him appertaining, Specially and particularly mentioned in the aforesaid Mortgage, for the purpose of securing certain sums with interest accrueing thereon arising out of transactions between them all finally liquidated, and whereas the said Moses Elias Levy hath from time to time through himself or his Agents in the United States, remitted unto the said Joseph Delevante in Bills on England, including those remitted in January last of Six hundred pounds sterling on Jas Smith & Son Manchester & which was due & paid on the twenty ninth of March last, & also one of five hundred pounds sterling on Ormrod and Hardcastle Bolton which was & paid on the thirtieth of March last these & former remittances were particularly specified in an account current rendered him, bearing interest from their respective dates, and in consideration of the above remittances including the two bills conjointly of eleven hundred pounds received by the above mentioned Joseph Delevante comprehending principal due to him in liquidation of the annexed mortgage on the lands in East Florida, he doth hereby for himself his heirs, Executors, administrators, & assigns, acquit and release all the lands mentioned in the annexed mortgage, as well as the above mentioned Moses Elias Levy Esq, his heirs Executors, administrators, and assigns, from any claim on his or their part forever & in full faith thereof he has signed and sealed this in presence of Jos Delevante - Consulate of the United States of America at London

I George W. Sanders consul of the United States of America for London, and the dependencies thereof, do hereby make known and certify to all whom it may concern that on the day of the date hereof before me personally appeared and came Joseph Delevante to me known to be the person described in and who has executed the annexed instrument and then and there as acknowledged the same to be his free act and deed In testimoney whereof I have hereunto set my hand and affixed the seal of the Consulate of the United States at London, aforesaid this twenty fourth day of May in the year of our Lord one thousand eight hundred and fifty four, and in the seventy eighth year of the Independance of the United States"

Recorded July 18th 1854
Robt Youngblood, Clerk
From Alachua County Ancient Records
Deed Record B pages 390-399

Peter Mitchel to Robert Mitchel as collateral for a $20,000 loan:
"This Indenture made this thirteenth day of October in the year of Our Lord eighteen hundred and twenty seven between Peter Mitchel of the place aforesaid of the first part and Robert Mitchel of the City of Savannah and the State of Georgia of the second part Whereas the said Peter Mitchel stands justly indebted unto the said said Robert Mitchel in the sum of twenty thousand Dollars and in security for the payment of said late mentioned sum of money hath given his promissory note bearing even date with these presents Now this Indenture witnesseth that the said Peter for and in consideration of

the premises for the better securing the payment to the said Robert of the said above mentioned sum of money according to the tenor of said note and for the sum of one Dollar to him in hand paid by the said Robert at or before the sealing & delivery of these presents the receipt whereof is hereby acknowledged hath granted bargained sold conveyed and confirmed and by these presents doth bargain sell convey and confirm unto the said Robert his heirs executors administrators and assigns all the right title interest and claim whatsoever of him the said Peter in and to all the real and personal property here in after set forth and designated that is to say an undivided interest consisting of fourteen seventy seventh parts or shares of of that tract of land situate lying and being in Alachua County known by the name of the Arredondo Grant and which Originally granted on the twenty second day of December eighteen hundred and seventeen to Arredondo and son and the said grant containing four Leagues in [unreadable] of land to each point of the compass and center thereof is in Micanopy Also all that house and lot of land situate in the City of St. Augustine on the west side of St. Georges Street by which and the public square it is bounded on the East and on the North by Brody Creek and on the south by the house and lot belonging to Paul H. Pemaull and the said house is occupied by the said Peter Mitchel and family and subject nevertheless to a Judgment and mortgage to (Recorded in the County) Francis R. Sanchez to secure the said Sanchez the payment of three thousand and forty four Dollars as by Referance to said Mortgage on Record in the County Court of the County of St. Johns will more fully appear Also the following Negroes slaves to wit **Milinda London Maria Cornelia and her two children Jim and Jane together with the future issue and increase of the females of said slaves** also one Piano one Sopha four Mahogana Tables and the other household and Kitchen furniture in the Kitchen and house house ocupied as aforesaid by the said Peter also three hundred volumes of Books in said house. Together with all and singular the houses out houses Edifices buildings improvements herridetements and appurtenances to the said property appertaining or belonging, the Remainder and remainders, revision and Revisions rents issues and profits thereof. To have and to hold the above with the appurtenances unto him the said Robert Mitchel, his heirs executors administrators and assigns forever upon condition Nevertheless and according to the intent of these presents that if the said Peter Mitchell his heirs Executors Administrators shall and do well and truly pay or cause to be paid to the said Robert Mitchell the said sum of twenty thousand Dollars according to the time of said note of said Peter Mitchell on or before the first day of October next which shall be in the year of Our Lord eighteen hundred and twenty and twenty eight then these presents and every and every matter or thing herein Contained shall cease determine and be null and void

Otherwise to remain in full force and virtue."

October 13, 1827
District of East Florida, County of Saint Johns
From Alachua County Ancient Records
Deed Book A pages 044-046

Territory of Florida vs Monday (a negro man) - Indictment for a rape on the body of Sarah Cason: "Now on this day came as well Thomas Douglas Esquire who prosecutes the pleas of the Territory in this behalf as the prisoner who was brought to the Bar by the Marshall. When Charles Downing, Esq. was assigned by the Court as his Council. Whereupon said Prisoner was arraigned on said indictment and for a plea in this case says he is not guilty and for trial puts himself on his country. Where upon came a Jury of Twelve good and lawful men who were duly empannelled and sworn to try the issue joined. (viz) Henry W. Maxey Fernando Lowe, Wiley Daniel Thomas Colding William Harn Henry Harn James Burnett Jonas Ellis, Robert Payne, Joshua Stafford, John Standley and Joseph Warren Who upon their oaths do say that the Defendant is guilty in manner and form as in the Indictment is charged. and further say that the defendant is a slave of David Smith Esq. of Georgia and assess his value at two hundred dollars."

December 24, 1829
From Alachua County Ancient Records
Superior Court Minutes 1 pages 021-022

Enslaved man named Monday sentenced to death for the rape of Sarah Cason: "Now, on this day came Thomas Douglas, who prosecutes the Pleas of the Territory in this behalf & the said Monday, having been led to the bar of the Court, by the Marshall, & it being demanded of him, If he had anything to say, why Indictment Should not be pronounced against him, upon the verdict of the Jury, heretofore rendered against him in this case, and he saying nothing, in bar of said Indictment. Therefore, it is considered & ordered by the Court, that this Said Monday, be taken from the bar of this Court, to the prison from whence he came, to be detained in Safe & close custody, until Wednesday the twentieth day if January next, & that on the said twentieth day of January next, between the hours of twelve Oclock & four O'clock of said day, he be taken from the said prison to the place of Execution & there be hanged by the neck until he be dead."

December 25, 1829
From Alachua County Ancient Records
Superior Court Minutes 1 pages 024-025

Sally of the Florida Indians Sister of Tuskeneha to Gad Humphreys for $700: "Know all men by these presents that I Sally of the Florida Indians Sister of Tuskeneha have granted bargained and sold and by these presents do grant bargain and sell to Gad Humphreys of Florida the following named and described Negro Slaves my property to wit **Peggy aged about forty years and Hager & Joe her two children the first aged about fourteen years & the last about sixteen years** For and in consideration of the sum of Seven Hundred dollars to me in hand paid by the said Gad the receipt whereof is hereby acknowledged. To have and to hold to the said Gad his heirs assigns &C &C the said Slaves as their property and for their own proper use and behoof forever"

June 12, 1827
Territory of Florida, Alachua County
From Alachua County Ancient Records
Deed Book B page 077

1830's

William Broadaway to Bennett M. Dell for $925: "I have this day received of Bennett M. Dell nine hundred and twenty five dollars for **two Negro boys named and Summersett** and in these presence doth acknowledge the reception of the same in full payment of the aforesaid Negroes.

June 3, 1835
Territory of Florida, Alachua County
From Alachua County Ancient Records
Deed Book B page 196

William A. G. Broadaway to Philip Dell for $1,550: "Know all men by these presents that I William A. G. Broadaway for and in consideration of the sum of Fifteen hundred and fifty dollars to me in hand paid at and before the Sealing and delivery of these presents by Philip Dell the receipt I do hereby acknowledge have bargained and sold and by these presents do bargain sell and deliver to the said Philip Dell **a negro fellow named Cuffy also a negro girl named Matilda,** to have and to hold the said slaves Cuffy and Matilda unto the said Philip Dell his heirs executors Administrators and Assigns to his and their only proper use and behoof forever"

July 8, 1839 and in the sixty fourth year of the Independence of the United States of America
East Florida, Alachua County
From Alachua County Ancient Records
Deed Book B pages 272-273

Ashley H. Brooks to father Willy Brooks to hold in trust and to manage on Ashley's behalf: "Know ye that I Ashley H. Brooks of the County of Alachua and Territory of Florida being possessed & owner of two certain **negro Girls (to wit) Elsy about Eleven years and Flora aged about nine years** & being anxious that the said negros shall be managed for my greatest advantage & to this effect being anxious to have the benefit of the service & experiences of my father Willy Brooks. Do by these presents & in consideration of five dollars to me in hand paid by my said father before the ensealing and delivery of these said presents hereby bargain sell & deliver to him the said Willy Brooks the said two negro girls Elsy & Flora and I the said Ashley H. Brooks for myself my heirs executors & administrators do hereby forever warrant and defend the same & my right to bargain sell and deliver the said negros unto the said Willy Brooks & to his heirs Executors etc, etc, To have and to hold the said negros **together with**

their increase (if any they shall have) in trust to use for my sole & only use for the term of my natural life & after my death in trust to my children if any I should have, till said children shall come of age, but if I should die without children these said negros with their increase be held by my said father in trust aforesaid for the use & benefit of my surviving brothers & sisters (should there be any, but not for the benefit of my other legal heirs"

May 27, 1834
From Alachua County Ancient Records
Deed Book B pages 224-225

John Chesnut Last Will & Testament: "In the name of God Amen, I John Chesnut of the Town of Camden District & state aforesaid being of Sound Mind & Memory, do make and publish this my last will and Testament

I direct that all my Estate-both personal and Real Shall be Kept together by my Executrix and Executors hereinafter to be named and my plantation interest to be carried on and the proceeds of the Sale to be applied as heretofore to the Support of my family, the Education of my children and the payment of my debts, And when my debts Shall be finally paid and not before my estate Shall be Subject to the following disposition

I direct that my Estate both Real and personal shall be Kept together as it now is untill One of my daughters Shall be married or untill my oldest Sons Shall become of age then as soon as one of my daughters shall be married or my oldest Son become of age my debts being paid I direct that my Executrix and Executors Shall take an inventory of my personal estate Household & Kitchen furniture Stock on the plantation Horses and Carriages and all things pertaining to the

Establishment of my yards at Camden and Cold Spring not to be included and from Such an Inventory Shall make as many shares and all Equal as then any children of mine as that time living and one more for my wife and Shall assign one of the Shared So made to my daughter being married or to my Son who Shall become of age as his or her portion of my Said personal Estate and I further direct that as my other daughters Shall be married or my or his sons respectively become of age then a like inventory shall be taken of the remaining part of my said personal Estate with the Exceptions aforesaid and shall assign a share being made as before Directed to my daughter who shall be married or to my son becoming of age as his or her portions of my said personal Estate at that time but if when my daughter or any of them shall become entitled under the provisions before made as their Share of my said personal Estate it Shall seem fit in this opinion of Executrix and Executor to purchase with the funds of the Estate Negros equal in number and in the same place of that which shall fall in the share or shares of my daughters or any of them becoming entitled as aforesaid my Executrix and Exectors are authorized So to purchase and Substitute

3rd Item I further direct that when my daughters respectively Shall become Entitled under the provisions of the will to their portion of my Estate they Shall be provided with a good Cook a good Seamstress, and a good hand Servant which Cook Seamstress and hand servant Shall be contained in the number of those Negrors which Shall fall to their Shares or be purchased with the funds of the Estate and be Substituted in the place of them which then shall be returned to the Estate

4th I direct that my Executrix and Executor Shall purchase a fine gold watch for each of my daughters as respectively they shall complete their Education

5th I direct that before my daughters Shall be put in possession of the property to which they shall become entitled under the provisions of this will my Exectrix and Executors Shall Secure it to them So that it Shall not in any way be liable to the disposition for the debts of her husband and if any of my daughters Shall die without issue the property of the daughter or daughters So dying to which She or they shall become entitled under this will Shall revert to my other children in equal proportions

6th I give and bequeath unto my wife Ellen Chesnut a life Estate in my dwelling House at Camden and also a life Estate in my dwelling House at Cool Springs together with all the furniture in and appurtenances belonging to the establishment at both places

7th I give and bequeath unto my wife Ellen Chesnut my Carriage and Carriage Horses and the carriages and Carriage Horses of any then to which Shall belong to my Estate at the time of this final divisions to her own proper use and behoof forever

8th I direct that my exectrix and Executor shall in the divisions of my Said personal estate as before directed place in the Share of Negrors which Shall be assigned to my wife Ellen Chesnut all those with their present and future issue and increase which were named by her from the Estate of her father Thomas Whitaker and also two others Viz **Phillis and Nelson** which are to replace two that were Sold from that number . I direct that Exutrix and Executors Shall after my debts are paid carry into effect the following disposition of my Real and Remainder of my personal Estate

9th I give and bequeath unto my Son James Chesnut and his heirs forever all the land which I posses lying on the West side of the Wateree River and also the Ferry Known as "Chesnut Ferry with enough of land on the East Side of said River to make a good and Convenient landing place, the quantity land necessary for this purpose will be indicated by the Executors

10th I give and bequeath unto my Son James Chesnut to his own proper use and behoof forever all of my Mules, Horses, Cattle, Hogs & c which belong to my plantation on the West Side of the Waters

River with the exception of One third or if it shall Seem More fit in the opinion of my Executors they may an estimate of the value of Said Stock and take One third of the value So estimated to be raised out of the monies which may be assigned in the Share of My Son James Chesnut in the division of my Said personal property as before directed and apply the same so raised to a purpose hereinafter to be mentioned giving under the arrangement the entire Stock aforesaid to my Son James

11th I direct that my Executrix and Executor shall place among the Negrors which are to make the Share of my Son James Chesnut in the division of my said personal property as before directed the following viz **John & his wife Betty and their children Hety, Hampton and Grace his wife Harry Ban and Shadrick (children of Dye) Catoe & Edy his wife and their children Charity, Saby and his wife Betsey and their children Martha and Dye with the present & future issue and increase of the above named Negrors** to be held by my Son James to his own proper use and behoof forever 12th I direct that my Exectrix and Executors Shall purchase with the funds of the Estate at a time when they may deem proper a good gold watch for my Son James Chesnut 13th I give and bequeath unto my son James Chesnut my double barrel gun

14th I give and bequeath unto my son John Chesnut Jr. all my real estate lying in the East side of the Wateree River in the district & State aforesaid reserving all the right vested in the Estate which I have bequeathed to his Mother Ellen Chesnut and all the right which may attatcd to the Ferry which I have left to my son James Chesnut My Son John Chesnut Jr. shall receive and hold to him and his heirs forever the whole of my real Estate lying as aforesaid in the East side of the Wateree River upon the following conditions, That the burying ground of the family Situated on the Nights Hill tract Shall be left open for the use of the descendants of my Grand Father Col. John Chesnut, That he shall not despose of the Nights Hill tract of land to any person except to one of his brothers or to their children, who shall be required to take it liable to the same conditions under which it was held by my Son John Chesnut Jr.

15th I give and bequeath to my Son John Chesnut Jr. all the Stock which shall belong to my plantation on the East Side of the Wateree River, to his own proper use and behoof forever, with The Exception of One third or if it Shall Seem fit in the opinion of my Executrix they may make an estimate of the whole value of said Stock and Shall take One third of the value of said Stock in lieu of the third of the Stock itself from the monies which may fall to the Share of my Son John Chesnut in the division of my said personal Estate as before directed and which money when So raised shall be applied to a purpose hereinafter to be mentioned, leaving under this last arrangement the entire Stock on the plantation aforesaid to my son John Chesnut

16th I give and bequeath unto my Son John Chesnut to him and his heirs forever the remainder of the life Estate which I have left to his Mother Ellen Chesnut in my dwelling house at Camden and Cool Springs together with all the appurtinances unto them belonging and the furniture Contained in the Houses at both places,, the furniture which was left to me by Grand Father Col. John Chesnut I desire will take and Keep with Special care

17th I direct that my exectrix and Executors Shall place among the number of those which shall fall to my son John Chesnut Jr. in the division of my Said personal estate as before directed **the following Negrors with all their future issue and increase Viz Motty and all her children Viz Pat and her husband Turpin with their child Juan Tist and her child Josey, Bill and his wife Sary with their children Ellen, Matty, Scip and Sue, Also Ceasar, Patrick and Charles (Tist the daughter of Dye) and Ned the Blacksmith**

I give and bequeath unto my Son John Chesnut the Sword which was presented to me by the Kershaw Volunteers whom I had the Honor to Command in the late Indian War in Florida. I Bequeath it to him with the special desire and trust that he will Keep and honor it as the pledge of the friendship and Confidence of the friends and brave Companions of his Father

18th I direct as soon as my Son Thomas Whitaker Chesnut Shall become of age my Executrix and Executors Shall my debts being paid make a division of my said personal Estate as before directed and assign him his portion thereof,

And that they shall Also made and assignment of the value of the Several plantations which I have given to my Sons James & John Chesnut and Shall take funds from the Estate to the amount of the value of either of the Plantations aforesaid and lay out the same in lands for the use of my son Thomas Whitaker Chesnut to him and his heirs forever

19th I direct further that my executrix and Executors Shall take the one third of the Stock which was before reserved from the gift of the Stock on the Several plantations given to my Sons James & John Chesnut or if Shall seen more fit in the Opinion of Executrix and Executors they may take One third of the value of the Stock on each the plantations aforesaid in money to the value raised as before provided and apply the same to the purchase of Stock for my Son Thomas Whitaker Chesnut

20th I direct that my Executrix and Executors Shall require of each of my Sons as they become entitled to their respective portions of my Estate under this will to bear his proportions in the gift of two thousand dollars which Shall be given to each of my daughters in line of the lands which were bequeathed to the Sons in land or otherwise at the discretion of my Executors

21st I direct that my Executrix and Executor Shall place in the lot of Negrors which shall be assigned to my Son Thomas Whitaker Chesnut the following Viz **Frank his wife Ama[unreadable] and their children Edward (and house Servant) and his sister Betsy with issue and increase [...]**

42

I direct that the Negros **Betsy and her brother Edward house Servants** Shall not be taken by my Son Thomas Whitaker Chesnut during the life time of his mother Ellen Chesnut without her Consent

CODICIL
South Carolina

I John Chesnut of Camden in the State aforesaid having already made and declared my last will and Testament and Confirming the same with this codicil as a part thereof Viz; I do hereby give to my Executors in my said last will named the full power and authority to sell all my lands lying on the other or West Side of the Waters River at any time when in their Judgment a Sale of the Same may be advantagious to the interest of my estate on such time as they may deem most for the interest of my estate reserving in the rest of Such sale the full right to the Ferry and Sufficient land on the West Side of the river for the uses of the Ferry which Ferry with the full right of the same with the lands so reserved shall in case of such sale go and pass with the Knights Hill Place as a part of the same as divided by me in my last will and Testament, and I direct my said Executors in case they make the sale aforesaid to Purchase other lands from the funds of my Estate which land So purchased shall Be Substituted for and pass in lieu of the land So sold in the same manner and to the same persons as the land in this Codicil authorized to be sold and divided in my last will and testament

And I hereby give to and rest in my said Executors and full power to Execute legal title to the lands So to be purchased without applications for any other or further Authority to any Court of Justice

And I do further declare by way of Codicil to my last will and Testament aforesaid that it is my will and direction that nine of the house hold servants whom I may bequeath to any of my children in my last will and Testament aforesaid Shall be taken from my wife during her life time but during her life such Servants Shall remain with her and She Shall be entitled to their Services unless she her Self Shall choose

43

to relinquish them,, The bequest of said Servants to take effect after her death as declared in my last will and Testament And I do hereby Confirm My said last will and Testament by the Testament aforesaid with the Codicil as a part of the Same" 10th May 1839

May 3, 1839 and May 10, 1839
State of South Carolina, Kershaw District
From Alachua County Ancient Records
Will Book B pages 034-047

Duncan L. Clinch Col. of the Army of the United States to John L. Engle Lieutenant in the Army of the United States Administrator of the Estate of F. P. Fatio as collateral for $3,150 in loans: "Whereas I the said Duncan L. Clinch in and by my two certain Bonds bearing even date herewith am held and firmly bound jointly and severally with Joseph Lawton and Charles Lawton trading together at Charleston in the State of South Carolina under the style and firm of J&C Lawton unto John L Engle Lieutenant in the Army of the United States Administrator of the Estate of F. P. Fatio in the several penal sums of three thousand one hundred and fifty dollars [...] Now know ye that I the said Duncan L. Clinch for the better securing the payment of the said bonds and the sums of money therein mentioned unto the said John L. Engle his heirs executors administrators or assigns together with interest according to the true intent and meaning of the said bonds have bargained and sold and by these presents do bargain and sell and in open market deliver unto the said John L Engle the twenty one Negro slaves named as follows (to wit) **Adam, Frank and Dolly his wife and their children Adam, Frances, George, Mary Jane and Sopha; Dorcas and her children Dick, Lewis, and Teresa; Friday and Molly his wife and their children Charlotte, John, Christianna, and Dabline; and Hercules. Hannah and Mason. To have and to hold the said twenty one**

Negroes (to wit) Adam, Frank Dolly, Adam, Frances, George, Mary Jane, Sopha, Dorcas, Dick, Lewis, Teresa, Freddy, Molly, Charlotte, John, Christianna, Dabline, Hercules, Hannah, and Mason unto the said John L. Engle his heirs Executors Administrators and assigns Forever Provided always nevertheless that if the said Duncan L. Clinch my heirs executors administrators or assigns shall and do well and truly pay or cause to be paid unto the said John L. Engle his certain attorney executors administrators or assigns the full and just sums of money in the said bonds mentioned according to the true intent and meaning of the same and the conditions thereof and of these presents together with lawful interest as therein provided then this deed bargain and sale and all and every cause article and thing therein contained shall cease determine and be utterly void and of none affect any thing herein contained to the contrary thereof in any wise notwithstanding […] if default shall happen to be made of or in payment of the said bonds or the sum of money and interest as therein and in the conditions thereof is provided according to the true intent and meaning thereof that then and in such case it shall and may be lawful to and for the said John L Engle his executors, administrators and assigns or his or their attorney or agent from time to time and at all times hereafter peaceably and quietly to enter into any or all the messuages lands tenements of me the said Duncan L. Clinch and to take the said Negro slaves all or any of them into his possession and the same to hold and detain to his and their own use and behoof as his and their own proper goods and chattles from here forth and forever or the same to sell and dispose of at will and pleasure returning the overplus if any should happen to be after paying the said bonds and he conditions thereof mentioned unto me the said Duncan L. Clinch my executors administrators or assigns"

May 12, 1834
From Alachua County Ancient Records
Deed Book B pages 129-131

Duncan L. Clinch Colonel in the Army of the United States to Martha J. P. Bench widow of Daniel E. Bench as collateral for $13,110.16 in loans: "This Indenture made the third day of May 1834 between Duncan L. Clinch Colonel in the Army of the United States now the City of Mobile of the first part and Martha J. P. Bench of the City of New Orleans widow of Daniel E. Bench late of New Orleans deceased by her legally constituted Attorney Doct. J. P. C. Mahon of the second part Whereas the party of the first part was, on the first day of October 1833 justly indebted to the said party of the second part in the sum of thirteen thousand one hundred and ten 16/100 dollars (say $13 110. 16) and whereas it was then agreed by and between the said parties of the first and second parts that the said party of the first part should retain the use of said sum of money for and during the tenor of six years from that date payable by annual installments of one fifth part each year the first part to be paid on the first day of October eighteen hundred and thirty five and an annual Interest rate of seven per cent the said interest to be paid annually on the whole sum with the privilege secured to the party of the first part of paying the said debt or any part thereof with the interest at any time or times before the expiration of the said period of credit with which the said party of the second part declares herself to be content and whereas the said party of the first part hath this day Executed & delivered to the said party of the second part five several promissory notes expressed to be for value received each bearing date the first day of October 1833 payable to the order of the said Martha J. H. Bench at the Louisiana State Bank in New Orleans the first for four thousand four hundred and fifty seven 45 1/5/100 dollars (say $4457.45 1/5/100) due two years after date the second for three thousand three hundred and fifty six 19 1/5100 dollars (say $3356.19 1/5/100) due three years after date the third for three thousand one hundred and seventy two 65 1/5/100 dollars (say $3172.65 1/5/100 due four years after date the fourth for two thousand nine hundred and eighty nine 11 1/5/100 dollars (say $2805.57 1/5) due six years after date which said note amount in all to the sum of sixteen thousand seven hundred and eighty 98/100 dollars ($16780.98) they being for the principal and interest of the said debt calculated at the rate of seven per cent upon the amount of the principal debt above mentioned And whereas the said party of the first part is willing and desirous to secure the payment of said debt & the interest thereon - Now therefore for the above consideration And further consideration of one dollar to him in hand paid by the party of the second part at & before the sealing and delivery of these presents - the said party of the first part hath given granted bargained sold aliened enfeoffed released & confirmed and by these presents doth give grant bargain sell alien enfeoff release & confirm unto the party of the second part her heirs and assigns forever all that certain piece or parcel of land situate in the Teritory of East Florida on the westward of the big Alachua Savannah containing three thousand acres of land being a part of a four thousand acre grant made to Charles W. Clark by the Spanish Government and sold by him to G. I. F. Clark & by him sold to the said party of the first part, also the following slaves **one female slave named Renah aged thirty six years one male slave named Henry aged fourteen years one male slave named Tem aged 12 years one female slave named Mary aged 36 years one male slave named Affie aged 18 years one male slave named Andrew aged nine years one female slave aged 12 years named Nancy one female slave named Diace aged 12 years one male slave named Davy aged 29 years one male slave named Harry aged 26 years one female slave named Sirah aged 20 years one female slave named Kate aged 22 years one male slave named Abram aged 18 years one male slave named Jimmy aged 15 years one female slave named Clarinda aged 14 years one female slave named Beck aged 34 years one female slave named Susan aged 12 years one male slave named Jimmy aged 31 years one female slave named Nelly aged 24 years one male slave named Kinto aged 26 years one slave named aged 12 years one female slave named Syvia aged 38 years one male slave named Billy aged 32 years one female slave named Mary aged 27 years one male slave named Stephen aged 29 years one female slave named Peggy aged 32 years one male slave named Frank aged 35 years one male slave named Charley aged 12 years one female slave named Mary aged 50 years one female slave named Binah aged 27 years one male slave named Toby aged 25 years one male slave named**

Primus aged 20 years one female slave named Abby aged 16 years one male slave named Sam aged 25 years one male slave named Frank aged 55 years one female slave named Abby aged 50 years one male slave named January aged 35 years one male slave named Jacob aged 34 years one male slave named Pagus aged 24 years one male slave named Newton aged 40 years one male slave named George aged 28 years one male slave named Lewis aged 32 years one male slave named Sam aged 26 years one male slave named Bob aged 25 years one male slave named Jack aged 25 years one male slave named Joe aged 25 years one male slave named Larkin aged 22 years one male slave named Solomon aged 40 years one female slave named Delphi aged 36 years one male slave named Daniel aged 40 years one female slave named Sarah aged 25 years one female slave named Kitty Ann aged 8 years one male slave named John aged 6 years one female slave named Susan aged 4 years With all and singular the appurtenances to the said tract or parcel of land belonging and the further increase of the females of the said slaves To have and to hold the hereby granted or intended to be hereby granted tract or parcel of land & premises with the appurtenances together with the aforesaid slaves and the future increase of the females thereof unto the party of the second part her heirs executors and Administrators and assigns forever And the said party of the first part for himself his heirs executors and administrators the above described and hereby granted & released premises and every part and parcel thereof with the appurtenances together with the aforesaid slaves and the future increase of the females thereof unto the said party of the second part her heirs and assigns against the said party of the first part his heirs against all and every person and persons lawfully claiming or to claim the same shall and will warrant & by these presents forever defend and the said party of the first part doth further warrant the said slaves above conveyed to be sound in body and mind And the said Clinch wife of the said Duncan L. Clinch in consideration of ten cents to her in hand paid by the said party of the second part the receipt whereof is hereby acknowledged by her doth hereby relinquish to the said party of the second part her heirs and assigns all her right and title of dower in and to the above named premises Provided nevertheless and these presents are upon this express condition that if the said party of the first part his heirs executors administrators shall and do well and truly pay or cause to be paid unto the said party of the second part their executors administrators or assigns the said several sums of money in the above five promissory notes mentioned at the times when then respectively fall due according to the true intent and meaning of the said several notes then and from thenceforth these presents & every thing here in contained shall be utterly null and void to all intents and purposes"

May 3, 1834
From Alachua County Ancient Records
Deed Book B pages 091-095

Mary Dewees last will and testament: "In the Name of God amen. I Mary Dawees of Alachua county Widow, do make and publish this as my last Will & Testament hereby revoking and making void all former Wills by me at an time heretofore made

First I direct that my body decently buried in a manner corresponding with my Situation in life, And I direct that all my debts and funeral expenses be paid by my executors as hereafter prescribed And of my Worldly Estate which it has pleased God to entrust me with I dispose of the same as follows

I direct that all my real Estate of which I shall die seized or possessed shall be sold by my executors for its reasonable value for Cash, or on such credit as to my said executors may seem advisable taking care to secure payment for the same by good bonds & Mortgages or as some other proper and Sufficient manner to ensure the full & punctual payment Thereof, and to effectuate this my intention, I do hereby vest in my executors full power and authority to dispose of my Real Estate in fee simple or otherwise in as full and large a manner in every respect as I could myself do if living,

And I direct that the proceeds arising from the Sale of my said Real Estate be appropriated first to the payment of my funeral expenses, and my other debts if any, and then that the residue or balance of that purchase money of my real Estate aforesaid be equally divided between my Son Henry W. Maxey and my Daughter Louisa Mattair the Wife of Lewis A. Mattair of Columbia County

I give & bequeath to my Said Son Henry W. Maxey my Slave **Stephen**

Also I give & bequeath to my Brothers Bennett Maxey Dell and Simeon Dell of Alachua and to my Nephew Philip J. Dell son of Col. James Dell, herein after named Executors by this my Will the following named Negroe Slaves to Wit. **Clarissa, Nell, Silvey, Bell, January, Leonida and Julia, the last named being the children of said Clarissa and Jim The Husband of said Clarissa together with the Issue of the said Slaves** to have and to hold to them the said Bennett M. Dell Simeon Dell & Philip J. Dell and to the Survivor of them, and to the heirs executors or Administrators of such Survivors. To be held by them in trust, for the sole use benefit and behoof as follows- first for the use and behoof of my Said daughter Louisa Mattair to for and during her natural life; And after the death of my said Daughter Louisa Mattair then to and for the use of any child of her Body then living, but should my said Daughter Louisa die without any child or heir of her body living at the time then and in that case, my Slaves above named are to be held in trust to and for use and benefit of my said Son Henry W. Maxey during his life and after his death for the use of any child or children of the said Henry W. Maxey lawfully begotten, and should my son Henry die without legal heirs of his body, then the said foregoing Slaves shall be equally divided between my Brothers and Sisters living at the time, and the children of such of my Brothers and Sisters as may be dead according to the Laws of the Land and in such Shares and proportions as by said Laws are prescribed, after which the trust herein before created shall cease,

And it is my Will that my said Daughter Louisa, shall have during her life, the possession use and avail of said Slaves, without the same being in any manner or shape subject to the power or control of her present or any future Husband She may have or in any manner or form liable for the present or future debts of said present or future Husbands or of the said Louisa, and when the happening of either or any of the Contingencies above provided for then the possession shall accompany and go with the use and benefit of said slaves, but in no case shall said Slaves or any of them be liable for the debts or Contracts of those to whom said use shall…

Codicil to my foregoing WILL - Should it please God to spare my life for a few years longer and bless or trust me with any additional increase of property, I Will and bequeath it, to be equally divided betwixt my aforesaid Son and Daughter, with all the instructions to be observed towards it as regards further conveyance as is placed in the Conveyance of the property above given and bequeathed."

January 3, 1835
From Alachua County Ancient Records
Will Book A pages 004-006

Bennett M. Dell to Simeon Dell in trust for Sarah Brooks wife of Wiley Brooks: "This Indenture made and entered into this Twenty fifth day of December in the year of our Lord One Thousand Eight hundred & Thirty Three between Bennett M. Dell of the County of Columbia & Territory of Florida & Wiley Brooks and Sarah his wife of the second part they being of the County of Alachua in the aforesaid Territory, and Simeon Dell of the County of Columbia aforesaid of the third part Witnesseth that for and in consideration of the sum of Ten dollars to the said Bennett M. Dell in hand paid at and before the ensealing and delivery of these presents by the said Simeon Dell the party of the third part to & for the use benefit & comfort of the said Sarah Brooks the receipt whereof is hereby acknowledged hath bargained sold and delivered & by these presents do bargain sell & deliver to the said Simeon Dell & his assigns forever the following named Negro Slaves -- To wit **Patty a woman about Thirty years old, Jess a boy about three years & Newton a boy about Ten months old** Also Six Indian Ponies branded with the letters AB, four mares and Two horses & one hundred & fifty head of Stock Cattle with a crop in one ear & hole in the other branded with the said letters AB Upon trust Nevertheless to the use benefit comfort support & maintenance of the said Sarah Brooks for and during the term of her natural life and after death should he survive her to the use benefit comfort and support and maintenance of the said Wiley Brooks for and during the term of his natural life. And at the death of the said Wiley Brooks and Sarah Brooks his wife and the survivors of them then to their heirs share and share alike. And the said Simeon Dell doth agree and bind himself to convey to any other trustee to the uses and for the purposes in this deed expressed all the aforementioned property **together with the increase** at the request in writing of the said Wiley Brooks & Sarah Brooks his wife to him made & by them or the survivor of them required whenever thereto requested and that he will execute the trust in this deed conferred on him according to its true intent and tenor"

December 25, 1833
From Alachua County Ancient Records
Deed Book B pages 063-064

Bennett M. Dell acting guardian, to W. Broadway: "Received of Bennett M. Dell my acting guardian **Two Negro boys Volintine or Toby and Summunt** with a one hundred head Stock Cattle with all the papers and money which he held in his possession and all other property coming to me from my father Aabner G. Broadway Estate also of my mother Delia Broadway late Delia Stafford"

May 16, 1835
From Alachua County Ancient Records
Deed Book B page 186

Bennett M. Dell to Jane Ann Clark for $1,100: "Know all men by these presents that I Bennett M. Dell of Alachua County in the Territory of Florida for and in consideration of the sum of Eleven hundred dollars to me in hand paid by Jane Ann Clark wife of Asa Clark of the County aforesaid at or before the sealing and delivery of these presents this receipt whereof I do hereby Acknowledge have granted bargained and sold and by these presents do grant bargain and sell unto the said Jane Ann Clark and her children by the said Asa Clark begotten or to be hereafter begotten and their heirs **One Negro woman named Sarah aged about twenty five years, one negro boy named Frank aged about eight years and one female infant child a daughter of the said Sarah aged about six month** To have and to hold the above mentioned negro slaves **together with their increase** to the said Jane Ann Clark during her life and after her death to her children aforesaid begotten or to be begotten of her said husband Asa Clark and their heirs Executors and assigns forever"

August 12, 1837
From Alachua County Ancient Records
Deed Book B pages 221-222

Barthelow Gany to Simeon Dell as collateral for a $125 loan: "Know all men by these presents that I Barthelow Gany has this day executed to Simeon Dell, this day my Promissory Note for One hundred & Twenty five Dollars for Value Rec'd payable on the first day of January next bearing even date with this Mortgage for the true payment of the above named note I do mortgage unto Simeon Dell a certain **Negro man by the name Jim aged about twenty one**. The Condition of the above Obligation is such that if the said Gainy shall well and truly pay to the above named Simeon Dell the above Note for One hundred & twenty five Dollars then the above Obligation to be Null & void Else to stand in full force

The said Dell shall be Authorized to take the said Negro And Expose to Publik sale And pay him self And all expenses And all Surplus money or monies to be paid Over to said Gainey or to his order or agent."

June 2, 1835
Territory of Florida
From Alachua County Ancient Records
Deed Book B pages 211-212

Eliza Ann Ganny to Simeon Dell for $1,000: "Know men by these presents that I Eliza Ann Ganny for and in consideration of the sum of one thousand dollars to me in hand paid at and before the sealing and delivery of these presents by Simeon Dell the receipt whereof I do hereby acknowledge have bargained and sold, and do by these --- bargain sell and deliver said Simeon Dell **my Negro man Jim** To have and to hold the said negro man Given unto the said Simeon Dell his heirs executors administrators and assigns to his and their own proper use and benefit forever"

January 26, 1839
State of Georgia
From Alachua County Ancient Records
Deed Book B page 237

Isaac Garrason to John F. Miller for $300: "Know all men by these presents that I Isaac Garrason of the Territory and County aforesaid for and in consideration of the sum of Three Hundred Dollars to me in hand paid (the receipt whereof I do hereby acknowledge) by the John F. Miller of the aforesaid County & Territory have bargained sold and delivered and by these presents do bargain sell and deliver to the said John F. Miller a certain **Negro boy named Peter aged about fourteen years**"

March 30, 1833
Territory of Florida, Alachua County
From Alachua County Ancient Records
Deed Book B pages 022-023

Isaac Garrason to Darius Garrason Michael Garrason, Samuel Piles, William Piles, and James Harn as collateral for a $600 loan: "This Indenture made and entered into this twenty ninth day of September A.D. 1834 Between Isaac Garrason of the one part and Darius Garrason, Michael Garrason, Samuel Piles William Piles & James Harn of the other part all of the County of Alachua Witnesseth that whereas the parties of the second part Have heretofore furnished a letter of credit to the party of the first part authorizing him to purchase goods wares and merchandise at the City of Savannah for the sum of not exceeding six hundred dollars and whereas the said Isaac Garrason the party of the first part by virtue of said letter of credit did go to the City of Savannah and did purchase of the house of A Champain goods wares and merchandise to the amount of [] dollars and did also purchase of the house of [] goods, wares & merchandise to the amount of [] dollars amounting in the whole to the sum of Six hundred dollars using said letter of credit to affect said purpose whereby the said parties of the second part have become bound and are liable in law to pay the aforesaid debt of the said Isaac Garrason the party of the first part and whereas the parties of the second part have organized a mortgage from the said Isaac Garrason to indemnify & secure them against their said liability so as aforesaid created & existing and he is willing to execute the same. Therefore in consideration of the promises and in consideration of the further sum of one dollar in hand paid to the said Garrason the party of the first part at and before the sealing and delivery of these presents the receipt whereof is hereby acknowledged We the said Isaac Garrason hath bargained sold and delivered and doth by these present bargain sell and deliver to the said Darius Garrason M Garrason Samuel Piles William Piles and James Harn the parties of the part a certain **Negro man named Sylvester aged about twenty four years** a cotton saw Gin and the improvement on which the said Isaac Garrason now resides together with crop grown and growing there on during the present year and three head of Horses to wit one sorrel Horse a sorrel mare and a black mare and indian poney To have and to hold the above named and described property all and singular to the parties of the second part their heirs and assigns forever free from the claim of him said Isaac Garrason his heirs and assigns &c forever provided however it is expressly understood by and between the parties hereto that this Indenture is to be taken and construed and held as a mortgage to secure to the parties aforesaid the payment of the sum of one dollar as aforesaid and also as an indenture against the liability of the said parties of the second part so as here in before expressed was incurred by them for the said Isaac Garrason on or before the first day of May that will be in the year of our Lord Eighteen hundred & Thirty five well and truly pay the parties of the second part for all sum & demands herein set forth then at the proper cost and charges of the said Isaac the said parties of the second part shall reconvey to him the said Isaac all and singular the property herein granted and conveyed and provided also that it is expressly understood by and between the parties hereto that the said Isaac shall be intitled to keep the possession of property herein and hereby granted until the first day of May 1835 at which time if the said Isaac shall have failed to pay the said and discharged and exonerated the liabilities of the said parties of the second part then and in that case it shall and may be lawful for the said parties of the second part to enter & take possession of all the property herein & thereby granted as of their own Estate and the proceeds thereof to appropriate to the payment of the demands aforesaid and the surplus if any to pay over to the said Isaac the party of the first part."

September 29, 1834
Teritory of Florida
From Alachua County Ancient Records
Deed Book B pages 084-086

Llewellyn Gilliland to Augustus Steele as collateral for a $400 loan: "Know all men by these presents that I Llewellyn Gilliland of the Territory of Florida and County of Alachua for and in consideration of the sum of four Hundred dollars, paid to me by Augustus Steele of Tampa the receipt whereof I hereby acknowledge, do hereby give grant bargain sell & convey unto the said Augustus Steele his heirs and assigns forever a certain **Negro Woman named Malissa aged about Seventeen years**. To have and to hold the said Negro woman to the said Augustus Steele his heirs and assigns to his & their use & behoof forever hereby warranting & defending the said Negro woman to the said Augustus Steele his heirs and assigns forever. Against the lawful claims of all persons whatsoever. Provided Nevertheless that if I the said Llewellen Gilliland my heirs Executors or administrators shall well and truly pay or cause to be paid to the said Augustus Steele on or before the first day of march One Thousand Eight hundred & Thirty four the sum of Three hundred and ninety seven dollars and seventy five cents - then the above shall be null & void otherwise remain in full force and virtue"

December 22, 1833
From Alachua County Ancient Records
Deed Book B page 059

L. Gilliland to Jesse Standly as collateral for a $500 loan: "Know all men by these presents that I L. Gilliland of Hillsborough County & Teritory aforesaid for and in consideration of the sum of Five hundred Dollars to me in hand paid at & before the sealing & delivery of these presents the receipt whereof is hereby acknowledged have bargained granted & sold & by these presents do grant bargain convey and sell to Jesse Standly also of said Teritory & County first above named One **Negro Woman named Permelia aged about Twenty years & her child Jim aged about three years** which aforesaid property I hereby bind myself heirs assigns &c to warrant & defend to the aforesaid Standly his heirs assigns &c against the claim of all others whomsoever. The condition of the above conveyance is such that if the said Gilliland does pay or cause to be paid to the aforesaid Standly the sum of Five Hundred Dollars on or before the first day of June next the above Bill of sale is void else to remain in full force."

August 25, 1834
Teritory of Florida, County of Columbia
From Alachua County Ancient Records
Deed Book B pages 175-176

John Hague Last Will and Testament: "In the Name of God Amen. I John Hague being of sound mind & memory and knowing that it appointed to man Once to die Do make and Ordain the following my last Will and Testament

First, I will my soul unto God, and my Body to be decently Buried.

Secondly As concerning my Worldly affairs I Will and bequeath is follows

And first That all my Just Debts shall be paid

Second That my beloved Wife Maria Hague shall have the privilege of living on my place on Turkey Creek during her Widowhood, and shall be allowed apart of all of my Estate according to Law, and that the Hire of **my Negroe Slaves**, shall go to the maintenance of my children, I have had by her my said Wife during their Minority.

Thirdly That all my children shall have an equal share of all my Estate the names of which are as follows. James Hague, John R. Hague, Gideon Hague, Mary Kelly, Rufina Hague, Archibald Hague, Vicey Hague, Amelia Hague and John Cooper Hague.

Fourthly Also that said Negroe Slaves shall not be hired out of my Family, and that Archalus Lipsey and Doctor James Kelly Shall have no Control of any part of my property Nor receive any benefits from it."

September 8, 1836
From Alachua County Ancient Records
Will Book A page 001

Thomas A. Halliday charged with buying from an enslaved person: "The Grand Jury returned into Court the following...Territory of Florida vs Thomas A. Halliday - buying from Slave without ticket - True Bill"

March 28, 1833
From Alachua County Ancient Records
Superior Court Minutes 1 page 106

Thomas A. Halliday charged with buying from an enslaved person without a ticket from Master: "The Grand Jury came into Court & presented the following [...]Territory of Florida vs Thomas A. Halliday - Buying from Slave without ticket from Master - No Bill"

March 30, 1833
From Alachua County Ancient Records
Superior Court Minutes 1 page 108

Thomas A. Halliday charged with buying from an enslaved person without a Ticket from his Master: "Territory of Florida vs Thomas A. Halliday - Buying from slave without Ticket from his Master - The Defendant entered into recognizance in the sum of two hundred Dollars & two sureties in the sum of One Hundred Dollars each conditioned for the appearance of the said Defendant to answer the Charge against him and not depart without leave of the Court"

December 28, 1833
From Alachua County Ancient Records
Superior Court Minutes 1 pages 120-121

Thomas A. Halliday charged with selling to an enslaved person: "The Territory of Florida vs Thomas A. Halliday - Selling to a Slave - In this case came the Territory by W. District Attorney and the Defendant in proper person & the said Mr. District Attorney declines to further prosecute the said Defendant and it is ordered that a Nol Proseq be accordingly entered in the said case"

April 23, 1835
From Alachua County Ancient Records
Superior Court Minutes 1 page 178

Thomas A. Halliday charged with selling to an enslaved person: "The Territory of Florida vs Thomas A. Halliday - Selling to a Slave - No Bill"

April 28, 1835
From Alachua County Ancient Records
Superior Court Minutes 1 page 204

J. M. Hanson acknowledges that Co'l Gad Humphreys paid off his January 9, 1832 loan for $955.96: "given by him to me on sundry Slaves to wit. **Sampson, Katy & Bob** to secure to me a certain sum of money therein specified [...] Humphreys having fully paid and satisfied me for the money thereby intended to be secured"

April 29, 1833
St Augustine
From Alachua County Ancient Records
Deed Book B page 063

Benjamin Harn to Charles Waldron as collateral for a $223.57 loan: "This Indenture made this twenty second day of November one thousand and eight hundred & thirty four between Benjamin Harn of the County and Territory aforesaid of the one part and Charles Waldron of the same place Witnesseth that the said Benjamin Harn hath this day made and delivered to the said Charles Waldron his certain promissory note subscribed by his hand and bearing date even with these presents whereby the said Benjamin Harn hath promised to pay the said Charles Waldron or bearer Two hundred & twenty three 57/100 dollars on or before the thirty first day of January next entering the date hereof for value received

Now for and in consideration of the sum of five dollars by the said Charles Waldron to the said Benjamin Harn in hand paid the receipt whereof is hereby acknowledged as well as for the better securing the payment of the aforesaid promissory note the said Benjamin Harn hath granted bargained and sold and by these presents doth grant bargain and sell unto the said Charles Waldron his heirs and assigns **a certain mulatto slave named Mary aged about twenty one years about five feet ten inches in height**

To have and to hold the said slave to the said Charles Waldron his heirs and assigns to his and their own proper use, benefit and behoof forever

And the said Benjamin Harn for himself his heirs executors and administrators the said bargained slave unto the said Charles Waldron will warrant and forever defend against the claim of himself and his heirs and against the claim of all other persons whatsoever

Provided nevertheless that if the said Benjamin Harn his heirs executors and administrators shall and do well and truly pay or cause to be paid unto the said Charles Waldron his heirs and assigns the afore mentioned sum of Two hundred & twenty three 57/100 dollars on the day and time mentioned and appointed for the payment thereof in the said promissory note mentioned with interest for the same at ten per centum, according to the tenor of said note then & from thenceforth as well as this present indenture and the right to the property thereby conveyed as the said promissory note shall cease determine and be void to all intents and purposes

November 22, 1834
Florida Teritory, Alachua County
From Alachua County Ancient Records
Deed Book B pages 099-100

Henry Harn to Charles Waldron for $500: "Know all men by these presents that for and in consideration of the sum of five Hundred dollars to me in hand well and truly paid before the signing hereof, I do Sell bargain & grant unto Charles Waldron his heirs executors & administrators one **Negro man named Orange aged about thirty years, about six feet in height**"

March 4, 1834
Territory of Florida, Alachua County
From Alachua County Ancient Records
Deed Book B page 072

William Harn to Bennett M. Dell for $450: "Know all men by these presents that I William Harn hath bargained and sold and by these presents do bargain & sell a certain **Negro woman by the name of Deffy And child Charles** to Bennett M. Dell for the sum of four hundred and fifty dollars"

November 27, 1835
Territory of Florida, Alachua County
From Alachua County Ancient Records
Deed Book B page 213

Samuel Harville Last Will and Testament: "In the name of the Most High Amen. I Samuel Harville of the State of Georgia in Liberty County Do Ordain this my last Will and Testament

First, I desire my Debts be punctually paid.

Secondly I leave under the care of my three Sons Warren Harville John Elliot Harville, and Edward McVean Harville My Trustees, or either of them, the following property, both real and personal, for the use and Support of my beloved Wife Rebecca Harville during her natural Life

All the Lands I own in Liberty County, Horses, Outhouses Plantation Tools and implements of Husbandry, Three Slaves viz, **Sally, Cloe, & Jackson**, One brown Horse, my Cattle, Hogs and Sheep, Household and Kitchen Furniture, lacking special care not to waste, And at the death of my beloved Wife R. Harville as aforesaid, the above property and **its increase if any**, to be equally divided between my three sons as aforesaid, Warren, Elliot and McVean

I give to my Daughter Rebecca Lowther a female slave named **Jenny**, I give to my Daughter Celia Zoucks a female slave named **Lucy**, I give to my Daughter Elizabeth Cash a Slave Boy named **Stephen**, (unreadable) Harville my Daughter, **Washington** a boy Slave, I give to my youngest Daughter Sarah Smylie Harville a Negro Girl by the name of **Georgia**, I give to Richard T. Baker One Cow & Calf. I give to Warren Harville my oldest Son, One Negro boy by the name of **Abram**, my Gun also. I give to my Son John Elliot Harville One Negro boy named **Cyrus**, I give to my youngest Son Edward McVean Harville, my Negro boy **Cerno**.

I desire my Land in Houston County be sold, and whatever it may bring be equally divided between Berrien Harville & Samuel Rivers Harville my Grandsons,

If I should draw a prise in the present contemplated Land Lottery, I desire it should be divided, between Warren Harville John Elliot Harville Edward McVean Harville, Stephen Fuller Baker and Mary Harville Baker."

April 12, 1832
From Alachua County Ancient Records
Will Book A pages 002-003

Thomas A. Holiday to William O. Thomas for $650: "Know all men by these presents that I Thomas A. Holiday hath this day for and in consideration of the sum of Six hundred and fifty dollars to me in hand paid the receipt whereof I do hereby Acknowledge bargained and sold and do by these presents bargain and sell unto William O. Thomas A negro man slave named **Jim** "

June 14, 1837
Territory of Florida, Alachua County
From Alachua County Ancient Records
Deed Book B pages 220-221

Col. Gad Humphreys to John M. Hanson as collateral for a $335 loan: "This Indenture made this fourteenth day of March in the year of our Lord One thousand Eight hundred and thirty two between Co'l Gad Humphreys of the County of Alachua and Territory Aforesaid of the one part and John M. Hanson of St. Augustine and county of St. Johns Aforesaid of the other part, Witnesseth, whereas the said Humphreys stands justly indebted to said Hanson in the sum of Three hundred & thirty five dollars agreeably to the tenor of his Promissory Note bearing even date with these presents, Now therefore the said Humphreys in Consideration of the Premises for the better securing the payment to said Hanson of the said sum of three hundred and thirty five dollars And for the sum of five dollars by the said Hanson to the said Humphreys in hand paid at and before the sealing and delivery of these presents the receipt whereof is hereby acknowledged, hath granted bargained and sold and by these presents doth grant bargain and sell unto said Hanson his executors Administrators and assigns three Negro Slaves to wit, **Sam about thirty five years**

of age and his wife **Dolly about thirty years of age and her child named Lucy a female about Eight years of age together with all the future issue and increase of the said female Dolly** To have and to hold said above bargained & sold Negro Slaves together with all the future issue and increase of the said female Dolly unto the said Hanson his executors, administrators and assigns forever. Provided Nevertheless and these presents are upon this Condition that if the said Humphreys shall and doth well and truly pay or cause to be paid unto the said Hanson the said sum of three Hundred and thirty five Dollars on or before the first day of January Next then these presents and every matter and thing herein contained shall cease and be utterly void Otherwise to be and remain in full force and virtue"

March 14, 1832
Territory of Florida, County of St. Johns
From Alachua County Ancient Records
Deed Book B pages 012-013

Col. Gad Humphreys to J. & C. Lawton as collateral for a $1,000 loan: "This Indenture made the Twentieth day of November Eighteen hundred & Thirty Two between Gad Humphreys of the Territory & County aforesaid of the one part & Mess'rs J.& C. Lawton of the City of Charleston State of South Carolina Witnesseth that the said G. Humphreys hath promised to pay the said J.& C. Lawton one Thousand dollars on or before the first day of April next ensuing for value received. Now for and in consideration of the sum of five dollars by the said J.& C. Lawton to the said G. Humphreys in hand paid the receipt whereof is hereby acknowledged as well as for the better securing the payment of the aforesaid promissory note the said Humphreys hath granted bargained & sold and doth by these presents grant bargain & sell unto the said J.& C. Lawton their heirs and assigns his thirty seven Negroes now in the County of Alachua

Territory aforesaid named as follows. **Cornelia, Lancaster, Morris, Sampson, Joe, Andrew, Peter 1st, Peter 2nd, Sam 1st, Sam 2nd, Ansel, Hardy, August, Mungo, Dick, Worley, Toney, Beck, Sally, Nancy, Sophy, Dolly, Katy 1st, Katy 2nd, Jane, Amy, Cyrus, Elsy, Cooter, Nursey, Limus, Tom, Stepney, Lucy, Flora, Frank, July.** To have & to hold the said bargained Negroes unto the said J.& C. Lawton their heirs and assigns to their own proper use and benefit forever And the said G. Humphreys for himself his heirs and Executors administrators the said bargained Negroes unto the said J.& C. Lawton will warrant and forever defend against the claims of himself & his heirs and against the claim of all other persons whatsoever Provided Nevertheless that if the said Humphreys his heirs Executors & administrators shall & do well & truly pay or cause to be paid unto the said J.& C. Lawton their heirs and assigns the aforesaid sum of One Thousand dollars on the day mentioned & appointed for the payment thereof in the promissory note then & from thenceforth as well this present Indenture and the right to the property thereby conveyed on the said promissory note shall cease determine & be void to all intents & purposes."

November 20, 1832
Territory of Florida, Alachua County
From Alachua County Ancient Records
Deed Book B page 065

Colonel Gad Humphreys to John M. Hanson as collateral for $955.96 in loans: "This Indenture made the ninth day of January One thousand Eight hundred and thirty two between Co'l Gad Humphreys at present of the City of St. Augustine of the first part and John M. Hanson of the same place of the second part. Whereas the said Gad Humphreys was on the twenty second day of January One thousand Eight hundred and thirty one indebted unto the following persons in the following sums of money that is to say unto Lieu't F. D. Newcomb of the United States Army in the sum of four hundred and fourteen dollars on the draft of the said Gad Humphreys with interest from the time the same became due; to Abraham Bellamy by the Note of the said Gad Humphreys in the sum of two hundred dollars with interest from the time it became due; to the above named John M. Hanson by Book Account in the sum of sixty one dollars and ninety six cents; to Isaiah J. Hart of Jacksonville in the sum of Eighty dollars and unto James Baker in the sum of two hundred dollars with interest; and whereas the said Gad Humphreys did on the twenty second day of January one thousand Eight hundred & thirty one for the purpose of paying the said debts assign to the said John M. Hanson the wages of certain Negroes then recently hired to Dan'l S. Griswald by the said Gad Humphreys and whereas although a part only of the said wages of the said Negroes have been received by the said John M. Hanson, he may have rendered himself responsible to the above named creditors of the said Gad Humphreys so far as their respective claims remain unsatisfied; and whereas the said John M. Hanson hath at the request of the said Gad Humphreys relinquished his right under the aforesaid assignment to receive the balance of the wages owing by the said Daniel S. Griswald for the said Negroes; and whereas it is reasonable and proper not only that the said John M. Hanson should be secured against all claims on the part of the above named creditors of the said Gad Humphreys growing out of the aforesaid assignment, but that the said Creditors of the said Gad Humphreys should be secured in their just demands against him. Now therefore this Indenture Witnesseth that the said Gad Humphreys for and in consideration of the premises and in consideration also of the sum of Ten dollars by the said John M. Hanson to him in hand well and truly paid at or before the sealing and delivery of these presents the receipt whereof is hereby acknowledged Hath granted bargained sold, transferred, and delivered and by these presents doth grant bargain, sell transfer, and deliver unto the said John M. Hanson, his executors Administrators and assigns forever his certain Negro Slaves, following that is to say **Sampson aged about twenty four years Katy aged about Eighteen years and Bob aged about ten years with the future issue**

and increase of the said female Slave. To have and to hold the said Slaves and the future increase and issue of the female Slave unto the said John M. Hanson his executors administrators and assigns forever, in trust nevertheless and to and for the special uses purposes and intents, hereinafter mentioned, that is to say, that the said John M. Hanson his executors or administrators shall cause the said Negro Slaves to be sold in front of the court house in the City of St. Augustine to the highest bidder for cash at Public Auction on any day he may think proper in the month of January One thousand Eight hundred and thirty three after the tenth day of said month provided the said Gad Humphreys or his executors or administrators shall not have paid and satisfied in full the debts owing by him as herein above specified and shall not have produced to the said John M. Hanson his executors or administrators satisfactory evidence of the payment of said debts on or before the first day of January One thousand Eight hundred and thirty three and provided also that public notice posted at the aforesaid court house or published in the newspaper of St. Augustine of the time and place of the sale of the said negroes, shall have been given for at least one week previous to the said sale, and that first from the proceeds of the sale of the said Negroes the said John M. Hanson his executors or administrators shall reimburse to himself or themselves all such costs charges & damages as he or they may or shall have been put to or have received by reason of the aforementioned assignment and the and the relinquishment thereof by the said John M. Hanson and that secondly from the proceeds of the sale of the said Negroes the said John M. Hanson shall immediately pay and discharge the aforesaid debts or such part thereof as shall be unpaid or owing as aforesaid by the said Gad Humphreys together with the expenses incurred in carrying into efect the provision of this indenture so far as the said proceeds will extend and that the said John M. Hanson or his executors or administrators shall pay over the residue of said proceeds if any there shall be to the said Gad Humphreys his executors administrators or assigns and the said John M. Hanson doth by these presents covenant promise and agree to allow and pay to the said Gad Humphreys his executors administrators or assigns ten dollars per month for the Labor of the said three Slaves for such time as they shall actually work for him and to find them in provisions the said Gad Humphreys hereby agreeing to be at the expense of clothing the said Negroes and in case of sickness of such medical aid as the said John M. Hanson shall think they require and shall furnish. And the said John M. Hanson for himself his executors and administrators doth hereby further covenant and agree to and with the said Gad Humphreys his executors and administrators that if the said Gad Humphreys or his executors or Administrators shall and do pay and discharge the aforesaid debts and furnish to the said John M. Hanson or his executors or administrators satisfactory proof thereof on or before the first day of January One thousand Eight hundred and thirty three so that a sale of said Negroes shall not take place in virtue of these presents he the said John M. Hanson or his executors or administrators shall and will reconvey and deliver the said Negroes to the said Gad Humphreys or to his executors administrators or assigns so soon as the said John M. Hanson or his executors or administrators shall be repaid and reimbursed from the labor of said Slaves or otherwise all such damages Costs expenses and charges as the said John M. Hanson or his executors or administrators shall have been put to or have suffered by reason of the aforesaid assignment and the relinquishment thereof as aforesaid or which may have arisen from the making of these presents or the carrying the provisions of the same into effect and it is hereby agreed between the said parties that this clause and the covenants and agreements therein contained shall be considered and taken as a part of the foregoing indenture precisely as if the same had been inserted therein."

January 9, 1832
From Alachua County Ancient Records
Deed Book B pages 014-017

Gad Humphreys to Joseph L. Smith as collateral for $768.14 in loans: "Know all men by these presents that I Gad Humphreys of the County of Alachua in the territory of Florida for the consideration of Six hundred dollars received to my full satisfaction of -- Joseph L. Smith of the City of St Augustine in east Florida Do give bargain sell and deliver and by these presents have given bargained, sold and delivered into the possession of the said Joseph L. Smith the five Negro Slaves bearing the description which follows to wit **Ansel aged about Twenty Two years Toney aged about Eighteen years Joe aged about Twenty four years Andrew aged about Twenty Two years and Bob aged about thirteen years. All of the said Negro Slaves bring of the value of One Thousand Dollars** to have and to hold the said Slaves to him the said Joseph L. Smith and to his heirs and Executors administrators and assigns forever to his and their own proper use and behoof And the said Gad Humphreys do by these presents bind myself my heirs Executors and administrators forever to warrant and defend the said five Negro Slaves bargained sold and delivered as above written unto the said Joseph L. Smith and unto his heirs Executors administrators and assigns against all claims of whatsoever name or nature Provided Nevertheless If I the said Gad Humphreys my heirs Executor or administrators shall well and truly pay the said Joseph L. Smith his heirs Executors administrators or assigns a certain promissory note in Writing by me the said Gad Humphreys well executed and delivered bearing even date with these presents for the sum of six hundred dollars lawful money of the United States for value received payable to said Joseph L. Smith or to his order on or before the Twenty Seventh day of April AD 1834 with Ten per cent interest after the said note shall become due according to the tenor and true intent and meaning thereof And also Shall well and truly pay to the said Joseph L. Smith his heirs Executors administrators and assigns a certain other promissory note in writing by me the said Gad Humphreys well executed and delivered of the same date for the sum of One hundred and Sixty Eight dollars 14/100 dollars lawful money of the United States for value received also payable to the said Joseph L. Smith or to his order on or before the first day of March AD 1834 with ten per cent interest after the same shall come due -- according to the tenor and true intent and meaning thereof, then such payment being made this deed is to be void and of no effect otherwise to remain in full force forever."

April 27, 1833
From Alachua County Ancient Records
Deed Book B pages 061-062

Gad Humphreys to Francis D. Newcomb as collateral for a $286.49 loan: "This Indenture made this twenty ninth day of April in the year of our Lord one Thousand Eight hundred & thirty three Between Gad Humphreys of the County of Alachua and Territory aforesaid of the one part, and Francis D. Newcomb of the County of Monroe Territory aforesaid, of the other part. Witnesseth, whereas the said Gad Humphreys stands justly indebted to the said Francis D. Newcomb of the county aforesaid in the full and just sum of Two Hundred Eighty Six dollars and forty Nine Cents according to the tenor of his certain promissory bearing even date with these presents for the sum of Two hundred Eighty Six dollars and forty nine cents payable on the first day of January next, that is to say One Thousand Eight hundred and thirty four with interest thereon at the rate of six percent per annum. Now therefore Gad Humphreys for and in consideration of the premises and for the better securing the payment of the said sum of money in said note mentioned and of the sum of One dollar to him in hand paid by the said Francis D. Newcomb at or before the sealing and delivery of these presents the receipt whereof is hereby acknowledged, hath granted, bargained, sold, aliened, and conveyed, and by these presents doth grant, bargain, sell, alien, and, convey and confirm unto the said Francis D. Newcomb and to his heirs and assigns forever Two Negro Slaves viz **Sampson a man aged about twenty five years, and Kety his wife aged about Twenty Two years, together with her future increase** To have and to hold the said bargained Slaves to the said party of the second part his heirs and assigns to the sole and only proper use benifit and behoof of the said party of the second part his heirs and assigns forever. Provided nevertheless and these presents are upon this express condition, that if the said Gad Humphreys shall and doth well and truly pay or cause to be paid unto the said Francis D. Newcomb his executors, administrators and assigns the said sum of money in said promissory note mentioned, that is to say the said sum of money in the above said note mentioned with the lawful interest thereon that is to say at the rate of six per cent per annum from the date of said note which will be payable on the first day of January next which will be in the year of our Lord One Thousand Eight hundred & thirty four then these presents and every matter and thing herein contained shall cease and become null and void otherwise to be and remain in full force and virtue."

April 29, 1833
Territory of Florida, County of St. Johns
From Alachua County Ancient Records
Deed Book B pages 048-049

Gad Humphreys repaid loan from F. D. Newcomb that used two enslaved people as collateral: "I do hereby Acknowledge and Certify that a mortgage given by Gad Humphreys to F. D. Newcomb on two Negroes to secure the payment of a sum of money, has been cancelled and paid in full by said Humphreys through me to Capt. W. M. Graham agent of said Newcomb and that said Humphries has satisfied and paid me in full for the same"

February 25, 1836
Oaksands
From Alachua County Ancient Records
Deed Book B pages 207-208

Gad Humphreys to Ashley H. Brooks for $500: "Know all men by these presents that I Gad Humphreys of the County and Territory aforesaid for & in consideration of the sum of Five hundred dollars to me in hand paid the receipt whereof is hereby acknowledged have bargained sold & delivered unto Ashley H. Brooks of the same & Territory. Two certain **negro slaves (females) Elsy & Flora the first about Eleven & the other about nine years of age** To have and to hold the said negro slaves unto the said Ashley H. Brooks & unto his heirs to his and their own proper use & behoof"

May 26, 1834
Territory of Florida, Alachua County
From Alachua County Ancient Records
Deed Book B page 223

Gad Humphreys to John Parhill Esquire as collateral for a $6,000 loan: "Know all men by these presents that I Gad Humphreys of the Teritory and county aforesaid for diverse god causes and reasons me there with moving and hereafter stated have this day alienated released transferred and conveyed (in Trust) to John Parhill Esquire cashier of the Union Bank of Florida for the purposes of securing the payment of a certain note of hand for the sum of six thousand dollars baring date the 21st day of July 1835 (with the interest which may accrue thereon) made by me payable to the order of George Center Esq'r of Micanopa in the County aforesaid and payable six months after date at the Union Bank of Florida Which note is endorsed by said Center and Charles Waldron Esq'r residents and merchants at Micanopy aforesaid The following property to wit My plantation of (unreadable) hundred and fifty acres of Land the improvements thereon lying and being situate at a place called Big Swamp in the County aforesaid also the Negro slaves named and described in the list and appraisement here unto annexed To have and to hold all the said lands, Negroes &c unto him the said John Parkill in trust as aforesaid for the purposes aforesaid and for the further purposes of securing indemnity to the said George Center & Charles Waldron as endorsers upon my note aforesaid and it is hereby expressly understood and agreed by me that in the event of any defalcation or failure to pay the aforesaid at maturing or when due then and in that case it shall be the right and privilege of the said John Parkhill (Trustee as aforesaid) upon giving sixty days notice in the paper called the Floridian published in the City of Tallahassee and given also written public notice at the village of Micanopa aforesaid to offer and sell at public outcry to the highest bidder the Land & Negroes aforesaid or so much thereof as may be necessary to satisfy and pay the full amount of the note aforesaid together with the interest and all regular expenses incident to the collection of the - It being expressly understood and provided however that if the said note should be canceled and paid when due then this deed shall cease to have effect and become null and void otherwise to remain in full force and virtue"

1. **Peter 1st - age 40**
2. **Peter 2nd - age 34**
3. **Jam 1st - age 40**
4. **Jam 2nd - age 35**
5. **August - age 40**
6. **Dick - age 35**
7. **Lancaster - age 28**
8. **Merris - age 26**
9. **Sampson - age 24**
10. **Joe - age 22**
11. **Andrew - age 20**
12. **Hardy - age 22**
13. **Worley - age 30**
14. **Ancel - age 20**
15. **Israel - age 18**
16. **Jem - age 17**
17. **Tony - age 18**
18. **Cyres - age 16**
19. **Joe 2nd - age 20**
20. **Tom - age 50**
21. **Mingo - age 40**
22. **Cornelius - age 50**
23. **Katy 1st - age 45**
24. **Katy 2nd - age 22**
25. **Jane - age 35**
26. **Dolly - age 30**
27. **Sophy - age 28**
28. **Beck - age 25**
29. **Amy - age 30**
30. **Lally - age 25**

31. **Nancy - age 22**
32. **Peggy - age 35**
33. **Hagar - age 20**
34. **Bob - age 11**
35. **Nursey - age 8**
36. **Cooler - age 7**
37. **Lymus - age 6**
38. **Tim - age 5**
39. **Stepny - age 4**

40. **Frank - age 3**
41. **York - age 3**
42. **Affy - age 3**
43. **Philip - age 3**
44. **Betty - age 3**
45. **Sampson 2nd - age 2**
46. **and 5 children under 2 years** Total = 50

Examined and appraised as before stated @ five hundred dollars each"

July 21, 1835
Teritory of Florida, Alachua County
From Alachua County Ancient Records
Deed Book B pages 163-166

James A. D. Lawrence to George E. McClelland as collateral for a $500 promissory note: "Know ye that I James A. D. Lawrence of the County of Alachua in the Territory of Florida, for the Consideration of five hundred dollars, Lawful Money of the United States to me in hand paid by George E. McClelland before the sealing and delivery of these presents, the receipt whereof is hereby fully Acknowledged do give grant bargain and sell unto the said George E. McClellan my two Negro Slaves, **Dick a male aged about fifty years and Charlotte about thirty five years of age a female with all her future increase**, also my sorrel horse about seven years of age and also all my stock of Cattle Carefully Collected and Counted Amounting to twenty four head Marked and branded with the letter L said stock being all that are owned and possessed by me, It being my intention hereby to Convey unto the said George E. McClellan all the stock that belong to me, though it shall be found at any future Collection and Counting that thereof number exceeds the amount herein above stated To have and to hold the above granted and bargained premises unto him the said Geo E. McClellan, or to his executors administrators or assigns for ever to his and their proper use and behoof. And I the said James A.D. Lawrence do for myself my executors and Administrators do covenant with the said George E. McClellan his executors Administrators and Assigns that I have good and lawful right to grant bargain and sell the premises above granted bargained and Sold in manner and form as above written and that the same are free from all incumberances whatsoever And I do also hereby bind myself my executors and Administrators forever to Warrant and defend the above granted and bargained premises unto him the said George E. McClellan his Executors, Administrators and Assigns forever against all claims & demands whatsoever Provided nevertheless if I the said James A. D. Lawrence my executors Administrators or any person for me or them shall well and truly pay unto the said George E. McClellan his executors Administrators or Assigns My certain promissory Note by me made and delivered unto the said George E. McClellean for Value Received and bearing date the first day of January AD 1832 for the sum of five hundred Dollars payable one day after date with Interest as Eight percent according to the terms thereof or any time within one year from the date hereof, then this Deed to be void otherwise to remain in full force"

November 19, 1835
From Alachua County Ancient Records
Deed Book B pages 209-210

Susannah Lowe to son Fernando E. Lowe: "Know all men by these presents that I Susannah Lowe of Alachua County in Consideration of the Love and affection which I have to my Kind and dutiful son Fernando E. Lowe of said County and in Consideration of the many and long services and attention that he has always rendered to and [unreadable] aforesaid a dutiful and loving son and also in the further consideration of five dollars to me in hand paid by the said Fernando E. Lowe before the sealing and and delivery of these presents The receipt whereof is hereby Acknowledged by us and he the said Fernando E. Lowe forever acquited therefore Do give grant and deliver unto the said Fernando E. Lowe & by these presents have given granted granted and delivered unto him my Certain Negro man Slave named **Bill aged thirty five years** To have and to hold unto him the said Fernando E. Lowe his executors and administrators and assigns to his and their own proper use benefit and behoof forever. And I do warrant unto him his executors administrators and assigns that I have good and legal right so to give grant and deliver unto him the said Lowe in manner and form as is above written & that I and my executors administrators and assigns will forever defend the same against all claims and demands whatsoever But it is this agreement of the said Fernando E. Lowe that the said gift grant and delivery of the said slave not withstanding that to keep and use the said slave till my death allowing the said Fernando E. Lowe at the rate of five dollars per year therefore to be paid after my death."

May 3, 1836
From Alachua County Ancient Records
Deed Book B pages 217-219

John H. McIntosh Jr. to Joseph Lawton and Charles Lawton as collateral for a $4,065.11 loan: "This Indenture made this nineteenth day of June One thousand eight hundred and thirty two between John H. McIntosh Jun'r of Oaklands Plantation County of Alachua and Territory of Florida of the one part and Joseph Lawton and Charles Lawton merchants and partners trading under the firm of J. & C. Lawton of the City of Charleston, South Carolina of the second part

Whereas the said J. H. McIntosh Jun'r is justly indebted to the said parties of the second part in the sum of Four thousand sixty five and 11/100 Dollars lawful money of the United States aforesaid to be paid by his bond or obligation bearing even date herewith in the penal sum of Eight thousand one hundred and thirty 22/100 Dollars lawful money aforesaid conditioned for the payment of the first mentioned sum of Four thousand sixty five 11/100 Dollars With legal interest from the first day of July next as by the said bond or obligation and the condition thereof may appear

Now this Indenture Witnesseth that the said party of the first part for the better securing of the said sum of money according to the condition of the said bond or obligation and in consideration of ten Dollars to him in hand paid by the said parties of the second part the receipt whereof is hereby acknowledged have granted, bargained, sold, aliened, released, conveyed, and confirmed, and by these presents do grant, bargain, sell, alien, release, convey, and confirm unto the said parties of the second part their heirs and assigns forever all that Tract or parcel of Land called Oaklands and on which the said John H. McIntosh Jun'r now resides lying and being in the County of Alachua of the Territory of Florida aforesaid on Orange Lake containing Twenty five hundred acres more or less and having the following boundaries to wit

On the East by Orange Lake, on the north by Lands belonging to Arredondo and others, on the west by a tract of Land owned by D. L. Clinch, and on the south by Lands belonging to Arredondo and others it being the same tract or parcel of Land sold and conveyed by one George I. F. Clark to J. H. McIntosh Sen'r as by reference to said deed will more fully appear Together with all and singular the tenements hereditaments and appurtenances, the sugar Works and improvements, implements, Waggons, Carts, Carriages, Horses, Mules, and cattle of every kind thereunto belonging or any wise appertaining and also all the estate right title, interest property possession claim and demand in law or in Equity of the said party of the first part of in and to the same and the reversion and reversions, remainder and remainders rents issues and profits thereof and the said J.H. McIntosh Jun'r of the first part hath furthermore bargained and sold and by these presents doth bargain and sell unto the said parties of the second part all and singular the following Negroes and other Slaves - to Wit **Lewis and his wife Lucy, Hector and his wife Delia and her six children, Captain and his wife and her six children, Situs and Helen his wife, Andrew and Iris his wife and her one child, Quoa and his wife Betty, Pizarro and his wife Cornelia, Colonel and his wife Fatina, Little Lewis and his wife Hagar, Old Hagar, Sandy and Adam**. To Have and to Hold all and singular the herein before granted and released premises with the appurtenances and all of the above named slaves **with all the future increase and issue of the female slaves aforesaid** unto the said Joseph and Charles Lawton aforesaid their Heirs Executors administrators and assigns forever and to their own proper use and behoof forever provided always and these presents are upon this condition nevertheless that if the said J. H. McIntosh Jun'r of the first part his heirs executors or administrators or any of them shall well and truly pay unto the said parties of the second part their executors administrators or assigns the said sum of money mentioned in the condition of the aforesaid Bond or Obligation of him the said J. H. McIntosh Jun'r at the time and in the manner therein specified according to the true intent and meaning thereof that then and from thence forth these presents and the Estate hereby granted and every thing herein contained shall cease and determine and be absolutely void to all intents and purposes and the said John H. McIntosh Jun'r for himself heirs Executors and administrators doth Covenant grant promise and agree to and with the said parties of the second part their executors administrators and assigns the sum of money aforesaid (Four Thousand sixty five 11/100 Dollars) at the time and in the manner herein before mentioned according to the condition of the said Bond or Obligation well and truly to pay."

June 19, 1832
From Alachua County Ancient Records
Deed Book B pages 028-030

John H. McIntosh Jr. manumits and emancipates three enslaved children: "Whereas my father John H. McIntosh of Camden County Georgia did deliver to me in this Territory in the month of January Eighteen Hundred & Twenty Seven **three Coloured female Slave Children, all of them sisters called Bella who is about Ten years of age, Maria, who is now about Eight years of age & the other who is called Sue who is now between six & seven years old**, for the express & sole purpose and intention of having them emancipated & manumitted with their issue forever according to the laws of said Territory, and whereas I did declare & consider them, Emancipated and manumitted & their issue forever to all intents and purposes Though I did not at that time execute any instrument of writing to that effect and which might have been of record. Now Know all men By these presents that I John H. McIntosh Jr. of Florida for and in consideration of the sum of one dollar to me in hand paid the receipt whereof I do hereby acknowledge, hath agreed and declared to manumit three Coloured female Slave Children with their issue forever are manumitted and Emancipated. And I for myself my heirs executors and administators will warrant and defend the manumission and emancipation of the said Children & their issue forever against any person or persons whatsoever"

October 11, 1833
Territory of Florida, Alachua County
From Alachua County Ancient Records
Deed Book B pages 043-044

John Houston McIntosh Jr. to Ralph King and William King as collateral for a $1,960.27 loan: "This Indenture made this twenty fourth day of February in the year of our Lord one thousand eight hundred and thirty four Between John Houston McIntosh Jr. of Alachua County East Florida of the first part and Ralph King and William King merchants and copartners trading under the style of R A W King of Savannah in said State of the second part Witnesseth that the party of the first part as well for the better securing to the parties of the second the faithful payment of debt, which the said John H. McIntosh Jr. the said party of the first part justly owes to the parties of the second part in manner herein after mentioned or in consideration of the sum of one dollar to him in hand paid by the parties of the second part the receipt whereof is hereby acknowledged hath granted bargained sold aliened released and confirmed and by these presents doth grant bargain sell alien release and confirm unto the parties of the second part their heirs and assigns forever All that tract of Land situate lying and being in the County of Alachua in east Florida bounded east by Orange Lake West by Col D. L. Clinch's land north and south by public land and also doth bargain & sell the following Negro Slaves to wit **Big Lone (1) and Lucy (2) Young Lone (3) Young Hagar (4) and two children (6) Captain (7) Nancy (8) and three children (11) Grace (12) Amy (13) Newton (14) Hector (15) Dilin (16) and two children (18) Gino (19) Amelia (20) Juba (21) Iris (22) and two children (24) Rhoda (25) Titus (26) Helen (27) Pezarro (28) Cornelia (29) Jug (30) Biss (31) Harriett (32) Andrew (33) Adam (34) Ben (35) Hagar (old)(36) Julian (37) Sandy and Lydia together with their future issue and increase of the said female slaves** The said land and Negroes having been previously mortgaged by the said party of the first part to J&C Lawton of Charleston South Carolina to secure the payment of Four thousand one hundred dollars Together with all and singular the edifices buildings rights members and hereditaments & appurtenances to the same belonging or in any wise appertaining and all estate right title interest property claim and demand whatsoever of the said party of the first part of in or to the same and the reversion and reversions remainder and remainders thereof To have and to hold the said premises herein granted and released with the rights members hereditament and appurtenances thereunto belonging and in every part and parcil thereof unto the parties of the second part their heirs and assigns to the only proper use and behoof of the said parties of the second part their heirs and assigns forever

Upon condition nevertheless that if the said John H. McIntosh Jr. of said party of the first part his heirs executors Administrators or assigns shall faithfully pay to the said parties of the second part on or before the first day of January next (1835) nineteen hundred and sixty dollars & twenty seven cents according to the tennor and true intent and meaning of his certain promissory not bearing date even with these presents and duly made and executed the said John Houston McIntosh Jr. The said party of the first part to the party of the second part and also shall pay or cause to be paid all future notes bills drafts or other Instruments for or in removal of said notes or any part thereof together with with all interest expenses or charges of any description arising therein therefrom or there out Then this present Indenture and the Estate hereby granted and every article and clause herein contained as well the said promissory note shall cease and become utterly void […] if default be made in the payment of the principle secured to be paid to the said parties of the second part and the interest which shall accrue thereupon at any time or times on which they shall be due or of any part of such principal or interest that then and from thence forth it shall be lawful for the parties of the second part their Heirs and Executors Administrators or Assigns to grant bargain sell and dispose of the said hereby granted premises and all benefit and equaty and equaty of redemption of the said party of the first his Heirs Executors Administrators or assigns therein according to the direction of the Act of the Legislature in that case made and provided rendering the overplus of the purchase monies to be obtained for the same after full satisfaction of the principal and interest to be due on such note or notes thereof in manner aforesaid and to the charges of advertisement and sale (if any overplus there shall be) unto the said John Houston McIntosh Jr. the said party of the first part his Heirs Executors Administrators or Assigns"

February 24, 1834
State of Georgia
From Alachua County Ancient Records
Deed Book B pages 087-091

Micanopy Chief of the Seminole Tribe to John Paine and his wife Susan Paine for $140: "Know all men by these presents that I Micanopy Chief of the Seminole tribe of Indians in the Territory of Florida for and in consideration of One Hundred & forty dollars to me in hand paid before the sealing of these presents the receipt whereof I hereby acknowledge have bargained sold and conveyed and by these presents do bargain sell and convey to John Paine and Susan Paine wife of the said John Paine a certain Negro girl named **Catherine** daughter of the said John and Susan Paine born in the month of March 1829. The condition of this conveyance is that the said John Paine is to exercise the right of Parent and guardian over the said Catherine until the age of Twenty One Years when the said Catherine is by these presents to free. And I the said Micanopa aforesaid do hereby warrant this my said conveyance to be good, and engage to defend the said John from all claims to said Catherine whatsoever during and after her minority."

May 6, 1834
From Alachua County Ancient Records
Deed Book B page 076

Shikes Nelomus and Penelope H. Nelomus to Benett M. Dell for $1,500: "Know all men by these presents that we Shikes Nelomus and Penelope H. Nelomus for and in consideration of the sum of $1500 dollars to me in hand paid at and before the sealing and delivery of these presents by Benett M. Dell the receipt whereof we do hereby acknowledge have bargained and sold and by these presents do bargain sell and deliver to the said Bennett M. Dell my Negro Slaves, to wit, **Silvey a negro woman and her children Charles, George, Charlotte, Jacob and Israel** To have and to hold the said negro woman Silvey and her children Charles, George, Charlotte, Jacob and Israel unto the said Benett M. Dell his heirs Executors Administrators and assigns to his and their only proper use and benefit forever"

January 26, 1839
State of Georgia
From Alachua County Ancient Records
Deed Book B pages 239-240

Francis D. Newcomb to Gad Humphreys for $414: "Know all men by these presents that I Francis D. Newcomb of the Territory and County aforesaid have this day bargained sold and delivered to Gad Humphreys **a Negro or Mulatto Girl named Katy aged about Seventeen years** for and in consideration of the sum of four Hundred and fourteen dollars to me in hand paid the receipt of which is hereby acknowledged & I hereby warrant & defend the title to the said Girl."

April 14, 1830
Territory of Florida, Alachua County
From Alachua County Ancient Records
Deed Book B page 136

James Perryman to Gad Humphreys for $650: "Know all men by these presents that I James Perryman of the State of Georgia have this day sold granted bargained and delivered to Gad Humphreys of Florida for and in consideration of the sum of Six Hundred & fifty dollars to me in hand paid by the said Humphreys (the receipt whereof is hereby acknowledged) the following named and described ~~property~~ Negro Slaves now residing in the Seminole Nation of Indians viz **Lydia the wife of a Negro fellow called March aged about thirty years and all the increase or children of the said Lydia Except her oldest daughter named Sarah** which I have sold to the Chief Tugatskee commonly called Charles To have and to hold to the said Humphreys his heirs and assigns &C &C for their own proper use and behoof forever the said Negroes as Slaves for life And I the said Perryman do by these presents obligate myself my heirs assigns &C &C to forever warrant and defend to the said Humphreys his heirs and assigns &C &C the title to the said Slaves against all claims Whatever

November 22, 1833
Territory of Florida, Alachua County
From Alachua County Ancient Records
Deed Book B pages 078-079

John Phagan to Bennett M. Dell and Erastus Rogers for $1,250: "Know all men by these presents that I John Phagan of the Seminole Agency County of Alachua & Territory of Florida have bargained sold and delivered to Bennett M. Dell and Erastus Rogers the following named property for and in consideration of the sum of twelve hundred and fifty dollars to wit Five head of Horses, One mule, Thirty head of cattle **One Negro Boy about thirty five years of**

age named Nat and One Negro woman about sixty years of age named Betty. All of the above mentioned property I do warrant and defend against my heirs executors administrators and assigns to the said B.M. Dell and E. Rogers"

October 4, 1833
Seminole Agency Fla
From Alachua County Ancient Records
Deed Book B page 058

W. H. G. Sanders to Thomas Colding to be held in trust for Zelpha Caroline Colding who W. H. G. Sanders is to marry: "This Indenture made this eighteenth day of December 1834 Between W.H.G. Sanders of the Teritory and County aforesaid of the one part and Thomas Colding (sen) of the same place of the other part Witnesseth, whereas a marriage is shortly intended to be had and solemnized between the said W.H.G. Sanders and Zelpha Caroline Colding of the Teritory and County aforesaid and whereof the W.H.G. Sanders being possessed and owning certain personal property hereafter discribed is desirous previous to said marriage being had and solemnized and in consideration thereof between him and the said Zelpha Caroline of settling and securing the same the same unto the said Zelpha Caroline for her and during her life

Now therefore this Indenture witnesseth that for and in consideration of the premises and the said marriage to be had and solemnized as aforesaid and of the sum of ten dollars to him the said W.H.G. Sanders in hand paid by the said Tho's Colding, sen at and before the sealing (& delivery) of these presents the receipt whereof is hereby acknowledged he the said W.H.G. Sanders has granted bargained sold and by these presents doth grant bargain and sell unto him the said Tho's Colding sen his executors administrators the following personal property that is to say **one Negro male slave named Fortune about twenty five years of age one female slave - Nancy about sixteen years of age and her child Robert about seven moths old and one male slave named Cathom about five five years old one male slave named Hary aged thirty years and one female slave named Maria about thirty years of age** forty head of stock cattle and one Bay Horse - **and the future issue of the females of said slaves and cattle** To have and to hold all the above bargained sold and discribed property unto him the said Tho's Colding Sen his Executors and administrators in trust nevertheless and for the use benefit and behoof of her the said Zelpha Caroline Colding and during the time of her natural life and upon the death of the said Caroline then in trust for him the said W.H.G. Sanders and if he the said W.H.G. Sanders depart this life before the said Zelpha Caroline then upon the death of the said Zelpha Caroline in trust for the legal heirs of him the said W.H.G. Sanders and it is specially agreed & understood between the parties to these presents that all of the above granted bargained sold and discribed property shall be and remain in the possession and under the control and direction of her the the said Zelpha Caroline and she shall without any interference on the part of him the said Tho's Colding Sen, use said property and receive and enjoy the service and avails and proceeds of the slaves and increase and increase of the stock aforesaid"

December 18, 1834
Territory of Florida, Alachua County
From Alachua County Ancient Records
Deed Book B pages 101-102

John M. Stafford to Susanna Stafford his wife upon their final separation as patrimony for herself and their children Lafayette Stafford and Columbus Stafford: "This Indenture made & entered into this Twenty ninth day of June in the year of our Lord one thousand Eight hundred and thirty three between John M. Stafford and Susanna his wife of the County of Alachua and territory of Florida of the one part and George Branning of Duval County in the Aforesaid Territory of the other part Witnesseth that whereas on the Twentieth of May in the year now present, a final separation took place between the aforesaid John M. Stafford and his aforesaid wife Susanna, formerly Susanna Branningand sister of the aforesaid George Branning, and whereas the aforesaid John M. Stafford is willing to make a lawful provision for the support maintenance and comfort of his aforesaid wife and hath agreed for that purpose to refund to the said George for her use, all the property and estate hereinafter named, being the entire property received as her Patrimony at or since their marriage for this cause and for and in consideration of a Bond Executed by the said George Branning with William Branning as his security to bear the said John M Stafford free and harmless from the further support and maintenance of the said Susanna his wife, and for other purposes in said Bond expressed reference thereto being had bearing even date with these presents will more fully appear and for and in consideration of the sum of five dollars to him the said John M. Stafford in hand paid at and before the ensealing, and delivery of these presents the receipt whereof is hereby acknowledged. He the said John M. Stafford hath bargained sold and delivered unto the said George Branning the following named property to wit Two Negroes **Milley a girl about eighteen years of age and Wiley a boy about four years old together with the future issue and increase of the female if any**, also thirty nine head of stock cattle the old ones whereof are marked with a poplar leaf in one ear and a split in the other and branded AB, the younger ones marked with a poplar leaf in one ear and a split and under bit in the other branded F Also two notes of William Branning payable to the John M. Stafford or bearer dated 22 January 1833 the One for Eighty three dollars thirty three and a third cents $83 33 1/3/100 payable six months after date and the other for Eighty six dollars sixty six and two thirds cents $86 66 2/3/100 payable Eighteen months after date. Also a note of George Branning of same date payable three months after date for the sum of Thirty one dollars, forty three cents and one yellow Bay mare of the Indian pony racer about three years of age Branded $, and the said John M. Stafford doth by these presents bargain sell and deliver the aforesaid and named property and [unreadable] to the said George Branning and his assigns forever Upon trust nevertheless and, and, to the use and for the purposes herein after named that is to say the afore mentioned Negroes Milley and Wiley upon trust for the sole and separate use benefit & and behoof and for the comfort and maintenance of the aforesaid Susanna Stafford for and during the term of her natural life and at her death if that event should take place during the minority of the infant children of the said John and Susanna now born or in being in trust during the minority of such child or children, to be hired out and the money apropriated according to law at interest and the same and interest to be paid over to the said children when they respectively come of age

In trust also if the said Susanna shall survive until all of said children them in being shall arrive at Lawful age to be by the said Branning delivered up at her death to such child or children or their heirs according to the terms & provisions of a deed of gift of the said John M. Stafford and Susanna his wife of Sundry Negroes therein named, made to Lafayette Stafford, and Columbus Stafford and such other child or children of the said John M. And Susanna as shall be born on or before the twentieth day of February which will be in the year Eighteen hundred & thirty four.

Upon trust further if the said Susanna shall survive all the children of the said John aforesaid named or referred to, or their lineal descendants then at her death the said Negroes with the increase shall vest in her right heirs by consanguinity

And this deed is upon the especial trust more ever, that all the property & *oses in action herein and hereby conveyed, shall be and remain for and during the natural life of the said Susanna for her use benefit and behoof and for her support, maintenance, and comfort and at her death to vest fully and entirely in her heirs at law, Provided that this clause of this deed shall not be construed in any manner to affect the disposition herein before made of the Negroes hereby conveyed

Upon trust also that this conveyance and the delivery of the Negroes therein named to the said Branning shall shall sustain and not abridge in any manner weaken the deed of gift of the same made to Lafayette & Columbus Stafford and such past humons children of the said John M. And Susanna as may be born on or before the twentieth day of February 1834 Reference to the said deed bearing even date with theses presents will fully appear -- but the aforesaid deed of is made upon the full knowledge priority and consent & agreement of the parties hereto

Provided however it is expressly understood by parties hereto if the said George Branning should die before the trust herein confided shall be executed and finished, that his executor or executors shall succeed to said trust and if he should die without an executor or for any other cause, no trustee shall be in being it shall and may be lawful by appointment of any Court Of Chancery, having jurisdiction to supply such vacancy upon application of any person interested"

June 29, 1833
From Alachua County Ancient Records
Deed Book B pages 035-038

John M. Stafford and Susanna Stafford his wife to their infant children Lafayette Stafford and Columbus Stafford, held in trust by George Branning: "Know all men by these presents that we John M. Stafford and Susanna Stafford his wife for and in consideration of the natural love and affection which we bear to our two infant children Lafayette Stafford and Columbus Stafford and for and in consideration of one dollar to us in hand paid by George Branning for and on behalf of said infant children at and before the ensealing and delivery of these presents have bargained, and sold and do by these presents bargain and sell to the said Lafayette Stafford and Columbus Stafford, the following Negro Slaves to wit **Milley a girl aged about Eighteen years, Wiley a boy about four years of age Fanny a girl about eight years of age and Jack about seven years old together with the future issue and increase of the females if any there should be**. Reserving however to the said Susanna Stafford the right of using and having and enjoying the use and profits of the two Negroes Milley and Wiley for and during the term of her natural life and also in like manner and for the like term the increase of the female slave if any there should be and reserving also to the said John M. Stafford a life estate of the use and profits of the two slaves Fanny & Jack and the increase of the female if any it being expressly understood that at the time of the death of Susanna the estate herein or hereby Granted to the said children Lafayette and Columbus shall take effect and operation so far as respects the Negroes, for which a life estate is reserved to her and in like manner at the time of death of the said John M. Stafford the estate herein and hereby Granted to the said children shall take effect and operation, so far as respects the Negroes for which a life estate is reserved to him the said John

Provided however if the said Susanna Stafford shall be delivered of any other child or children by the said by the said John M. her husband on or before the twentieth day of February which will be in the year of our Lord Eighteen hundred and thirty four, that this conveyance shall operate equally to the use and right of such posthumous child or children, as if such child or children were now born and herein named so as to vest the right of such Negroes herein and hereby granted to the said Lafayette and Columbus equally in such posthumous child or children born as aforesaid together with the said Lafayette and Columbus share & share alike and provided also if any or either of such child or children herein spoken of or referred to should die before the particular estates herein and hereby reserved shall determine that his or her share in said Negroes shall vest in the remaining child or children herein named or referred to so as to vest in the remaining children if more than one equal shares and if but one the whole property Granted but if all said children should die before the particular estates or either hereby reserved, shall determine the estate hereby Granted shall so operate that the Negroes Milley and Wiley and the increase of the female shall vest at the death of said Susanna Stafford in her right heirs by consanguinity, and in like manner the title in the Negroes Fanny & Jack and the increase of the female shall revert to the said John M. Stafford or his right heirs at law,

Provided also that if the said John Stafford should die during the minority of the Grantees herein named or referred to or during the minority of either of them that he reserve to himself the right of appointing a guardian to such minor or minors as the case may be, to manage that part of the estate hereby granted and in which a life estate has reserved to said John M. for the use of such minor or minors during minority in such manner as by appointment he may think necessary and must to interest of said minor or minors,

Provided also that this deed is made subject to the limitations contained in a deed of trust made by the said John M. Stafford and Susanna his wife to the said George Branning herein before named, So far as respects the Negroes Milley and Wiley and the increase of the female, which said deed of trust bears even date with these presents and is intended to perfect a final separation between the aforesaid John M. Stafford and his aforesaid wife and for the purpose of a division of their estate between them.

June 29, 1833
From Alachua County Ancient Records
Deed Book B pages 039-041

H. H. Tarver to Ashley Brooks for $200: "Rec'd of Ashley Brooks Two Hundred dollars in full of the purchase of a **Negro Man named Toney** which I will warrant & forever defend the wright & title of unto the said Brooks his heirs &c"

December 6, 1833
From Alachua County Ancient Records
Deed Book B page 058

Theophilus Weeks applying for a Revolutionary War pension: "Theophilus Weeks vs. The United States - Application for a Pension

Now on this day came the said Theophilus Weeks in his own proper person and made the following Original Claim, "Declaration in order to be placed on the Pension List under the Act of the 18th March 1818 County of Alachua fl.

On this 20th day of April in the Year of our Lord one thousand eight hundred and thirty personally appeared in open court being a court of record for the District of East Florida Theophilus Weeks, resident in said County aged sixty nine years who being First duly sworn according to law doth on his oath make the following declaration in order to obtain the provision made by the acts of Congress of the 18th March 1818 and the first of May 1820 That he the said Theophilus Weeks enlisted for the term of two and one half years on or about the twentieth day of May in the year of our Lord one thousand seven hundred and seventy six (as such as this deponent can now recollect, but having lost all his papers connected with this case he cannot State with certainty the time of his said enlistment or of his discharge) in the State of North Carolina in the Company commanded by Captain George Mitchell in the Regiment commanded by Colonel Lytle, or Colonel Taylor. one of whom was Colonel and the other Lieut Colonel but this deponent cannot now say with certainty which commanded at the time of his enlistment as aforesaid, in the line of the State of North Carolina on the continental establishment, that he continued to serve in the said Corps about one year when he was transferred to the company commanded by Captain Griffin John McCrea in the Regiment commanded by Colonel John Clark & that he continued to serve in the last mentioned Corps until about the twentieth day of November in the year of our Lord one thousand Seven hundred and Seventy eight but of the exact time he cannot be certain for the reason aforesaid, when he was honorably discharged from the Service in the State of New York, (the period of his said enlistment having having expired) and that he hereby relinquishes every claim whatever to a claim except the present. that his name is not on the role of any State except North Carolina; and that the following are the reasons for not making earlier application for a pension, to wit, that he had been informed and believed that he could not obtain a pension without making oath that he could not Support himself without a pension and that he was not willing to make such oath.

In pursuance of the Act of first May 1820 I do solemnly swear that I was a resident Citizen of the United States on the 18th day of March 1818 and that I have not since that time by gift, sale, or in any manner disposed of my property or any part thereof with intent thereby so to diminish it as to bring myself within the provisions of an act of Congress entitled an "act to provide for certain persons engaged in the land and Naval Service of the United States in the revolutionary war." Issued on the 18th day of March 1818 and that I have not nor has any person in trust for me any property or securities contracts, or debts due to me; nor have I any income other than what is contained in the Schedule hereto annexed and by me Subscribed, that since the 18th day of March 1818 the following changes have been made in my property (to wit) I have lost two horses by death and have Sold a tract of land which I owned in the State of georgia for the sum of one hundred dollars which Sum has been expended in the necessary Support of my family the members of which now residing with me are my wife aged about Sixty eight years who is quite Feeble, a grand daughter eleven years of age a son aged twenty five years a Farmer by profession who supports himself by his own labor having no property except a horse and five Cows and calves besides these I have living with me **one Negro Woman a Slave** who however does not belong to me; I am by trade a Cooper but am unable to do much work.

Sworn to and declared on this 20th day of April 1830 in open Court

Schedule above referred to (viz) 20 head of hogs - 4 iron pots - 1 oven - 1Teakettle - 5 chairs - 2 Tables - one old chest - one old cart- and a set of Coopers tools

Sworn to in open Court on this 20th day of April 1830 as a complete and perfect Schedule.

Now on this day the said Theophilus Weeks having made the declaration and oath required by Law in his said Application for a Pension, as a private Soldier of the Revolution - and this Court having considered said declaration an oath of the Said Weeks and the other evidence in Support thereof Exibited in Court- and here placed on file and it appearing to the satisfaction of this court that the said Theophilus Weeks Served in the Revolution as aforesaid against the common enemy - It is hereby ordered that the Clerk of this Court do certify in due form and transmit the testimony in this case, and the proceedings had thereon to the Secretary of the War Dept. The Court having heard testimony as to the value of the property contained and Set forth in the foregoing Schidule is of opinion that the amount and Value thereof is forty five dollars and no more - which well also be certified by the Clerk of this Court to the said Secretary."

April 20, 1830
From Alachua County Ancient Records
Superior Court Minutes 1 pages 034-038

1840's

Cornelius Barber to John W. Pearson as collateral for a $145.04 loan: "Know all men by these presents that I Cornelius Barber of Alachua County, State of Florida in consideration of the sum of one Dollar to me in hand paid by John W Pearson of the County and State aforesaid the Receipt whereof is hereby acknowledged, Have granted bargained and sold and by these presents do grant bargain & sell unto the said J.W. Pearson the following property to wit, **one negro woman named Lucy aged about 48 years** also ten milch cows with their calves or yearlings, marks poplar leaf in one ear swallow fork poplar leaf & hole in the other ear, brand C.B. to have and to hold all and singular the said negro woman name Lucy and the named cattle unto the said Jno W. Pearsonhis Executor Administrators and assigns to his and their whole & sole use forever and I the said Cornelius Barber for myself my Executors and administrators and assigns do covenant to and with the said J. W. Pearson his Executors administrators and assigns that I am lawfully possessed of the said negro woman and ten cows & their calves as of my own property that the same are free from all encumbrance and that I will and my Executors &c shall warrant and for ever defend the same to the said John W. Pearson his Executors administrators &c against the lawful claiming and demands of all persons. Provided nevertheless that if the said Cornelius Barber his Executors administrators &c shall well and truly pay unto the said John W. Pearson his executors administrators &c a certain note of hand bearing date 22 Jany 1848 for the amount of one hundred forty five dollars & 4 cents Then this conveyance shall be void otherwise to remain in full force and effect and provided also that until default by the said Cornelius Barber his Executors assigns &c in the performance of the condition aforesaid it shall and may be lawful for him or them to keep possession of the said property and to use and enjoy the same but if the same shall be attached at any time before payment &c by any other creditor of the said Cornelius Barber or if the said Cornelius Barber of if his executor administrators &c shall attempt to sell the same without notice to the Said John W. Pearson or his Executor &c and without his or their agreement to such sale in writing expressed then it shall be lawfull for the said John W. Pearson his assigns &c to take immediate possession of said granted property to his and their own use."

March 30, 1848
From Alachua County Ancient Records
Mortgage Record A pages 012-013

Rebecca Bates to Fernando A. Underwood for $500: "Know all men by these presents, that I Rebecca Bates of Alachua County, for and in consideration of the just sum of five hundred dollars to me in hand paid by Fernando A. Underwood, the receipt whereof I do hereby acknowledge, have bargained, and sold, and by these presents do bargain, convey, and confirm unto the said Underwood one certain Negro man named **Ben**, being the same heretofore conveyed to me by an instrument of writing now on record from said Underwood. To have and to hold unto him the said Underwood, his heirs, and assigns forever said bargained premises."

January 21, 1843
From Alachua County Ancient Records
Bills of Sale A page 014

Robert D. Bradley to James Bradley as collateral for a $6,440 loan: "This Indenture made June the first in the year of our Lord One thousand eight hundred and forty two Know all men by these presents that I Robert D. Bradley of the Territory and County Aforesaid of the one part and James Bradley of the same Territory & County of the second part Witnesseth that I Robert D. Bradley of the first part for and in consideration of the sum of Six thousand four hundred and forty Dollars lawful money of the United States to me in hand paid at and before the Sealing and delivery of these presents by the said James Bradley of the second part of the Territory and County Aforesaid, the receipt whereof I do hereby Acknowledge have bargained and sold, and by these presents do bargain Sell and deliver unto the said James Bradley Seven Negroes, To Wit **David, Moses, Bill, Caroline, and Elizer with her two children Wiley and Willis**, To have and to hold the said Seven Negroes viz David, Moses, Bill, Caroline, and Elizer with her two children Wiley and Willis, and unto the said James Bradley his heirs Executors, Administrators and Assigns to them and to their only proper use and behoof forever, And I the said Robert D. Bradley my heirs Executors and Administrators, to the said Bargained Premises, unto the said James Bradley his heirs, executors, Administrators and Assigns from & against all and every person or persons whosoever, shall and will Warrant and forever defend by these presents. Now the Condition of the above Mortgage is such that if the said Robert D. Bradley by himself or his heirs, executors, Administrators and Assigns, shall well and truly pay or cause to be paid unto the said James Bradley his heirs, executors, Administrators and Assigns the sum of Six thousand four hundred and forty Dollars lawful money of the United States by the first day of January Eighteen hundred three, then this Mortgage to be Null and void otherwise to remain in full force and virtue."

June 1, 1842
Territory of Florida, County of Alachua
From Alachua County Ancient Records
Deed Book B pages 417-419

George L. Brown to Samuel Clark Esqr. in Trust for Olympia Clark for $650: "Know all men by these presents that I George L. Brown of Alachua County, State of Florida, for and in consideration of the sum of six hundred and fifty dollars to me in hand paid by Samuel Clark Esqr, the receipt whereof I do by these presents acknowledge, have bargained, and sold, and by these presents do bargain, sell and deliver the following Negro Slaves, to wit: **a woman named Polly aged about fifty years, Susan, aged about fifteen years, and her infant child John aged about six months**. To have and to hold the said Negro Slaves, **together with their future issue and increase** unto the said Samuel Clark Esqr, in Trust nevertheless to and for the sole use, benefit and behalf of Olympia wife of William H Clark, her heirs begotten by the said William H. Clark, her husband as aforesaid, forever."

February 14, 1848
State of Florida, Alachua County
From Alachua County Ancient Records
Mortgage Record A page 018

Nehemiah Brush Last Will and Testament: "The last will and Testament of Nehemiah Brush at present of the City, State, and County of New York. I Nehemiah Brush considering the uncertainty of this mortal life and being of Sound mind and memory blessed be God, do make and publish this my last will and Testament in manner and form following.

That is to Say, I give and bequeath to my beloved wife Margaret Brush and my Children, viz, Julia Van Ness, John H. Brush, Caroline E.

Brush and Charles W. Brush each respectively four Hundred Dollars which Said Sums of money Shall be paid to each of the said legatees within two years after my decease, or sooner if the State of the funds permit them, I then further give and devise to my said Daughter Julia Van Ness her heirs and assigns, all my right title, interest, in and to a tract of land being about twelve Hundred and fifty acres more or less, the same having been conveyed to me by my said Daughter Julia and Eugene Van Ness her Husband, and fifty acres thereof which was conveyed *** **** the Sheriff or tax collector of St. Johns County Territory of Florida, Situate on the Matanzes Rier and Pallicers creek, granted it is believed originally to one Tucker containing Eight hundred acres more or less, also, another tract or part of a grant Situate in Mosqueto or Reid County in Said Territory at or near a place known by the name of New Smyrna originally granted to one Samuel Betts, containing two Thousand acres which said part, portion and interest had been conveyed to me by my said Daughter Julia and Eugene Van Ness her Husband in a certain deed recorded in the Book of records in Said St. Johns County will more fully Show, reference being thereunto had, both of the Said described parts and portions of land and devised premises, to hold to the Said Julia Van Ness her heirs and assigns forever, I further give and devise to my said Son John H. Brush my entire real Estate in the State of Illinois amounting to Seven Military bounty lots more or less, to his heirs and assigns to hold to the said John H Brush his heirs and assigns forever, I further give and devise to my said Daughter Caroline E. Brush her heirs and assigns, all my interest claim title to a tract of land in the St. Johns County, in the territory of Florida, Situate on the side of the St. Johns River, and opposite to a place known by the name of Palatka, called New Buna Vista, or more lately Orange Point, containing three hundred and fifty Acres, more or less to hold to the said Caroline E. Brush, her heirs and assigns forever, I further give and devise to my Said Son Charles W. Brush all my interest, claim, title, and interest in and to certain tracts of land, said to be Situate at, or near a place on the west side of the St. John River, in Florida Known as Bryants Point opposite to Old Buna Vista, one of said tracts was granted by the Spanish Government, or authorities, I believe, to one Tate containing four hundred and fifty acres, another to one Fleming in all said to be there located*, was seven hundred and Eighty acres more or less, or wherever Situate or to be located, Also two fractional Sections of land Situate on the North of the above described land lying upon the Said River St. Johns, the same was purchased by Eugene Van Ness of the U. S. Army for my benefit, to hold to the Said Charles W. Brush, his heirs and assigns forever. I will and order that my Executors hereafter named do pay all my past debts and respective legatees first named from and not of my other and remaining property or Estate, when, I then further give, bequeath, and devise unto my said wife Margaret Brush, Julia Van Ness, John H. Brush, Caroline E. Brush, and Charles W. Brush, Respectively all the balance, remainder, and residue of my real and personal Estate, good and chattels of every kind and description whatever and wheresoever in the United States, or elsewhere in the following manner and form, viz, To hold to the Said Margaret Brush her heirs and assigns, the same to be in lieu of her Dower, the one fifth part or portion, or the avails hereof when Sold, forever, to the said Julia Van Ness, and her heirs, another fifth part or portion or the avails thereof of said property when Sold, Which I will Shall be put out on good and sure Bond and Mortgage, or invested equally safe and advantageous, the said Julia Van Ness drawing the interest dividend and of the same and her heirs, to hold to the Said Julia Van Ness and her heirs forever, to the said John H. Brush, his heirs and assigns another fifth part and portion or the avails thereof of said property when Sold, to hold to the said John H. Brush, his heirs and assigns forever, to the said Caroline E. Brush drawing the interest or dividends of the same and her heirs, to hold to the said Caroline E. Brush and her heirs and assigns after the death of her Mother as already Stated forever, also to the said Charles W. Brush his heirs and assigns another and the last fifth part and portion or the avails whereof when sold of said property, to hold to the said Charles W. Brush his heirs and assigns forever. I further give bequeath and devise to my said wife Margaret Brush, in case my said Daughter Caroline E. Brush, Should die leaving no child, the said fifth part and portion of said property when sold, as before named, belonging to my Said Daughter Caroline E. Brush, during her natural life, that is to hold to the said Margaret Brush So long as she shall live. I will that my Executors hereinafter named be charged with all the respective duties of selling, investing, collecting, recurring, and paying money as above given & bequeathed to the several, and respective named as interested therein, which they Shall exercise their best judgment in, but shall not be liable for any less thereby under the circumstance as stated, that is, where due diligence and their best Judgment is and they, my hereinafter named Executors, Shall Sell and dispose of all my thus named, bequeathed, and devised, and last named property, Estate real and personal, goods and chattles as mentioned already for the term of two years, and forever if it can be effected to advantage, and shall make dividend yearly of all the sales that shall be made of parts and portions of said property or estate till the whole shall be sold, I do hereby nominate my two said sons John H. Brush and Charles W. Brush, my Executors to this my last will and Testament, revoking all former wills made by me and lastly, my express will and meaning is, and I do hereby order, and appoint that, if any difference, dispute, question or controversy Shall be moved, arise or happen, concerning any gift, bequeath, matter or thing in this will given and bequeathed, expressed or contained, that then no suit or suits in law or Equity or otherwise shall be brought, commenced prosecuted for and concerning the same, but the same shall be referred wholly to the award, order, and determination of my friends William Woodhull of the City of New York, and Peter P. Monfort of Dutchess County, N. York that and what they, or the Survivor of either of them shall award, direct or determine therein, Shall be binding and conclusive to all and every person and persons therein contained, This tenth day of March in the year 1843....

A Codicil to my last WILL and TESTAMENT, WHEREAS I Nehemiah Brush of the Town of Fish Kill County of Dutchess and State of New York Physician, being of sound mind and memory, and having made my last WILL and TESTAMENT in writing bearing the date the Tenth day of March in the year of our Lord One Thousand Eight Hundred and forty three, which said WILL was executed by me in the City of New York, and having thereby made constituted and appointed

Peter P. Monfort of the Town of Fishkill, County of Dutchess and State of New York Farmer, and William Woodhull of the City, County and State of New York, Merchant, advisor to my Executors therein appointed, in case they have any difficulty in Settling my Estate,

NOW I do by this writing, which I declare to be a codicil to my said last WILL and TESTAMENT and to be taken as a part thereof revoke the power of the said Peter P. Monfort and of the Said William Wood-hull to act as advisors to my said Executors as aforesaid.

AND WHEREAS in and by my last WILL and TESTAMENT I have made constituted and appointed my sons John Henry Brush, and Charles Wortzer Brush both of the City, County, and State of New York Executors of my last WILL and TESTAMENT I hereby also make, constitute, and appoint my Son in law Eugene Van Ness of the United States, Army, at present residing in the Town of New Burgh, County of Orange and State of New York, Executor of my last WILL and TESTAMENT in addition to my Sons appointed as aforesaid.

AND I do hereby order and declare that my will is that **my two Slaves, George and Legarda**, residing in Town of Palatka, East Florida, Shall have their freedom at the expiration of the term of five years from the date of this codicil, provided that during the said period, they prove to be good and faithful Slaves, otherwise to remain in bondage at the discretion of my said Executors, AND I do hereby also order and declare that it is my will that **Eve, Sarah, Antonia and Francis** Children of my Said Slaves George and Legarda, all of the Town of Palatka as aforesaid and all others they may have at the expiration of the term of five years as aforesaid, Shall each of them have their freedom, as they respectively attain the age of forty years, AND I do hereby also order and declare, that it is my will that my Share of the bank Stock now invested in the Vestry Street Methodist Church in the City, County and State of New York, be transferred to the Methodist Church in the Town of Cormac County of Suffolk Long Island for the maintenance and Support of said Church only. AND lastly it is my desire that this my present

Codicil be annexed to, and made a part of my last WILL and TESTA-
MENT to all intents and purposes."

March 10, 1843 and August 31, 1843
From Alachua County Ancient Records
Deed Record A pages 110-117

**Calvin Bryan to Ozias Buddington as collateral for a $780.52
loan:** "Know all men by these presents that I Calvin Bryan of Alachua County Florida, do hereby for and in consideration of the sum
of seven hundred and eighty dollars and fifty-two cents to me paid
by Ozias Buddington of said State the receipt whereof is hereby
acknowledged bargain sell and deliver to said Ozias Buddington the
following property, to wit: **Moses aged about forty years and Sapia
aged about thirty five years, Negro Slaves.** To have and to hold
said property unto the said Ozias Buddington his Executors administrators and assigns forever. Provided nevertheless and these presents
are made upon the express condition, that if the said Calvin Bryan his
Executors or administrators shall pay or cause to be paid unto the said
Ozias Buddington his Executors administrators or assigns the said
sum of seven hundred and eighty dollars and fifty two cents, together
with lawful interest therefor from date on or before the first of January AD 1849 according to the terms and effect of a certain promissory
note of said Calvin Bryan, payable to said Ozias Buddington for said
sum bearing even date herewith, then these presents and every claim
thereof to be void, else to remain in full force."

October 2, 1848
From Alachua County Ancient Records
Mortgage Record A page 020

Calvin Bryan to William Dell as collateral for a $500 loan: "Know all men by these presents that I Calvin Bryan of said Town and county State have This day Sold and delivered to William Dell of said Town County and State a certain **Negro Boy Slave aged about Twelve years dark complection named Charles** For and in consideration of the Sum of Three hundred Dollars to me in hand paid at and before the signing and Delivering of these presents by said William Dell, To have and to hold the said Negro Boy Slave to the said Dell and to his Executors administrators and assigns free and discharged of any and all incumberence whatever the conditions of the above Bill of Sale is such that whereas the said Calvin Bryan is indebted to the said Dell in and by a certain promisory note in the words and figures following to wit

Newnansville 30th Nov 1849 note for $50

Thirty days after date I promise to pay to William Dell or to his order Five hundred Dollars value Received in Borrowed money by his draft of this date on Boston and Gunby Savannah Georgia in favor of Manning Leavitt & Co of New York

Now if the said Calvin Bryan Shall Well and Truly pay to the said William Dell the said Sum of Five hundred dollars due by said note when the same shall become due and payable then the above Bill of Sale of said Negro Boy to be void Else to remain in full force and virtue."

November 13, 1849
Newnansville, Alachua County, State of Florida
From Alachua County Ancient Records
Mortgage Record A page 035

Calvin Bryan to John B. Stanley as for a $500 loan: "Memorandum of Agreement Between Calvin Bryan & John B. Stanley Witnesseth

1st Whereas John B. Stanley had this day loaned to Calvin Bryan by drafts On Boston & Ganby of Savannah Geo. in favor of Mannery Levit & Co., at sixty days after date dated Dec. 27th 1849 the Sum of five Hundred Dollars and the Said Calvin Bryan is desirous to Secure the Said Stanley for Said Loans and the Said Stanley is anxious to purchase two Negro Slaves of Said Bryan Named **Doply & Charles each aged about Eleven years**, and the said parties have fixed a price on Said Negro Slaves of Six Hundred Dollars to Wit Three Hundred Dollars Each now this agreement for the witnesseth that if the Said Calvin Bryan Shall fail to pay the Said amount of Five Hundred Dollars ($500) to the Said Stanly at or before the time when Said draft becomes due to Wit Sixty Days from the date thereof then the Said Stanley Shall take in to his possession in the payments to Said Bryan or for the sum one Hundred Dollars and hold as his property absolutely the Said Negro property So pledged and if the Said Bryan does pay the Said Amount to the Said Stanley aforesaid then the Said Stanley relinquishes all claims to the Said Negro property above described and pledged as aforesaid."

December 27, 1849
From Alachua County Ancient Records
Deed Record A page 206

David C. Cash to Jno W. Pearson as collateral for a $158.35 loan: "Know all men by these presents that I David C. Cash of Alachua County State of Florida in consideration of the sum of one dollar to me in hand paid by Jno W. Pearson of the County of Marion, State aforesaid, the receipt whereof is hereby acknowledged, have granted bargained and sold and by these presents do bargain and sell unto the said Jno W. Pearson the following property to wit: one **Negro man named Tony aged about 28 years** Black complected, to have and to hold all and singular the said Negro man Tony unto the said Jno W. Pearson his Executors administrators and assigns, to his and their sole use forever. And I the said David C. Cash for myself my heirs Executors administrators and assigns, do covenant to and with the said Jno W. Pearson, his Executors and administrators and assigns that I am lawfully possessed of the said Negro man Tony as of my own property, that the same are free from all incumbrances and that I will and my Executors &c shall warrant and forever defend the same to the said Jno W. Pearson his Executors and assigns against the lawful claims and demands of all persons. Provided nevertheless that if the said David C. Cash his Executors or assigns shall well and truly pay unto the said Jno W. Pearson his heirs and assigns a certain note of hand bearing date 18th Jany 1849 due one day after date for the sum of one hundred and fifty eight dollars 35th ($158.35) then this conveyance shall be void, otherwise to remain in full force and effect and provided also that until default by the said David C. Cash, his Executors administrators or assigns in the performance of the condition aforesaid it shall and may be lawfull for him or them to keep possession of said property and to use and enjoy the same but if the same shall be attached at any time before payment &c by any other creditor of the said David C. Cash or if the said David C. Cash or if his Executors administrators or assigns shall attempt to sell the same without the consent or notice to said Jno W. Pearson his Executors administrators without his or their consent to such sale in writing expressed then it shall be lawfull for the said Jno W. Pearson his Executors administrators &c to take immediate possession of said granted property to his or their own use."

February 5, 1849
From Alachua County Ancient Records
Mortgage Record A pages 026-027

David C. Cash to George B. Payne as collateral for a $170.75 loan: "Memorandum of an agreement made and entered into this 28th day of May, in the year of our Lord one thousand Eight hundred and forty nine, between David C. Cash of the County of Alachua and State of Florida of the one part, and George B. Payne of the said County and State, of the other part. Witnesseth, That whereas the David C. Cash acknowledges himself to be due and indebted to the said George B. Payne in the sum of one hundred and seventy 75/100 dollars, and for which amount the said David C. cash hath executed his certain promissory note bearing even tenor and date with these presents, Now for the better security of the said George B. Payne in the payment of the said sum of one hundred and seventy 75/100 Dollars so by the said promissory note acknowledged by the said David C. Cash to be due and owing from him to the said George B. Payne, as aforesaid, the said David C. Cash hath this day in consideration of the premises above set forth as well as for and in consideration of the sum of five dollars in hand to him paid by the said George B. Payne, at and before the sealing and delivery of these presents, hath bargained, sold, transferred and conveyed unto the said George B. Payne his heirs and assigns, a certain **male slave named Toney aged about thirty years**, and whereas it is understood between the said parties, to wit; David C. Cash and the said George B. Payne that the said David C. Cash did on the fifth day of February A.D. 1849 Execute to John W. Pearson a certain Deed or Mortgage upon the Negro slave above named and discribed to secure the said John W. Pearson in the payment by the said David C. Cash of a sum of money in said Deed or Mortgage named Now the said David C. Cash doth hereby covenant and agree with the said George B. Payne that the said Slave Toney above named shall be, and is hereby conveyed unto him the said George B. Payne his heirs or assigns, subject only to the claim of John W. Pearson as above set forth, and if the said David C. cash shall fail to pay or cause to be paid unto the said George B. Payne his heirs or assigns the amount of money named and expressed in the promissory as above set forth, then this instrument shall have all the force and effect of a Mortgage upon the said above named and described Slave, subject only to the claim of John W. Pearson as above set forth, but should the said David

C. Cash or his heirs or legal representative pay the said promissory above described according to the tenor and effect thereof, then this obligation shall be void and of no effect."

May 28, 1849
From Alachua County Ancient Records
Mortgage Record A pages 031-032

Mathew Cheshire to William A. Osteen in trust and for the exclusive use and benefit of Joseph Miles Osteen and Caroline Osteen: "Know all men by these presents that I Mathew Cheshire of the County and State aforesaid for and in consideration of the Sum of five dollars to me in hand paid by William A. Osteen the receipt whereof is hereby acknowleged as well as divers other good and valuable considerations me thereunto moving, have granted, aliened, enfeoffed and conveyed, and do hereby grant, alien, enfeoff, and convey, unto the Said William A. Osteen, his heirs and assigns, in the manner and for the trust hereinafter Stated, all my reversionary in and to three certain negro Slaves to wit; **Susan a woman and Henry and Hilliard her sons, Together with the future increase of the Said Susan** To have and to hold to the Said William A. Osteen his heirs and assigns in trust as follows viz; in trust and for the exclusive use and benefit of Joseph Miles Osteen Son of the Said William A. Osteen and his wife Caroline Osteen and the future issue Sons and Daughters or either of the said William A. Osteen, or the body of his said wife Caroline Osteen hereafter to be begotten, either born in the life time of the Said William A. Osteen or in due time after his decease, to be divided Equally between them."

December 12, 1848
State of Florida, Alachua County
From Alachua County Ancient Records
Deed Record A page 096

Archibald H. Cole to Annie L. Mays in anticipation of their marriage - a plantation and other property including cattle, hogs, and enslaved people: "This Indenture made the Twenty fifth day of April in the year of our Lord one Thousand Eight Hundred and Forty eight, Between Archibald H. Cole in the town of Columbus, in the County of Columbia and state of Florida of the first part, and Annie L. Mays eldest daughter of Doctor R. G. Mays of the county of Madison, in said State of Florida of the second part; Witnesseth that Whereas an agreement or promise of Marriage hath been entered into between the said parties in pursuance of which a marriage is shortly to be solemnized between them, Now therefore in consideration of the said marriage about to be entered into between the said parties, and also in the further consideration of one Dollar to the said party of the first part in hand paid, the receipt whereof is hereby acknowledged, he the said Archibald H. Cole, hath granted, bargained, sold, aliened, conveyed and confirmed, and by these presents doth grant, bargain, sell, alien, convey, and confirm unto the said Annie L. Mays, the following described Real Estate, slaves and personal property, to wit. The lands and Plantation of the said party of the first part, situated on the Easterly side of "Lake Grandin" in the County of Alachua in said state of Florida, and in Township nine, south Range twenty four East - on fractional sections Numbers Two, Ten, Eleven, thirteen, Fourteen, twenty three, Twenty four, Twenty six, and thirty five, and comprising in all one Thousand seven hundred and Eighty seven acre and sixty eight hundredths of an acre, as will more fully appear by the certificates of the entries of the same at the Land offices - together with all the Buildings, Farming utensils, wagons mule horses, cattle hogs & c, now upon said plantation and thereunto belonging and all the rights, privileges, hereditaments and appurtenances unto the same belonging or in any wise appertaining - And also **the following Slaves now upon said plantation, together with their increase to wit, Peter and his wife Mary, and their children, Lilla, Dolly, Ben, Sicely and Jane, - Milly and her child named Jim, Sam Brown,**

and Tabby his wife, and their child named Joe, Jim (Peters son) and Julia his wife, Reuben and Agnes his wife, Little Sam (husband of Mary) Lucinda (a woman) Bill and Ellen his wife and their children viz Guildred, Ben, and Martha, - Joe and Ellen his wife, Nelson (a boy) Susan (sister of Nelson) and Mary (a little girl) making Twenty Eight in all.

To have and to hold the said Real and personal property and Slaves and their future increase above described and the rights and privileges and appurtenances thereto belonging, and the rents issues and profits thereof and all the estate right, title and interest therein unto the said Annie L. Mays and for her sole and separate use for and during her natural life,

And the said Archibald H. Cole for himself his heirs, executors and administrators doth covenant with the said Annie L. Mays, her heirs executors and administrators that he is Lawfully seized in fee of the aforegranted premises; that they are free from all incumbrances, that he has good right to sell and convey the same, and every part thereof, to the said Annie L. Mays as aforesaid; And that he will, and his heirs executors and administrators shall, warrant and defend the same and every part thereof to the said Annie L. Mays her heirs and assigns, during the term aforesaid, against the Lawful demands of all persons, by virtue of these presents."

April 25, 1848
From Alachua County Ancient Records
Deed Record A pages 064-066

Inventory of property held and owned by Margaret Crichton:
"The following is a true and full inventory of all property held and owned by Margaret Crichton of Alachua County Florida, wife of John

P. Crichton of said County, in her own right and to her Sole and Seperate use free from the controll, interferance disposal or debts of the said John P. Crichton Viz **One Negro woman Kate age 22 years, and her child Richard age 2 years, one Negro girl named Diana age about 12 years, also one Negro man named John age about 20 years, And the future issue and increase of Said Negros**"

August 16, 1848
From Alachua County Ancient Records
Deed Record A page 073

Richard R. Crum to Samuel L. Burritt as collateral for a $600 loan: "This Indenture made this Twenty Second day of April in the year of our Lord One thousand eight hundred & forty two Between Richard R. Crum of Alachua County and Territory of Florida of the first part and Samuel L. Burritt of said Territory of the second part,

Whereas the said party of the first part stands indebted to the said party of the second part, in the sum of six hundred Dollars lawful money of the United States, by his certain Bond or writing Obligatory bearing date the day and year aforesaid payable to the said Samuel L. Burritt, or his Assigns with interest thereon six months after the date thereof in said sum of Six hundred Dollars, as by the said Bond or writing Obligatory reference being thereunto had will more fully appear

Now this Indenture Witnesseth for the better Securing the payment of the said sum of money in the said Bond or writing Obligatory mentioned with the interest thereon acording to the tenor and effect of said Bond, And also in consideration of the sum of Ten Dollars lawful Money of the United States in hand paid to the said party of the first part, at or before the ensealing and delivery of these presents the receipt whereof is hereby Acknowledged The said party of the first part hath bargained and sold, and by these presents doth bargain and sell unto the said party of the second part his heirs and Assigns a certain **Negroe Male Slave (the property of the said party of the first part) named Cato aged forty years or thereabouts,** To have and to hold said slave Cato, unto him the said party of the second part, to the only purpose use benifit and behoof of the said party of the second part his heirs and Assigns forever Provided always neverthe- less and these presents are upon the express condition, that if the said party of the first part his executors Administrators or Assigns shall well & truly pay or cause to be paid unto the said Samuel L. Burritt his certain Attorney Executors Administrators or Assigns the said sum of money mentioned in the said Bond or writing Obligatory at the time and in the manner specified therein, According to the tenor and effect thereof and the Interest which may then be due thereon According to the Tenor and effect of the said Bond or writing Obligatory, and the interest which may then be due thereon Then as well, the Estate hereby granted as the said Bond and this Indenture shall cease deter- mine and be absolutely void, Else to remain in full force and virtue "

April 22, 1842
From Alachua County Ancient Records
Deed Book B pages 416-417

Wily Daniels to John W. Pearson as collateral for $364 in loans:
"Know all men by these presents that I Wily Daniels of Alachua County State of Florida in consideration of the sum of one Dollar to me in hand paid by John W. Pearson County and State aforesaid the receipt whereof is hereby acknowledged, I have granted I bargained and sold and by these presents do grant bargain and sell unto the said John W. Pearson the following property to wit one **negro man named Aleck aged about 21 years** to have and to hold all and singular the

said negro man Ale- unto the said John W. Pearson or his Executors Administrators and assigns to his and their sole use for ever and I the said Wily Daniels for myself my executors and administrators do covenant to and with the said J.W. Pearson his Executors Administrators and assigns that I am lawfully possessed of the said negro man Alex as of my own property that the same are free from all encumbrance and that I will and my executors &c shall warrant and defend the same to the said JW Pearson his executors and assigns against the lawfull claims and demands of all persons Provided nevertheless that if the said Wily Daniels his Executors administrators and assigns shall well and truly pay unto the said John W. Pearson his executors administrators and assigns a certain note of hand bearing date 1st January 1848 for the amount of two hundred and sixty four dollars also one note payable to B.M. Dell bearing date 27th February 1846 for one hundred dollars then this conveyance shall be void otherwise to remain in full force and effect and provided also that untill default by the said Wily Daniels his executors administrators in the performance of the conditions aforesaid note it shall and may be lawful for him or them to keep possession of the said property and to use and enjoy the same but if the same shall be attached at any time before payment &c by any other creditor of the said Wily Daniels or if the said Wily Daniels, or if his Executor, administrator and without his or their assent to such sale in writing expressed then it shall be lawful for the said John W Pearson his executors administrators &c to take immediate possession of said granted property to his and their own use."

March 6, 1848
From Alachua County Ancient Records
Mortgage Record A pages 013-015

Bennett M. Dell to daughter Sarah Angeline Dell, held in trust by Phillip Dell: "Know men by these presents, That I Bennett M. Dell of Alachua county and State of Florida for and in consideration of the natural love and affection which I have and do bear unto my daughter Sarah Angeline Dell, and for her better maintenence and the increase of her portion, and also in consideration of the Sum of one dollar to me paid by Phillip Dell of the Same State and County at and before the Sealing and delivery hereof the receipt whereof is hereby acknowledged, have given, granted, bargained, and Sold, and by these presents, do give, grant, bargain, and Sell unto the Said Phillip Dell the following Negro Slaves, to wit; **Charlotte a Mulatto woman Slave about twenty years of age, and her Son Charles about one year of age, Jacob a Negro Slave about fourteen years of age, and Polly a female Slave about eight years of age**; to have and hold all and Singular the premises hereby given and granted unto the Said Phillip Dell, his Executors and Administrators forever upon this Special Trust nevertheless that the Said Phillip Dell his Executors and Administrators Shall and do hold the aforesaid Negro Slaves to and for the sole and separate use benefit and behoof of the said Sarah Angeline Dell for and during the term of her natural life this provision being intended to take effect in addition to any provision which may be made in my last will and Testament for my said Daughter Sarah Angeline Dell and at her death the said negro Slaves to revert to me, & if I be dead, to be divided amongst my lawful heirs and distributies according to the law of, And I do hereby convey unto the Said Phillip Dell his Executors and Administrators full and ample power and authority to Execute the Trust herein created."

June 22, 1849
From Alachua County Ancient Records
Deed Record A page 148

James Dell Last Will and Testament: "In the name of God Amen. I James Dell of Jacksonville Duvall County Florida being in tolerable health and of sound & disposing mind & memory calling to mind the frality & uncertainty of human life & being desirous to settle my worldly affairs while I have strength & capasity so to do do make and publish this my last will & testament, and hereby revoking & making null & void all other last wills & testaments by me heretofore made and

First I conveyed my immortal soul to him who gave it and my body to the earth to be decently buried

And as to my worldly estate and all of the property real personal or mixed of which I shall be seized & possessed or to which I shall be entitled at the time of decease I divide & bequeath & dispose thereof in the following to wit

First My will is that all my just debts & funeral charges shall by my Executors hereinafter named be paid out of my estate as soon after my funeral as shall by them be found convenient.

I give devise & bequeath all my negro property of which I may die seized to my children William Thomas Dell Ann Louisa Dell James Gadsden Dell Martha Mary Delea Dell to be equally divided among them Except big Jim & Peggy who are to be disposed of as hereinafter mentioned or to these hands all the land of which I shall die seized & possessed or to which I shall be entitled at the of my decease I direct to be sold so soon as my Executors shall think it prudent so to do & the money arising from said sales to be funded in good stocks and the same to be Equally divided among my aforementioned Children or their heirs

Second I give & bequeath unto my daughter Martha Mary Delea Dell & her heirs my **negro girl Peggy** one good horse saddle & bridle & one good bedstead feather bed & necessary clothing for the same, over & above her equal division my desire is to deal equally with my children all alike near & dear to me & I think this extra portion will not more than make this my youngest equal with what the other older have had & in the event of the death of any of my children before his or her legacy may become due, my will is, that his her or their portion or portions be equally divided among the survivors

I direct my executors to pay over to my children as soon after my death as they may think consistent with the best interest of my estate or to each child at that time of age, his or her part & to those not of age to each his or her part as soon as he or she, shall become of age, or to either or any of them at the time of their marriage though on that contingency they may be of marriage.

Third I give & bequeath unto my son James Gadsden Dell the sum of one thousand dollars to be made good to him by the balance of my heirs at the division of my estate for the completion of his education and professional studies.

Fourth My will is that **big Jim** who has at all times in all troubles stood by me, shall have the elective either to remain a slave to some of my children or else to pay executors the sum of one hundred Dollars per year for four years (the same to be equally divided among my children) when he shall be free. And my Executors are charged with the trust in the event of his complying with this proposition to give to him emancipation and I hereby charge my my Estate to comply with the law So far as to carry this request into execution if the Election of Jim require it

Fifth My will is (if possible) that **Ester & her children** be kept together; & also **little Jim & his children** & that my executors make up the difference that may arise to any of my legatees by such a dis-position of them all the rest of my estate & the residue thereof real personal or mixed I direct to be sold & the proceeds of said sales to be equally divided among my surviving children (Except) my negros which I wish equally divided among my children (Except) the one allotted to my Daughter Martha

Sixth My will is that my son William shall not pay Intrust on the sum of fifteen hundred dollars advanced to him to be deducted out of his portion for part of the estate. And also that my Daughter Ann shall not pay intrust of the sum of six hundred Dollars advanced her to be deducted out of her portion or part of the Estate

Lastly I do nominate and appoint my brother Bennet Maxy Dell & my son William Thomas Dell and Samuel R. Piles to be the Executors of this my last will and testament

In witness whereof I the said James Dell have to this my last will and testament contained on four pieces of paper have here subscribed my name and affixed my seal this twenty fifth day of September in the year of our Lord one thousand eight hundred and forty four in the County of Alachua East Florida

It is my wish & desire that my executors Should make a title to Philip Dell or his heirs for one right of land where he now resides compliments number as follows N.W 1/2 N.West quarter Range 18 township seven section 26.

A Codicil to my last Will & Testament

Whereas since the execution by me of the foregoing instrument it has pleased the almighty to call from this earth my son William who departed this life in the state of Alabama on the thirtieth day of September last leaving a widow and three infant children now therefore, I declare it to be my Will that their share which by this provisions foregoing testimentory instrument would have gone to my said son William had he been living at the date of my death shall upon my decease be vested in the possession and care of my trusty friends Bennett M. Dell Samuel R. Piles & Charles L. Dell the said C. L. Dell having been appointed by me in the place of my son William deceased to be managed by them and distributed together with its increase equally to the said children of my said deceased son, as they shall respectively reach the age of twenty one years or shall marry, and should any of them die before becoming entitled to his or her distributive share the survivor or survivors shall receive such share equally and in Case of the death of all before becoming entitled to receive under this codicil then and in that case it is my will that the whole shall pass to my three children now living or their legal representatives in the year of our our Lord 14th February 1845"

September 25, 1844 and February 14, 1845
From Alachua County Ancient Records
Will Book A pages 025-029

Big Jim enslaved by James Dell, deceased, pays the $400 (see record above): "Received January 10th, 1850 of Jim, a slave late the slave and property of Col. James Dell deceased the sum of four hundred dollars"

January 10, 1850
From Alachua County Ancient Records
Deed Record A page 224

William Dell received from Cornelius Rain (late guardian of Geo. W. Wells Jr., a minor): "Nine Negroes, and the Sum of Two hundred and thirty Seven dollars, and Eighty Cents, Secured by his note, bearing interest at Eight per cent from date in full of the property of Said minor in his hands"

February 9, 1848
Newnansville
From Alachua County Ancient Records
Deed Record A page 083

Mary Dixon to James D. Starke in trust for Mary Dixon: "Know all men by these presents that I Mary Dixon of Kershaw District in the State aforesaid in consideration of the good will for my friend and relative Madison S. Perry of Fairfield District in the State aforesaid and in consideration of one dollar of one dollar to me paid by James D. Starkes of Fairfield District State aforesaid have granted, bargained, sold and delivered, and by these presents do grant, bargain sell and deliver to the said James D. Starke the following Negro slaves, nameley **Bill about fifty years old, Charity about fifty years old, Fanny about eight years old, Charlotte about sixty years old, and Betty about sixty years old**, Also one sorrel mare, one Barauche and harness, one wagon and gear, all my stock of cattle & hogs all my plantation utensils, and all my household and Kitchen furniture; To have and to hold all and Singular the above named Negro slaves **and their future issue and increase**, and all & singular the other property above mentioned, unto the said James D. Starke, his Executors, administrators and assigns forever; In Trust nevertheless, for the uses and purposes hereinafter specified That is to say In Trust for the use, benefit and behoof of the said Mary Dixon for and during the term of her natural life; and from and immediately after the death of the said Mary Dixon, then in Trust for such person or persons and for such uses and purposes as the said Madison S. Perry shall at anytime hereafter by any instrument in writing signed by himself, or by his last will and testament appoint and designate; and unless, or until the said Madison S. Perry shall otherwise direct and appoint,

In Trust after the death of the said Mary Dixon to permit the said Madison S. Perry to have The use and services of the said Negro slaves and their issue, and the use and benefit of all and singular the other property above mentioned according to his own will and pleasure during the term of his natural life; and in case the said Madison S. Perry shall fail to make any such appointment during his life as above authorised then In Trust after the death of the said Madison S. Perry to deliver to deliver the said Negro slaves and their issue, and all and singular the other property above mentioned to the children of the said Madison S. Perry, if more than one, equally to be divided among them, and if only one child, then to deliver the same to said child, the issue of any deceased child of the said Madison S. Perry should there be any such to represent the parent, and take the share which the parent would be entitled to if living."

December 23, 1846 in the seventy first year of the independence of the united States of America
The State of South Carolina
From Alachua County Ancient Records
Deed Record A pages 232-233

Michael D. Duskin Last Will and Testament: "In the name of God Amen - I, Michael D. Duskin of said State and County being of advanced age and knowing that I must shortly depart from this world deem it right and proper both as respects myself and my family that I should make a disposition of the property with which a kind provider has blessed me, I therefore make this my last Will and testament, hereby revoking and annulling all other heretofore made by me

Item 1st I desire and direct that my body be burried in a decent manner and christian like manner suitable to my circumstances and condition. My soul I trust shall return to be with God who gave it as I hope of eternal salvation through the blessed Lord and Savior Jesus Christ whose religion I have professed and as I humbly trust for years past

Item 2nd I desire and direct that all my just debts should be paid without delay by my Executors hereinafter named, as I am unwilling my creditors should be delayed of their rights especially as there is necessity for delay

Item 3rd I give and bequeath unto my beloved wife Elizabeth Duskin with whom I have lived in the strictest and loved for thirty two years Lot of land Number one hundred and seventy five in the Twenty second District of originally Lee, now, Stewart County containing two hundred and two and a half acres more or less, with all the rights, members and appurtances to said lot of land in anywise appertaining free from all charges or Consideration whatever to her own proper use benfit and behoof forever, for her to hold the above described land during her natural life and at her death for it to be equally divided amongst all my children

Item 4th I give and bequeath to my beloved wife for and during her natural life **all my Negroes except these hereafter named** and for her to give off to my children as they marry or become of age one Young Negro apiece as she may choose to give and at her death for an equal division of all my negroes to be made among all my children and if my wife should marry again and if my wife should marry again then for an equal division to be made of my Negroes forthwith among all my children and for my wife to draw a childs part and to Keep it during her life and then for it to be equally divided among all my children

Item 5th The negroes that was to be hereinafter named is two that I have already given to my beloved daughter Mary Gordon Miller and Elizabeth Jane Bartlett **Lucinda about ten years old** I have given to my beloved daughter Mary Gordon and **Jimey about 16 years old** I have given to my beloved daughter Elizabeth Jane

Item 6th I bequeath to my beloved son John L. B. Duskin a **negro boy Henry about Eight years old** to him & to his heirs forever, and if any of my children should marry and have no heirs the property that I give them is to be returned back to those of my family that is living

Item 7th All of the above named property is to remain with my children and their lawful heirs and not to be traded in anywise whatever

Item 8th I constitute and appoint my beloved wife Elizabeth my Executrix and my beloved son John L. B. Duskin Executor to this my last Will and testament this March 3rd 1845.

Item 8th It is my will and desire that if my wife should die or marry before the youngest children become of age or marry that the youngest children be made equal with the older children before a division and the remainder of my Estate be equally divided among my children share and share alike"

March 3, 1845
State of Georgia, Stewart County
From Alachua County Ancient Records
Will Book A pages 019-022

John H. Ellis & Sand Ellis, Infants by James Gibbons their Guardian vs. John Helveston agent & Mary C. Stanley admr of John R. Stanley Decd - "Appeal from proceeding before three

Justices under the Act of 12th Feb 1837 entitled "An act to present the unlawful & violent taking of personal property."

On reading & filing a record of the proceedings in this case before the Justices, and after hearing Counsel for said Infants, and also for the Defendants it is ordered on motion of Plaintiffs Counsel that the defendants do immediately deliver to the Guardian of the above named Infants, the negro woman and child in question, or give a Bond with two sureties to be approved by the Clerk of this Court in the Penalty of ten hundred, Dollars, and issued that if the said Infants or their guardian shall institute any suit or proceeding at Law, or in equity, to recover or obtain the said negro woman and child, or the value of them; and if in any such suit or proceeding Judgement shall be given for said Infants: or if it shall be adjudged or decreed, or decided that they are the owners of said negro woman and her children, - or that they recover them or their value - then if the said Defendants in any such suit shall restore and deliver the said negro woman and children, and her increase if any, - to the said Infants or their Guardian, and pay to said Infants or their guardian the damages which they may retain by reason of the loss of the service of said negro woman while she may be so held by the said Defendants or any of them - or in case of failure to restore or deliver the said negro woman as aforesaid if the said Defendants shall pay to the said Infants or their guardian the full value of said negro & her increase if any - and the value of her services as aforesaid then &c &c

And it is further ordered that in case the Defendants deliver up **the said negro woman & her children** to the Infants or their guardian, then he shall give a like Bond to the Administrator of the Estate of John R. Stanley conditioned as above and so as to secure the restoration of the negroes in question or their value - & the value of their Services to the admr in case Judgement should pass in their favor

May 14, 1843
From Alachua County Ancient Records
Superior Court Minutes 2 pages 284-286

An inventory of all property owned by Sarah Ann Ellis: "The following is a true and full inventory of all property held and owned by Sarah Ann Ellis of Alachua County Florida, wife of Thomas C. Ellis of Said County in her own right and to her Sole and Separate use free from the control interference disposal or debts of the Said Thomas C. Ellis, viz; **One Negro woman Eliza and her children named Jane and Mary, one Negro woman Ann and he Child Halbert, and the future issue and increase of Said Negroes.**"

August 16, 1848
From Alachua County Ancient Records
Deed Record A pages 079-080

Moriah Floyd to her daughter Florida Ann Floyd: "Know all men by these presents that I Moriah Floyd of Alachua County in said State for and in the consideration of the natural love and Affection which I have and do bear unto my daughter Florida Ann Floyd of said State and County, and for the love and Affection which I have for the lawful heirs of her body, and for and in consideration of the Sum of one dollar to me in hand paid, at and before the sealing and delivery of these presents, the receipt whereof is hereby acknowledged hath granted, bargained, and by these presents, do freely give, grant, and convey unto her my Said Daughter Florida Ann Floyd, and the lawful heirs of her body, the following described property to wit, one **Negro woman Slave named Jane aged about Sixteen years** and ten cows and their calves, **together with their future Issue and increase,** which Said property I do hereby warrant, and forever defend against myself, my heirs, executors, administrators and assigns. To have and to hold the above named and described property as aforesaid, and I the Said Moriah Floyd, for myself, my heirs, Executors, administrators and assigns, Shall and will warrant and forever defend the given and granted property as aforesaid, against all and every other person or persons whomsoever, unto her my said Daughter Florida Ann Floyd, and the lawful heirs of her body, and to their heirs and assigns forever in fee Simple."

January 3, 1849
State of Florida, Alachua County
From Alachua County Ancient Records
Deed Record A page 098

Moriah Floyd to her son Raford M. Floyd: "Know all men by these presents, that I Moriah Floyd of Alachua County in said State for and in consideration of the natural love and Effection which I have and bear unto my Son Raford M. Floyd of Said State and County, and for the love and Effection which I have for the lawful heirs of his body, and for and in consideration of the Sum of one dollar to me in hand paid, at and before the Sealing and delivery of these presents, the receipt whereof is hereby acknowledged, hath granted, bargained, and by these presents, do freely give, grant, and convey, unto him, my said Son Raford M. Floyd, and the lawful heirs of his body, the following described property to wit; one **negro woman named Lucy aged about Eighteen years**, and ten cows and calves, **together with their future issue and increase** which Said property I do hereby warrant and forever defend against myself, my heirs, Executors, administrators and assigns, To have and to hold the above named property as aforesaid, and I the Said Moriah Floyd, for my self, my heirs, Executors, administrators and assigns, Shall and will warrant, and forever defend, the given and granted property as aforesaid, against all and every other person or persons whomsoever, unto him (my said Son Raford M.

Floyd) and the lawful heirs of his body, and to their heirs and assigns forever in fee Simple."

January 3, 1849
State of Florida, Alachua County
From Alachua County Ancient Records
Deed Record A page 098

Samuel Geiger to Margery Ann Tucker: "Know all men by these presents, that I Samuel Geiger of Alachua County in the State of Florida, for and in consideration of the natural love and effection which I have and bear unto Margery Ann Tucker wife of Elijah Tucker of Said County have given and delivered, and by these presents do give and deliver unto the Said Margery Tucker **One negro woman Slave, named Lucy** now in the possession of the Said Margery Ann Tucker Said negro Slave **aged about 40 year**, also a Stock of Cattle now in the County of Alachua, Say thirty head more or less, marked, Strait Spilt and uper bit in one ear, Strait Split in the other, branded T, and figure 9 and one mare and Colt, to have and to hold Said property above given and delivered with its future increases unto the Said Margery Ann Tucker to her Sole and seperate use free from and independent of the control and debts of her said husband"

December 13, 1848
From Alachua County Ancient Records
Deed Record A page 097

William D. Grimes to Robert O. Dale as collateral for a $4,382.81 loan: "This indenture made this the fourth day of March in the year of our Lord One thousand eight hundred and forty three between William D. Grimes of the County of Alachua and Territory of Florida of the one part and Robert O. Dale of the County of Marbour and the state of Alabama of the other part Witnesseth that the said William D. Grimes for and in consideration of the sum of four thousand three hundred and eighty two Dollars and eighty one cents to him in hand paid by the said Robert O. Dale at or before the Sealing and delivery of these presents, the receipt whereof is hereby Acknowledged, hath granted bargained and sold and by these presents doth grant bargain and sell unto the said Robert O. Dale his executors Administrators and Assigns, all and Singular the Negro Slaves hereinafter particularly named and described, that is to say. **Jim a Man about twenty years of age, Willis a Man about twenty one years of age, Jerry a man about thirty years of age, Dick a Man about forty five years of age, Griffin a boy about sixteen years of age, Dennis a boy about seventeen years of age, Greene a boy about sixteen years of age, Levin a boy about eighteen years of age, Alfred a man about twenty two years of age, Bob a man about thirty years of age, Harrison a man about twenty eight years of age, Toney a man about thirty five years of age, Bony a man about twenty five years of age, Ary a girl about fourteen years of age, Celia a woman about twenty one years of age, Sarah a woman of about twenty years of age, Caroline a woman about thirty years of age and her four children viz. Anderson a boy about five years of age, Martha a girl about three years of age, William about two years of age and Charles a boy about one year of age, Ann a woman of about twenty two years of age and her four children viz. Allen a boy about five years of age, Jefferson a boy about two years of age Anthony a boy about three years of age and her infant girl child about five months old, Clarissa a woman about thirty years of age and her four children viz. Maria a girl about ten years of age, Fort a boy about eight years of age, Charity a girl about five years of age and her infant girl child, Richardson a boy about twelve years of age together with all of their further increase of the above described slaves** To have and to hold all and Singular the aforesaid Negro Slaves together with all of their future increase therein before granted, bargained and sold unto said Robert O. Dale his executors, Administrators and assigns to the only and proper use and behoof of the said Robert O. Dale his Executors Administrators and assigns forever And I the said William D. Grimes do hereby further Covenant and agree with the said Robert O. Dale his Executors Administrators & Assigns that the said Negro Slaves above Mortgaged shall not be removed beyond the limits of Alachua County, Territory of Florida without due Notice given to the said Robert O. Dale his Executors Administrators and assigns, or his or their agent or agents duly appointed and authorized. And I the said William D. Grimes do hereby further Covenant and agree to pay all costs and charges that have Accrued or may Accrue which said Costs are estimated by the consent of all parties at the sum of four hundred and thirty nine Dollars exclusive of Tax = Fee

The Condition of the above Obligation is such that whereas the aforesaid William D. Grimes did on the twenty second day of February One thousand eight hundred and forty three make a certain promissory note of the following term and effect viz. One day after date I promise to pay Robert O. dale or bearer Four thousand three hundred and eighty two Dollars and eighty one cents for value received. Now if the said William D. Grimes his heirs, Executors and Administrators shall and do will and truly pay or cause to be paid to the said Robert O. Dale his heirs executors Administrators or assigns the full and just sum of four thousand three hundred and eighty two Dollars and eighty one cents together with all interest that has accrued or may Accrue thereon, at the rate of eight per cent per annum till paid As well also if the said William D. Grimes perform or cause to be thing herein contained, determine and be utterly void, any thing contained to the contrary thereof in any wise Not withstanding Otherwise to remain in full force Virtue and Effect"

March 4, 1843
Territory of Florida, Alachua County
From Alachua County Ancient Records
Deed Book B pages 446-447

William D. Grimes to Thomas C. Grimes as collateral for $10,500 in loans: "Know all men by these presents that Where as I William D. Grimes of Alachua County Territory of Florida am indebted to Thomas C. Grimes of Hancock County Georgia in the sum of Ten thousand Five Hundred Dollars upon several Promisary Notes and other Wrightings upon which I am Held and Bound to the said Thomas C. Grimes and also in the consideration of the sum of one Thousand Dollars in hand Paid By the said Thomas C. Grimes at or before the sealing and Delivery of these presents, the receipt whereof is hereby Acknowledged, Have Bargained Granted and Sold and by these Presents do Grant Bargain & Sell unto the said Thomas C. Grimes his executors Administrators and assigns All and singular the Negro Slaves Here in After Particularly Named and described, That is to say **Jim a Man About Twenty years of Age & Willis a Man About Twenty one years of Age, Jerry a Man About Thirty years of Age, Dick a Man about Forty Five years of Age, Griffin a Boy About Sixteen years of Age, Dennis a Boy About Seventeen years of Age, Green a Boy About Sixteen years of Age, Levin a Boy About Eighteen years of Age, Alfred a Man About Twenty Two years of Age, Jourdan a Boy About Twelve years of Age, Bob a Man About Thirty years of Age, Harrison a man About Twenty Eight years of Age, Tonee a Man About Thirty Five years of Age, Boney a man About Twenty Five years of Age, Isaac a Boy About Eighteen years of Age, Ary a Girl About Fourteen years of Age, Selia A Woman About Twenty One years of Age, Sarah A Woman About Twenty years of Age, Mary A Woman About Forty years of Age and a Boy Child Simeon About Two years of Age, Caroline a Woman About thirty years of Age and her four children Anderson a Boy About Five years of Age Martha a Girl of About Three years of Age William a Boy About Two years of Age Charles a Boy About One year of Age Ann a Woman About Twenty Two years of Age and her four Children, Clarisa A Woman About Thirty years of Age And her Children To Wit Mariah A Girl About Ten years of**

Age Fort A Boy About Eight years of Age and Her infant Girl Child & Also her Daughter Charity About Five Years of Age, Richerson A Boy About Twelve years of Age, Rody A Girl About Fourteen years of Age, Together with All of the Future Increase of the Above Discribed Negroe Slaves To have and to Hold All and Singular the aforesaid Negroe Slaves With All of the Future Increase Here and Before Granted bargained and Sold unto the said Thomas C. Grimes his Executors Administrators and Assigns Forever, And I the said William D. Grimes For Myself My Executors and Administrators do covenant to and With the said Thomas C. Grimes his Executors Administrators and Assigns That the said Negroe Property is Free From All Incumberences With the Exception of a Mortgage of the Said Slaves Negroe Property Given to Robert O. Dale on the Twenty Second day of February One Thousand Eight Hundred and Forty Three at Maderson County Florida For the Sum of Four Thousand Three Hundred and Eighty Two Dollars and Eighty one cents Given to Secure A Debt to That Amount to the said Robert O. Dale And That I Will and My Executors & co Shall Warrant and Defend the Same to the Said Thomas C. Grimes his Executors Administrators and Assigns Against the Lawful Claims and Demands With the Foregoing Exception of All Persons Now the Condition of the Above Instrument is Such That If the said William D. Grimes his Executors Administrators Shall Well and Truly Pay unto the Said Thomas C. Grimes his Executors Administrators and Assigns The Said Debt in Such Sums as the Said Thomas C. Grimes Shall require to Secure Himself From Such Demands as have Been Shall be may be Prosecuted to A Judgement Against Him, Then This Conveyance to be void Otherwise to remain in full Force and Affect And Provided Also that until Defaults By the Said William D. Grimes his Executors or Administrators in the Performance of the Condition Aforesaid, it Shall and may Be Lawfull for him or Them to Keep Possession of the Afore Granted Property And to use And Enjoy the Same"

March 8, 1843
From Alachua County Ancient Records
Deed Book B pages 449-451

Isaiah D. Hart to Orian R. Hart for $330 in trust for Mary Ann Andrew: "This indenture made this twenty sixth day of December in the year of our Lord one thousand Eight hundred and forty two Between Isaiah D. Hart of the Town of Jacksonville in Duval County and Territory of Florida of the first part, and Orian R. Hart of the same place of the Second part Witnesseth that the said party of the Second part for and in consideration of the Sum of three hundred and thirty dollars good and lawful money to him in hand paid by the party of the second part at and before the ensealing and delivery of these presents the receipt whereof is hereby acknowledged, hath granted, bargained, sold, aliened, remised, released, conveyed, and confirmed, and do by these presents grant, bargain, sell, alien, remise, release, convey and confirm unto him the said party of the Second part and to his assigns all that certain lot or parcel of land Situated lying and being in said Town of Jacksonville and Known and described in the plan or plat of said Town as lot number four (No 4) in Square number eleven (No 11) and containing one hundred and five feet each way, and bounded as follows to wit; on the North by Adams Street, on the East by lot Number five (No 5) on the South by lot Number one (No 1) all in said Square, and on the west Ocean Street. And also **one Negro woman slave named Susan aged about twenty four years, and her two children, are named Henry age two years, and the other an infant at the breast not yet two weeks old**. To have and to hold the above granted, bargained, and described premises or lot of Land, and all and the tenements hereditaments, and appurtenances thereunto belonging or in any wise appertaining, together with the above mentioned Negro Slaves, **and all the increase of the aforesaid Negro woman Slave Susan**, and all the rents, issues, profits and income whatsoever from the same arising unto him the said party of the second part and to his assigns forever. In trust never the less to and for the sole use benefit and behoof of Mary Ann Andrew wife of Joseph Andrews all of said Town, and the heirs of her body forever to pay over to her and assigns all the income arising out of the use of said property."

December 26, 1842
From Alachua County Ancient Records
Deed Record A pages 055-056

William B. Hart to Benjamin Hopkins as collateral for a $450 loan: "Know all men by these presents that I William B. Hart of the county and state aforesaid for the better security of the sum of four hundred & fifty Dollars by note with interest from date due Benjamin Hopkins or bearer dated 25th day of June 1849 do hereby grant bargain and sell unto the said Benjamin Hopkins and his assigns the following property (Negro Slaves) **Susan William & Ama & Alford (Children of Susan)** to have and to hold said Negroes forever. Provided nevertheless that if the said note of four hundred & fifty Dollars be paid by me or by my assigns on or before the first day of January 1850, with lawful Interest from date to the said Benjamin Hopkins or bearer or to his assigns then and in that event this Instrument of writing to be null & void Otherwise to be in full force and effect."

June 25, 1849
State of Florida, Alachua County
From Alachua County Ancient Records
Mortgage Record A page 034

Warren Harville and Elisa A. Harville to Dicey Standley for $1,200, to be held in trust for Elisa A. Harville: "An Indenture made between Warren Harville and Elisa A. Harville of Marion County in the State of Florida of the first part and Dicey Standley of Alachua County in said State of the Second part. Whereas the said Warren Harville and Elisa A. Harville are entitled to and own certain personal Estate consisting of **five negroes and their increase Viz Martha Francis Richard Melissa and Primus** and other personal estate to which they derive title under and by virtue of the last will and testament of Jesse Standley Deceased late of Alachua County aforesaid and other property of the Estate of said Jesse Standley Deceased to which they are entitled as heirs and legal representatives of said Jesse Standley Deceased and also about Two Hundred head of cattle marked with a crop and one half flower deluce in one ear and an upper and under slope in the other and branded twenty six in the following manner Viz ("26"), three head of horses and thirty head of hogs or thereabout marked in the same manner with the cattle above described together with all farming utensils now in possession of said Warren Harville, and whereas the said Warren and Elisa A. Harville are desirous that said property and its increase should be assigned over secured and settled to the sole and separate use of the said Elisa A. Harville and her children in the manner hereinafter set forth and that the said Warren Harville shall have no control over or power to interfere with the same. Now this indenture witnesseth that in consideration of Twelve Hundred Dollars paid to the said Warren and Eliza A. Harville by the said Dicey Standley the receipt whereof is hereby acknowledged, they the said Warren and Elisa A. Harville do hereby grant bargain sell and deliver unto the said Dicey Standley all the property herein before described mentioned or referred to and all property to which either the said Warren or Elisa A Harville are or may hereafter become entitled to or possessed of under or in virtue of said last will and testament or from the Estate of said Jesse Standley deceased or as heirs or legal representatives of said Jesse Standley and all the present and future issue and increase of any such property and do hereby assign and set over their and each of their right title interest claim and demand in and upon the same and each & every part thereof and the present and future issue and increase of the same as aforesaid. To have and hold the same unto the Said Dicey Standley her Executors Administrators or assigns upon the trusts and to the intent and purpose hereinafter Expressed, that is to say, upon trust that the said Elisa A. Harville shall have the possession and use and service or shall enjoy the income wages and profits arising from said property which ever she may deem most proper free from the control disposal, interference or debts of her husband the said Warren Harville for and during the term of her natural life and at her (the said Elisa A. Har-ville's) death leaving a child or children then to deliver surrender and release to any such child or children as may survive her (the said Elisa A.) all the property herein before described or mentioned or referred to with its increase as aforesaid together with all proceeds of any sale of the same which may be herein provided for or any investment of such proceeds and any profits or wages which may be on hand undis-posed of arising from said property to such child or children and if there be more than one child to be divided Equally among them And upon the further trust that the said Dicey Standley or such other per-son or persons as may be acting in her stead as Trustee or Trustees may if she or such Trustee or Trustees may may think it Expedient sell and dispose of any portion of said property and invest the pro-ceeds in such other manner in personal securities or real Estate upon the trusts herein set forth and to be set forth, and in the event that the said Dicey Standley may desire to resign or be relieved from the trusts herein set forth and to be set forth and when confided (which she is herein and hereby expressly allowed to do when ever she may so desire) that she the said Dicey Standley shall have power to and shall appoint by deed in writing one or more persons to act in her stead and to execute and fulfil the trust herein set forth and to be set forth and in case of her death as Trustee she may make such appointment by will. And the said property herein before described mentioned and referred to is bargained sold delivered and the interest therein assigned as aforesaid upon the further trust that if any such child or children as may survive the said Eliza A. Harville as aforesaid be at the time of her death under age the interest portion or share of such child under the trust aforesaid shall be reserved and witheld by said Dicey Standley or such person or persons as she may appoint as aforesaid until such child shall become of age or shall be married. And it is hereby agreed by all parties herein concerned that the said Dicey Standley or such person or persons as she may appoint as aforesaid shall be allowed all reasonable charges in the premises and that the seperate receipt or receipts of the said Eliza A. Harville shall be a full and complete discharge to the said Dicey Standley or to such person; or persons as she may appoint as aforesaid from all payments and deliveries that shall be made to the said Eliza A. Harville by virtue of and in pursuance of the premises. And the said Dicey Standley for herself her Executors and Administrators does hereby covenant to and with the said Warren & Eliza A. Harville severally and with their several and respective Executors and administrators that the said Dicey Standley will faithfully and truly perform and fulfil from time to time and at all times all and singular the truth aforesaid according to the true intent and meaning of these presents except so far as the same may conflict with any claim of dower or as widow of said Jesse Standley deceased or any other claim which she may have in her own right to any of the property herein before described mentioned or referred to and by the acceptance of these trusts she does not intend to surrender any such claims."

June 29, 1847
From Alachua County Ancient Records
Bills of Sale A pages 006-009

Levi Hickson to daughter Martha Hagood: "To all persons to whom these presents, Shall come; Levi Hickson of Barnwell District in the State aforesaid, Sends Greeting: Whereas the Said Levi Hickson is now the lawful owner in his own right of **a Certain female Slave named Louisa aged about Thirty Years and her five children (to wit) Rodd aged about Eleven years, Patience about Nine Years Phillis aged about Seven Years Emma aged about Five Years and**

Andrew aged about Two Years, which he is desirous on account of his affection for Martha M. Hagood his daughter to Give and assure in trust To the Said Martha M. Hagood and her children as is herein after expressed: Now Therefore Know Ye That the Said Levi Hickson in consideration of the Love and affection he hath and beareth unto the Said Martha M. Hagood, and also for and in Consideration of divers other good and valuable causes and Considerations him thereunto moving Hath by these presents acknowledge, Testify and declare that the Said Slaves Louisa and her children Rodd Patience, Phillis, Emma and Andrew, **and the future issue and increase of the females** is hereby given and assured bythe Said Levi Hickson, And Shall be held by him during his natural life, and after his death by William T. Hickson his Executors and administrators Subject to the following uses and trusts, and to and for no other use, Trust, or purpose, whatsoever

That is to Say in trust for the Sole and Separate use benefit and behoof of the Said Martha M. Hagood during her natural life, and in Such manner that the Said Slaves, and their future issue and increase of the females is hereby given and assured by the Said Levi Hickson and Shall be held by him during his natural life, and after his death by William T. Hickson his Executors and administrators Subject to the following uses and Trusts, and to and for no other use, Trust or purpose, whatsoever, That is to Say in Trust for the Sole and Separate use, benefit and behoof of the Said Martha M. Hagood during her natural life and in Such manner that the Said Slaves and their future issue and increase, and the wages, income and profits thereof Shall not be Subject to the Control, disposal, debts, Contracts or Engagements of the present or any future husband of the Said Martha M. Hagood, and after death, then in trust to and for the use and behoof of such child or children of the Said Martha M. Hagood, as Shall then be living, and the heirs of such Child or Children. (The Issue of any deceased child to Stand in the parents Stead, and take in like manner the parents Share.) And for default of Issue of the Said Martha M. Hagood living at the time of her death, then to the use and behoof of the right heirs of the Said Levi Hickson For ever,

Provided always that it Shall and may be lawful for the Said Levi Hickson, and after his death for the Said William T. Hickson, at the request of the Said Martha M. Hagood during her life, and of her Children after her death to Sell or otherwise dispose of the Said Slaves and their issue and increase or any part thereof, and invest the proceeds in other property real or personal which Substituted property Shall be subject to all the Trusts limitations and provisions herein Expressed and declared -- And Provided always Nevertheless that it Shall and may be lawful for the Said Levi Hickson at any time or times hereafter, as often as he Shall think fit by deed or writing under his hand and Seal or by his last will duly made and Subscribed, to appoint any other person or persons to be a Trustee or Trustees in the place of the Trustees Shall and may have and Exercise the Same powers and authorities to all intents and purposes whatsoever as if he or they had been originally appointed by these presents - And provided Lastly That the Said Slaves and their future Issue and increase Shall be deemed and held on advancement of One thousand Eight hundred and forty nine dollars of the Share or portion of the Said Martha M. Hagood in and out of the Estate of the Said Levi Hickson"

November 22, 1849 and in the Seventy fourth Year of the Independence of the United States of America
The State of South Carolina
From Alachua County Ancient Records
Deed Record E pages 314-316

Benjamin Hopkins, planter, to W. P. Hall of the firm of H. & W. P. Hall as collateral for a $2,150 loan: "This Indenture made and concluded this fourteenth day of March in the year on thousand Eight hundred and forty Eight, between Benjamin Hopkins of the first part, of the County and State aforesaid, planter, and W. P. Hall of the firm of H. & W. P. Hall Factors Charleston South Carolina, of the second part, Sheweth that the aforesaid Benjamin Hopkins is justly indebted to the party of the Second part, in the lawful sum of two thousand one hundred and fifty dollars, for which said sum of money, he the party of the Second holds his the party of the first part note of hand payable on the first day January Eighteen hundred and forty nine, bearing date with this instrument, Now this Indenture witnesseth, that the said party of the first part for the better security of said note of hand, have granted, bargained, and sold, and by these presents doth grant, bargain, sell, convey and confirm unto the party of the second part, his heirs, Executors and assigns the following property vis, a certain house and lot in the Town of Palatka, wherein the party of the first party now resides [...] together with the buildings thereunto attached, and all appertenances, also the undivided half of seven hundred acres of first quality of Hammock land lying and being in the County and State aforesaid on the Durkin Swamp, together with the following Negro Slaves, **Caroline aged twenty four, Dilea aged twenty six, George aged Seventeen, Charles aged forty-seven, William aged seven, Laura aged three, Susan the mother of William and Laura aged twenty one, Dorcas aged forty seven, Mariam aged Seventeen, Prisilla aged twenty, with the future issue of the female slaves**, to have and to hold the above granted property, to the party of the second his heirs and assigns forever, provided nevertheless, that should the party of the first part pay or cause to be paid to the party of the second part, the full amount of said note, at the time it becomes due, then these presents, and the property herein granted, shall cease and determine, and be null and void. other to remain in full force and effect, according to law."

March 14, 1848
St Johns County, State of Florida
From Alachua County Ancient Records
Mortgage Record A pages 010-011

Joe, an enslaved man, charged with assault with intent to kill a white person: "Territory of Florida vs Joe, a slave - Assault with intent to kill a white person. A True Bill."

December 20, 1843
From Alachua County Ancient Records
Superior Court Minutes 2 page 313

Samuel W. Jones to George L. Brown as collateral for a $555.49 loan: "Be it known that I Samuel W. Jones of Alachua County Florida being indebted to George L. Brown of said County in the just and full sum of Five Hundred and fifty five dollars and forty nine cents according to a certain promissory note for said amount made by me payable to said George L. Brown bearing even date with these presents and being desirous to secure to said George L. Brown the payment of said note, have this day and by these presents bargained sold and delivered to said George L. Brown the following Negro slaves of mine. Viz, **Jerry and Binah** to have and to hold said negro slaves **with their increase** unto the said George L. Brown, his executors, Administrators and assigns forever.

These presents are given and made nevertheless upon this express condition, that if the said Samuel W. Jones his executors or administrators do pay or cause to be paid on or before the first day of January next after date the said amount of money with interest according to the terms and effects of said promissory note then these presents and every clause article and thing therein contained shall be void and of no effect, otherwise to remain in full force and virtue."

June 25, 1847
From Alachua County Ancient Records
Mortgage Record A page 007

Samuel W. Jones to George L. Brown for $650: "Know all men by these presents that I Samuel W. Jones of Alachua County Florida in consideration of Six hundred and fifty dollars to me paid by George L. Brown of Said County the receipt whereof is hereby acknowledged, do hereby bargain, sell, and deliver to said George L. Brown **one negro woman named Binah, and her child Ben, the former aged about twenty one years, and the latter about five years**. To have and to hold said negroes unto said George L. Brown his Executors Administrators and assigns forever."

February 10, 1849
From Alachua County Ancient Records
Bills of Sale A page 012

William Lewis Senior to his son John Lewis: "Know all men by these presents that I William Lewis Senior of the State and district aforesaid for and in consideration of the natural love and affection which I have for my son John Lewis, and also in consideration of the sum of one Dollar to me in hand paid at & before the signing of these presents the receipt whereof is hereby acknowledged have given bargained sold and Delivered in trust however during the term of his natural life for his own use and behoof and upon the Death of the said John then to whatever child or children of the said John may be living at the time of his Death - the following Negros to wit **Ben, Viney, Washington, Black Ben, Margret, Kizzy & her children, Maria, Sarah and William & Bob together with their future increase**, To have and to hold all & singular the nine Negros above named according to the uses & trust above mentioned, And I do hereby bind myself & my executors Administrators or assigns forever to warrant and defend the title of the said Negros to the said John Lewis during his natural life, and at his Death to his children according to the former conditions & provisions of this Deed."

February 9, 1841
South Carolina, Fairfield District
From Alachua County Ancient Records
Deed Record D pages 216-217

John McCrorey, husband of Dorcas McCrorey, received from Dorcas's dad John Mobley: "This is to witness that I John McCrorey of Fairfield district have received of John Mobley the Father of my wife Dorcas **Six Negroes Amstead Cumber and her four children viz Jacin, Alfred, Albert, & Jane all valued at One thousand and Six hundred dollars**, Also Eleven hundred dollars recvd in Cash which I am to hold for the Sole and Separate use of my Said wife Dorcas, and of which my said wife Dorcas is to have the Sole use & benefit of for and during her natural and should my said wife Dorcas die before me leaving children living, then the Said property is to be for the Sole use and benefit of her Children to be equaly divided among them,

And Should my Said wife Survive me, the Same is to be for her benefit during her life, free from the debts or liabilities of any husband or husbands She may marry. And at the death of my Said wife the Same is to be equally divided among her Children whom She may have living at the time of her Death

And Should my Said wife Dorcas depart this life without leaving Children living the Said property is to revert to the Said John Mobley Should he be living and if he Should die before Such an event the

Same property is to be equally divided among his heirs at Law who may be then living"

August 22, 1846
The State of South Carolina, Fairfield District
From Alachua County Ancient Records
Deed Record E pages 218-219

John McKinlay to Horace Merry as collateral for a $1,500 loan: "Whereas on the 15th day of November 1848 a certain John McKinley of the County of Alachua and State of Florida, by his certain Indenture, bearing the day and year aforesaid and of record in the office of the Clerk of said County of Alachua, bargained, Sold, and delivered to Horrace Merry of said County and state the following described Negroes, to wit; **Emily a female aged about twenty two years Cuffy a male aged about six years son of Emily, George a male aged about three years also son of Emily, and Tenna a female aged about twenty one years,** to have and to hold said Slaves to the said Horace Merry his heirs and assigns forever, with condition annexed in and by said Indenture; that if the Said John McKinley shall well and truly pay to the said Horrace Merry the Sum of fifteen hundred dollars the amount of a promissory note, bearing like date with said indenture executed by said John McKinley to said Horrace Merry for said amount, and payable as set forth in said promissory note and executed in said indenture, then the said indenture to be veri and obligative without effect, otherwise to continue in full force, and the title to said Slaves to vest and remain absolutely in Said Horrace Merry, all of which will more fully appear by reference to said deed and promissory note, of record as aforesaid in Clerks Office of said County of Alachua, to which is here made, and the same is to be taken and regarded as a part of this indenture, and when the said John McKinley and Horrace Merry have annulled and cancelled the conditions by reason of which the said Sum of fifteen hundred dollars become due and payable from the former to the latter, and the said Horrace Merry hath Surrendered and delivered up to the said John McKinley said promissory note for fifteen hundred dollars, and release to the Said John McKinley all claims on account thereof, now this indenture witnesseth, that the said Horrace Merry, in consideration of the Premises, and the further consideration of five dollars to him in hand paid by the said John McKinley at and before the Sealing and delivery of these Presents, the receipt whereof is hereby acknowledged, hath bargained, sold, and released, and by these presents doth bargain sell, and release, to the said John McKinley, Said Slaves to wit; Emily, Cuffy, George, Tinna, To have and to hold Said named Slaves to said McKinley his heirs &C as fully and to every interest as if said indenture and promissory note herein before described had never been made and executed and the said Horrace Merry for himself his heirs, &C agrees to defend Said Slaves to the Said McKinley his heirs &C, against all claim on the part of Said Merry, and others claiming by him or under him, and against such claim only."

November 15, 1848
State of Florida, Alachua County
From Alachua County Ancient Records
Mortgage Record A pages 022-023
Also see Deed Record A pages 117-118

James McNabb, Samuel Wood, & William Roach charged with aiding an enslaved person to run away: "The grand Jury came into Court & presented the following Bills…Territory vs James McNabb, Samuel Wood, & William Roach - Aiding &c a slave to runaway &c - A True Bill"

December 19, 1843
From Alachua County Ancient Records
Superior Court Minutes 2 page 307

Archibald McNeill and his wife to George Field as collateral for a $3,182 loan: "This indenture made the twelfth day of August in the year One thousand eight hundred and forty, Between Archibald McNeill of Alachua county in the Territory of Florida and his wife of the first part and George Field president of the Southern Life Insurance Company of the second part - Whereas the said Arch. McNeill is justly indebted to the said party of the second part, in the sum of Three thousand One Hundred and Eighty two Dollars Current money of the United States of America, Secured to be paid in and by a certain Bond or Writing Obligatory bearing even date herewith executed by the party of the first part, as by said Bond or Writing Obligatory, reference being thereto had will more fully appear -

Now this Indenture Witnesseth that the said party of the first part, for the more perfect security of the payment of the said money, according to the true interest and meaning thereof, and in consideration of one Dollar in hand paid, at and before the ensealing and delivery of these presents, hath granted, bargained, sold, Aliened, released, conveyed and confirmed, and by these presents, do grant Bargain, Sell, alien, release, convey and Confirm, unto the said party of the second part, and to his successors in office and assigns forever, those certain Slaves of him the said Archibald McNeill following to wit, **George, a male**

aged thirty five years, Ebenarzer, a male aged Twelve years, Sampson, a male aged Five years, Philida, a female aged Twenty eight years, Beck, a female aged three years, Ann, a female Twenty Seven years, Peggy, a female aged Eighteen years, Dorcas, a female aged thirty years, Rose, a female aged fourteen years, and Lydia, a female aged Twenty years - Together with all and Singular the future increase of said female Slaves.

Together with all and Singular the tenements, hereditaments and appurtenances, thereunto belonging and the reversion and reversions remainder and remainders, rents, issues and profits thereof, and all the Estate, right, title, interest, dower and right of dower, property claim and demand in law or equity, of the party of the first part.

To have and to hold the above bargained premises unto the party of the second part, his successors and assigns, to the sole and only use of the party of the second part his successors and assigns forever

Provided always, and these presents are upon this express condition, that if the party of the first part, his Executors or Administrators shall and do well and fully pay or cause to be paid unto the said party of the second part, his successors or assigns the said sum of money mentioned and specified in the said Bond or Writing Obligatory and the interest thereof according to the tenor and effect, true intent and meaning of the said Bond or writing Obligatory and According to the covenants and agreements herein after contained then and from thenceforth, these presents and the estate hereby granted Shall cease determine, and be utterly null and void.

And the said parties of the first part, covenant, grant, promise and agree to and with the party of the second part, and his successors and assigns, the said sum of money with lawful interest there on, as the time and or manner Specified, that is to say, The said principal Sum of Three Thousand One hundred and eighty two Dollars, on or before the Expiration of Three years from the date hereof, with the interest to grow due there on. Time = Annually on the first days of January &

July in each and every year, shall and will well and truly pay or cause to be paid to the party of the second part, his successors in office or Assigns.

And it is hereby mutually covenanted and agreed by & between the parties of these presents, that if default shall be made in the payment of the aforementioned sum, or the interest or any part or parts thereof, at the time, and or in the manner specified - That then it shall be lawful for the party of the second part, or his Successors or Assigns, to enter into and upon the premises, and take possession of the whole or any part of the same, and grant, sell and bargain the same, and all of the benefits, and equity of redemption of the party of the first part his heirs or assigns, or any person claiming by through or under them at public auction, to the highest bidder, according to the manner prescribed by the Act of the Legislative Council of Florida, entitled, An Act to incorporate the Southern Life Insurance and Trust Company

And as the Attorney of the party of the first part, for that purpose by these presents, duly authorized to make, seal execute and deliver, to the purchaser or purchasers thereof, a good and valid deed or deeds of conveyance in law, in fee simple for the same to retain the principal and interest of the moneys then in arrears and unpaid and all the cost of charges and of advertisements. Sale and other expenses in the premises, rendering the Overplus (if any) to the party of the first part, or his legal representative on demand, Which sale so to be made shall be a perpetual bar both in law and equity, against the party of the first part, and all persons claiming by through or under him, And the party of the first part hereby Covenant and agree, to and with the party of the second part, his Successors in Office and Assigns, that the said party of the first lawfully is Seized, of a perfect, Absolute, indefeasible estate of inheritance, in fee simple of in and unto said premises"

August 12, 1840
From Alachua County Ancient Records
Deed Book B pages 350-352

Abraham Mott to Dicy Standly as collateral for a $300 loan:
"Know all Men by these presents that I Abraham Mott of Alachua
County Florida have by these presents bargained and sold to Dicy
Standly in consideration of Three Hundred Dollars to me by her paid,
my **Negro woman named Tenah aged about thirty years**. To have
and to hold said Negro woman **with her future issue** to her the said
Dicy Standly her Executor, Administrator and assigns forever. The
consideration of the above instrument of writing is such that if the
said Abraham Mott his executors or administrators shall pay or cause
to be paid to the said Dicy Standly her executors, administrator or
assigns the sum of Three Hundred Dollars with lawful interest from
the date of these presents on or before the first day of January next
according to the term and effect of a certain promissory note for said
amount signed by me and bearing even date with these presents then
these presents and any clause and article thereof shall be void and of
null effect; otherwise to remain in full force and effect."

May 28, 1847
From Alachua County Ancient Records
Mortgage Record A page 006

Allen B. Mundin to John Waterston for $600: "Know all men by
these presents that I Allen B. Mundin for and in consideration of the
sum of six hundred Dollars to me in hand at and before the sealing
and delivery of these presents by John Waterston the receipt whereof
I do hereby acknowledge to have bargained sold and delivered and by
these presents do bargain sell and deliver unto the said John Waterston a certain **Negro slave named Martha June aged about twenty
years** to have and to hold the said slave Martha June unto the said

John Waterston his heirs Executors Administrators and assigns to his and their only proper use and benefits forever."

April 6, 1846
From Alachua County Ancient Records
Bills of Sale A page 001

Alonzo B. Noyes to John S. Livingston as collateral for $1,500.42 in loans: "Know all men by these presents that I Alonzo B. Noyes of Micanopy in the County of Alachua being justly Indebted to John S. Livingston of the same place in the sum of Fifteen hundred Dollars and forty two Cents upon three promissory Notes made by me [...] payable to John S. Livingston with interest, have for the purpose of Securing the payment of said Debts, granted, bargained, sold & Mortgaged and by these presents do Bargain, grant, sell, and Mortgage unto the said John S. Livingston, the following personal property To Wit **My Negroe fellow Alexander aged twenty five years, Also my Negroe Woman Hyacinth aged twenty two years, and her child Amanda aged Eleven months, All Slaves for life**, Also the issue of said Slaves if any from and after this date, Also Two Grey Mules also two Sorrel Mules, and One Sorel Mare and colt, One Wagon & four Sets of harness, Also One Barrouch with two sets of Harness Together with the House I now Occupy at Micanopy and all the Out houses and Appurtenances and improvements thereunto belonging To have and to hold forever [...] if I the said Alonzo B. Noyes shall pay or cause to be paid unto the said John S. Livingston the debts with interest on or before the first day of January AD 1844 then this instrument shall be void and of no effect And I the said Alonzo B. Noyes agree to pay the same Accordingly But if default be made in such payment the said John S. Livingston is hereby Authorized to sell at Public Auction after the like Notice as is by Law required for Sheriffs Sales, the Goods, Chattels, and personal property herein before mentioned or so much thereof as may be necessary to satisfy the said debt, Interest and reasonable expenses, and to retain the same out of the proceeds of such sale the Overplus or residue if any to belong and be returned to me And the said John S. Livingston is hereby Authorized to take possession of the said goods, chattels and personal property on or before the first day of January AD 1844 unless the said debt shall be sooner paid."

October 10, 1842
Territory of Florida, Alachua County
From Alachua County Ancient Records
Deed Book B pages 428-429

Alonzo B. Noyes to Augustus E. Noyes as collateral for a $500 loan: "Know all me by these presents that I Alonzo B. Noyes of the Town of Micanopy in the County of Alachua being justly indebted unto Augustus E. Noyes of Wacasessee in the County of Alachua in the Sum of Five hundred Dollars [...] Now for the purpose of Securing the payments of said Debts, granted, bargained, Sold and Mortgaged and by these presents do grant, bargain, Sell and Mortgage, unto the Said Augustus E. Noyes, the following personable property To Wit, **My Negroe fellow Abraham aged thirty Seven years a Slave for life**, Also Eight Cows and Calves and Five Yearling Steers, to have and to hold the same forever Provided Always, and the Condition of these presents is such that if I the said Alonzo B. Noyes shall pay or cause to be paid to the said Augustus E. Noyes the debt Aforesaid with Interest, On or before the first day of March AD (1844) Eighteen hundred and forty four next, then this Instrument shall be void and of no effect, And I the said Alonzo B. Noyes agree to pay the same accordingly But if default be made in such payment the said Augustus E. Noyes is hereby Authorized to Sell at Public Auction after the like Notice as by Law required for Sheriffs Sale, the personal property herein before mentioned or so much thereof as may be necessary to satisfy the said Debt interest and reasonable expenses, And to return the same out of the proceeds of Such Sale the Overplus or residue if any to belong and be returned to me And the Said Augustus E. Noyes is hereby Authorized to take possession of the said personal property on or before the first day of March AD 1844 One thousand eight hundred and forty four unless such debts shall be sooner paid."

October 10, 1842
Territory of Florida, Alachua County
From Alachua County Ancient Records
Deed Book B pages 426-427

Thomas Paisly to daughter Margaret W. Paisly for $500: "I Thomas Paisly of the Territory and County aforesaid this day I bargin and sell unto my Daughter, Margaret W. Paisly a **Negro woman Judy, aged forty or forty five, with two small children Dinah aged six years old, Letta two years old** for the sum of five hundred Dollars good money ***** of said negroes I warrant and defend against myself my heirs Executor and Administrators assigns forever."

December 28, 1843
Territory of Fla, Gadsden County
From Alachua County Ancient Records
Deed Record B page 195

Eliza D. Payne enumerates the property belonging to her: "In Inventory of Slaves and other property showing their names & belonging to Mrs. Eliza D. Payne, formerly of Buckingham County Virginia, and now of Alachua County Florida which are held for the exclusive benefit of said E. D. Payne by Geo M. Payne and other trustees, viz; **Edy, Billy, Frank, Solomon, Anna, Sopha, Emily, China, Brunnell, Charles, Alick, Lucy, Albert, Beccy, Martin, Tom, Frank Jr., Washington, Martha, Lindy, Susan, Henry, John William, Dick, Amos Jnr, Tom Jnr, Squire, John & London with their increase and annual profits**, also stock of mules, horses, cattle, plantation furniture &C

June 5, 1848
From Alachua County Ancient Records
Deed Record A page 062

Edmond Penn's daughter Jane Penn to marry Edwin H. Jordan. This document lays out what Jane Penn is bringing into the marriage: "This Indenture made and entered into this 19th day of June 1843, by and between Edmond Penn and his Daughter Jane Penn of the first part, and Edwin H. Jordan of the other part, all of the County of Amherst, whereas a marriage is Shortly intended to have and Solemnised Between the Said Edwin H. Jordan, and the Said Jane Penn, and it hath been agreed by and between the said Edwin H. Jordan and the said Jane Penn and the Said Edmond Penn her Father that all the property, rights, interest and estate of the Said Jane Penn Shall be Secured to her and her issue as hereinafter provided, So as not to be in any manner liable to the debts or contracts or liabilities of the Said Edwin H. Jordan, Now this Indenture witnesseth, that the Said Jane Penn by and with the approbation and consent of her Father the Said Edmond and her intended Husband the Said Edwin H. Jordan Signified by their becoming parties hereto, and Signing and

Sealing this Indenture for and in consideration of the premises, and the further consideration of one dollar lawful money of Virginia to her in hand paid, at and before the Sealing and delivery of this Indenture by the Said Edwin H. Jordan, the receipt of which is hereby fully acknowledged, hath granted, bargained, Sold, aliened, enfeoffed and confirmed, and doth by these presents grant, bargain, Sell, enfeoff and confirm unto the Said Edwin H. Jordan all the Estate real and personal of her the Said Jane Penn in possession, reversion, or remainder and all debts, choses in action, rights and interest unto her belonging, or to which She is or may become in any manner entitled, her Said Estate consisting of an undivided equal Share or interest in common with Same or all of her Sisters as the case may be, in the lands and Slaves, Stock and other Estate real and personal now in the possession and enjoyment of the family of the Said Edmond Penn, or held in trust for their use and benefit, and all other estate real & personal, rights, & interest, to her belonging, or to which She is entitled, or may become entitled, whether herein enumerated or not, and all property or estate, of what kind or nature whatever, to which She may hereafter become entitled by inheritance, or devise, bequest, or donation, or under the acts of distribution, To have and to hold the Estate, rights and interest, of her the Said Jane Penn herein conveyed to the Said Edwin H. Jordan, his heirs and assigns forever, upon trust nevertheless that the Said Edwin H. Jordan Shall hold the Estate hereby conveyed, and every part thereof, until the Solemnization of the Said intended marriage to the use and benefit of the Said Jane Penn, and after the Solemnization of the intended Marriage Separate use and benefit of the Said Jane Penn, free from the claims of any his present or future creditors & applying the profits thereof to the Sole and Separate Support and maintenance of the Said Jane, and the issue of the marriage during the coverture, with the advice and consent of her Husband, the Said Edwin H. Jordan, and in the event of the Said Jane dying during the life of the Said Edwin H. Jordan having issue, he Shall thence forward hold the Said Estate or So much thereof as had not been disposed of as aforesaid, to the use and benefit of the issue of the marriage, and if She dies without issue living at the time of her death, the Same Shall go to the Said Edwin H. Jordan. If the Said Edwin H. Jordan Shall die first having issue of the marriage, the said trust, Estate or what may remain undisposed of as aforesaid, it then to be divided in to two Equal parts and one moity thereof transferred and conveyed to the Said Jane to be her absolute estate, and the other moiety to their issue to be their absolute estate. And in the event of the death of the Said Edwin H. Jordan, before the Said Jane having no issue of the marriage, the trust estate, or what may remain undisposed of as aforesaid Shall thereupon become the absolute Estate of her the Said Jane. And the Said Edwin H. Jordan hereby covenants and agrees to and with the Said Edmond Penn, the Father, and the Said Jane, the Daughter, Jointly and separately that he will notwithstanding the marriage faithfully perform all the duties hereby imposed upon him as trustee, and permit the Said Jane and the issue of the Marriage, to have the benefit of her estate as herein before provided, free from the claims of any and all of his present or future creditors, and that he will, if need be, when thereto reasonably requested make and execute any Such further conveyances or assurances as may necessary fully to Secure and protect for the uses and purposes herein before declared, all the estate of every Kind and description of which the Said Jane is now possessed, or to which She is entitled, as also like conveyances and assurances of all Such property or estate as may hereafter come to the Said Jane by inheritance or devise, bequest or donation, or under the acts of distribution to be held by the Said trustee for the uses and purposes herein before Set forth."

June 19, 1843
From Alachua County Ancient Records
Deed Record D pages 133-134

Henry Pennington on trial for murder. 9 people were sworn in to give evidence before the grand Jury, including an enslaved man named Moses: "Territory of Florida vs Henry Pennington - Murder - The said Henry Pennington having been arraigned, to wit; on Tuesday the 20th day of December A.D. 1842: & having pleaded "Not Guilty" to the Indictment against him, & having put himself upon the country for his trial: There came, on this day, a Jury, to wit; Fleming Bates, R. S. Stoughton, Wm T. Brown, John R. Hague, Joel B. Smith, Richard R. Crum, Abraham Daniels, James Weeks, James Harn (Talisman), James B. Bates (Talisman), and Wm Mayo (Talisman) who were sworn well & truly to try and true deliverance make between the Territory of Florida and the prisoner at the bar, and a true verdict to give, according to law and evidence.

Wm D. Andrews, David C. Cash, & Elizabeth Cash were sworn as witnesses on the part of the prosecution.

The Court then took a recess of one hour, during which the Jury in this cause sworn, were placed under the charge of Ethelbert Hagan & Thomas Coverly, who were sworn for the purpose.

The Court having met, James Walker, Mary V. Andrews, Wm Johns, & Abraham Daniels, were sworn as witnesses on the part of the prosecution, & Melintha Lanier, Laburn Burnett, Enoch Daniels - were sworn in behalf of the prisoner.

The following persons were today sworn to give evidence before the grand Jury, to wit; Meyer Helfer, John J. Sanchez, Enoch Daniels, Wm G. Ferris, John B. Allen, James A. Bardin, James M. Flinn, James T. Thomas, Moses (a slave)

There not being sufficient time to go through with the trial of Henry Pennington to-day; the prisoner is remanded to the custody of the Marshal, & by consent of the parties, & under the charge of the Court the Jury empannelled for the trial of the said Henry Pennington on the

Indictment against him for murder; were allowed to separate to be in Court tomorrow morning at 9 oclk."

December 21, 1843
From Alachua County Ancient Records
Superior Court Minutes 2 pages 317-318

Charlotte L. Pyles marrying George Helvinston, with Charlotte's property being held in trust by Samuel R. Pyles: "This Indenture of three parts made this twenty fourth day of September in the year One thousand eight hundred & forty five between Charlotte L. Pyles of Alachua County, gentlewoman of the first part, Samuel R. Pyles Esquire of said County of the second part, and George Helvinston gentleman of the third part, Witnesseth; That Whereas a marriage is intended to be had and Solemnized between the said parties of the first and third parts, and the said party of the first part is possessed of certain personal Estate "to wit, four Negro slaves - viz - **Maria, Primus Lill & Randall**, which said Slaves, the said party of the first part with the Consent of the said party of the third part, is minded and disposed to transfer to the said party of the second part in trust for her own proper use and benefit Now therefore in Consideration of the premises and of one dollar paid by the said party of the Second part to the said party of the first part (the receipt whereof is hereby acknowledged) the said party of the first part doth bargain, sell, assign and transfer to the said party of the second part the said named Negro slaves with all their and each of their further issue and increase to hold the same to him the said party of the second part and his Executors & Administrators upon the special trusts and for the uses and purposes following, namely;

In the first place that until the solemnization of the said marriage the said party of the second part shall pay on to the said party of the first part or shall empower her to receive for her own use all the income & profits owing from the services of said Negro slaves and from any other Estate which my be substituted therefore as is herein after provided.

Secondly, That from and after the Solemnization of the said marriage and during the coventure of the said party of the first part the said party of the second part shall permit and allow the said party of the first part to hold and enjoy the said negro slaves and their increase and the issues & profits arising from the services of said slaves and to have such use & control of said slaves as she the said party of the first part may desire, and that the parties of the second and third parts shall not interfere with such use and Control of said slaves, and that the said slaves and their increase or any part thereof shall not be liable for the debts or other liabilities of said party of the third part or at his disposal.

Thirdly, That in case of the death of the said party of the first part after the solemnization of said marriage and during the life of her said husband the said slaves and their increase and all monies and profits from their service arising in the hands of said party of the second part at the time of such death shall be transferred & paid over to such person or persons as she the said party of the first part may by her last will & testament appoint to receive the same and in default of her making such last will & testament the said Slaves and their increase and said monies & profits in the hands of said party of the second part at the time of such death shall be transferred according to the Laws of Florida in existence at the time of such death, that the said party of the Third part nevertheless shall be entitled to receive and to have transferred to him such portion (by the said party of the second part) of said slaves their increase & the monies & profits arising from the services or sale of said slaves & their increase or of such property as may be substituted therefore as by law he is more entitled in the event of such death

Fourthly, that in the event of the decease of the said party of the third part leaving the said party of the first part all the property then held in trusts under this Indenture shall be transferred & conveyed back to the said party of the first part and until so transferred the said party of the second part shall pay over to her or empower her to receive the incomes & profits arising there from for her own use

Fifthly, that the said party of the second part shall have power with the approbation or at the request of the said party of the first part expressed in writing to sell and dispose of the property above mentioned or any part of it and the proceeds to invest in other personal or in real Estate according to the written direction of the said party of the first part and the Estate so purchased shall be had and held by the said party of the second part for the same uses & purposes as an declared in & by this Indenture of and concerning the property and Estate first above mentioned And may be sold and the proceeds invested from time to time in trust in manner aforesaid.

Sixthly, that in case of the decease of the said party of the second part or his resignation of said trust, he or his Executors or Administrators shall convey transfer & pay over the whole of the trust Estate then held by him to such person or persons as may be appointed in writing by the said party of the first part to be the trustee or trustees under the Indenture and such new Trustee or Trustees shall have all the powers and Shall hold the trust Estate subject to all the provisions herein set forth and Expressed, and the receipt of such new Trustee or Trustees shall be a complete acquittance to the said party of the second part his Executors & administrators and in like manner (other) & new Trustee may be appointed from time to time as occasion may require.

And the said party of the second part doth hereby signify his acceptance of the said trust and doth engage to hold and manage said property & Estate for the uses trust & purposes herein mentioned

And the said party of the third part doth hereby signify his Consent to the provisions of this Indenture and doth Covenant to and with the said party of the second part and his successors in the said Trust, not to interfere with the said trust or with the property hereinbefore mentioned otherwise than in conformity to the provisions of this Indenture"

September 24, 1845
From Alachua County Ancient Records
Deed Record A pages 017-019

John J. Sanchez and Alexander B. Sanchez to Fernando A. Underwood of Alachua County for $900: "Know all men by these presents that we John J. Sanchez and Alexander B. Sanchez for and in consideration of the sum of nine hundred ($900) dollars to us paid by Fernando A. Underwood of Alachua County, the receipt whereof we do hereby acknowledge, have granted, bargained, sold, and delivered, and by these presents, do grant, bargain, sell, and deliver unto the said Fernando A. Underwood **two Negro Slaves named Louis and Ann**. To have and to hold said Negro Slaves **with their future increase** unto the said Fernando A. Underwood his Executors, Administrators, and assigns forever without any claim or hindrance of any person whatsoever, and without any account to us, or to any other person hereafter to be rendered. So that neither we the said John J. Sanchez, or Alexander B. Sanchez, or any other person any right or interest in or to said Negro Slaves or their increase shall or will claim or demand at any time hereafter. And we the said John J. and Alexander B. Sanchez our Executors and Administrators, the said Slaves unto the said Fernando A. Underwood his Executors and Administrators against all and every other person or persons whatsoever shall and will warrant and forever defend by these presents."

November 4, 1845
State of Florida, Alachua County
From Alachua County Ancient Records
Bills of Sale A page 015

John J. Sanchez to Sarah A. Sanchez as collateral for a $1,000 loan: "Know all men by these presents that I John J Sanchez of the County and State aforesaid for and in consideration of the sum of one thousand dollars to me in hand paid the receipt whereof is hereby acknowledged have bargained and sold unto Sarah A Sanchez of the same place all the following named and described Negro slaves; to wit: **Bill a Negro Boy about seventeen years of age, Moses a dark complexioned Negro man about forty five years of age, Edward a Negro Boy about twenty three years of age, Nat a Negro Boy about twenty two years of age and February a Negro boy about eighteen years of age.** To have and to hold said bargained and sold Negro slaves unto her the said Sarah A. Sanchez her heirs and assigns unto her and their own proper use and benefit forever. And I the said John J. Sanchez for myself, my heirs and assigns do covenant to and with the said Sarah A. Sanchez her heirs and assigns that I am legally possessed of my own right to said Negro slaves with full power and authority to dispose of the same. Provided nevertheless that whereas the said John J. Sanchez and George W. Sanchez have made, executed and delivered unto the said Sarah A Sanchez their joint and several promissory notes bearing even date with these presents, payable to the said Sarah A Sanchez or bearer on the first day of January, eighteen hundred and forty eight for the sum of one thousand dollars with interest thereon at the rate of eight percentum per annum from the date thereof. The consideration whereof is the above named and described Negro slaves this day sold and delivered unto the said John J. Sanchez by the said Sarah A Sanchez. Made in case the said John J. Sanchez and the said George W Sanchez or either of them shall well and truly pay unto the said Sarah A. Sanchez or the bearer thereof the above named and described promissory note on the day and date therein specified with interest thereon according to the tenor and effect thereof Then the above Sale to be null and void otherwise to remain in full force and virtue to all intents and purposes."

January 14, 1847
State of Florida, Alachua County
From Alachua County Ancient Records
Mortgage Record A pages 003-004

John J. Sanchez, administrator of the Estate of Francis R. Sanchez dec'd to Sarah Ann Sanchez for $400: "Know all men by these presents that I John J. Sanchez administrator on the Estate of Francis R. Sanchez dec'd for and in consideration of the sum of Four Hundred dollars $400 to me in hand paid (as agent for Francis R. Sanchez on the 1st day of January 1845) the receipt whereof is hereby acknowledged have bargained sold and delivered and by these presents do bargain sell and deliver unto Sarah Ann Sanchez wife of George W. Sanchez her heirs and assigns the following named Negro Slave to wit one **negro Boy named Bill aged about fifteen years**. To have and to hold the said Negro Slave Bill unto her the Said Sarah Ann Sanchez her heirs and assigns for ever and I the Said John J. Sanchez administrator as aforesaid for myself my heirs Executor and administrator, all and singular the said Negro Slave Bill unto the Said Sarah Ann Sanchez her heirs, administrators and assigns against me the said John J. Sanchez administrator, my Executors and administrators and against all and every other person and persons whatsoever, Shall and will warrant and forever defend by these presents."

December 8, 1849
State of Florida, County of Alachua
From Alachua County Ancient Records
Bills of Sale A page 016

Sarah Ann Sanchez, widow of Francis R. Sanchez, moved from FL to NY and appointed attorney Robert G. Livingston of Newnansville FL to handle her business in Florida: "Know all men by these presents that I Sarah Ann Sanchez late of San Palaska in the State of Florida, and now of Brutus in the County of Cayuga and State of New York have made constituted and appointed, and by these presents, do make constitute and appoint, Robert G. Livingston of Newnansville in the State of Florida aforesaid, Counsellor at Law, my true and lawful attorney, for one, and **in my name, place and stead, to govern, direct, control, let on him, all the Negroes being in Florida as aforesaid belonging to me under and by virtue of a marriage contract executed by and between Francis R. Sanchez** (now deceased) late of San Palacka aforesaid, and myself the said Sarah Ann Sanchez (then Sarah Ann Houckin the year 1841* and recorded in the Office of the Clerk or Register of the County of Alachua in the said State of Florida and I do hereby fully authorize and empower my said attorney to execute all necessary papers for the letting and hiring of the said Negroes, and to collect and receive all monies now due or hereafter to become due for the labor and service and to take all legal ways and means for the recovery thereof; if payment of the same, or of any part thereof shall be rented and on such receipt and recovery as aforesaid, to execute and deliver all proper acquittance and acknowledgements in the premises. And I do further make, constitute and appoint the said Robert G. Livingston my true and lawful attorney, for me, and in my name place and stead to ask, demand, sue for recover, and receive, all in trusts claims, dower, and rights of dower, which I can or may have in to or against the Estate of the said Francis R. Sanchez, deceased, late of San Palacka as aforesaid; to institute and prosecute all necessary suits and take all lawful ways and means for the recovery thereof; to compromise, confirm and agree for the same; And upon each receipt, recovery, compromise, com*****, or agreement to execute and deliver sufficient discharges thereof, And I do hereby give and grant to my said attorney, full power of substitution and revocation, deed ample and complete authority to do and perform all and every act and thing whatsoever requested and necessary to be done in and about the premises above recited, as fully to all interests and purposes as I might or could do if personally present, hereby ratifying and confirming all that my said attorney or his substitute shall lawfully do, or cause to be done by virtue thereof."

August 25, 1845
From Alachua County Ancient Records
Deed Record A pages 035-036

Sarah A. Sanchez widow of Francis R. Sanchez regarding his estate: "Be it Known that I Sarah A. Sanchez of Alachua County Florida Widow of Francis R. Sanchez late of said County deceased in consideration of the sum of Two Hundred and Fifty Dollars to me paid by John J. Sanchez Administrator of the Estate of said Francis R. Sanchez deceased **for the hire of five Negro slaves** for and during the year One thousand Eight hundred and forty five for the purpose of cultivating attending to and gathering the crop which the said Francis R. Sanchez had a short time before his death planted, and in consideration of the further sum of Twenty Six Dollars and seventy five cents paid to me by the said John J. Sanchez Administrator as aforesaid with the understanding and in consideration on his part that I would release unto him as Administrator all my claims and demands upon the Estate and property of the said deceased and dismiss my petition or proceeding wherein and whereby the same may have been asserted in any of the Courts of the State of Florida and any appeal or writ of error which may have been taken or brought upon any decree which may have been rendered with reference to any claim or demand of mine so asserted as Widow as aforesaid, the receipt of both which amounts I hereby acknowledge do hereby release, renounce, assign, and forever quit claim unto the said John J. Sanchez as administrator for the use of said Estate all my right, title, interest or claim, either at law or in equity in or upon the property, lands, tenements and Estate of the said Francis R. Sanchez and more particularly any claim of Dower or to a childs portion and upon said Estate or upon any property upon which the said Francis R. Sanchez at the time of his death had or the said John J. Sanchez as administrator as aforesaid her any claim or lien whatsoever. To have and to hold any right title interest and claim so assigned as aforesaid unto the said John J. Sanchez as administrator as aforesaid for the use of said Estate free from any interference of mine forever. And I the said Sarah A. Sanchez for myself my Executors and Administrators to dismiss any each proceeding, petition, appeal or writ of Error as above described whenas ***** by the said John J. Sanchez Administrator or his successors in the administration of said Estate."

September 19, 1846
From Alachua County Ancient Records
Deed Record A page 037

James H. Smith to William Dell in Trust for Smith's wife Mary Smith and their children: "This Indenture made this sixteenth day of June eighteen hundred and forty nine, between James H. Smith of the County and State aforesaid of the first part, and William Dell of the County of Alachua aforesaid of the other part; Witnesseth, that whereas a marriage has heretofore been had and Solemnized between Mary Smith formerly Mary Thomas now Mary Smith, and the Said part of the first part Jas. H. Smith, and whereas the Said Jas. H. Smith and the Said Mary hath begotten the following named children viz; Wm. F. Bryan, Lavenia, Fanny, James, Hampton, Milton, Florida, America, & Curling Smith, and whereas the Said Jas. H. Smith of the first part is legally possessed in his own right and title the following named and described property, viz; **One Negro man named Jim, one Negro woman named Sarah, together with four children**

Monday Moses, Mary, and Stephen also the following land to wit; The S.W. 1/4 of the S.E. 1/4 of Section one, & N.W. 1/4 of N.E. 1/4 Section (12) and S.E. 1/4 of S.W. 1/4 Section one, all of Township (8) Range (19) also one Bay mare two year old, and Sorrel mare five years old also one hundred and Sixty head of stock Cattle, in the following marks and brands, viz; Same crop and Split in one ear, the other ear whole, Branded with a heart and figure 2, same in the same mark Branded 22, Same crop and split In one ear, the other ear cropped off. Branded with a heart and figure 2, and DIL also one hundred and twenty five head of hogs more or less, and being free from all debts and liabilities to any person whomsoever of whatever character, and fortune are uncertain, and the probabilities of loss many, therefore in consideration of the love and affection which he the Said Jas. H., of the first part hath and has towards his Said wife Mary, and his said children, as well as other good and valuable considerations him hereunto moving, and being desirous and for the purpose of making a Suitable provision for his said wife Mary, and his Said Children above named, is minded and disposed to Set over and transfer to the Said William Dell of the Second part, all the above mentioned named and described property, and the increase thereof for the uses and purposes, and upon the conditions and limatation hereinafter set fourth and expressed. NOW THEREFORE in consideration of the premises, and for the further consideration of five dollars to the Said Jas. H. Smith of the first part in hand paid by the Said William Dell of the Second part, the receipt whereof is hereby acknowledged, the said party of the first Part doth herby assign, transfer, and set over to the Said party of the Second Part, his Executors, Administrators and assigns, all the above mentioned named and described property, to hold the same the Said William Dell his Executors, Administrators, and assigns upon Special Trust, to the use and benefit of the Said Mary for and during her natural life, and pay over or cause to be paid over to the Said Mary all the increase, rents, incomes, or dividends arising from or out of the said trust property, for her own Sole use and benefit and after the death of the said Mary the whole of the Said trust property, and the increase thereof Shall vest immediately and absolutely and without any restriction limitation or condition in the aforesaid named children, for their own proper use and benefit and enjoyment forever, Provided nevertheless, that in case the Said Mary Shall Survive the Said Jas. H. her Husband, and Shall afterwards marry a Second Husband, then and in that case, the aforesaid mentioned and described property Shall immediately vest as aforesaid in the above named Children upon Said Second marriage, and in case of further issue of the Said Mary by her Present husband Jas. H. Smith, the Said Issue to Share all equal proportion of Said trust Property with the above named Children aforesaid upon the Same conditions and limitations above named and provided, and the Said William Dell of the Second Part, doth hereby Signify his acceptance of the Said trust, and doth engage to hold and manage the Same upon the trust and for the uses and purposes herein mentioned, and doth covenant to and with the said Party of the first Part, to Permit the said Mary to receive and enjoy the said increase and Profits of the Said trust property, to her sole and separate use and benefit, in manner and form, and upon the conditions hereinbefore provided, and doth further covenant not to interfere with the Said property otherwise than in conformity with the provisions of this Indenture."

June 16, 1849
State of Florida, Alachua County
From Alachua County Ancient Records
Deed Record A pages 145-147

Robert Stafford to William Crosby for $500: "Know all men by these Presents, That I Robert Stafford of Wayne County and State of Georgia hath this day bargained and sold for the consideration sum of five hundred dollars to me in hand paid by the said William Crosby a certain **Negro boy by the name of Davy,** to have and to hold the said Negro unto him the said William Crosby his heirs and assigns forever."

September 13, 1842
Columbia County, East Florida
From Alachua County Ancient Records
Bills of Sale A page 010

Jesse Standley Last Will and Testament: "Know all men by these presents that I Jesse Standley of the Territory of Fla and County of Alachua, for the affection and good Will which I bear towards my Children, Eliza Harvil Mariah Floyd, Sebron J. Standley, William S. Standley, and Thomas C. Standley of the same place; I do voluntarily and of my own free Will and accord after my death and the death of my wife Dicey Standley do give to said Children the following property naimly

To my daughter Eliza Harvil I give **my Negro woman Martha and her children Frances and Richard and her increase and my negro, Millissa and negro boy Primas.**

To my daughter Mariah Floyd I give **my Negro womin Hannah and her increase, and negro girl Lucy and Jane.**

After my death, I give all of my children an equal share of my stock catel except the Two Year old Steers and afterwards, I give to my wife Dicy and the benefit of her family, said cattle to be divided as follows,

My sons Sebron, William, and Thomas will first take out ten Cows and calves and the number of increase that I have already given to my daughters Eliza and Mariah so as to make an equal division between all my children herein mentioned.

All the money I have in hand and all the debts due me, either by note, Books of accrued or otherwise, I give to my wife Dicy for the benefit of raising William and Thomas, to have and to hold said property herein mentioned unto the said Eliza Harvil and her children, Mariah Floyd and her children, Sebron J. Standley William S. Standley and Thomas C. Standley their heirs and assigns for there own proper use and benefit, and to no other person whatever."

September 4, 1844
East Florida, Alachua County
From Alachua County Ancient Records
Will Book A pages 008-011

James D. Starke to his father Thomas Starke Sr. as collateral for $6,800 in loans: "Know all men by these presents that I James D. Starke of Fairfield District in the State aforesaid in consideration of one dollar to me paid by my father Thomas Starke Sr. of the District of Kershaw and State aforesaid and for divers other good causes and considerations me thereunto moving have granted bargained sold and delivered and by these presents do grant, bargain sell and deliver unto the said Thomas Starke Sr. the following negro Slaves namely, **Andy about forty years old, Charlotte about forty two years old, Unity about Eighteen years old, Tillman about sixteen years old, Cynthia about twelve years old, Cato about seven years old, Andy about five years old, Levingston about three years old, Mary about twenty five years old, Henry about six years old, Lucy about four years old, Mose about two years old,**

Edwin about thirty two years old, Martha about twenty three years old, Scinda about four years old, Jim about two years old, Edward about twenty six years old, Reuben about twenty two years old, Nance about Sixty years old, Nance about fifty five years old and Stephen about Sixty years old Also a mare called Lucy Abbot and her Monarch colt, a Stallion called Rowton and a mare called Margaret and five other head of horses and three mules, also three bedsteads and the bed mattrasses and bed clothes. To have and to hold the aforesaid negro Slaves **and their issue and increase** together with all and singular the other property to the said Thomas Starke Sr. his Executors, Administrators and assigns forever, In Trust nevertheless for the uses and Purposes hereinafter specified, that is to say From the next yearly profits and income of labors of said slaves, horses and mules to pay and refund to the said James D. Starke the amount of two notes of which said James D. Starke is maker and N.A. Peay John Harrison Senr and John W. Starke are endorsers both payable to Robinsons and Caldwell, one for the sum of three thousand six hundred dollars (or about that sum, as nearly as now remembered) made payable on the first day in the year Eighteen Hundred and forty seven, the other for the sum of Three thousand two hundred dollars (or about that Sum as nearly remembered made payable on this first day of January in the year eighteen hundred and forty eight. And for the purpose of carrying into effect the uses and purposes of this deed the said Thomas Starke is authorized and empowered to give the custody management and control of the labors of said slaves horses and mules and the use of the other property above specified to my friend and brother in law Madison S. Perry now of Fairfield District in the State aforesaid as Agent on the premises and after the amount of the aforesaid two notes shall have been paid or refunded to the said James D. Starke then in Trust to hold said negro slaves and their issue and increase together with the said horses, mules and other property for the use benefit & behoof of such person or persons and upon such other and further Trusts and Limitations and for such uses and purposes as the said Madison S. Perry shall at any time hereafter by any instrument in writing required by himself or by his last will and testament appoint and designate. And until the said Madison S.

Perry Shall make such appointment, in Trust to permit the said Madison S. Perry to hold said negro slaves and their issue and increase together with said horses mules and other Property for the uses benefits and support of himself and family and in case the said Madison S. Perry shall fail to make any such appointment or designation as above authorized during his life either by will or other wise then in Trust immediately after the death of the said Madison S. Perry to divide said negro slaves and their increase together with all and singular the other property above specified between Martha Perry wife of the said Madison S. Perry in case she shall survive him and the child or Children of the said Madison S. Perry share and share alike and in case the said Martha Perry shall not survive the said Madison S. Perry then the whole of said property to be divided among the children of the said Madison S. Perry share and share alike if more than one and of but one then the whole to the delivered to that one in case however of the death of a child having issue living, Such issue is to represent the parent and take the share which the parent would have been entitled to if living."

December 22, 1846, and in the seventy first year of the Independence of the United States of America
The State of South Carolina
From Alachua County Ancient Records
Bills of Sale A pages 002-004

John S. Taylor to Loyal Scranton and William Olmstead of Savannah as collateral for an $800 loan: "This Indenture made the Twenty Second day of January One thousand eight hundred and forty one Between John S. Taylor of Newnansville of the one part and Loyal Scranton and William Olmstead of Savannah of the second part Witnesseth that the said party of the first part for and in consideration of the sum of Eight hundred Dollars lawful money of the United States of America to him duly paid hath bargained, Sold, assigned transferred & set over and by these presents Doth grant bargain Sell Assign transfer & set over unto the Said parties of the second part **One likely Negro Slave man named Ben of light complexion aged about Twenty years old** purchased by said John S. Taylor of Spencer Price of Alachua County Florida said Negro Slave now in my possession Together with all the Rights title and interest of the said party of the first part of in and to the same Provided always nevertheless that if the said John S. Taylor shall well and truly pay the said Loyal Scranton & William Olmstead the just and full sum of Eight hundred Dollars lawful money as aforesaid on or before the first day of March next According to a certain Bond or Obligation bearing even date herewith then this Obligation or Conveyance shall be null and void"

January 22, 1841
From Alachua County Ancient Records
Deed Book B page 372

Lite Townsend to daughter Mary Kendrick: "Know all men by these presents that I Lite Townsend of the County of Alachua and State of Florida for and in consideration of the natural love and affection which I bear unto my daughter Mary Kendrick and for her better prefferment in marriage and the increase of her Portion and also in consideration of the sum of one Dollar to me in hand paid by my said daughter Mary Kendrick at and before the sealing and delivery hereof the receipt whereof I do hereby acknowledge have given granted bargained and Sold and by these Presents do grant bargain and Sell unto my said daughter Mary Kendrick the following named negroes to wit; **One Negro Man by the name of Dennis of Yellow complexion age about twenty eight years and also one negro woman by the name of Eliza and her two children by the name of Nelson &**

Sarah and also One negro woman by the name of Sela and her Child Frank and also one negro woman by the name of Libby. To have and to hold all and singular the above named Negroes hereby giving and granting unto my daughter Mary Kendrick and the lawful heirs of her body, her Executors and Administrators for ever as her and their own lawful property"

January 4, 1847
From Alachua County Ancient Records
Deed Record A page 029

Light Townsend to daughter Margaret Crichton: "Know all men by these present that I Light Townsend of Alachua County Florida, for and in consideration of the natural love and effection which I have with my Daughter Margaret Crichton wife of John P. Crichton of said County have given and delivered and by these presents do give and deliver unto the said Margaret Crichton the following Slaves to wit; **Kate a woman age about 22 years and her child Richard age about 2 years, also a Negro girl named Diana age about 12 years, and also a Negro man named John age about 20 years, together with all the future issue and increase of said Slaves,** to have and to hold the said Slaves with their future issue and increase unto the Sole and Seperate use of the Said Margaret Crichton free from the control interferance disposal or debts of the said John P. Crichton her husband for and during the time of the natural life of her the Said Margaret Crichton, and at her death I do hereby give the remainder in said Slaves and their future issue and increase and the same Shall go to the child or Children of the said Margaret Crichton living at the time of her death, to be divided equally among Said Children, if there be more than one Child Share And Share alike to have and to hold said interest in remainder unto the Said Child or Children, and unto his or

175

their Executor or Executors, administrator or administrators, assign or assigns forever "

August 16, 1848
From Alachua County Ancient Records
Deed Record A pages 072-073

Light Townsend to daughter Elizabeth Brown: "Know all men by these presents that I Light Townsend of Alachua County Florida for and in Consideration of the natural love and affections which I have unto my daughter Elizabeth Brown wife of William T. Brown of Benton County Florida, have given and delivered, and by these presents do give and deliver unto the said Elizabeth Brown the following Slaves to wit; **Charlotte a negro woman about 28 years, and her children George a Boy age about 14 years Sam a Boy age about 12 years, Eliza a girl age about 10 years, Dick a Boy age about 8 years, Rose a girl age about 3 years, and also one age and name not known. Together with all the future issue and increase of Said Slaves**, to have and to hold the Said Slaves with their future issue and increase unto the Sole and Separate use of Said Elizabeth Brown, free from the Control, interference disposal or debts of the said William T. Brown her husband for and during the term of the natural life of her the said Elizabeth Brown, and at her death I do hereby give the remainder in said Slaves and their future issue and increase and the same Shall of to the Child or children of the Said Elizabeth Brown living at the time of her death to be divided equally among Said Children, if there be more than one child Share and Share alike, to have and to hold the Said interest in remainder unto Said Child or Children, and with his her or their Executor or Executors, administrator or administrators assign or assigns, for ever"

August 16, 1848
From Alachua County Ancient Records
Deed Record A page 078

Light Townsend to daughter Sarah Ann Ellis: "Know all men by these presents that I Light Townsend of Alachua County Florida for and in consideration of the natural love and affections which I have unto my Daughter Sarah Ann Ellis, wife of Thomas C. Ellis, of Said County have given and delivered and by these presents do give and deliver unto the said Sarah Ann Ellis, the following Slaves to wit; **Ann a woman age about twenty five years, and Child Albert age about two years also Eliza a negro woman and her children, Jane age about two years, and Mary age about one year, together with all the future issue and increase of said Slaves** To have and to hold said Slaves with their future issue and increase unto the Sole and Separate use of her the Said Sarah Ann Ellis free from the control interference disposal or debts of the said Thomas C. Ellis her husband for and during the term of the natural life of her the Said Sarah Ann Ellis, and at her death I do hereby give the remainder in Said Slaves, and their future issue and increase and the Same Shall go to the child or Children of the said Sarah Ann Ellis living at the time of her death, to be divided equally among Said Children if there be more than one Child, Share and Share alike, to have and to hold Said interest in remainder unto the said Child or Children and unto his her or their Executor or Executors, administrator or administrators, assign or assigns forever."

August 16, 1848
From Alachua County Ancient Records
Deed Record A page 079

Light Townsend to son William Townsend: "Know all men by these presents that I Light Townsend of the County of Alachua in Said State, for and in consideration of the natural love and Effection which I have and do bear for my Son William Townsend of the County of Columbia, aforesaid in Said State and for the love and Effection which I have for the lawful heirs of his body, and for and in consideration of the sum of one dollar to me in hand paid at and before the Sealing and delivery of these presents, the receipts whereof is hereby acknowledged, hath granted, bargained and by these presents do freely give, grant and convey unto him my Said Son William Townsend and the lawful heirs of his body, the following described property To wit; **One certain Negro man Slave named Michael about thirty five years of age, also one certain Negro woman Slave named Mary about thirty years of age**, Which said Negro Slaves as aforesaid I do hereby warrant and forever defend against myself, my heirs Executors, administrators and assigns. To have and to hold the above named Negro Slaves as aforesaid, and I the Said Light Townsend for myself my heirs Executors, administrators and assigns, Shall and will warrant and forever defend the Said given and granted Negro Slaves as aforesaid, against all and every other person or persons whomsoever unto him my Said William Townsend and the lawful heirs of his body and to their heirs and assigns forever in fee simple."

October 31, 1848
State of Florida, Columbia County
From Alachua County Ancient Records
Deed Record A page 092

Inventory of the property of Margery Ann Tucker: "Inventory of the property of Margery Ann Tucker wife of Elijah Tucker of Alachua County Florida, which She holds in her own right Seperate from her said husband independent of and beyond his control and free from his debts viz; **A negro woman Slave named Lucy aged about 40 years**, a Stock of Cattle 30 head more or less marked Strait

Split and uper cut in one ear, and Strait Split in the other, branded T and figure 9 also a mare and colt"

December 13, 1848
From Alachua County Ancient Records
Deed Record A pages 097-098

Moses Turner and Margaret Turner to George L. Brown as collateral for a $230.10 loan: "Know all men by these presents that we Moses Turner and Margaret Turner wife of said Moses Turner of Alachua County Florida in Consideration of the sum Two Hundred and Thirty Dollars and 10 cents ($230.10) to us in hand paid by George L. Brown of said County the receipt whereof is hereby acknowledged have granted bargained and sold and by these presents do grant bargain and sell unto the said George L. Brown the following named negro slaves to wit **Crusoe & Sopha & Maria & Elisa with all their future increase** To have and to hold said negro slaves unto the said George L. Brown his Executors Administrators and assigns to his and their only proper use and behoof for ever. Provided always and these presents are upon this condition that if the said Moses and Margaret Turner or either of them their or either of their Executors Administrators or assigns do well and truly pay or cause to be paid the full sum of Two hundred and Thirty Dollars and ten cents $230.10) with legal interest thereon from the date hereof on or before the first day of January next according to the true meaning and intent of a certain promisory note signed by said Mose and Margaret Turner for the said amount of money bearing even date herewith and payable on or before the first day of January next the payment of which note these presents are intended to secure then and in such case these presents and every thing herein contained shall cease determine and be void other wise to remain in full force and effect."

March 9, 1847
Alachua County, State of Florida
From Alachua County Ancient Records
Mortgage Record A pages 001-002

John G. Tyner to Archibald H. Cole as collateral for an $800 loan: "This Indenture made and entered into this Twenty first day of December in the year of our Lord One thousand eight hundred and forty two, Between John G. Tyner of Alachua County in the Territory of Florida of the first part and Archibald H. Cole of St. Johns County in said Territory of the second part Whereas the said party of the first part is justly indebted to the said party of the second part, in the sum of eight hundred Dollars lawful money Conditioned for the payment of four hundred Dollars with interest thereon at the rate of eight per Cent per annum, on or before the first day of May in the year of our Lord One thousand eight hundred & forty three as appears by his certain bond or written Obligatory bearing even date with these presents, Now this Indenture Witnesseth that for the better securing to the said party of the Second part the payment of the said Bond or Written Obligatory According to the true intent and meaning thereof, as also in consideration of the sum of ten Dollars by the said party of the second part in hand paid at & before the ensealing and delivery of these presents, the receipt whereof is hereby Acknowledged, The said party of the first part, hath bargained, Sold and delivered and by these presents doth bargain, Sell and deliver unto the said party of the second part, the following personal property of him the said party of the first part viz **One Negroe Man Slave (black) named Renta aged about forty five to fifty years**, the same formerly belonging to Henry Lindsey and now in the hands of Thomas Colding Administrator of the estate of said Lindsey deceased, Also One large four wheel Waggon, Also One mule of a brown Colour aged Seven years or thereabouts Also one black mule aged Ten years or thereabouts Also One Sorrel mare with a white face aged nine years or thereabouts together with a Colt the foal of said mare, nearly one year old, To have and to hold the said Negro Slave, four wheeled Waggon, Brown and Black Mules, Mare and Colt and every of them unto the said party o the second part his executors, Administrators & Assigns to the only proper use benefit and behoof of the said party of the second part his executors, Administrators and Assigns forever Provided Always Nevertheless, and these presents are upon the express Condition, that if the said party of the first part his Executors or Administrators, shall well & truly pay or cause to be paid unto the said party of the second part, his certain Attorney, executors, Administrators or Assigns, the said sum of money mentioned in the condition of the said bond or Written Obligatory, with the interest thereon at the time therein mentioned and according to the true intent & Meaning of the said Bond and the Condition thereof, then as well this present Indenture as the Estate herein Conveyed shall cease determine and be null & void, Else to be and remain in full force and Virtue"

December 21, 1842
From Alachua County Ancient Records
Deed Book B pages 433-434

Solomon Warren to Simeon Dell for $1,100: "Know all men by these presents that I Solomon Warren of the County of Alachua and State of Florida For and in consideration of the Sum of Eleven Hundred Dollars to me in hand paid by Simeon Dell of the Said County and State at or before the Sealing & Delivery of these presents the receipt Whereof I do hereby acknowledge have granted bargained and Sold and by these presents do grant bargain and Sell Unto the Said

Simeon Dell his Executors administrators and assigns the following described property to Wit **One Negro Woman Slave dark complection named Charlotte aged about Thirty-years And one Negro Boy (Slave) named Shepperd aged about 17 years** To have and to hold the Said Negro Slaves as above named to the said Simeon Dell his Executors administrators and assigns forever"

October 2, 1849
State of Florida, County of Alachua
From Alachua County Ancient Records
Deed Record A pages 168-169

Lucy B. Williams, spinster is marrying Samuel R. W. Furman. John T. Rowland and James O. Scriven are trustees over what she is bringing into the marriage until she marries Samuel R. W. Furman: "This Indenture made the first day of March in the year of our Lord, one thousand eight hundred and forty one, between Lucy B. Williams of the City of Savannah in the County and State aforesaid Spinster of the first; Samuel R.W. Furman of the State of South Carolina of the Second part, and John T. Rowland of the City of Savannah aforesaid, and James O. Screven of the County of Bryan in the State of Georgia aforesaid of the third part,

Whereas a Marriage is intended to be had and Solemnised, between the Said Lucy B. Williams, and the Said Samuel R. W. Furman, and whereas the Said Lucy B. Williams the party of the first part, is now possessed of, and entitled to an undivided half of the following Negro Slaves, to wit: **Will, Patience, Jacob, Mary, Lyndy, Sarah, Alexander, Daphney, Bason, Hannah, Peter, George, January, Sophy, Anica, Grace, Phillis, Aleck, Bacus, Tom, Aleck, Tom, Henry, Laidy, Warsaw, Nina, Stephen, Joly, Patience, Sophia, Abram, Billy, Bason, Paris, Sampson, Phillis, Dye, Siah, Reuben, and**

Ellen, forty in all, and also and undivided half in lot Number (17) Seventeen, Washington Ward, in the City of Savannah aforesaid, also other real and personal estate which cannot now be enumerated, designated, And whereas the Said Lucy B. is desirous of Selling, and diposing of all her property, real or personal, upon certain uses and trusts hereinafter mentioned and expressed; Now this Indenture Witnesseth, that the Said Lucy B. Williams by and with the consent of her Said intended Husband Signified by his becoming a party to and Signing and Sealing this Indenture, and for and in consideration of the Said intended marriage, and also the Sum of five dollars to her in hand well and truly paid by the Said parties of the third part, the receipt whereof, She doth hereby acknowledge, hath granted, bargained, Sold, aliened, remised, released, confirmed, and delivered, and by these presents doth hereby grant, bargain, Sell, alien, remise, release, and confirm & deliver, unto the John T. Rowland and James O. Screven, and to the Survivor of them, and to the Executors and Administrators of Such Survivor, all the right, title, interest, claim and demand, whatsoever of the Lucy B. of in and to the aforesaid Negro Slaves, and the aforesaid lot number (17) Seventeen, Washington Ward in the City of Savannah aforesaid to have and to hold the same, together with Such other estate Real and personal, to which Said Lucy B. may now in any manner be entitled to, or possessed of with the future issue and increase of the female Slaves, and all the improvements, buildings, hereditaments, and appurtenances, to the real estate belonging, or in any wise appertaining, and the rents, issues and profits thereof, unto the Said John T. Rowland and James P. Screven, and to the Survivor of them, and to the Executors and Administrators of Such Survivor, In trust nevertheless, that they the Said parties of the third part, will hold the Same to and for the Sole and Separate use, benefit, and behoof of the Said Lucy B. and her heirs and assigns until the Solemnization of the Said intended Marriage, and from and after the Solemnization thereof; to and for the joint use, benefit, and behoof of the Said Lucy B. and Samuel R.W. Furman and the Survivor of them, not Subject to the Separate debts, contracts, or engagements of the Said Samuel R.W. and from and after the death of the Survivor of the Said Lucy B. and Samuel R.W. then to Such child or children of the Said Lucy B. as may be living at the time of her death Share and Share alike, if more than one, to their heirs, Executors, Administrators, and assigns for ever, and if the Said Lucy B. Should die in the life time of the Said Samuel R.W. without leaving children living at the time of her death, then in trust for Such person or persons, and, in Such manner as She the Said Lucy B. may direct by instrument, in the nature of last Will and Testament Signed in the presence of three or more witnesses,

And if the Said Lucy B. Should die in the lifetime of the Said Samuel R.W. without leaving children living at the time of her death, and without making any disposition of her property by an executed as aforesaid, then in trust to hold the same after the death of the Said Samuel R.W. to the Sole and Separate use and behoof of Henrietta Mary Williams, the Sister of the Said Lucy B. her heirs, Executors, Administrators and assigns for ever, but if the Said Lucy B. Should Survive the Said Samuel, and there Should be no children issue of Said Marriage living at the death of the Said Samuel, or born within the legal time afterward, then in trust that they the Said parties of the third part, will reserving the Said property real and personal with all increase and addition that may hereafter take place, to the Said Lucy B. her heirs, Executors, Administrators and assigns, free from any trust, and is eventually covenanted and agreed by and between the parties to these presents, that it Shall and may be lawful for the third parties of the third part, and the Survivor of them, upon the written request of the Said Lucy B. Signed before Witnesses, to grant bargain and Sell, mortgage, or other wise dispose of any or all of the aforesaid property, reinvesting, and preserving the proceeds hereunto except So much as may be necessary to pay off any debts or liabilities now existing against the Said Lucy B. or of the estate from whence She derives the Same, which requests may be made out of the proceeds of Such Sale subject to the Same uses and trusts and for the Same purposes, as and hereinbefore expressed, and power is hereby given by the Said John T. Rowland to the Said James O. Screven and by the Said James O. Screven to the Said John T. Rowland if either of them Should be absent when any conveyance is necessary to be made, to convey any part of the property as aforesaid, to Sign the name of the trustee so absent, as aforesaid, So as fully to convey the legal estate therein, the Said absent Trustee whose name is thus Signed however not to be liable to any of the Cestiuque for any act thus done, this provision being inserted in order that no dificently may occur in making such titles

March 1, 1841
State of Georgia, Chatham County
From Alachua County Ancient Records
Deed Record D pages 046-048

Henrietta M. Williams a spinster, to marry Samuel K. W. Furman: "This Indenture made this twenty fifth day of January in the year of our Lord one thousand eight hundred and forty nine, Between Henrietta M. Williams of the County and State aforesaid, Spinster of the first part, Samuel K.W. Furman of the County and State aforesaid, of the Second part, and George W. Hardee of the County and State aforesaid of the third part, whereas a Marriage is intended to be had and Solemnised between the said Henrietta M. Williams, and the Said Samuel K.W. Furman, and whereas the Said Henrietta M. Williams the party of the first part, is now possessed of and entitled to an undivided half of the following Negro Slaves, to wit: **Will, Mary, Linda, Tom, Phillis, Bason, Daphne, Bachus, Patience, Stephen, Mona, Dye, Ellen, Sophy, Ulah, Sam, Nina, Lindy, Peter, Tenah, Sarah, George, January, Will, and Grace (R5) and also possessed of and entitled to three Negro Slaves in addition, viz. Suckey, Emma, and Abey,** and also thirty five head Stock cattle, more or less, thirty head Sheep, more or less, one yoke of oxen, three horses, household furniture notes and mortgages, and whereas, the Said Henrietta M. is desirous of Settling and disposing of all her property real or personal; upon certain uses and trusts hereinafter and expressed, Now this Indenture, Witnesseth, that the Said Henrietta M. Williams, by and with the consent of her said intended

Husband, Signified by his becoming a party to, and Signing and Sealing this Indenture, and for and in consideration of the Said intended Marriage, and also of the Sum of five dollars, to her in hand well and truly paid to the Said party of the third part, the receipt whereof, She doth hereby acknowledge, hath granted, bargained, Sold, aliened, remised, released, confirmed, and delivered, and by these presents doth hereby grant, bargain, Sell, alien, remise, release and confirm, and deliver unto the Said George W. Hardee and to the Survivor of him, and, to the Executors, administrators of Such Survivor, all the right, title, interest, claim and demand whatsoever of the Said Henrietta M. Williams of in, and to the aforesaid Negro Slaves, together with the Stock, household furniture, notes and mortgages aforesaid, To have and to hold the Same, together any other real and personal estate to which the said Henrietta M. Williams may now, or at any future time be possessed of, or in any manner entitled to, with the future issue and increase of the female Slaves, Stock &c unto the said George W. Hardee and to the Survivor of him, and to the executors and Administrators of Such Survivor, In trust nevertheless, that he the Said party of the third part, will hold the same to, and for the Sole and Separate use, benefit and behoof of the said Henrietta M. and her heirs and assigns, until the Solemnization of the said intended Marriage, and from and after the Solemnization thereof to and for the Joint use, benefit and behoof of the Said Henrietta M. and Samuel R. W. Furman, and the Survivor of them, not Subject however to the Separate debts, contracts or engagements or the Said Samuel K.W. Furman and from and after the death of the survivor of the said Henrietta M. and Samuel R.W. then to such child or children of the said Henrietta M. as may be living at the time of her death, share and share alike if more than one, to them their heirs, Executors, administrators and assigns for ever, and if the said Henrietta M. Should die in the life time of the said Samuel K.W. without leaving children living at the time of her death, then in trust for such person or persons and in such manner as she the said Henrietta W. may direct by instrument, in the nature of a last will and Testament, signed in the presence of three or more witnesses and if the said Henrietta M. Should die in the lifetime of the said Samuel K.W. without leaving children living at the time of her death, and without making disposition of her property by an instrument executed as aforesaid, then to have to hold the trust the same after the death of the said Samuel K.W. to the sole and separate use and behoof of Lucy Elizabeth, Samuel M. William B, and James S. Furman, their heirs, Executors, administrators and assigns for ever, but should the said Henrietta M. Survive the said Samuel K.W. and there should be no children issue of such marriage being at the time of the death of the death of the said Samuel, or born within the legal time afterward, then in trust that he the said party of the third, will reconvey the said property real and personal, with all increase and addition that may hereafter take place, to the said Henrietta M. her heirs, Executors Administrators and assigns, free from any trust; and it is mutually covenanted and agreed by and between the parties of these presents, that it shall and may be lawful for the said party of the third part, and the survivor of them, upon the written request of the said Henrietta M. signed before one witness to grant, bargain, and sell, mortgage, or otherwise dispose of any or all of the aforesaid property, reinvesting and preserving the proceeds however except so much as may be necessary to pay of any debts or liabilities now existing against the said Henrietta M. Williams which payments may be made out of the proceeds of such sale, subject to the same uses and trusts and for the same purposes as are hereinafter expressed

January 25, 1849
State of Georgia, Camden County
From Alachua County Ancient Records
Deed Record D pages 049-051

Henry C. Wilson & Lemuel Wilson to Bennett M. Dell as collateral for a $2,400 loan: "Know men these presents that Henry C. Wilson and Lemuel Wilson are held and firmly bound unto Bennett M. Dell, his Executor administrators and assigns in the sum of twenty

four hundred dollars, for the payment of which well and truly to be made, we bind ourselves our Executors and administrators and every of them jointly and severally by these presents sealed with our seals, signed and dated this 16th day of February AD 1848. The condition of the above obligation is such that if said Henry C. and Lemuel Wilson, or either of them, do pay or cause to be paid or made good unto the said Bennett M. Dell, his Executors administrators or assigns, any and every damages which may result to the said Bennett M. Dell his Executors administrators and assigns by or on account of said Bennett M. Dell's having this day signed with the said Henry C. and Lemuel Wilson a certain promissory note whereby he and the said Henry C. and Lemuel Wilson jointly and severally promise twelve months after the date thereof to pay to William Bailey or bearer the sum of Twelve hundred dollars ($1200) with interest from date said note having been made and signed for the purpose and with a view of enabling the said Henry C. and Lemuel Wilson by the transfer of the same to raise or obtain the loan of the said sum of twelve hundred dollars, then the above obligation and every clause article and thing therein contained to be void else to remain in full force and virtue.

Know all men by these presents that we Henry C. Wilson and Lemuel Wilson hereby bargain sell and deliver unto Bennett M. Dell of Alachua County Florida **two negro men slaves named George and Latimore the former aged about nineteen years, and the latter about twenty five years,** to have and to hold said negro slaves unto the said Bennett M. Dell his Executor administrators & assigns forever. Provided nevertheless that if the said Henry C. and Lemuel Wilson or either of them do well and truly perform or cause to be performed the conditions of the foregoing bond or obligation according to the true intent and meaning of the same then this deed or instrument of writing which is intended as a mortgage & also the said bond shall both be void, otherwise to remain in full force. And we the said Henry C. & Lemuel Wilson and each of us do covenant and agree for ourselves, Executors and administrators and each of them with the said Bennett M. Dell his Executors administrators or assigns that said negroes are free from encumbrances, that we have good right to sell them and that we will and our Executors and administrators shall warrant and defend the same unto the said Bennett M. Dell his Executors administrators and assigns forever."

February 16, 1848
From Alachua County Ancient Records
Mortgage Record A pages 008-009

Lemuel Wilson to Henry C. Wilson as collateral for a $536.55 loan: "To all whom these presents shall come. Know ye that I Lemuel Wilson of the State and County aforesaid, party of the first part, for securing the payment of the money mentioned and described in the promissory note hereinafter set forth and mentioned, and in consideration of the sum of one dollar to me duly paid by Henry C. Wilson of the County of Columbia in the said State, of the Second part, at and before the sealing and delivery hereof, the receipt whereof is hereby acknowledged, have bargained and sold and by these presents do bargain and sell unto the party of the second part, a certain **Negro man Slave named George, aged about (38) thirty eight years**, now in the possession of the said party of the second part. To have and to hold the above bargained and sold Negro, or intended to be bargained or sold, unto the said party of the second part his Executors administrators and assigns forever, and the said party of the first part, for myself my heirs Executors & administrators and assigns, against me the said party of the first part, and against all and every person or persons whomsoever, shall and will warrant and forever defend. Upon condition that I the said party of the first part, shall and do well and truly pay unto the said party of the second part, his executors administrators or assigns the full sum of five hundred and thirty six and fifty five hundredths Dollars ($536.55) according the terms and effect of a certain promissory note bearing date Newnansville July14th 1848, made by me the said party of the first part, to the said party of the second part, and which is in the words and figures following, to wit: Newnansville July 14th 1848 $536.55

One day after date I promise to pay to H.C. Wilson or bearer five hundred and thirty six dollars and fifty five cents, for and on account of goods received from him while merchandising in the year 1841, 1842 & 1843. Then these presents shall be void otherwise to remain in full force and virtue."

October 14, 1848
State of Florida, Alachua County
From Alachua County Ancient Records
Mortgage Record A pages 021-022

A prisoner named Windsor, an enslaved man indicted for consulting and advising an enslaved man Moses to murder, sentenced to fifty lashes: "Territory vs Windsor, a slave - Consulting & advising one Moses to Murder - Now on this day came Thos Douglass Esqr. who prosecutes the pleas of the Territory in this behalf, and Windsor, a slave, aforesaid who being arraigned Pleaded "Not Guilty" to the Indictment against him, & put himself on the country for trial; whereupon came a Jury … who were sworn well & truly to try & true deliverance make between the Territory of Florida & the prisoner at the bar, & a true verdict to give according to law & evidence.

Moses (a slave of James Dell) was sworn as a witness on the part of the prosecution, and H. C. Wilson & Charles L. Dell were sworn on behalf of the prisoner.

After hearing the proofs & allegations of the parties, the arguments of Counsel & the charge of the Court, the Jury retired accompanied by Ethelbert Hagan, an officer sworn for that purpose. After deliberating upon their verdict, the Jury returned into Court; they say they find the Prisoner "Guilty" and that he be punished with fifty lashes on his bare back.

December 23, 1843
From Alachua County Ancient Records
Superior Court Minutes 2, pages 325-326

Oliver D. Wood Guardian of his daughter Ellen H. Wood (Plaintiff) vs. Moses Curry (Defendant) - Foreclosure of $120 Mortgage: "It appearing to the satisfaction of the Court that the Plaintiff in this case did, on the 18th day of February A.D. 1843 file his petition for foreclosure, together with the mortgage; that due notice has been given to the Defendant of the institution of this suit, that no plea, answer, or demurrer, has been filed by said Defendant to the petition aforesaid, & it further appearing by the affidavit of Louis Aldrich of Counsel for the said Plaintiff, that there is due & owing on the note, to secure which the said mortgage was given, for principal & interest the sum of one hundred & twenty Dollars; Therefore it is considered by the Court that the said Plaintiff do recover against the said Defendant the said sum of One hundred & twenty Dollars, together with the further sum of the costs of said Plaintiff about this suit expended. And it is further considered & adjudged that the said Defendant & all persons claiming by or through him, be, and they hereby are foreclosed & forever barred of and from all right and equity of redemption in the **negro slave Eldridge** in the said mortgage mentioned.."

December 23, 1843
From Alachua County Ancient Records
Superior Court Minutes 2, pages 330-331

1850's

Washington Geiger appointed as trustee of William Adkins: "In the matter of the application of William Adkins to have Trustee appointed, In Circuit Court For Alachua County, December Term 1852 - The Petition of the said William Adkins, praying that Washington W. Gieger be appointed Trustee for certain purposes in said petition mentioned & set forth haveing been presented to the Court on this day, and the said Gieger haveing signified his willingness to accept said trust & filed his Bond as required by law, It is ordered adjudged and decreed by the Court that the said Washington W. Geiger be & he is hereby appointed Trustee for the said William Adkins and it is further ordered adjudged and decreed that he receive the said **Negro Girl Colen together with all issue and increase that she may have had since the Twenty fifth day of May in the year of our Lord one thousand eight hundred and forty six, and any issue or increase that the said Negro Girl Colen may hereafter have** and hold the same in Trust for the use and benefit of William Adkins according to the tenor and effect true intent and meaning of a certain Deed of trust made by one Sarah Adkins to one James L. Reed, bearing date the day and year last aforesaid and that the said Washington W. Geiger shall by good and sufficient title convey the said Negro Girl Colen and all of her said issue and increase to such child or Children of the said William Adkins lawfully begotten or may be liveing at the time of his death to them their heirs and assigns forever, according to the tenor and effect true intent and meaning of the said deeds, and that he report his actings and doings in regard to the said Negro Girl Colen and her said issue and increase annually to this Court at the December Term thereof"

December Term 1852
From Alachua County Ancient Records
Chancery Order Book A, page 071

George W. Aldrich indicted for selling liquor to enslaved people without a license: "State of Florida vs Geo W. Aldrich - Selling liquor to Slaves without license - Now on this day personally appeared in open Court George W. Aldrich Bennet M. Dell and Samuel Russell and acknowledged themselves to owe and stand indebted to the Governor of Florida, and his successors in office, that is to say George W. Aldrich in the sum of Five hundred Dollars, and Bennet M. Dell and Samuel Russell in the sum of Two hundred and fifty Dollars each, lawful money of the United States to be made and levied of their respective goods and chattels, lands, and tenements, if the said George W. Aldrich shall fail in performing the following condition, that is to say: that the said George W. Aldrich shall personally be and appear at the next Term of the Circuit Court to be held for the Counties of Alachua and Levy to answer to an indictment returned into said Court against him for selling liquor to a Slave without license, and not depart thence without leave of the Court, then this recognizance to be null and void, else to remain in full force and virtue."

December 10, 1850
From Alachua County Ancient Records
Judgment Record A page 027*

George W. Aldrich indicted for selling to an enslaved person without a license: "State of Florida vs George W. Aldrich - Indictment for selling to a Slave without license - On motion of the Solicitor a nolle prosequi is ordered to be entered in this case on condition that the defendant do pay all the costs of this prosecution"

May 5, 1851
From Alachua County Ancient Records
Judgment Record A page 041*

William Axer charged with malicious killing and wounding stock - enslaved people used as a part of collateral to ensure he showed up for Court: "State of Florida vs William Axer - Malicious wounding & killing stock - Continued to the next term of the Court and the defendant recognized in the sum of five hundred dollars for his appearance at the next term of the Court two hundred & fifty dollars for the principle and one hundred & twenty five for each Security William Axer, Daniel C. Hart Joseph Mickle appeared in open Court and acknowledged themselves to stand indebted to the State of Florida in the sum of five hundred dollars that is to say William Axer in the sum of two hundred & fifty dollars Daniel C. Hart in the sum of One hundred & twenty five dollars & Joseph Mickle in the sum of One hundred & twenty five dollars to be levied of their respective goods & Chattels, Slaves lands & tenements if default be made in the following Condition that is to say of the said William Axer Shall be and appear at the next term of this Court to answer to an indictment for malicious Killing & wounding Stock and Shall not thence depart the Court without lien thereof then this obligation to be null and void otherwise to remain in full force and virtue"

May 13, 1858
From Alachua County Ancient Records
Judgment Record B page 052

Barney Barfield indicted for larceny. Enslaved people were used as part of collateral to ensure he showed up for Court: "State of Florida vs Barney Barfield - Larceny - Continued to the next term of the Court and the defendant recognized in the sum of five hundred dollars for his appearance at the next term of the Court two hundred & fifty dollars for the principal and one hundred & twenty five for each Security

Barney Barfield, Hardy Stuckey, & Daniel S. Stuckey appeared in open Court and acknowledged themselves to stand indebted to the State of Florida in the sum of five hundred dollars, that is to say Barney Barfield in the sum of two hundred & fifty dollars Hardy Stuckey in the sum of One hundred & twenty five dollars & Daniel S. Stuckey I the sum of One hundred & twenty five dollars to be levied of their respective goods & Chattels lands & Slaves & tenements if default be made in the following Condition that is to say if the said Barney Barfield Shall be and appear at the next term of this Court to answer to an indictment for Larceny and Shall not thence depart the Court without lien thereof then this obligation to be null and void otherwise to remain in full force and virtue"

May 13, 1858
From Alachua County Ancient Records
Judgment Record B page 053

Andrew Bates to Joshua N. G. McNalb as trustee for Andrew's wife Sarah Bates: "This indenture made the twenty fifth day of October in the year one Thousand Eight hundred and fifty three Between Andrew Bates in the County of Alachua and State of

Florida of the first part and Joshua N.G. McNalb of the same place
of the second part whereas the said Andrew Bates is desirous to
make provisions for his wife Sarah Bates against future continen-
gences and for her maintenance and support and whereas the said
Andrew Bates is desirous that his said wife should enjoy the proceeds rents issues and income of her whole estate hereinafter more
particular described during the term of her natural life free from
the control liabilities or interference of any husband that she now
has or may hereafter have Now therefore this indenture Witnesseth
that the said Andrew Bates in consideration of the premises and the
sum of one dollars lawfull money of the United States to him in
hand paid by the said Joshua N.G. McNalb of the second part the
receipt whereof is hereby acknowledged hath bargained sold aliened
remised released conveyed and confirmed and by these presents
doth bargain sell alien remise release convey and confirm unto the
said Joshua N.G. McNalb of the second part the following property
to wit **One Negro woman named Caty aged twenty one or two
and two children named Margret and Lula** [1/4 quarter section
of land lying on the south side of little Orange lake Bounded on
the North by James F. Secrest and others West by Henry Sweeny
on the south by Jacob Thomas and others on the east by Daniel
one horse cart three (3) head of horses one grey mare and a black
mare and Colt Twenty three head of cattle twenty five head of hogs
together with all and singular the tenements heredetements and
appurtenances thereunto belonging or in any wise appertianing and
reversions and reversions remainders and remainders rents, issues
and proffets thereof, and also all the estate right title interest property possessions claim and demand whatsoever as well at law as in
equity of the said Andrew Bates of the first part of in or to the
above described property and every part and parcel thereof with the
appurtenances To have and to hold all and singular the above mentioned and described property together with the apurtenances unto
the said Joshua N.G. McNalb his successors assigns in trust however
to the said Joshua N.G. McNalb of the second part to keep and to
hold for the use benefit and behoof of the said Sarah his wife with
all the rents issues and profits thereof during the term of her natural

life and then the said deed of trust to cease and Determine and the estate above described shall belong in fee simple to the heirs of said Andrew Bates"

October 25, 1853
From Alachua County Ancient Records
Deed Record B page 240

Joseph G. Bell and Elizabeth Bell his wife to William Dell as collateral for a $950 loan: "This indenture made Sixth (6th) day of December in the Year of Our Lord One thousand Eight hundred and fifty One between Joseph G. Bell of Alachua County State of Florida And Elizabeth Bell his wife of the first part, and William Dell of Said County and State of the Second part Witnesseth, that the Said parties of the first part for and in Consideration of the premises herein after recited, have granted, bargained, aliened released, Conveyed and Confirmed, and by these presents do grant bargain, Sell, Alien, release, convey and confirm unto the Said party of the Second part and to his assigns forever, all that certain lot of land belonging to us by virtue of my wife Elizabeth as her Dower in the Estate of James L. Townsend and Known as the Townsend Plantation, Situated about four miles from Newnansville in Said County and State, also **a negro man named Thom, and a Negro woman named Phebe** of Said Estate, Sixty head of Stock Cattle more or less, three head of Horses, One hundred and fifty Bushels of Corn, fifteen hundred pounds of Fodder, Thirty Six head of Stock Hogs more or less one Bark Mill worth fifty Dollars One Buggy Wagon worth fifty Dollars, together with all the hereditaments and appurtenances thereunto belonging, or in any wise appertaining, and the reversion & reversions, remainder and remainders, rents, issues, and profits thereof, and also all the Estate, right, title, interest, dower, possession claim and demand whatsoever of the Said parties of the first part in and to the same, and every part therof with the appurtenances, to have and to hold the Said hereby granted premises with the appurtenances unto the Said party of the Second part, his heirs and assigns, and to his and their only proper use benefit and behoof forever, provided always, and these presents are upon this express Condition that if the said Joseph G. Bell and Elizabeth Bell his wife Shall well and truly pay to the Said William Dell a certain promissory note bearing even date executed by the Said Joseph G. Bell and Elizabeth Bell his wife and payable to the Said William Dell or bearer for the Sum of Nine Hundred and fifty Dollars, together with the interest thereon according to the tenor and effect of Said note then this Conveyance and the Estate hereby created Shall be null & void and of no effect, otherwise to remain in full force and effect"

December 6, 1851
State of Florida, Alachua County
From Alachua County Ancient Records
Deed Record A pages 424-426

Jesse Talbot Bernard & his wife Mary E. Bernard to Thomas A. Bradford Jr. and William H. Bradford and Samuel M. Wilson as collateral for a $3,000 loan: "This Indenture made and entered into this fifth day of February one thousand eight hundred and fifty three by Jesse Talbot Bernard, Mary E., his wife of the County of Alachua State of Florida of the first part, Thomas A. Bradford Jr and William H. Bradford of the said County and State of the second part and Samuel M. Wilson of the town of Portsmouth and State of Virginia of the third part; Witnesseth that whereas the said Jesse T. Bernard is justly indebted unto the said Samuel M. Wilson in the sum of three thousand dollars as will appear by his note under seal with Thos A. Bradford and John Talbot as Securities bearing date the 30th day of September 1852, with interest from date thereof payable on or before the first day of May 1853 the faithful payment of which sum of money he the said Jesse T. Bernard is desirous to secure to the said Samuel M. Wilson. Now therefore this indenture further witnesseth that the said Jesse T. Bernard and Mary E. his wife, as well for and in consideration of the promises, as well as for the sum of five dollars to them in hand paid by the said Thomas A. Bradford Jr and William H. Bradford the receipt whereof is hereby acknowledged they the said Jesse T. Bernard and Mary E. his wife have and by these presents do grant bargin sell and deliver unto the said Thomas A. Bradford and William Bradford their heirs and assigns all that tract of land situated one mile and a half from the Town of Newnansville, County of Alachua and State of Florida and designated by the United States Surveys as the South East Quarter of Section one, and the South East qr. of the North west of Sec one and the North half of Lot No. three (3) of Sec one and the North East quarter of Section Twelve in Township Eight South of Range Eighteen East, containing three hundred and sixteen 72/100 acres as per return made by U.S. Surveys to the Land Office at Newnansville Fla, being the land purchased with by Jesse T. Bernard of Arthur Floyd with a portion with a portion obtained by Bernard from other sources. Also the following negro slaves to wit, man **Sampson about 26 years of age, man Charles about 26 years of age and woman Tenes about 22 years old**, to have and to hold the above described land and premises and all and singular the appurtenances thereto belonging or in any wise appertaining together with the aforesaid slaves **and any future increase of the said woman slave** unto them the said Thomas A. Bradford and William H. Bradford their heirs and assigns upon trust nevertheless that the said Jesse T. Bernard shall be permitted quietly to occupy said land and enjoy the labor of said slaves until such time as the said Samuel M. Wilson or his heirs and assigns shall demand the Sum of money aforesaid, or any portion thereof remaining due and unpaid, and if said default is made in the payment of the same it shall and may be lawful for the said Thomas A. Bradford Jr and William H. Bradford or either of them, on being thereto required by the said Samuel M. Wilson his heirs or assigns to proceed to advertise the said land and negroes for four weeks at the door of the court House in the said County of Alachua and sell the lands or so much as may be required to raise the sum Remaining due to said Samuel M. Wilson his heirs or assigns the sale to be one third each and the balance three and six months, the property being held as security for the purchase, and out of the proceeds of such sale satisfy all charges and expenses attending the execution of this trust then pay if sufficient whatever may be due on the debt aforesaid, and render the balance if any to the said Jesse T. Bernard his heirs or assigns, the said Thomas A. Bradford Jr. and William H. Bradford so acting executing to the purchaser or purchasers of said land and negroes a conveyance or conveyances for the same when fully paid for. The said Jesse T. Bernard and Mary E. his wife, for themselves and their heirs the said land and negroes to the said Thomas A. Bradford Jr. and William H. Bradford and their assigns for the purposes of this Indenture will warrant free from the claim of these the said Jesse T. Bernard and Mary E. his wife and their heirs and against the lawful claim and demand of all persons whomsoever provided that in full payment of the said sum of money to the said Samuel M. Wilson his heirs or assigns with all the interest that may have accrued thereon, this Indenture shall cease and determine and be of no further force or effect"

February 5, 1853
From Alachua County Ancient Records
Deed Record B pages 108-109

J. T. Bernard to W. H. G. Sanders for $3,000: "Know all men by these presents, that I J. T. Bernard of the County and State above mentioned, have for the sum of three thousand dollars to me in hand paid by W. H. G. Sanders of the same place, at and before the sealing and delivery of these presents, the receipt whereof is hereby acknowledged, bargained, sold, and delivered, and by these presents do bargain Sell, and deliver, unto the said W. H. G. Sanders **three grown Negroes, and one child viz; Sampson a Mulatto man aged about 27 years of age, Charles aged about 26 years of age, Tenah aged about 28 years of age, and her Child aged about ten months named Georgianna**, to have and to hold the said Negroes unto the said W. H. G. Sanders, his Executors, administrators, and assigns, to his and their proper use and benefit forever, and I J. T. Bernard do further more warrant the said Negroes to be sound in mind, and I the Said J. T. Bernard, my heirs, Executors and Administrators, the said bargained premises unto the said W. H. G. Sanders, his Executors, Administrators, and assigns, to his and their own proper use and benefit forever"

March 28, 1854
Alachua County, State of Florida
From Alachua County Ancient Records
Deed Record B pages 377-378

Jesse T. Bernard to Charles L. Wilson as collateral for a $200 loan: "This Indenture made the Seventh day of May, in the year of our Lord one thousand eight hundred and fifty four, Between Jesse T. Bernard of the first part, and Charles L. Wilson of the Second part, both of the State and County aforesaid, Witnesseth, that the Said party of the first part, in consideration of the Sum of two hundred dollars ($200) lawful money of the United States, to him in hand paid, the receipt whereof, is hereby acknowledged, has granted, bargained, conveyed, and confirmed, and by these presents doth grant, bargain, convey and confirm, the following Negro Slaves to wit; **Negro boy Jim aged five years, and Negro boy Sam aged three years**, to have and to hold the above granted and described Negroes, unto the said party of the second part, his heirs and assigns, provided always, and these presents are upon this condition, that if the said party of the first part, Shall well and truly pay his certain promissory note bearing date the fourth day of May A.D. 1854, given to the said party of the second part, for the sum of two hundred dollars lawful money as aforesaid, according to the tenor of said notes then these presents shall become void."

May 7, 1854
State of Florida, County of Alachua
From Alachua County Ancient Records
Deed Record B page 382

Amy Blake to daughter Rachel W. Colson: "Know all men by these presents that I Amy Blake of the State and County aforesaid being of Sound disposing mind, having determined to divide my property amoung the heirs of my body, Doth in account of the kind reguard and affection which I have and do bear towards my Daughter Rachel W. Colson, Consort of Paul B. Colson, give and bequeath and by these presents do give and bequeath unto the Said Rachel W. Colson four Negroes (viz) **a man named Sam, aged about twenty Eight years of Age** (reserving use of Said Negro for myself during my natural life) and **Pleasant a woman aged about Twenty four Year, Patsey a girl about four Years of age & Sharlotte a girl about two years of age**, to have and to hold Said property for her the said Rachel W. Colson's own use and benefit, during her natural life, and in no wise subject to the debts of her husband Paul B. Colson and when the Said Rachel is no more an inhabitant of Earth, when She Shall Cease to live, and be no more amoung the living of the land, **the within named property with all of its increase** shall belong to the children of the Said Rachel W. Colson, by her first husband John D. Strobhar, names of children Laura L. Boston Consort of Geo W. Boston, Henry J. Strobhar Noble A. Strobhar and Should Either of the here last named Children die leaving no increase, The Surviving one or ones to have Said named property with its increase."

January 16, 1851
State of Georgia, Effingham County
From Alachua County Ancient Records
Deed Record A page 472

Laura L. Boston to Noble A. Strobhar for $500: "Know all men by these presents that I Laura L. Boston of the State and County above written have for and in consideration of the sum of Five hundred dollars to me in hand paid by Noble A. Strobhar of the Same place Granted bargained sould released, conveyed and confirmed, and by these presents, doth grant, bargain, sell, release, convey and confirm unto Noble A. Strobhar all of my right title and interest in **a Negro woman named Pleasant aged about twenty five years, and her three children, Patsy about seven years, Charlotte about four years, and Peter about 4 months old**. Said property deeded by my grandmother Ann Blake to my mother R.W. Colson during her natural life, and afterwards to be equally divided Between my Brothers N. A. Strobhar H. J. Strobhar and myself. To have and to Hold. Said property, to him N.A. Strobhar, his heirs Executors, Administrators assigns and I the said Laura L. Boston, shall and will forever warrant and defend same to the said N.A. Strobhar his heirs and assigns."

May 12, 1853
State of Florida, Alachua County
From Alachua County Ancient Records
Bills of Sale A page 035

Samuel Boykin to Narcissa Boykin Executrix of Last Will and Testament of Samuel Boykin Senior as collateral for a $4,000 loan: "Know all men by these presents that I Samuel Boykin of the County of Alachua, State of Florida, for and in consideration of the Sum of five dollars to me in hand paid, at and before the Sealing and delivery of these presents, the receipt whereof is hereby acknowledged, as well as for the better Securing the payment of a certain promissory note which the Said Samuel Boykin hath this day made and delivered to Narcissa Boykin Executrix of the last Will and Testament of Samuel Boykin Senior Deceased, of the County of Muscogee State of Georgia, Said note bearing even date with these presents, due one day after date, whereby the Said Samuel Boykin promises to pay to the Said Narcissa Boykin Executrix as aforesaid or order, the Sum of four thousand dollars for value received, have bargained and Sold, and do hereby bargain and Sell unto the Said Narcissa Boykin, Executrix as aforesaid, the following Negro Slaves, to wit: **Cuff a Negro man about 32 years old, Henny a woman about 30 years old, and her male Child, an infant, Ransom a boy about 17 years of age, Richard a boy about 12 years old, Morton a boy about 10 years of age, Ann a girl about 6 years old, Jim a boy about 3 years old, Clara a woman about 63 years old, Margaret about 24 years old, and her infant child, Dell a girl about 7 years old, Antoinetta a woman about 20 years of age, and her male child, George a boy about 16 years of age, Jenny a woman about 41 years old, Hampton a boy about 18 years old, Arabella a girl about 15 years old, Aranetta a girl about 7 years old, Paralee a woman about 22 years old, Isaac a boy about 18 years old,** To have and to hold, the Said bargained property to her the Said Narcissa Boykin, Executrix as aforesaid, her heirs, Executors and Administrators forever, And I the Said Samuel Boykin for my self, my heirs, Executors and administrators, the Said bargained property, unto the Said Narcissa Executrix as aforesaid, her heirs and assigns, against me, my heirs, Executors and administrators, and against all and every other person or persons whatsoever, Shall and will warrant, and defend by these presents, Provided nevertheless, that if the said Samuel Boykin Senior his heirs and assigns Shall, and do well & truly pay or cause to be paid to Said Narcissa Boykin,

Executrix as aforesaid, her heirs and assigns, the Said Sum of Money in Said promissory note Specified with lawful interest thereon, according to the tenor and effect thereof, then & from thenceforth, as well the mortgage or the right to the property hereby conveyed, as the Said promissory note, Shall cease, determine & be void to all intents and purposes."

April 4, 1855
State of Georgia, Muscogee County
From Alachua County Ancient Records
Deed Record D pages 104-105

Oliff Bradshaw to Lewis G. Pyles as trustee for Oliff Bradshaw's wife Quintine Bradshaw: "This Indenture, made the tenth day of February in the year Eighteen hundred & fifty Eight, between Oliff Bradshaw of the County of Alachua and State of Florida of the first part, and Lewis G. Pyles of the same County & State of the second part Witnesseth, Whereas the said Oliff Bradshaw is desirous to make provision for his wife Quintine Bradshaw against future contingencies and for her maintainance and support and whereas the said Ollif Bradshaw is desirous that his said wife should enjoy the proceeds hires issues and in come of the property hereinafter more particularly described during the term of her natural life free from the control liabilities of any future husband in the event of the death of the said Oliff Bradshaw and his said wife marrying again Now therefore this Indenture Witnesseth, that the said Oliff Bradshaw in Consideration of the premises and of the sum of One dollar lawfull money of the United States, to him in hand paid by the said party of the second part, the receipt whereof is hereby acknowledged, hath bargained, Sold, aliened remised, released, and conveyed, and by these presents doth bargain, sell, alien, remise, release, and convey unto the said party of the Second part, the following described property, to wit, **a negro**

man, named Edmund aged about Thirty five years old, negro girl Lucy, aged about Twenty years and an infant about eighteen months old the Child of said negro girl Lucy, together with all the future increase of said negro girl, also one open buggy now used by the party of the first part, two Horses, only one oxen, forty five head of hogs and their future increase one wagon, and one horse cart all of which property to wit one buggy, horses, oxen, wagon, and cart, are now in the possession of the said party of the first part, and all the estate, right, interest, title, claim, and demand whatever - as well at law as in Equity of the said party of the first part of in or to the above described, and alluded to property, To have and to hold all and singular the above mentioned described property together with all that is attended to and not particularly described unto the said Lewis G. Piles, his successors and assigns

In trust to and for the several uses intents and purpose hereinafter mentioned namely First In trust to take collect and receive the issues income and profits of the above described and alluded to property, and out of the same to pay all taxes, assessments and Charges that may be imposed thereon, together with all necessary expenses

Second, In trust to pay the residue of such issues, and income to my wife Quintine Bradshaw upon her sole and separate receipt, to the intent and purposes that she may enjoy possess and have the same free from the control liabilities or interference of any future husband she might have

Third, In trust, to hold the above mentioned described and alluded to property during the of the natural life of my wife Quintine, and for the her children after her death,

And upon the further trust, that if anytime it Should become necessary to dispose of any of the above described and alluded to property then the party of the second part shall have power to sell and convey the same, (the party of the first part consenting thereto) and the proceeds of said Sale, shall be subject to the same uses and trusts as any of the above described and alluded to property. And the said Olliff Bradshaw hereby declares that upon the decree of his said wife and the heirs of her Children, the said trust shall cease and determine and property herein described and alluded to, and the increase shall revert to him and his heirs to his and their sole use, benefit and behoof forever [...]"

February 10, 1858
From Alachua County Ancient Records
Deed Record C pages 158-159

George Branning to William M. Ledwith for $550 in trust for George Branning's niece Amanda M. Coker: "Know all men by these presents, that I George Branning, for and in consideration of the natural love and affection which I have to my niece Amanda M. Coker, wife of J. B. Coker of Newnansville in the County of Alachua and State of Florida, and also for and in consideration of the Sum of five hundred and fifty dollars, lawful money to me in hand paid by William M. Ledwith, at and before the ensealing and delivery of these presents, the receipt whereof I do hereby acknowledge, have bargained and Sold, and by these presents do bargain, Sell and deliver to the Said William M. Ledwith, and to his Executors Administrators and assigns, A certain **Negro Slave named Catharine with her future issue and increase**. To have and to hold the Said Slave with her future increase, unto the Said William M. Ledwith, his Executors administrators and assigns, to his and their own proper use, benefit and behoof forever. In trust nevertheless, to and for the use of the Said Amanda M. Coker wife of the Said J.B. Coker, for and during the term of her natural life, and after her death, in trust for Such child or children of the Said Amanda M. as may be living at her death, and the heirs of the Said child or children, And in case no child or children of the Said Amanda M. Shall Survive her, then the Said Slave and her increase to vest in the Said William M. Ledwith, and to be, and become his absolute property both in law and Equity."

July 21, 1855
From Alachua County Ancient Records
Deed Record D page 174
Also see Alachua County Ancient Records
Bills of Sale A page 025

J. A. Breedon Last will and testament: "This is the last Will and testament of Me J. A. Breeden of the district and state aforesaid, Whereas, I have lately intermarried with Martha Vasty O'Cain whose property consists of a **negro woman named Henny** and three notes of hand, amounting in all to five hundred dollars; to wit; one given by Henry Snelland and his two sons, one by Stephen Buzzard and the three by William Wanamaker Now in case I should die leaving my said wife surviving me, that She may not be deprived of What property came by her, I do hereby will and bequeath to my said wife Margaret Vasty Breedon, in case she survives me as aforesaid for her life time, and afterward to her child or children Should She have any, and Should She die without leaving any children alive or grand child or grand children then to any child or children I may have alive at my death the said negro female slave Henny, **and her issue**, and the said sum of five hundred dollars due on the said three notes of hand"

March 11, 1853
South Carolina, Orangeburg District
From Alachua County Ancient Records
Will Book B page 048A

Calvin Bryant to D. &. A. Wesson, Merchants, as collateral for a $364.72 loan: "Know all men by these presents that I Calvin Bryant, of the County and State aforesaid, for securing the payment of the money hereinafter mentioned, and in consideration of the sum of One Dollar to me in hand paid by D. & A. Wesson, Merchants and copartners doing business in the City of New York, at and before the sealing and delivery of these presents (the receipt whereof is hereby acknowledged) have bargained sold, aliened confirmed and delivered unto the said D. & A. Wesson a certain **negro man slave called John, aged about thirty years** To have and to hold the said negro man Slave unto them, their survivor or survivors, executors, administrators or assigns for ever. And I the said Calvin Bryant for myself my heirs, executors, administrators and assigns, the said negro man slave above sold and conveyed unto the said D. & A. Wesson their survivor or survivors, heirs, executors, administrators or assigns, against me and against all and every person or persons whomsoever, shall and will warrant and forever defend

Upon Condition that if I the said Calvin Bryan shall and do well and truly pay or cause or procure to be paid unto the said D. & A. Wesson their survivor or survivors, heirs, executors, administrators or assigns, the full sun of three hundred and sixty four Dollars and Seventy two cents with interest thereupon on the seventh day of December in the year of our Lord One thousand eight hundred and fifty one according to the tenor and effect of a certain promissory note bearing even date herewith made and signed by me in favor of the said D. & A. Wesson, then these presents shall be void [...] in case default shall be made in the payment of the said sum of money above mentioned, then it shall and may be lawful for the said D. & A. Wesson, their survivor or survivors, heirs, executors, administrators or assigns to proceed to sell said negro man slave according to the Statute in such case made and provided, and out of the money arising therefrom to retain and pay the said sum above mentioned and all charges touching the same rendering the overplus, if any to me or to my heirs executors, administrators or assigns"

December 7, 1850
State of Florida, Alachua County
From Alachua County Ancient Records
Mortgage Record A page 051

John Bryant to his wife Myrum Bryant and his 2 children: "Know all Men by these presents that I John Bryant of the County & State aforesaid for and in Consideration of the Natural love & affection Which I have & do bear for my wife & two Children, to wit, Myrum Bryant and my two Children to wit Risanvastine Bryant and John Westley Bryant all the foregoing described personall property, to wit. I give and grant unto my Said wife Myram Bryant the following described property to wit, **One Negro Man named Bob about Thirty two years of age, and One Negro girl named Lizy about Thirteen years of age**, also one Black mare and one Bay mare,

And I hereby give, grant bargain & Sell unto my said Son Risanvastine Bryant the following described property to wit one mare & Colt, twenty head of Stock Cattle marked Crop & two Splits in one ear & pale handle in the other Branded with a diamond, also twenty head of Stock Hogs in the same mark

And I hereby give, grant, bargain & Sell unto my said Son John Westley Bryant the following described property to wit One dark Bay filly & one Sorrel Horse also Twenty head of Stock Cattle marked with a Smooth Crop in one ear & a Crop & half Crop in the other and branded the Same as above also twenty head of Stock Hogs marked with Crop & two Splits in one ear & pale handle in the other, To Have & to hold the above & foregoing property unto them my said wife &

Children, together **with the future increase of the Stock of Cattle Hogs & Negro girl**, also the future increase of the horse hereby Conveyed And I the Said John Bryant for myself my heirs &c will warrant & forever defend the above described, given granted bargained & Sold property against myself my heirs Executors administrators & assigns, & against all & every other person or persons, whomsoever unto them my Said wife and two Children their heirs & assigns forever in fee Simple"

February 14, 1855
State of Florida, Alachua County
From Alachua County Ancient Records
Deed Record E page 184

Ozias Buddington (Plaintiff) vs Calvin Bryant (Defendant) - Petition for foreclosure to recover 2 enslaved people and debt of $855.30: "And now on this day came the Said plaintiff by his attorney and presents to the Court his petition together with the original mortgage of Said Negro Slaves and as being made to appear to the Court, that the Said petition & mortgage hath been filed in this Court more than two months before the present Term of this Court to wit On the 4th day of March 1850, and that notice of the intention of Said plaintiff to institute the Said Suit hath been Served upon the Said defendant at least two months before the present Term of this Court to Wit On the fourth day March One Thousand Eight hundred and fifty and the Said plaintiff haveing Exhibited to this Court the evidence of debt to recover which the Mortgage whereof foreclosed is Sought in this case was executed which it appears to the Court was here given by the Said defendant above named as Mortgagor and an affidavit being also made by the Said plaintiff by his attorney aforesaid Whereby it appears that there is now due and owing to Said plaintiff the Sum of Eight hundred and fifty five Dollars & Thirty cents for principal &

Interest of which Seven hundred Eighty Dollars & fifty two cents is principal and Seventy four Dollars & seventy Eight cents is Interest

And no objection haveing been Shown or filed by way of plea or answer to Said petition of foreclosure of the said plaintiff and the said defendant hereupon on motion of the Said plaintiffs attorney it is considered that the Said plaintiff do recover of the Said defendant the Sum of Eight Hundred & fifty five Dollars & thirty Cents so claimed to be due for principal and interest upon Said Mortgage with Interest thereon at the rate of *** per cent from the date hereof untill paid and also the further Sum   Dollars   Cents for his Costs and charges in this behalf Sustained

And it is further ordered and considered that the Said defendant and all persons claiming or to Claim by through or under ***** Shall be for ever foreclosed and debarred of all rights and equity of redemption of or in the Mortgage property Set forth and described in the Said petition and the Said Mortgage thereto attached to wit, **Moses aged about forty years and Scipio aged about thirty five years**, and that the plaintiff have execution of this Cause above rendered"

May 7, 1850
From Alachua County Ancient Records
Judgment Record A* page 009

Edmund Cale to Joseph B. Coker in trust for Edmund Cale's wife Lydia Cale: "Know all men by these presents that for and in consideration of the natural love and affection which I Edmund Cale have for my wife Lydia as well for and in consideration of the sum of five dollars to me in hand paid by Joseph B. Coker at or before the ensealing and delivery hereof the receipt I do hereby acknowledge have given granted bargained and sold and by these presents do grant give bargain and sell unto the said Joseph Coker in trust for my said wife Lydia her heirs executors administrattors and assigns all the goods and chattels following To with **One Negro man named Washington**, three head of Horses one wagon one cart seventeen head of hogs marked Swallow fork and under bit in one ear and under bit in the other one buggy all my household and Kitchen furniture four head of cattle one note on Owen Revels two notes on E. J. Boyett & two on David Fryer. To have and to hold all and singular the premises hereby given and granted unto the said Joseph Coker in trust for my wife Lydia as aforesaid."

March 29, 1856
From Alachua County Ancient Records
Deed Record D pages 290-291

Blake Anderson Carter to James M. T. Carter in Trust for Margaret Regina Miller: "This Indenture made this the Sixth day of January in the Year of Our Lord Eighteen hundred and fifty two between Blake Anderson Carter of the County and State aforesaid of the One part and James M. T. Carter of the Same place of the other part, Witnesseth that for and in Consideration of the natural love and affection which he the Said Blake A. Carter has and bears towards his daughter Margaret Regina Miller of the County of Alachua and State, aforesaid, Wife of Richard W. Miller, and for and in consideration of the Sum of Four hundred dollars Cash in hand paid by the Said Richard W. Miller, and Five (5) dollars cash in hand paid by the Said James M. T. Carter at and before the Sealing and delivery of these presents, the receipt whereof is hereby acknowledged hath bargained Sold, granted and conveyed, and by these presents doth bargain, Sell, grant and Convey unto the Said James M.T. Carter for the use benefit and advantage in trust for the Said Margaret Regina Miller the children She now has and those She may hereafter have by her present or a future husband, free from the controll or disposition of her present of future husband, all and Singular the right title And interest of him the Said Blake A. Carter of in and to the following named and described Negro Slaves, to wit **Una, Aruzi and Martha Jane, Una a woman about twenty years of age and Aruzi a Boy three years and Martha Jane a Girl about four months of age children of Said Una together with all and Singular their increase and future issue,** Said Woman Una and her two children Aruzi and Martha Jane being (or to be Estimated to be worth Six hundred dollars over and above the four hundred paid at and before the Sealing and delivery of these presents. Providing however nevertheless that if the Said Margaret Regina Miller Should die and have no legal or natural heir of her body living at the time of her death then the aforementioned Negro Slaves, and the right and title of and to them to return and revert back to the aforesaid Blake Anderson Carter and to his heirs and assigns, as though this Indenture had never been given. Provided he pays back to the said Richard W. Miller or to his heirs administrators or assigns the aforementioned Sum of Four Hundred Dollars paid to him by the Said Richard W. Miller as aforesaid To have and to hold the afore described property unto him the Said James M. Carter in Trust for said Margaret Regina Miller wife of said Richard M. Miller and all her children as aforesaid forever in fee Simple free from the debts liabilities and contract of her present or a future husband, to their only benefit And behoof"

January 6, 1852
State of Florida, Marion County
From Alachua County Ancient Records
Deed Record A pages 445-446

Ransom Cason Senr. Last Will and Testament: "In the name God Amen I Ransom Cason Senr. of the County and State aforesaid being in good health and Sound disposing mind and memory calling to the frailty and uncertainty of human life and being desirous of Settling my worldly affairs and directing how the estate with which it pleased God to bless me Shall be disposed of after my decease and the death of my wife Phoebe and not untill then. While I have strength and capecity So to do, do make and publish this my last will and testament hereby revoking and making null and void all other last wills and testaments by me heretofore made.

And first I commend my immortal being to him who gave it and my body to the earth be buried with little expense or ostentation by my executor hereinafter named

And as to my worldly estate and the property real and personal of mine of which I Shall die Seized and possessed or to which I Shall be entitled at the time of my decease and the decease of my wife Pheobe as aforesaid I devise, bequeath and dispose thereof in the manner following to us

First, My will is that all my just debts and funeral charges Shall by my executor hereinafter named by paid out of my estate as Soon after my decease as Shall by them found convenient.

Second I give and bequeath to my beloved daughter Martha Hallbrook **Lot No. 1. of Negroes viz. Jane Woman and her three Children named as follows. Temper and Emaline and George** to be for her Sole use during her natural life and then to revert to her heirs and the death of the heirs of the Said Martha Hallbrook.

Third; I give and bequeath to my Son John Cason **Lot no. 6 of negroes, named as follows viz. Sampson, Catherine, Ned and Mary Jane** to have and to hold during his natural life and at his death to revert to his heirs.

Fourth, I give and bequeath to my daughter Pheobe Cason wife of John R. Cason **Lot no. 4. of negroes, named as follows viz.**

Berrian, Jacob, Condsey and Anna, to have and to hold to her Sole use and benefit during her natural life then to the heirs of her body.

Fifth, I give and bequeath to my son Moses Cason **Lot no 5. of negroes named as follows viz. Simon, Little Simon, Ester and little Dolly,** to have and to hold during his natural life then to revert to the heirs of Said Moses Cason at his death.

Sixth, I give and bequeath to my Son James Cason **Lot no. 2. of negroes named as follows viz. Hagun woman and her three Children viz. Civil Polly and Jim,** to have and to hold during his natural life then to revert to the heirs of the said James Cason at this death.

Seventh, I give and bequeath unto my Son William Cason **Lot no 3. of negroes named as follows viz. Margret a woman and her child Sharlotty and Archable and Queen** to have and to hold during the natural life of Said William Cason after his death to revert to his heirs.

Eighth, I give and bequeath unto my daughter Clementine Douglass **Lot no 7. of negroes named as follows, viz. Adam, Clarissa, Clementine and Randol** to have and to hold during her natural life then to revert to the heirs of her body at her death

Ninth, I give and bequeath unto my children as named above **the increase of the different Lot** to Martha Hallbrook **the increase of Said Lot distinguished by Lot 1.** then to John Cason **the increase of Lot designated by no 6.**

Fourth to Pheobe Cason wife of John R. Cason **the increase of lot of negroes designated as Lot. 4.**

Fifth **the increase of the negroes named in Lot No 5.** to Moses Cason, and **the increases of Lot no 2.** to the Said James Cason to William Cason **the increase of those give to him,** and to my daughter Clementine Douglass **the increase of those give to her.**

Lastly, I do nominate and appoint my Son James Cason to be the executor of this my last Will and testament.

A Copy of the different Lots named in the Will.

Lot no. 1 Jane and her then Children named as follows Temperance, Emaline and George.
Lot no 2. Hagan and her three children named Civil Polly and Jane.
Lot no 3. Margaret child Sharlotty, and negroes Archibald and Queen.
Lot no. 4. Berrian, Jacob Canasse and Anna
Lot no. 5. Simion Little Simon, Ester and little Dolly
Lot no 6. Sampson Catherin, Ned and Mary Jane.
Lot no 7. Adam, Clarissa, Clementine and Randol"

November 12, 1853
State of Florida, County of Alachua
From Alachua County Ancient Records
Will Book A pages 035-038

William Cason to Simeon Dell as collateral for a $500 loan: "Know all men by these presents that I William Cason of Columbia County for and in Consideration of the Sum of Four hundred dollars to me in hand paid by Simeon Dell of County of Alachua the receipt whereof is hereby acknowledged have and by these presents do grant bargain Sell assign and Set over unto the said Simeon Dell and his assigns forever the following personal property one **Negro girl Mary aged about Seventeen years** Whereas I have this day given my promisory note in writing for the Sum of Five hundred dollars dated of this date and due January the first A. D. Eighteen hundred & fifty nine bearing Eight per Cent interest and the Same to Simeon Dell and to be paid to the said Simeon Dell or his assigns. Now the Condition of the above Sale is such that if the said William Cason Shall well and truly pay to the said Simeon Dell or to his agent or attorney or assigns the amount of the said promisory note with Eight per Cent interest according to the Effect and tenor therof, then the above bill of Sale shall be void Otherwise on the neglect or the failure of the said William Cason to pay the said promisory note according to the Effect and tenor thereof then and in that Case the said Simeon Dell or his assigns are hereby authorized to Sell the said Negro girl Mary and retain from the proceeds of said Sale sufficient to pay the said promisory note with interest and all costs expenses charges &c that may be incurred in consequence of the failure of the said William Cason to pay said note rendering the overplus to the said William Cason or his assigns – the said William Cason hereby authorizes the said Simeon Dell to take the said negro into his possession at any time he may think propure"

June 18, 1858
From Alachua County Ancient Records
Mortgage Record A pages 142-143

William J. Caston indicted for assault with intent to kill; enslaved people used as part of collateral to ensure he showed up for Court: "State of Florida vs William J. Caston - Assault with Intent to Kill - Continued upon affidavit of Deft

Recognized in the sum of one thousand dollars, five hundred for principal, and five hundred dollars for the security I. J. Carter William J. Caston and I. J. Carter appeared in open Court and acknowledged themselves to owe and stand indebted to the State of Florida in the sum of one thousand dollars, that is to Say the said William J. Caston in the sum of five hundred dollars, and the said I. J. Carter in the sum of five hundred dollars, to be levied of their respective goods and chattels, Slaves lands and Tenements, If default be made in the following condition, that is to say, if the said William J. Caston shall be and appear at the next term of this Court, to answer an Indictment against him for an Assault with intent to kill, and Shall not thence depart from the Court without leave, then this obligation to be null and void, else to remain in full force and virtue"

December 15, 1853
From Alachua County Ancient Records
Judgment Record A* page 163

Last Will and Testament of Ellen Chesnut widow of the late John Chesnut: In the name of God Amen, I Ellen Chesnut widow of the late John Chesnut deceased, do make and ordain this to be my last will and testament. That is to Say.

1st The negroes which I received from the estate of my brother William Whitaker, with their present and future issue and increase, and also all the negroes which I brought into Coven-ture, together with their present and future issue and increase, to which under the Will and testament of my Said husband, I Shall again become entitled at the division of his estate I give and bequeath to my Six Children, to wit. Serena Haile the wife of Thomas E. Haile, Mary Whitaker Chesnut, Ellen Chesnut, Thos.W. Chesnut, James Chesnut, and John Chesnut, Equally to be divided among them Share and Share alike.

The Share hereby given to each of my daughters to be held by her to her own Seperate use and behoof, not Subject or liable to the debts or Contracts of her present or future husband, during the term of her natural life and from and immediately after her death to the heirs of her body, living at the time of her death, but if She Should die without leaving Such heirs living at the time of her death then to the issue of Such heirs, who may be then living, and in Case She Should without leaving any Such heirs or issue of Such heirs living at the time of her death, then to my other Children who may be then living, and the issue of Such as may be dead, the issue taking among them the Share their parents would have taken if alive.

The Share in the Clause of will bequeathed to each of my Sons is an absolute gift, Subject only to the following Condition that is to Say, that if either of My Sons Should die before arriving at the age of twenty one years, And leaving no issue living at the time of his death, then the Share hereby bequeathed to him Shall be divided equally among my other Children who may be then living, and the issue of such as may be dead. the issue taking among them the Share their parents would be entitled to if alive.

2d. I give And bequeath to My daughters Mary Whitaker Chesnut and Ellen Chesnut my carriages and Carriage horses to be held by them jointly, to them And their heirs forever.

3d. I give And bequeath to my niece Ellen Chesnut Reynolds daughter of Mary E. Reynolds, one hundred dollars, And direct My Executors hereinafter named within One year after my death, to invest the same in good bond or profitable Stock for her benefit. And to hold the Same in trust for her untill She Shall arrive at the age of eighteen or be married, to be then transferred to her absolutely.

4th. To My Niece Ellen Whitaker, I give and bequeath one hundred dollars, And direct My executors within one year after My death, to invest the Same in good bonds or profitable Stock, And to hold the Same in trust for her benefit or untill She Shall arrive at the age of eighteen years or be married, to be transferred to her absolutely the Niece Mentioned in this Clause is the daughter of my brother John Whitaker

5th. I hereby direct My Executors to purchase a gold watch for my Grand Son John Chesnut Haile; to be given to him when ever they think proper

221

6th The fourteen negroes which I received from the estate of my brother William Whitaker have been working in Common for Some years on the estate of My late husband and I am in consequence entitled to an accounting with the executors of the Said estate for the proceeds of their labor but in as much as accounts incurred by me for the building of the house which I now occupy at Cool Spring have been charged to the said estate I hereby authorize and direct my Executors to balance and extinguish the two Claims so Arising

7th I direct that my Executors Shall make distribution of the property bequeathed in the first Clause of this testament at the time and in the manner which in the last will and testament of my Said husband, and made for this distribution of his estate among his Children.

8th All the rest and residue of my estate and whatsoever consisting, and wheresoever being, I give, devise and bequeath to my Six Children, to be equally divided among them. To them and their heirs forever.

9th Lastly I nominate, Constitute and appoint my Father James Chesnut Senr. my brother Thomas Whitaker, my Sons, Thomas W. Chesnut and James Chesnut & my brother in Law James Chesnut Junr. Executors of this my last Will and testament.

In Witness Whereof I have hereunto Set my hand And Seal this fifteenth day of October in the year of our Lord one thousand eight hundred and fifty.

CODICIL
South Carolina

I Ellen Chesnut widow of John Chesnut, having on the 15th day of October A. D. 1850, made and executed my last will and testament which I do hereby confirm, do now make publish and declare this codicill to be my said will, having by an instrument in the hand writing of my Sister Sarah Chesnut, bearing the date the 22nd day of January

Annodomini 1851 Signed by me and attested by the witnesses of this codicil distributed certain household articles among my children I hereby declare it to be my intention and will that said Articles shall not be a part of my Estate in the hands of my Executors, but that the same, at my death, and not before, shall be taken possession by the persons specified in said Instrument, as therein provided, to each absolutely and without any of the usual forms of law, I direct that the said Articles shall not be included in any Schedule, inventory or appraisement of my estate, and I hereby release, acquit and discharge my Executors from any and all responsibility, in any way, and of any kind whatsoever, for or on account of said articles."

October 15, 1850 and February 12, 1851
State of South Carolina, Kershaw District
From Alachua County Ancient Records
Will Book A pages 039-044 and also
Deed Record B pages 350-352

James Chesnut and Thomas Whitaker, Executors of Last Will and Testament of John Chesnut (1839), To Mary Whitaker Haile: "Whereas James Chesnut and Thomas Whitaker by Testamentary appointment, and Qualification according to deceased, which bears date the 3rd day of May A. D. 1839, and whereas the said John Chesnut, in the fifth clause of the said last will and Testament, enjoins a certain duty, and thereby confers a power upon his said Executors in the following words, to wit; I direct that before my Daughters shall be put in possession of the property to which they shall become entitled under the provisions of this will, my Executrix, and Executors shall secure it to them, so that it shall not in any way be liable to the disposal, or for the debts of their Husbands, and if any of my Daughters shall die without issue, the property of the Daughter or Daughters so dying, to which She or they shall become entitled under this will, shall revert to my other children in equal proportions. And whereas the said Executors in the manner prescribed by the Testater, have proceeded to divide that portion of his personal Estate which is subject to division and are according the directions of the said last Will and Testament prepared to assign one of the Shares of the said Estate, so divided, for Mary Whitaker Haile Second Daughter of Testater, and now wife of Edward Haile of the District and State aforesaid. To the End Therefore, that the property, hereinafter specified, are comprised in the said Share, shall be secured to the said Mary Whitaker, before it goes into her possession, and that the provisions of the Will of the Testater in relation to the same may in all respects be fully carried into effect.

Know all men by these presents, that we James Chesnut and Thomas Whitaker, Executors as aforesaid of the said last Will and testament, pursuing the directions of our Testator, and by virtue of power and authority in us vested by the said Will and Testament, in consideration of ten dollars to us in hand paid, at and before the ensealing and delivery of these presents L. L. Whitaker of the District and State aforesaid, and also in consideration of premises, have bargained, sold, and delivered, and by these presents do bargain, Sell, and deliver unto the said L. L. Whitaker the following named Slaves, to wit: **Lewis, Easter, Mose, Hetty, Tom, Dolly, Grace, Fanny, Janeth, Relicas, Sally, Rose, Lawson, Lavila, Patsy, Mose, Henry, Patsy, Sarah, Lucy, Phillis, Columbus, Jerry, Isaac, Claricy, Cresy, Aaron, Emiline, Amy, Jinny, Willis, Epsy**, also ten shares of the capital Stock of the Bank of Camden South Carolina, To have and to hold the said Slaves **with the future issue and increase of them**, and the said Shares of the said Bank, to the said L. Whitaker, in the Special Trust and Confidence, nevertheless, that he the said L. Whitaker, will permit the said Slaves with their increase to go into the possession of the said Mary Whitaker Haile, so that she may enjoy the possession, use and profits of them and not in any way to be liable to the disposal or for the debts of her present or any future Husband and in trust that he will hold the said Shares of the said Bank for the benefit of the said Mary Whitaker Haile, and pay to her without any further accountability on his part, the profits and dividends arising from the same as often as they may be declared, and in further trust and confidence that he the said L. L. Whitaker in case the said Mary Whitaker Haile shall die without issue, will hold the said Slaves with future issue and increase of them, and also the said Shares of the Capital Stock of the Bank of Camden South Carolina, to be transferred to such person or persons as may be entitled thereto under the said last Will and testament of John Chesnut deceased or to such person as may be legally entitled…

We Edward Haile, and Mary W. Haile his wife, do hereby acknowledge that we have received the Slaves mentioned in this deed, and hold these subject to the conditions & provisions of said Deed …"

February 9, 1852
State of South Carolina, Kershaw District
From Alachua County Ancient Records
Deed Record B pages 345-346

James Chesnut and Thomas Whitaker, Executors of Last Will and Testament of John Chesnut (1839), To Esther Serena Haile: "Whereas James Chesnut and Thomas Whitaker, by Testamentary Appointment, and Qualifications according to law, became executors of the last will and Testament of John Chesnut, Deceased, which bears date of 3rd day of May A. D. 1839, and whereas the said John Chesnut, in the fifth clause of the said last Will and Testament, enjoins a certain duty, and thereby confers a power upon his said Executors, in the following words, to wit, I direct before my Daughters Shall be put in possession of the property to which they shall become entitled under the provisions of this will, my Executrix and Executors Shall secure it to them, so that it shall not in ay way be liable to disposal for the debts of their Husbands, and if any of my Daughters Shall die without Issue, the property of the Daughter or Daughters so dying, to which she or they shall become entitled under this will shall revert to my other children, in equal proportions. And Whereas the said executors in the manner prescribed by the Testator, have proceeded to divide that portion of his personal Estate which is Subject to division, and are according to the directions of the said last Will and testament, prepared the assigns of one of the Shares of the said Estate so divided for Esther Serena Haile, Eldest Daughter of Testator, and now wife of Thomas E. Haile of the District and State aforesaid. To the End therefore, that the property hereinafter Specified and comprised in the said Share, Shall be secured to the said Esther Serena, before it goes into her possession, and that the provisions of the will of the testator in relation to the same may in all respects be fully carried into effect. Know all men by these presents, that we, James Chesnut, and Thomas Whitaker, executors as aforesaid of the said last Will and Testament pursuing the directions of our Testator, and by virtue of power and authority in us vested by the said Will and Testament, in consideration of ten dollars to us in hand paid, at and before the ensealing and delivery of these presents, by L. L. Whitaker of the District and State afore said, and also in consideration of the premises, have bargained, Sold, and delivered and by these presents, do bargain, Sell and deliver unto the said L. L. Whitaker, the following named Slaves to wit: **Edmund, July, Leaty, Elsey, March, Phillis, Mary, Martha, Margaret, Patey, Nelson, Jack, Hannah, Beu, Mary Johnson, Billy, Nancy, William, Louisa, Jesse, Anthony, Richard, Aleck, Malinda, John, Sam, Lucy, Robert, Elizabeth, Margaret, Hampton, Washington, Hannah & Joe**, also the Shares of the Capital Stock of the Bank of Camden South Carolina, four Shares of the South Carolina Rail Road Company, and South Western Road Bank Company, and five Shares of the Capital Stock of the Camden Bridge Company, and one fourth of a Share of the last mentioned Stock, To Have and to hold the said Slaves **with future issue and increase of them**, and the said Shares of the said Bank, and Rail Road and Bank, and Bridge Company, to the said L. L. Whitaker in the special trust and confidence, nevertheless, that he the said L. L. Whitaker will permit the said Slaves with their increase to go into the possession of the said Esther Serena Haile, so that she may enjoy the possession, use, and profits of them, and not in any way to be liable to the disposal or for the debts of her present or any future Husband, and in trust that he will hold the said Shares of Stock of the said Bank, of the said Rail Road and Bank, and of the Said Bridge Company, for the benefit of the said Esther Serena Haile, and pay to her without any further accountability on his part the dividend and profits arising from the same as after as they may be declared, and in the further trust and confidence that he, the said L. L. Whitaker in case the said Esther Serena Haile shall die without Issue will hold the said Slaves with the future issue and increase of them, and also the said Shares of the capital Stock of the Bank of Camden South Carolina, of the South Carolina Rail Road Company, and South Western Rail Road Bank, and of the Camden Bridge Company, to be transferred to such person or persons as may be entitled thereto under the said last will and Testament of John Chesnut deceased or to such person or persons as may be legally entitled....

We Thomas E. Haile and Esther Serena Haile, his wife, do hereby acknowledge that we have received the Slaves mentioned within and hold them subject to the provisions & conditions of the within Deed..."

February 9, 1852
State of South Carolina, Kershaw District
From Alachua County Ancient Records
Deed Record B pages 348-349

Last Will and Testament of James Child: "Last Will & Testament of James Child made & published at Micanopy Alachua County State of Florida this twenty fourth (24) day of June one thousand Eight hundred and fifty

Item I give to my deceased sisters two children my nephew Rufus T.I. Humphreys & my niece Margaret Jane Humphreys all contingents interests I have or may have in or to the life estate of my mother in & to the estate of my Deceased father Alexander Child the same to be held by their natural Guardian as trustee until their majority

Item I give to my beloved sister Emma C. Child **my negro Boy Washington & my negro Girl Sally together with their future increase** the same to be held in trust by my Brother Robert A. Child & by him protected for the benefit & use of my sister as long as she may remain unmarried upon her marriage (if ever) the property to go into her possession but the trust hereby created to remain firm & unbroken forever

Item I give to my Beloved Brother Robert A. Child **my negro man Gardner** without trust reserve or limitation.

Item It is my decision that out of the remaining property of which I may die seised or possessed all my Just debts be paid by my Executor hereafter to be named & the Balance of said property to be Equally divided Between my beloved Brother Robert A. Child & Emma C. Child that moity to my sister Emma C. Child in trust as in a foregoing Item Expressed

Item I hereby appoint my Brother Robert A. Child as Executor to this my last Will & Testament & having full confidence in his integrity as such Executor I hereby direct that he shall be required to give no Security"

June 24, 1850
From Alachua County Ancient Records
Will Book A pages 033-034

Asa Clark to wife Jane Ann Clark: "Know all men by these presents that I Asa Clark of said State and County for and consideration of natural love affection which I have and bear to my wife Jane Ann Clark by the same place and for and in consideration of the sum of five dollars cash in hand paid by the said Jane Ann Clark the receipt whereof is hereby acknowledged, do by these presents give and grand unto my said wife Jane Ann Clark a certain **negro man by the name of Lias forty years of age of yellow complexion and one by the name of Sarah forty years of age of yellow complexion and one by the name of Ester 11 years of age of yellow complexion and one by the name of Victoria 8 years of age of yellow complexion and one by the name of Carditimes six years of age of yellow complexion, and one by the name of Nat four years of age yellow complexion, and one by the name of Bob two years of age of yellow complexion and one by the name of Satriah a babe of yellow complexion and one negro man by the name of Sam dark complexion twenty two years of age** and my plantation of One Hundred and twenty acres of land and one house worth one hundred dollars and one buggy worth seventy five dollars and all of my household and kitchen furniture and fifty head of cattle to have and to hold the said negros, House, buggy, cattle, and land and house hould and kitchen furniture for her my wife Jane Ann Clark and the heirs of her body to her the said Jane Ann Clark her heirs and assigns forever"

April 26, 1850
State of Florida, Alachua County
From Alachua County Ancient Records
Deed Record A pages 253-254

Asa Clark to wife Jane Ann Clark and her heirs and assigns:
"This indenture made this twenty third day of December in the year
of our Lord one thousand Eight hundred and fifty one between Asa
Clark of the State and County aforesaid of the one part and Jane Ann
Clark, wife of the Said Asa Clark, of the other part, Witnesseth: That
the Said Asa Clark, as well for and in Consideration of the Natural
Love and affection which he the Said Asa Clark, hath and beareth unto
the Said Jane Ann Clark, as also for the better maintenance Support,
and livelyhood of her the Said Jane Ann Clark hath given, granted,
aliened, enfeoffed and confirmed And by these presents doth give,
grant, alien, enfeoff, and confirm, unto the Said Jane Ann Clark, her
heirs and assigns all that messuage or tract of Land Situated in the
County of Alachua and State aforesaid, Containing One Hundred and
twenty Acres more or less and known as Clarks Plantation near Coutre
Pond Situated about 12 miles from the Town of Newnansville in an
Easterly direction, Together with all and Singular the Hereditaments
and Appurtenances thereunto belonging, or in any wise appertaining;
and the reversion and reversions, remainder and remainders rents,
issues, and profits thereof, and all the Estate, right, title, interest property, claim, and demand Whatsoever of him the Said Asa Clark, of,
in and to the Said Messuage tenements, and premises and of, in, and
to every part and parcel thereof, with their and every of their appurtenances; And also One House worth One hundred Dollars And
One Buggy worth Seventy five Dollars and all of my House hold and
kitchen furniture, and fifty head of Stock Cattle And also the following Described Negro property to wit: **One Negro man named Elias
aged about Forty years, One Negro woman named Sarah aged
about Forty years, One Negro Girl named Easter aged about
Eleven years, One Negro Girl named Victoria aged about Eight
years One Negro Boy named Hard times aged about Six years
One Negro Boy named Nat aged about four years and One
Negro girl by the name of Satirah an infant And One Negro
man named Sam aged about Twenty Two Years** to have and to
hold the Said Messuges tenements, and All and Singular the premises,
Farming utensils, Kitchen furniture And Negroes, hereby granted, and
Confirmed, or mentioned or intended So to be, with their, and every

of their appurtenances Unto the Said Jane Ann Clark her heirs and assigns, to the only proper Use and behoof of her the Said Jane Ann Clark his heirs And assigns forever

And the Said Asa Clark for himself his heirs executors and administrators doth conveenant, grant, and agree to and with the Said Jane Ann Clark her heirs and Assigns by these presents that She the Said Jane Ann Clark, her heirs and Assigns, Shall, and lawfully may from time to time, and at all times hereafter peaceably and quietly have, hold, use, occupy, possess and enjoy the Said messuage, farm, land tenements, hereditaments And premises, And negroes, Cattle, Kitchen furniture &c hereby granted and Confirmed, or mentioned or intended to be hereby granted and confirmed, with their and every of their appurtenances, free, clear, and freely discharged or Well and Sufficiently Saved, kept harmeless, and indemnified of, from, and against all former and other gifts, grants, bargains, Sales, Jointures, feoffments, dowers and Estates, and of from and against all former and other titles, troubles, Charges, and encumbrances, WhatSoever had, done, or Suffered, or to be had made done or Suffered by him the Said Asa Clark his heirs and assigns, or any other person or persons, lawfully Claiming or to Claim, by or under him, them or any of them"

December 23, 1851
State of Florida, Alachua County
From Alachua County Ancient Records
Deed Record A pages 433-434

Asa Clark to his daughter Elizabeth Jane Ann Wellhoner:
"This Indenture made this 24th day of June in the year of our Lord One thousand Eight hundred and fifty two between Asa Clark of the State and County aforesaid of the one part and Elizebeth Jane Ann Wellhoner, daughter of the said Asa Clark, of the other part

Witnesseth: That said Asa Clark, as well for and in consideration of the natural love and affection which he the said Asa Clark hath and beareth unto the said Elizabeth Jane Ann Wellhoner, as well as also for the better maintainence, support and livelyhood of her the said Elizebeth Jane Wellhoner, hath given, granted, aliened, enfeoffed and confirmed and by these presents doth give, grant, alien, enfeoff and confirm with said Elizebeth Jane Ann Wellhoner her heirs and assigns. The following described negroes and their increase Viz **One negro women named Kate, seventeen years of age, of yellow complection, one by the name of Miley, ten years old, of yellow complection and one by the name of Frank, one year old, of yellow complection** and twelve cows and calves marked, crop and ear bob in each ear, branded with the letters LW, together with their increase. To have & to hold **the said Negroes and cattle with their increase** hereby granted and confirmed, or mentioned or intended so to be with their and evey of their appurtenances unto the said Elizabeth Jane Ann Wellhoner her heirs and assigns to the only proper use and behoof of her the said Elizebeth Jane Ann Wellhoner her heirs and assigns forever. And the said Asa Clark for himself his heirs, executors administrators doth covenant, grant and agree to and with the said Elizabeth Jane Ann Wellhoner her heirs and assigns by these presents, that she the said Elizabeth Jane Ann Wellhoner her heirs and assigns shall and lawfully, May from time to time and at all times hereafter peaceably and quietly have, hold use, occupy, possess and enjoy the said negroes slaves heretofore mentioned, granted and confirmed, in mentioned or intended to be hereby granted and confirmed with their or every of their increase, clear and free and fully discharged as well and sufficiently saved kept harmless and indemnified of from and against all former and other gifts, grants, bargins, sales, joitures, feoffments, dower and Estate and of from and against all former and other title trouble charges and encumberances, whatsoever had, done or suffered or to be had, made, done or suffered by him the said Asa Clark, his heirs and assigns, or any other person or persons lawfully claiming or to claim, by or under him, them or any of them.

The above named negeros and cattle to be a portion of her share of my estate & at my death to be deducted out of the division of said estate."

June 24, 1852
State of Florida, County of Alachua
From Alachua County Ancient Records
Deed Record B pages 035-036

Asa Clark to Philip Dell and Asa Clark to hold in trust for Asa's wife Jane Ann Clark: "Whereas the said party of the first part is desirous of making provision for the support and maintenance of his wife Jane Clark, and the heirs of his body, against future contingencies […] have bargained and sold and by these presents do bargain and sell unto the said parties of the second part the following described property To wit, The following negro Slaves, Viz. **Frank, Orange, Moses, Charles, Simon, Eliza, Rose, Harriet, Stephen, Henry, & Bob**, together with three horses and Two hundred head of Cattle the property of the above named Grantor, also the following described land to wit, the North west quarter of North west of Section five and the North half of Lot two of Section Six Township 8 of Range 20, South & East containing Eighty acres more or less, To have and to hold all and singular the above described property, with the appurtinnances thereunto belonging, to the said parties of the second part, their successors and assigns, In Trust to manage the above described property as they may deem best for the interest of those for whose interest the said property is given & and in trust to convey absolutely the property given to my said wife"

May 5, 1856
From Alachua County Ancient Records
Deed Record D page 351

Asa Clark and wife Jane A. Clark to Mary Clark, wife of Asa Clark Jr: "This Indenture made this the 28th day of November A.D. one thousand eight hundred and fifty six between Asa Clark Sr. and Jane A. Clark (his wife) of the County of Alachua and State aforesaid of the first part and Mary Clark wife of Asa Clark Jr. of the County and State aforesaid of the second part, Witnesseth, That the said parties of the first part for and in consideration of the natural love and affection they bear and have for the said Mary Clark wife of the said Asa Clark Jr. aforesaid and for the further consideration of the sum of Five dollars to them in hand paid at and before the ensealing and delivery of these presents the receipt whereof is hereby acknowledged, hath given, granted, bargained, and sold and delivered and by these presents do give, grant, bargain, sell and convey unto the said Mary Clark, and to the heirs of her body both present and future, by her present husband the said Asa Clark Jr. the following described Negro slaves to wit, **One negro man named Morris aged about twenty two years, complexion dark, and one negro boy named Charles aged about Seven years, complexion dark**. To have and to hold the said negro slaves with their future increase unto the said Mary Clark wife of the said Asa Clark Jr. and to the heirs of her body as aforesaid forever"

November 28, 1856
State of Florida, Alachua County
From Alachua County Ancient Records
Deed Record D page 379

Asa Clark to John C. Richard Jr. for $100: "Know all men by these presents, that I Asa Clark Sr. have this day received of John C. Richard Jr. one hundred dollars being in full of all demands for a **negro man**

named George aged twenty three years. I do hereby warrant and defend the said negro against all claims whatsoever unto the said John C. Richard Jr. forever."

May 6, 1857
State of Florida, County of Alachua
From Alachua County Ancient Records
Bills Of Sale A page 036

Jane A. Clark to son John E. Clark: "Know all men by these presents that I Jane A. Clark of the County of Alachua and State of Florida for and in Consideration of the natural love and affection I have for my Son John E. Clark as well as the Sum of five dollars to me in hand paid at and before the Sealing and delivery the receipt whereof is hereby acknowledged have given granted bargained Sold and doth So give, grant bargain, and Sell, unto my Son John E. Clark his heirs Executors administrators and assigns the following described property To wit **Victoria a Negro woman Slave about the age of nineteen years old together with her future increase, Ephraim a Negro man Slave about the age of thirty years old, Hardtimes a Negro boy Slave about fifteen years old, Nat a Negro Boy Slave about thirteen years old, Bob a Negro Boy Slave about Eleven years old, Satira a Negro girl Slave about Eight years old, Harriet a Negro slave about Eight years old, Stephen a Negro boy Slave about Six years old, Henry a Negro boy Slave about five years old, Ned a Negro boy Slave about two years old, James a Negro boy Slave about one year old, Together with their future increase**, also the following described lands Situate lying and being in the County and State aforesaid containing one hundred & twenty acres more or less and Known as Clarks Plantation near Coutre Pond Situate about twelve miles from Newnansville in an Easterly direction To have and to hold together with all and singular the tenements hereditaments and appurtinances thereunto belonging or in any wise appertaining. Together also with all and Singular the Household and Kitchen furniture To have and to hold the above described property both real and personal together with the future increase thereof –

Provided nevertheless that the Said Jane A. Clark Shall retain possession and full Control of the above described property during the period of her natural life, and at her death to pass into the possession of John E. Clark according to the full intent and purposes hereof"

February 18, 1859
State of Florida, Alachua Co.
From Alachua County Ancient Records
Deed Record C pages 386-387

William D. Clark to John C. Richard Jr. for $3,000: "Know all men by these presents that I William D. Clark of Alachua County in the State of Florida for & in consideration of the sum of three thousand dollars to me in hand paid at or before the enseling and delivery of these presents by John C. Richard Jr. of Duval County & State of Florida the receipt whereof is hereby acknowledged have bargained & sold & by these presents do grant and convey unto the said John C. Richard Jr. his executors administrators & assigns, **Two Negro Slaves one of them named Sam about thirty four years of age & one of them named George about twenty two years of age** seven horses the same which I now own One 2 Horse wagon and about Three hundred head of cattle more or less being all the cattle now owned by me & in differrent marks and brands, To have & to hold the same unto the said J. C. Richard Jr. his heirs Executors administrators & assigns forever"

March 10, 1856
From Alachua County Ancient Records
Deed Record D pages 291-292

Samuel Clary - indictment for trading with enslaved people:
"State of Florida vs Samuel Clary - trading with slaves - Continued to the next term of Court and the defendant recognized in the sum of five hundred dollars for his appearance at the next term of the Court two hundred & fifty for the principal and one hundred & twenty five for each Security

Samuel Clary, Hope H. Colson & William Colson Jr. appeared in open Court and acknowledged themselves to owe & Stand indebted to the State of Florida in the Sum of five hundred dollars, That is to say Samuel Clary in the sum of two hundred & fifty dollars, Hope H. Colson in the Sum of one hundred & twenty five dollars and William Colson Jr. in the sum of One hundred & twenty five dollars to be levied of their respective goods & chattels, Slaves lands and tenements, if default be made in the following condition that is to say of the said Samuel Clary, shall be and appear at this next term of the Court to answer to an indictment for trading with Slaves and Shall not thence depart the Court without barr thereof then this obligation to be null and void otherwise to remain in full force and virtue"

May 13, 1858
From Alachua County Ancient Records
Judgment Record B pages 051-052

Daniel Conyers to daughters Aeseneth Conyers and Mary A. Richman: "Know all men by these presents that I Daniel Conyers of said State and County for and in consideration of the natural love and affection which I have and bear to my daughter Aeseneth Conyers of the same place, and for and in consideration of Five Dollars cash in hand paid by the said Aeseneth Conyers, the receipt whereof is hereby acknowledged, do by these presents give and grant unto my said daughter Aeseneth Conyers certain negroes to wit **one negro man named Sam about sixty years of age of black complexion, and one negro woman named Nancy about Fifty years of age black complexion:** To Have and to Hold the said negroes Sam and Nancy to her the said Aeseneth Conyers and to her children forever. Also one sorrel horse saddle and bridle, one bed and furniture belonging thereto: Also one buggy and harness,

I do further for the love and affection I have and bear for my daughter Mary A. Richman I give and grant to her the said Mary A. Richman one half of the profits of the labour of the above named negroes, Sam and Nancy for fifteen years, her the said Mary A. Richman to pay one half of the expense that may occur from sickness or anything happening to the said negroes Sam and Nancy."

April 21, 1856
State of Florida, Alachua County
From Alachua County Ancient Records
Deed Record D pages 531-532

Franklin R. Cox to Samuel R. Pyles as collateral for a $261 loan: "This Indenture made this the first day of January in the year of our Lord one thousand eight hundred and fifty five, Between Franklin R. Cox of the State and County above written, of the first part, and Samuel R. Pyles of the Same place of the Second part. Witnesseth, that I the Said Franklin R. Cox party of the first part, for and in consideration of the Sum of Two hundred and Sixty one dollars lawful money to me in hand paid, the receipt whereof is hereby acknowledged, doth bargain and Sell, and by these presents do bargain and Sell unto the Said Samuel R. Pyles party of the Second part, a **Negro man named**

Bailam, aged about twenty Six years old, To have and to hold, Said Negro Bailam unto the said Samuel R. Pyles, his heirs, and assigns for ever, provided always, and theses premises are upon these conditions, That if the Said Franklin R. Cox, Shall well and truly pay his certain promissory note, bearing January 1st 1855, payable January 1st 1856, with eight per ct interest from date, given by Said Franklin R. Cox for the Sum of ($261) two hundred & Sixty one dollars, lawful money as aforesaid, according to the true tenor of said note, then these presents Shall become void, and the property hereby sold, or grand, Shall cease and utterly determine"

January 1, 1855
State of Florida, Alachua County
From Alachua County Ancient Records
Deed Record C pages 008-009

Isaiah Crankfield to David H. Montgomery to hold in trust for Isaiah Crankfield's daughter Ann C. Feaster: "Know all men by these presents that I Isaiah Crankfield of the County and aforesaid in consideration of the natural love and affection which I have and do bear towards my beloved daughter Ann C. Feaster and also in consideration of the sum of one dollar to me in hand paid by David H. Montgomery of the State and County aforesaid the receipt of which is hereby acknowledged, have given, bargained, sold and delivered, and by these presents do give, bargain, sell and deliver to the said David H. Montgomery the following negro slaves, to wit: **Jesse and his wife Linder and their two children, Charles and Peter, together with all the future issue and increase from the female part thereof.** To have and to Hold the said negroes unto the said David H. Montgomery forever. In trust nevertheless, to and for the uses interest and purposes hereinafter mentioned: That is to say, in trust for the sole use benefit and possession of my said daughter Ann C. Feaster of the

Said State and County to remain in the possession of the said Ann C. Feaster, for her use benefit and enjoyment during her natural life, and to go to, and be equally divided among her children at her death, but should it so happen that the said Ann C. Feaster should die leaving no children or child living at the time of her death, then and in that case, the said negroes Jesse, Linder, Charles and Peter with all the future increase to return back to my estate, and be equally divided among my heirs at law. But in no case whatever are the aforesaid negroes or any part of their increase to be subject to the Contracts, debts or other liabilities of the present or any future husband of the said Ann C. Feaster, but it is further and expressly declared that the said Ann C. Feaster, shall have the undisturbed use, possession and enjoyment of the said negroes during her natural life."

January 21, 1856 - in the 79th year of American Independence
State of Florida, Marion County
From Alachua County Ancient Records
Bills of Sale A pages 027-028

Richard R. Davis to Samuel R. Pyles as collateral for $1,619.43 in loans: "This Indenture made this the twelfth day of March and the year of our Lord one thousand eight hundred and fifty nine Between Richard R. Davis of the County of Alachua and the State of Florida of the first part and Samuel R. Pyles of the same place of Second part Witness that the said Richard R Davis for and in consideration of the Sum of Twelve hundred dollars to him in hand paid by the said Samuel R Pyles as well as for the securing of the payment of the note here in after described has granted bargained sold delivered transferred and conveyed and by these presents doth grant bargain Sell deliver transfer and convey unto the said Samuel R. Pyles his heirs and assigns all those certain portions and tracts of Lands Situated lying and being in the Said County of Alachua more particularly known and described according to the maps and plats in the United States Land Office as the East half of the North East quarter of Section nine Township Seven south of range X eighteen East containing eighty acres more or less also the South east quarter of the north west quarter and the west quarter of the north east quarter of Section nine Township seven South of range eighteen East containing eight acres more or less. Also the South East quarter of the north east quarter and the west quarter of the north east quarter of Section nine Township seven South of range eighteen East containing eighty acres more or less. Also the South west quarter of the north east quarter of Section nine Township seven South of range eighteen East containing thirty nine 99/100 acres more or less making or containing in all Two hundred acres more or less Together with all the rights tenements appurtanances and heridetaments There unto an anywise appertaning or belonging and the Said Richard R Davis doth also bargain Sell and convey unto the Said Samuel R Pyles his heirs and assigns **a Negro man named Jeff of dark complection and about twenty two or three years old and a Negro girl named Sallie of dark complection and about Seventeen years of age and Boy named Lewis about thirteen years of age and of dark complection** To have and to hold the Said tracts of Land above described and the Negroes above named to the Said Samuel R Pyles his heirs and assigns forever and the Said Richard A Davis well and his heirs Executors and administrators Shall the afore granted premises to the Said Samuel R Pyles his heirs Executors and administrators forever warrant and defend by virtue of these presents and the Said Richard R. Davis covenants with the Said Samuel R. Pyles his heirs and assigns Executors and administrators that the Said Negros Jeff Sally and Lewis are Slave born and in sound health body and mind and that the Said Richard R Davis his heirs Executors and administrator Shall the Said negros to the Said Samuel R Pyles his heirs Executors and administrators warrant and defend

Provided nevertheless that if the Said Richard R Davis his heirs Executors administrators Shall pay unto the said Samuel R Pyles his heirs Executors administrators or assigns the amount of a certain promissory note made by the Said Richard R Davis payable to the Said Samuel R Pyles or bearer bearing even date these presents and due nine months after note for the sum of Sixteen hundred and nineteen dollars 43/100. Now if the Said Richard R Davis his heirs Executors or administrators shall pay unto the Said Samuel R Pyles his heirs Executors or administrators or assigns the note above mentioned and described nine months after date with all expenses incurred by the said Samuel R Pyles in collecting the Same then as well this deed as the above described promissory note to be utterly void otherwise to remain in full force"

March 12, 1859
From Alachua County Ancient Records
Mortgage Record A pages 182-183

James B. Dawkins to Giles U. Ellis as collateral for a $10,000 loan: "This Indenture made the twenty-eight day of May in the year of our Lord one thousand Eight hundred and fifty-eight Between James B. Dawkins of Alachua County and State of Florida of the first part and Giles U. Ellis of the County of Columbia and State aforesaid of the Second part Whereas the said James B. Dawkins is justly indebted to the said party of the Second part in the Sum of ten thousand Dollars lawful money of the United States of America Secured to be paid by his certain Bonds or obligations bearing said date with these presents on the final sum of Twenty Thousand Dollars conditions for the payments of the said first mentioned sum of Ten thousand Dollars lawful money as aforesaid to the said party of the Second part his Executors administrators or assigns, in three equal instalments of three thousand three hundred & thirty three 33/100 Dollars each one of which will fall due on the fifteenth day of January in the year of our Lord one thousand eight hundred & Sixty and the Second to fall due on the Fifteenth day of January

Eighteen hundred & Sixty one, and the third to fall due on the Fifteenth day of January Eighteen hundred & Sixty two and the interest on the said Ten thousand Dollars to be computed from the Fifteenth day of January Eighteen hundred and fifty-eight and paid annually at and after the rate of Six per Cent per annum as by the said bond or obligation reference being thereunto had may more fully appear. Now this Indenture witnesseth that the party of the first part for the better securing the payment of the said sum of money mentioned in the conditions of the said bonds or obligations with interest thereon according to the true intent and meaning thereof and also for and in consideration of the sum of one to him in hand paid by the said party of the Second part at or before the ensealing and delivery of these presents the receipt whereof is hereby acknowledged have granted bargained, sold, aliened, released conveyed and confirmed and by these presents do Grant bargain Sell, release, convey and confirm unto the said party of the Second part and to his heirs and assigns forever all that Certain tract or parcel of land situate in the County of Alachua and State of Florida Known and distinguished Section Thirty one (31) Township Nine Range 19 South East quarter Section Twenty five (five) Township nine Range Eighteen (18) Together with all and singular the tenements and heriditaments and appurtinances thereunto belonging or in any wise appertaining To have and to hold all and Singular the above mentioned and described together with the appurtenances unto the said party of the Second part his heirs and assigns forever Also in Consideration as aforesaid the said party of the first part doth by these presents grant bargain Sell alien and Convey unto the said party of the Second part and to his heirs and assigns forever the following negro Slaves to wit **Henry, Edy, Jude Tener Sina, Minta Mary Jane Dave Isaac Wade Suckey Curry Margaret Venus and Charle**s Provided always and these presents are upon this Express Condition that if the said party of the first part his heirs Executors or administrators shall well and truly pay unto the said party of the Second part his Executors, administrators or assigns the said Sum of Money mentioned in the Condition of said Bond or obligation and the interest thereon at the time and in the manner mentioned in the Said Condition according to the true intent

243

and meaning thereof that then these presents and the estate hereby granted Shall Cease determine and be void"

May 28, 1858
From Alachua County Ancient Records
Mortgage Record A pages 145-146

Bennett M. Dell and Samuel R. Piles Executors of last will and testament of James Dell deceased: "This Indenture made this the Tenth day January in the Year One Thousand Eight Hundred & fifty between Bennett M. Dell and Samuel R. Piles Executors of the last will and testament of James Dell deceased and Samuel R. Piles and his Wife Ann L. Piles late Ann L. Dell Daughter of Said James Dell and Samuel R. Piles Guardian of James Philip Dell, Florida Ann Dell & William Thomas Dell infant Children of William Thomas Dell who was also a son of the late James Dell deceased and Martha Mary Delia Dell Daughter of Said James Dell deceased heirs legatees distributees and Claimants under the last will and Testament of Said James Dell deceased of the first part and James Gadsden Dell who is also an heir legatee distributee and Claimant under the Said will of the Second part Witnesseth, That whereas of the last will and Testament of Said James Dell there is a request and direction to this affect, to Wit

My will is that **Big Jim** who has as all times and in all troubles Stood by me Shall have the election either to remain a slave to Some of my Children else to pay my executors the Sum of one Hundred Dollars per year, the Same to be equally divided Among my Children,

When he Shall be free and my executors are charged with the trust in the event of his complying with this proposition to give to him emancipation and I hereby Charge My Estate to Comply with the law So far as to carry this request in to execution of the Election of Jim require it and whereas the Said Jim has paid to Said executors the said Sum of four Hundred Dollars which Said Sum is acknowledged to have So paid by the receipts of Said executors therefore hereto attached and whereas as the payment of said Sum to Said Claimants under said will is hereby acknowledged to have been made by Said executors to them or their guardian by their receipts hereto attached and whereas All Said parties Well Knowing the faithful Services of Said Slave Jim and being anxious in consideration thereof to have a compliance with the intention of said teststator So far As they lawfully can do So

And Whereof the Said Slave Jim has elected to remain the Slave of James Gadsden Dell Son of Said James Dell deceased

And Whereas the said parties of the first And Second part desire to Secure to Said Slave Jim a comfortable Support and maintenance and to Secure him against any and all accident and contingences likely to derive him of Said support and Maintenance,

This indenture therefore further Witnesseth that the said parties of the first part and in consideration of the premises and of the further Sum of one dollar to these paid before the Sealing and delivery hereof the receipt whereof is hereby acknowledged by the party of the Second part Hath bargained and Sold and as by these present bargain sell and release to the party of Second part all their rights title interest and Claim of Any and every Sort in and to the Said Negro Slave Jim in Special trust And Confidance never the less that the Said party of the Second part Shall cause Negro Slave Jim to be employed in Some useful manner such a position of his time as will be Sufficient to afford him a comfortable Support, and only to employ him for Such time and for Such purposes and Shall direct and apply the whole of the proceeds derived from such employment to the comfortable Support and maintenance of Said Slave Jim, And the Said parties of the first and second part for themselves and their heirs executors and administrators doth covenant and agree to and with each other and the parties of the first part each for the other for the faithful performance of the matters and things and the Several Stipulations herein Contained"

January 10, 1850
From Alachua County Ancient Records
Deed Record A pages 222-224

Bennett Maxey Dell Last Will and Testament: "In the name of God, Amen. I Bennett Maxey Dell of the County of Alachua and State of Florida, being weak in body, and of sound and disposing mind and memory and calling to mind the frailty and uncertainty of human life, and being desirous of settling my worldly affairs and dividing proper the estate with which it has pleased God to bless me, shall be disposed of after my decease while I have strength and capassity so to do, do make and publish this my last will and testament, hereby revoking, and making null and void all other last will and testament by me heretofore made.

And first I commence my immortal being to Him that gave it, and my body to the earth to be buried in the family burying ground in a decent and suitable manner suitable to my rank and Estate in life.

And as to my worldly estate, and all the property real, personal as mixes of which I shall be seized and possessed or to which I shall be entitled at the time of my death I devise bequeath and dispose thereof in the manner following to wit;

My Will is that all My just debts and funeral charges shall by my executors hereinafter nominated be paid out of my estate as soon after my decease as shall be by them found convenient.

Item, To my present much beloved wife Eliza Dorothy Dell, I give devise and bequeath the following negro slaves, that is to say **Jack, Julian and her four children Lewis Henry, Frances, Billy and Grace, Somerset, Betsy, and her two children Jim and Sappbo, Adam and Peggy and her child Matibel with their increase** to have to hold and enjoy during her natural life, Would she not marry after my decease but if she does marry after my decease it is my will that the above mentioned negro slaves shall immediately upon such marriage revert to and be equally divided among my children or their children subject to certain restrictions and conditions hereinafter set forth and mentioned, and it is further my will that my wife the said Eliza Dorothy, from the time of the marriage referred to whose shall receive annually the sum of five hundred dollars to be paid to her by my executors hereinafter nominated, out of such portions of my estate or shall seem most proper to them during her natural life, but if my wife the said Eliza Dorothy does not marry after my decease, then it is my will that she shall possess, hold and enjoy the aforementioned and a have ********* negro slaves, with their increase during her natural life, and upon her death the said Negro slaves with their increase shall be equally divided among my present surviving her death or their children share and share alike subject to the restrictions above refered to and hereinafter mentioned and set forth.

Item, It is also my will that my said wife Eliza Dorothy shall be permitted to choose for her residence my plantation now occupied by me near Newnansville and know as Standley, or any other place which I might the time of my death be possessed of or entitled to and shall be allowed five horses and a carriage, and all necessary farming utensils and implements for the place which she may select, she shall also be allowed one hundred head of cattle also all the hogs belonging to my place near Newnansville, known as Stanly, and also all the household and Kitchen furniture which may be upon my place known as Stanly at the time of my death, the said place which she may so select and the said carriage and horses and the said farming utensils and the said cattle and the said hogs and the said household and kitchen furniture to be held and enjoyed by her during her natural life subject at her marriage or death to be possessed of as in the above first Item specified and subject to the same restrictions and provisions as above refered to and hereinafter set forth and mentioned.

Item, I hereby give devise and bequeath to my much beloved daughter Sarah Angelina Dell the following named negro slaves, that is to say, **Charlotte and her two children Charles and Washington, Jacob and Polly with their increase** to have to hold and enjoy during her natural life and at her death to be equally divided among My present Children or their Children surviving her death, subject to the same conditions and restrictions as refered to above and hereinafter set forth and specified upon

I hereby nominate constitute and appoint my executors hereinafter nominated Trustees for my said beloved daughter Sarah Angelina and earnestly recomend her to their special care and protection.

Item, I also give devise and bequeath unto the children of my son Charles L. Dell wife lately there in Texas so much of my estate as their father would have received under this will had he survived me to be paid in money when they the said children of my son the said Charles L. Shall respectively arrive at the age of twenty one years, and I hereby nominate constitute and appoint my executor hereinafter nominated, Trustees for the said minor children of my said son Charles L. deceased with full Power to convert such portion of my estate as they may be entitled to into money, or invest the same as may be most advantagious, to the said children aforesaid, but if they the said children of my son the said Charles L. deceased, die before arriving at the age of twenty one years, then the property to which they may be severelly entitled under this will, shall revert to and be equally divided among my present children or their children surviving the death of the death of the children of my son the aforesaid Charles L. deceased share and share alike, subject to the same restrictions and provisions refered to above in this will, and hereinafter set forth and mentioned.

Item, It is my will that my part of land lying on or near Pains Prarie and known the Garey Tract, be not sold untill it is worth twenty five dollars per acre.

Item, It is further my will that such portion of my estate as shall come to my present wife Eliza Dorothy under the will or to her children, shall be kept together during the life or until the marriage of my present wife the said Eliza Dorothy under the direction of my executors hereinafter nominated, but upon the arrival at twenty one years of age of any of my children there may if they see fit seperate their portion of my estate, which may come to them under this will from that of my present wife Eliza Dorothy and my other minor children.

Item, The balance of my land not disposed of by this will and all of my stock of cattle hogs and horses, not disposed of in this will and all the cattle hogs horses and other stock of which I may die possessed, I direct my executors hereinafter nominated to sell upon the most advantagious terms, and divide the proceeds thereof equally among my children surviving my death or their children giving to each his or her share after age of twenty-one respectively and I hereby nominate constitute and appoint my executors hereinafter nominated Trustees for my children or their children who may be under the age of twenty one years at the time of my death untill they May respectively arrive at the age of twenty one years with full power and instructions to place the said proceeds of interest and use of the same in the education of my said children or their children in proportion to their respective shares.

Item, I will further that all of my slaves not hereinbefore disposed of or of which I may die possessed shall be at my death equally divided among surviving children or their children in manner and form as hereinbefore specified, not just to conditions and restrictions hereinbefore refered to and hereinafter set forth and mentioned.

Item, It is also my will that such portion of my estate as shall under this will come to my Daughter Mary S. Duer wife of Christion F. Duer now residing in Texas or to her children or their children shall be held by my executors hereinafter nominated in trust for my said Daughter or her children during the lifetime of the said Christion F. Duer and I direct my executors as trustees to invest such of their portion as shall be in money and pay over the interest annually as well as the proceeds of such as shall be slaves to my said daughter or for the benefit of her children and at death of the said Christion F. Duer to pay over the whole portion to my said daughter for her children, not just to the condition refered to above and hereinafter set forth and fully explained.

Item, I also bequeath to my executors hereinafter nominated, in trust for the Methodist Episcopal Church in the place where my wife Shall chose to reside, provided my wife shall chose to reside at Stanly or some other place in East Florida the sum of one thousand dollars to be possessed of such portion of my estate as may seem most proper to my executors hereinafter nominated and to be put out at interest by them and the interest paid annually for the benefit of said church, but under no circumstances to be paid to any man raised north of Mason and Dixsons line or [unreadable] with ab- abilionism in the least degree, and if the said church where my wife may chose to reside should employ any man as above described then the interest of the said sum of one thousand dollars shall be applied to a common school in the county where my wife may chose to reside during the time any man as above described is employed.

Item, I hereby declare my will in regard to all my property whether personal real or mixed disposed of by this will so far as my children or their children are concerned

Where my property is given devised or bequeathed in any manner disposed of by this will to any of my children or their children it is my express will that it shall be enjoyed by them during their natural life time and upon their deaths it shall go to and be vested in their children, if any and upon failure of children of any of my children or their children, then the property to which my said children or their children might have been entitled under this will shall be divided among my surviving children or their children and in no case where my property is described willed or bequeathed or in any manner disposed of, to any of my children shall they sell or convey the same nor shall it be subject to their debts but the property shall be held for life and upon the death of any of my children or grand children whose my property is directly willed to them the same shall go to and vest in their children and upon failure of such children then the property thus held by them upon their deaths shall be equally divided among my surviving children or their children.

Item, It is further my will that the property which may come to my son Chas L. under this will shall be under the control and management of my executors hereinafter nominated, and shall not under any circumstances be subject to his debts, but he shall only enjoy it during his natural life and upon his death it shall go to his children subject to the restrictions as in the above last item specified

Item Finally, I hereby nominate constitute and appoint my sons, Philip and John executors and my wife Eliza Dorothy Executrix of this My last will and testament with full power and instructions to execute the same and the trusts therein named, but it is my will that my wife Eliza Dorothy shall only act as executrix untill my son John arrives at the age of twenty one years."

February 21, 1855
From Alachua County Ancient Records
Will Book A pages 050-064

Mary E. Dell vs. Phillip Dell fighting over the estate of Amos L. Dell: "The petition of Mary E. Dell would respectfully show unto your Honor that Amos L. Dell died sometime about the 1st

of August 1856 that he left an only son an infant aged about three years that the said Amos L. Dell died in possession of about **twelve negroes slaves** and some Horses that Philip Dell of said County and Brother of said Amos L. Dell deceased claiming to be trustee for said infant William O. Dell took possession of said property soon after the death of said Amos L. Dell the the said Philip Dell claims to be trustee under the wills of Bennett M. Dell and William Dell Decd That Ferdinand McLeod administrator of estate of said Amos L. Dell Decd has commenced legal proceedings on the Chancery side of this Court for recovery of said property and to make the same part of the assets of said estate that said suits have been now pending for a long time and with better prospects for a speedy termination or adjudication

Your petitioners would further show that the entire portion of the said Amos L. Dell was not set apart to the said Amos L. Dell during his life time and that the estate will be greatly increased by the next deaths of Dorothy Dell widow of late B. M. Dell your petitioner further shows that by the taking of said property she was left entirely destitute and dependant on her friends, that she been compelled to procure a nurse for said infant and to secure board for said infant and nurse

Your petitioner further shows that the said negroes now in possession of said Philip Dell Claimed by him as trustee for said infant were hired last year and also for this year at about Eight hundred dollars yearly

your petitioner therefore as next friend and natural guardian of said infant would respectfully petition your Honor to set aside and allow your petitioner out of the proceeds of said property held as aforesaid to be paid by the said Philip Dell for the maintenance clothing nursing &c of said infant under order of this Court in such amount as to your honor may seem best and proper and in accordance with the circumstances means & conditions in life of said infant that said allowances may commence at this time of the taking of said property in possession by the said Philip Dell and to be paid yearly untill the litigation between the said administrator in & the said Philip Dell shall be adjucated or untill the further order of this Court & your petitioner will ever pray &c

In answer to the forgoing petition Respondent Philip Dell believes and is advised that by virtue of the will of Maxey Dell the father of respondent and Amos L. Dell deceased as also by virtue of the will of William Dell deceased a Brother in the respondent is charged with the Care Custody Control and management of the property as Executor & trustee which he has in his possession and responsible as such for the same, that he is willing to contribute to the support of said child named in said petition as such Trustee and would have done so but that proceedings on the Chancery side of this Court have been instituted by Ferdenand McLeod as administrator &c the Estate of Amos L. Dell deceased claiming said property as belonging to said estate and to be made assets in his hands and that he did not feel safe in distributing said assets or income arising from said property so held by him untill said rights are determined by its proper authority that he is willing to pay such an amount for the support and maintainance of said child quarterly as may be necessary upon this Court issuing such order as will protect him on the premises

Upon the reading of said petition and also the answer of the respondent Philip Dell and it appearing to the satisfaction of the Court that the matter & things set forth in said petition are true and that the said Philip Dell has in his possession property claimed by him to be held as trustee for said infant William O. Dell the proceeds of which are more than sufficient for the maintainance and support of said infant and it appearing to the Court that the Means and Conditions of said infant entitles him to the allowance prayed for It is therefore ordered and adjudged that said Philip Dell to the said petition or order the sum of Three hundred & fifty dollars as equally allowance for support and maintainance of said William O. Dell the allowance to commence on the thirteenth day of November AD 1856 and to be paid yearly untill the further order of this Court It is further ordered that said petitioner

Mary E. Dell do account to the said Philip Dell of the disbursement of said allowance

May 13, 1858
In the Eastern Circuit Court, Alachua County
From Alachua County Ancient Records
Chancery Order Book A pages 137-139

Philip Dell to Frank Lubback and Christian F. Duer in trust for the use of Philip's sister Mary S. Duer: "Know all men by these presents, that I Philip Dell, for and in consideration of the natural love and affection which I have to my sister, Mary S. Duer, wife of Christian F. Duer of Texas, as well as for and in consideration of the sum of one dollar to me in hand paid by Frank Lubback and Christian F. Duer at and before the ensealing and delivery of these presents, the receipt whereof is hereby acknowledged, and by virtue of the authority in me vested by the last will and testament of one William Dell, deceased, late of Alachua County Florida, of which said will and testament the said Philip Dell is Executor by appointment of the said William Dell deceased have given, granted, bargained and sold, and by these presents do give, grant, bargain and sell and deliver to the said Frank Lubback and Christian F. Duer, and to their Executors, administrators and assigns the following described negro slaves, to wit: **John, a man aged about twenty eight years, Nancy his wife aged about twenty eight years, Cornelia a girl aged about ten years, Chloestina aged about eight years, and Mitchell a boy aged about eight years, with their future issue and increase**. To have and to hold the said slaves with their future increase unto the said Frank Lubback and Christian F. Duer, their executors, administrators and assigns, to their own proper use benefit and behoof forever. In trust nevertheless to and for the use of the said Mary S. Duer, wife of the said Christian F. Duer, for and during the term of her natural life, and after her death in trust for such child or children or grand children of the said Mary S. as may be living at her death and the heirs of the same child or children and in case no child or children of the said Mary S. shall surviver her, then the slaves and their increase to rest in the said Philip Dell and one Amos L. Dell and be and become their absolute property, both in law and equity."

February 6, 1856
From Alachua County Ancient Records
Bills of Sale A pages 022-023

Simeon Dell to Solomon Warren for $1,200: "Know all men by these presents that I Simeon Dell of the County and State aforesaid for and in consideration of the sum of Twelve hundred dollars lawful money to me in hand paid by Solomon Warren of the same county and state, the Receipt whereof is hereby acknowledged, have bargained, sold and conveyed, and do by these presents, bargain, sell and convey unto the said Solomon Warren, the following negro slaves to wit; **negro man Shepherd aged about Twenty-six years and negro woman Charlotte aged about forty years**, to him the said Solomon Warren his heirs and assigns, to have and to hold the said negroes **together with the future increase of said negro woman**. And the said Simeon Dell, for myself, my heirs, and assigns, do hereby warrant said negroes to the said Solomon Warren his heirs and assigns to be sound in body and mind and slaves for life."

May 11, 1858
State of Florida, County of Alachua
From Alachua County Ancient Records
Bills of Sale A pages 067-068

Clementeen Douglass to her son James Douglass: "Know all men by these presents that I Clementeen Douglass of the County and State aforesaid for and in Consideration of the natural love and affection which I bear to my Son James Douglass as well also for his better support and Maintenance hath given granted and Confirmed and by these presents do give grant and Confirm unto the Said James Douglass his heirs and assigns forever a certain **Negro Boy named Randall aged about Twenty years,** To Have and to hold the Said Negro boy Randall to his proper use his heirs and assigns forever"

September 21, 1857
State of Florida, Alachua County
From Alachua County Ancient Records
Deed Record E page 413

James W. Earle to Elizabeth H. Earle as collateral for $3821.88 loan: "To all whom these presents Shall come, I James W. Earle of the County and State aforesaid, Send Greeting, Whereas, I the Said James W. Earle by my certain note under Seal bearing date the ninth day of November A.D. 1854, am indebted to Elizabeth H. Earle in the Sum of thirty Eight hundred and twenty one Dollars and eighty eight cents, with interest from date and due twelve months after date. Now know Ye, That I the Said James W. Earle for the better Securing the payment of the Said Sum of Thirty eight hundred and twenty one Dollars and eighty eight cents, unto the Said Elizabeth H. Earle, her heirs, Executors, administrators or assigns, together with lawful interest for the Same, have bargained and Sold, and by these presents do bargain and Sell, {and in plain and open market, deliver unto the Said Elizabeth H. Earle, the following Slaves, to wit: **Clarisa and her three Children (vis) Louisa, Henrietta and Ellen, Sophy and her three children (vis) Green, William, and Moria, Charity and her two children (vis) Ann & Furman, Peter & Henry** - To have and to hold the Said Slaves above named, unto the Said Elizabeth H. Earle, her Executors, Administrators and assigns, for ever, provided always nevertheless, That if the Said James W. Earle, his heirs, Executors, or administrators, Shall, and do well and truly pay, or cause to be paid unto the Said Elizabeth H. Earle, her certain Attorney, Executors, or assigns, the full and just Sum of thirty Eight hundred and twenty one dollars and eighty eight cents, according to the true meaning of Said note, and of these presents, together with lawful interest upon the Said Sum of money, from the date before mentioned then this Deed of bargain and sale, and all and every clause, article, and thing therein contained Shall cease, determine, and be utterly void and of none effect, anything herein contained to the contrary thereof in any wise notwithstanding, And it is hereby declared by and between the Said parties and the Said James W. Earle, his Executors, Administrators and assigns, do covenant promise and agree to and with the said Elizabeth H. Earle, her Executors Administrators and assigns, by these presents, that if default shall happen to be made of or in payment of the said Sum of money as aforesaid, according to the true meaning and intent of the said note, that then and in such case, it shall and may be lawful to and for the said Elizabeth H. Earle, her Executors, Administrators, attorneys or agents from time to time and at all times hereafter peaceably and quietly to enter into any or all the messuages, land or tenements of the said James W. Earle and to take the said Slaves unto her custody and possession and the same to hold and detain to her own use and behoof as her own proper goods and chattels from thenceforth and for ever, or the Same to Sell and dispose of at will and pleasure, returning the over pluss if any should happen to be, after paying the said sum of thirty eight hundred and twenty one Dollars and eighty eight cents and interest unto the Said James W. Earle, his Executors, Administrators or assigns."

April 18, 1855 and in the Seventy ninth year of the Sovereignty and Independence of the United States of America
The State of Florida, Alachua County
From Alachua County Ancient Records
Deed Record D pages 130-131

Agreement between Giles U. Ellis and his intended wife, Nancy L. Townsend: "This Indenture made the Twenty fifth day of March in the year of Our Lord One thousand eight hundred and fifty six between Giles U. Ellis of the county of Alachua and said state of the first part and Nancy L. Townsend of the county of Columbia & State aforesaid of the second part. Whereas a marriage by Gods permission is intended shortly to be had and solemnized between the said Giles U. Ellis and the said Nancy L. Townsend, and the said Nancy L. Townsend being at this time entitled to certain undivided property both real and personal consisting of lands Negroes & lying and being in the said county of Columbia in the state aforesaid which she has elected as dower in the Estate of her deceased husband the late William Townsend Esquire of Columbia County all which reference being had to the records of the Probate court of said county will more fully and particularly appear To all which property herein referred to together with all and singular such property real or personal which she now possesses in her own right, the said Giles U. Ellis does by these presents relinquish every right title use benefit or claim that he may or might have to the same after the said intended marriage.

And Whereas Also the said Giles U. Ellis hath given granted bargained, and confirmed and doth by these presents give, grant bargain and confirm should the said intended marriage be solemnized and consummated with the said Nancy L. Townsend to and for the term of her natural life **a Negro woman named Nice and a Negro man named Ben together with the increase of said Negroes** to the sole and only use of the said Nancy Townsend should she so long remain his widow in case she survives him the said Giles U. Ellis but upon the demise of the said Giles U. Ellis and subsequent marriage of said Nancy L. Townsend the said Negress together with her increase and the Negro Ben to revert to the heirs of the said Giles U. Ellis.

And Whereas furthermore it is agreed between the parties that in the event of the said Nancy Townsend surviving her intended husband the said Giles U. Ellis she the said Nancy Townsend as the widow of the said Giles U. Ellis shall be entitled to Keep and retain possession of the dwelling house in which the parties to these presents may happen to reside at the time of the demise of the said Giles U. Ellis together with the plantation thereto attached or so much thereof as she may desire or require so long as she shall remain to the dire and faithful performance of which agreement to and with the said Nancy L. Townsend the said Giles U. Ellis his heirs executors or administrators do by these presents convenant and agree.

And Whereas it is yet further agreed by the said parties that in case it should so happen that there should be issue of the said intended marriage or their children who altogether shall represent their parent living at the demise of the said Giles U. Ellis that such issue shall possess and inherit share and share alike with the children or their representatives of the said Giles U. Ellis of his former marriage, less however their amount or proportion which said issue may inherit from his her or their mother the said Nancy Townsend out of such property as she now possesses in her own right or may hereafter possess by gift purchase inheritance or otherwise upon a division of such estate and distribution thereof the said Nancy Townsend agreeing and declaring that in the event of issue of the said intended marriage an equal portion of any property she may possess shall with her other children be awarded to him her or them; and the said Nancy Townsend covenants and agrees to and with the said Giles U. Ellis his heirs executors or administrators that she will make no disposition conveyance or transfer of any such property whereby the issue of said marriage might be prejudiced and all this in order and with the interest and property that the children of the said Giles U. Ellis of his first as well as of this his intended marriage may possess equal and proportional inheritance

Now this Indenture Witnesseth that for and in consideration of the above recited relinquishment gift contract agreement premises and provisions securing unto the said Nancy L. Townsend a competent maintenance secured from the debts or claims of her intended husband and of property which she now possesses as dower from the Estate of her late husband and otherwise so long as she may live, and confirming to her out of the estate of her intended husband the said Giles U. Ellis certain gifts grants and benefits for her use and comfort and assistance as long as she shall remain his widow and all of which are relinquished given and granted in full satisfaction and his charge of all and every right and title the dower which she the said Nancy Townsend might have in claim to the estate real or personal of the said Giles U. Ellis in the event of surviving her intended husband and which in every way in accordance with her free will and instructions as well as in consideration of said intended marriage the said Nancy L. Townsend hath renounced released and relinquished and by these presents doth renounce release relinquish and forever quit claim with her intended husband the said Giles U. Ellis his heirs executors or administrators all the dower and therein rights and title of dower and third and all and ever claim and demand whatsoever in Law and Equity which she the said Nancy Townsend her heirs executors or administrators upon this consummation of said intended marriage and in the event of surviving her intended husband the said Giles U. Ellis might have in to or out of the estate real or personal of the said Giles U. Ellis that she the said Nancy L. Townsend her heirs executors or administrators or any other person or persons for her them or any of them shall not have claim chalenge or demand or pretend to have claim Chalenge or demand any dower or thirds or any other right title claim or demand whatsoever of in and to the estate of the said Giles U. Ellis real or personal but shall be utterly barred and excluded for and by these presents,

And the said Giles U. Ellis in view of said contingences for himself his heirs executors and administrators covenates and agrees with the said Nancy Townsend her heirs executors or administrators in consideration of the premises the said gifts grants relinquishments and agreements to on his part given granted relinquished and agreed to warrant protect confirm and observe

And the said Nancy L. Townsend her heirs executor or administrator covenant promise and agree to and with the said Giles U. Ellis his heirs executors or administrators testified by her executing these presents to observe protect carry out access to and confirm the agreement to acceptance and relinquishments on her part above agreed accepted and relinquished and covenants and agree to receive the provisions made to and with her and for his use and benefit in this deed of indenture and Settlement by her intended husband the said Giles U. Ellis in lien of her whole dower in to or out of the estate of the said Giles U. Ellis either real or personal and of every other claim right or title to any childs part or distributive share or any interest whatever which she might otherwise have had therein upon the solemnization of this intended marriage and in the right she would possess in the event of ever being the widow of her said intended husband."

March 25, 1856
From Alachua County Public Records
Deed Record D pages 295-298

John H. Ellis Guardian of Thomas S. Ellis from John B Stanley for $6,000: "Know all men these presents that I John B. Stanley of the State and County aforesaid am held and firmly bound unto John H. Ellis Guardian of Thomas S. Ellis in the Sum of Six thousand dollars for the payment whereof well and truly to be maid, I bind myself my heirs Executors and administrators firmly by these presance Signed and Sealed this 5th day of February 1857. That if the Said Thomas S. Ellis on his attaining the age of twenty one years Shall ratify Said contract by consenting to Said Sale as transfer of his interest therein then the above bound John B. Stanly is to pay the Said Sum of Three

Thousand Dollars with interest as aforesaid; And if Said Thomas S. Ellis Should fail to ratify his interest as aforesaid then this obligation to be void and of no affect"

February 5, 1857
State of Florida, Alachua County
From Alachua County Ancient Records
Deed Record D pages 420-421

William H. Ellis and wife Lydia Ellis (plaintiffs) vs. Jesse T. Bernard (defendant): "And now on this day to wit the Eleventh day of December A.D. 1856, came the parties by their respective attorneys and issue being Joined, On motion of Defendants attorneys said cause was dismissed for want of prosecution, Whereupon came a Jury who were duly sworn to inquire what damages the defendant had sustained by reason of the detention of said negro Slaves in said writ mentioned from the possession of the said defendant ... who after having heard the testimony of Witnesses without leaving their Seats returned the following verdict,

We the Jury find for the defendant and assess his damages at one Cent and Costs of suit. Whereupon It is ordered Considered and adjudged by the Court that the said defendant do have and recover of and from the said plaintiffs said negro Slaves in said Writ of replevin mentioned to wit **Susan, a woman Jim a Boy, Sam a Boy William a Boy & Mary a girl and Infant born since the commencement of this suit** said defendant having Elected a return of the property; and

It is further ordered by the Court that the Clerk of this Court do issue a writ of restitution for said property forthwith, and that the Sheriff of said County do Execute the same by placing said negro slaves in the possession of said defendant, and

It is further ordered and adjudged by the Court that the said defendant do have and recover of and from the plaintiff the sum of one cent for his damages together with his Cost in this behalf expended, Taxed at Thirty four Dollars and fourteen Cents and the plaintiff in mercy &c"

December 11, 1856
From Alachua County Ancient Records
Judgment Record A pages 446-447

John M. Feaster to daughter Elizabeth M. Reeves: "Know all men by these presents that I John M. Feaster of the State and County afore-said, for and in consideration of the natural love and affection I have and bear to my daughter Elizabeth M. Reeves, wife of Benjamin T. Reeves of the State and County aforesaid have granted, Bargained and sold and do by these presents do give, grant bargain, sell and deliver to the said Elizabeth M. Reeves the following named negro Slaves To wit, **Sarah aged about twenty one Clary aged nineteen Lucy aged thirteen, and Frank aged about two years**. To have and to hold the said negro Slaves **and their future issue and increase**, hereby given, granted, bargained sold, and delivered unto the said Elizabeth M. Reeves, and the heirs of her body forever Now these presents are on the specific trust and confidence that the said negro Slaves aforesaid shall in no wise be liable for the debt and contracts of the said Benja-min T. Reeves nor shall they ever be sold or incumbered neither shall their future issue and increase, nor their labor be sold and incumbered or be in any wise liable for the debt or contract of the same Benjamin T. Reeves. That the said Benjamin T. Reeves shall have the control and management of the negro slaves aforesaid during his natural life, and that after his death they be under the control of such persons as shall, by will, or otherwise appoint. That on the death of the said Elizabeth M. Reeves the negro slaves aforesaid and their future issue and increase shall be divided among the lawful children of the said

Elizabeth M. Reeves or the heirs of their bodies to have and to hold the same unto their heirs and assigns forever"

June 6, 1853
State of Florida, Alachua County
From Alachua County Ancient Records
Deed Record B page 189

Arthur Floyd to Jesse T. Bernard as collateral for $6,000 in loans: "Know all men by these presents that I Arthur Floyd of the Said State & County am held and firmly bound unto Jesse T. Bernard his heirs and assigns in the Sum of Six Thousand Dollars for the payment whereof well and truly to be made I bind myself my heirs executors and administrators firmly by these presents: Signed and Sealed this Second day of December A.D. 1851 The Condition of the above obligation is Such that Whereas the above bound Arthur Floyd has Sold to the Said Jesse T. Bernard the plantation whereon the Said Floyd now resides one and a half miles from the Town of Newnansville County & State aforesaid, and designated by the United States Survey as the South East quarter of Section One and the North half of lot No. Three (3) of Section One of the South East quarter of the North West quarter of Section One in Township Eight South of Range Eighteen East Containing Two hundred & forty and 15/100 acres as per returns made by the U.S. Survey to the Land Office at Newnansville Florida together: with all appurtenances and Hereditaments thereunto belonging Also Three Negro Slaves Viz **One Negro Man named Sampson aged about Twenty Six years, one Negro Man named Charles aged about Twenty Six Years and One Negro Woman named Tenah aged about Twenty Two years** and the Said Jesse T. Bernard has agreed to pay the Said Arthur Floyd the Sum of Three Thousand Two hundred Dollars for the Said Described tract of Land and the Said Slaves above mentioned which amount of money is to be paid in the following manner to wit; Six hundred and fifty Dollars on the first day of January in the Year One Thousand Eight hundred & fifty Two and Two Thousand five hundred and fifty Dollars on the first day of January One thousand Eight hundred & fifty three with interest at the rate of Eight per cent from the first day of January 1852 Now if the Said Arthur Floyd his heirs executors or administrators Shall upon the receipt of the last Mentioned payment Make of Cause to be made to the Said Jesse T. Bernard his heirs or assigns good and Sufficient titles in law to the Said Property hereinbefore Mentioned then this obligation to be null & void, else to remain in full force and virtue and effect"

December 2, 1851
State of Florida, Alachua County
From Alachua County Ancient Records
Deed Record A pages 419-420

Change in trustee for Mariah Floyd, wife of Isaiah Floyd: "Upon the reading of the petition in this cause, and upon it appearing to the satisfaction of assent to act as trustee, and there appearing no reason why the said John B. Standley not be discharged, It is ordered adjudged and decreed that the said John B. Standley be discharged from the said trust upon his delivering up to George L. Brown the negroes named in said petition and that George L. Brown be appointed trustee of the said Mariah Floyd in the place and Stead of the said John B. Standly and with all the powers and restrictions which appertain or belonged to said Standly as such trustee"

December 15, 1855
In Chancery for Alachua County, Eastern Circuit of Florida
From Alachua County Ancient Records
Chancery Order Book A page 109

George Galpin was charged with receiving money from enslaved people: "State of Florida vs Geo Galpin - receiving money from Slaves - A true bill."

December 11, 1851
From Alachua County Ancient Records
Judgment Record A page 069

George M. Galpin found guilty for receiving money from enslaved people: "State of Florida vs George M. Galpin - Receiving Money from Slaves - The defendant in this cause having been returned guilty on yesterday by the Jury sworn and empanneled in this cause, it is considered ordered and adjudged by this Court that the defendant do pay a fine of Twenty five dollars and the costs of this prosecution and the said defendant in mercy &c"

December 11, 1852
From Alachua County Ancient Records
Judgment Record A* page 103

Samuel Geiger to John Jos. Sanchez & William Dell in trust for his wife Caroline Geiger: "This Indenture made this Nineteenth day of January in the Year of One Thousand Eight hundred and fifty-between Samuel Gieger of the first part and John Jos. Sanchez William Dell, Trustees of the second part and Caroline Gieger wife of the Said Samuel

Geiger of the Third part, Witnesseth, That the party of the part for and in consideration of the Sum of one dollar paid by the part of the Second part, and other good and valuable considerations herein of the expressed, Have bargained Sold and conveyed and by these presents do bargain Sell and Convey to the party of the Second part The following negro Slave and other personal property to wit; **A Negro woman named Feribe aged about Twenty Years. A negro Child named Nancy aged about Two years A negro Child named Ellen aged about one year** One Sorrel mare And Colt Ten Cows and Calves Marked Swallow fork and under bit in one ear over Slope in the other and branded S.G. also ten head of sheep and all his house hold and Kitchen furniture now in his possession, to have and to hold the above discribed property to the party of the Second part and to their Executors, administrators and assigns;

In Special Trust and confidence never the less That whereas The party of Third part does (in consideration of the Conveyance to her by the Trustee named on this deed of the property herein discribed and named) By these presents, Assign Set over renounce relinquish and release to the trustees aforesaid all her rights, title interest estate claim and property in and to any right of dower childs part distribution or any other interest which She now has or might hereafter become entitled to in the real or personal Estate of the Said Samuel Geiger Which she now possesses or may hereafter acquire

Now it is understood and agreed by and between the parties to these presents, that the Said John Jos. Sanchez & William Dell trustees, Shall after the Signing & sealing hereof and in pursuance of the Said Trust convey the aforesaid property above named to the Said party of Third part, for her own proper and seperate right, her benefit and control free and discharged of any all interest, and estate of the Said party of the first part and Shall deliver the same to her in her own proper person"

January 19, 1850
State of Florida, Alachua County
From Alachua County Ancient Records
Deed Record A pages 226-227

Samuel Geiger to son Enoch J. Geiger: "This indenture made this Twenty-third of November Eighteen hundred & fifty-seven. Between Samuel Geiger of the County and State aforesaid of the one part and Enoch J. Geiger of the Same place of the other part. Witnesseth for and in consideration of the natural love and affection which he the said Samuel Geiger has and grant to his son Enoch J. Geiger of this County and State aforesaid and for and in consideration of the sum of Ten dollars cash in hand paid by the said Enoch J. Geiger at and before the sealing and delivering of these presents the receipt whereof is hereby acknowledged hath bargained, sold, granted, and conveyed and by these presents, doth bargain, sell, and convey unto the Said Enoch J. Geiger, and his heirs all and singular the rites title and interest of him the Said Samuel Geiger of in and to the following named and described Negroes, Slaves to wit **Edmund a man about Thirty years old and Mary about Six years old** also fifty head cattle, also a boy named Solomon about ten years old. Said property estimated to be worth Fifteen hundred dollars. To have and to hold the above described property unto him the Said Enoch J. Geiger and his heirs **and all the increase of said Negroes** in witness whereof the said Samuel Geiger hath hereunto set his hand and affixed his seal the day and year above written."

November 23, 1857
State of Florida, Alachua County
From Alachua County Ancient Records
Bills of Sale A page 040

Samuel Geiger to son Joseph Samuel Geiger (Abraham E. Geiger trustee): "This Indenture made this Twenty-third day of November A.D. 1857 between Samuel Geiger of the County and State aforesaid of the one part and Joseph Samuel Geiger of the same place of the other part. Witnesseth that for and in consideration of the natural love and affection which he the said Samuel Geiger has and bears to his son Joseph Samuel Geiger of the County and State aforesaid and for and in consideration of the sum of Five dollars cash in hand paid by Abraham E. Geiger at and before the sealing and delivering of these presents the receipt whereof is hereby acknowledged hath bargained sold granted and by these presents doth bargain sell grant and convey unto the said Abraham E. Geiger for the use benefit and advantage in trust for said Joseph Samuel Geiger of in and to the following named Negroes slaves to wit **a boy named George about fourteen years old and a girl named Mary about Eleven years** old also thirty head of cattle **Together with all and Singular their increase and future increase in said slaves and cattle**, estimated to be worth fifteen hundred dollars to have and to hold the above described property unto him the said Abraham E. Geiger in Trust for said Joseph Samuel Geiger for his only benefit and behalf."

November 23, 1857
State of Florida, Alachua County
From Alachua County Public Records
Bills of Sale A pages 049-050

Samuel Geiger to daughter Louisa Jane Edwards (Enoch J. Geiger trustee): "This Indenture made this Twenty-third day of Novr A.D. Eighteen hundred and fifty-seven Between Samuel Geiger of the County and State aforesaid of the one part and Louisa Jane Edwards of Levy County State of Florida of the other part. Witnesseth, that for and in consideration of the natural love and affection which he the said Samuel Geiger has and bears to his daughter Louisa Jane Edwards of the County of Levy State of Florida wife of Simion H. Edwards and for and in consideration of the sum of ten dollars cash in hand paid by Enoch J. Geiger for the benefit advantage in trust for said Louisa Jane Edwards and the children she now has and those she may have by her present or future husband free from the disposuor of her present or future husband all & singular the rites titles and interest of him the said Samuel Geiger of in and to the following named and described Negroes, to wit **a girl named Jane about Ten years old and a boy named Ned about three years old and a girl named Henrietta about ten years old**. Also thirty head of cattle. **Together with all and singular their increase and future issue said slaves and cattle**, being estimated to be worth Fifteen hundred dollars, to have and to hold the above described property to him the said Enoch J. Geiger in trust for said Louisa Jane Edwards, wife of Simion H. Edwards and to her children as aforesaid forever in fee simple, free from the debts and liabilities and contracts of her present or future husband to their only benefit and behoof"

November 23, 1857
State of Florida, Alachua County
From Alachua County Ancient Records
Bills of Sale A page 044

Samuel Geiger to daughter Lousianna Geiger (Enoch J. Geiger trustee): "This Indenture made this the Twenty third day of November A.D. 1857 between Samuel Geiger of the County and State aforesaid of the one part and Lousianna Geiger of the County and State aforesaid of the other Witnesseth that for and in consideration of the natural love and affection which he the said Samuel Geiger has and bears to his daughter Louisianna Geiger of the County and State aforesaid and for and in consideration of the sum of five dollars cash in hand paid by Enoch J. Geiger at and before the sealing and delivering of these presents the receipt whereof is hereby acknowledged hath bargained sold and granted and conveyed and by these presents doth bargain, sell grant and convey unto the said Enoch J. Geiger for the use benefit and advantage in trust for said Louisannah Geiger all and singular the rites titles and interest of him the said Samuel Geiger of in and to the following named negro Slaves to wit **a boy named Elick about seven years old a girl named Sopha about six years old and a girl named Eliza about four months old** also about fifty head of cattle also all my household and kitchen furniture **together with all and singular their increase and future issue in said slaves cattle** being estimated to be worth fifteen hundred dollars to have and to hold the above described property to him the said Enoch J. Geiger in trust for said Louisannah Geiger to her only benefit and behoof "

November 23, 1857
State of Florida, Alachua County
From Alachua County Ancient Records
Bills of Sale A pages 048-049

Samuel Geiger to daughter Margery Ann Tucker (Enoch J. Geiger trustee): "This indenture being made this Twenty-third of Novr A.D. Eighteen hundred fifty seven between Samuel Geiger of the County and State aforesaid of the one part and Margery Ann Tucker of Levy County State of Florida of the other part. Witnesseth, that for and in consideration of the natural love and affection which he the said Samuel Geiger has and bears to his daughter Margery Ann Tucker wife of Elijah Tucker and for and in consideration of the sum of Five dollars cash to me in hand paid by Enoch J. Geiger at and before the sealing and delivering of these presents the receipt whereof is hereby acknowledged hath bargained, sold, granted, and conveyed, and by these presents doth bargain, sell, and grant, and convey unto Enoch J.

Geiger for the benefit advantage in trust for said Margery Ann Tucker and her children she now has and those she may hereafter have, by her present and future husband free from the disposure of her present or a future husband, all and singular the rites titles and interest of him the said Samuel Geiger of in and to the following named Negro Slaves to wit **a woman named Vine about forty years old a girl named Ann about four years old and a boy named Willis about two years old. Together with all and singular their increase and future issue** said Slaves being estimated to be worth Fifteen hundred dollars to have and to hold the above described property unto him the said Enoch J. Geiger in trust for said Margery Ann Tucker, wife of Elijah Tucker and all her children as aforesaid forever in fee simple free from the debts, liabilities and contracts of her present and future husband to thier only benefit and behoof."

November 23, 1857
State of Florida, Alachua County
From Alachua County Ancient Records
Bills of Sale A page 045

Samuel Geiger to daughter Martha Elizabeth Geiger (Enoch J. Geiger trustee): "This Indenture made this twenty third of Novr A.D. Eighteen hundred and fifty-seven between Samuel Geiger of the County and State aforesaid of the one part and Martha Elizabeth Geiger of Nassau County State of Florida of the other part. Witnesseth that for in consideration of the natural love and affection which he the said Samuel Geiger has and bears to his daughter Martha Elizabeth Geiger of Nassau County State of Florida wife of Henry J. Geiger and for and in consideration of the sum of Five dollars cash in hand paid by Enoch J. Geiger at and before the sealing and delivering of these presents the receipt whereof is hereby acknowledged hath bargained sold granted and conveyed and by these presents doth bargain, sell and grant and convey unto the said Enoch J. Geiger for the use benefit advantage in trust for said Martha Elizabeth Geiger and her children that she may have by her present or future husband free from the disposal of her present or future husband all and singular the titles and interest of him the said Samuel Geiger of in and to the following named and described Negro Slaves to wit **a man named Anderson about fifty years old and a girl named Charlotte about fifteen years old and a girl named Ellie about ten years old**. Also Thirty head of cattle. **Together with all and singular their increase and future issue said Slaves and cattle** being estimated to be worth Fifteen hundred dollars to have and to hold the above described property unto him the said Enoch J. Geiger in trust for said Martha Elizabeth Geiger wife of said Henry J. Geiger and all her children as aforesaid forever in fee simple free from the debts and liabilities and contracts of her present or future husband to her only benefit and behoof"

November 23, 1857
State of Florida, Alachua County
From Alachua County Ancient Records
Bills of Sale A page 042

Samuel Geiger to daughter Mary Ann Turner (Abraham E. Geiger trustee): "This Indenture made this twenty third day of Nov A.D. One Eight hundred fifty seven Between Samuel Geiger of the County and State aforesaid of the one part and Mary Ann Turner of the same place of the other party Witnesseth that for and in consideration of the natural love and affection which he the said Samuel Geiger has and bears to his daughter Mary Ann Turner of the County of Alachua State of Florida wife of Johnathan Turner and for and in consideration of the sum of Ten dollars cash in hand paid by Abraham E. Geiger at and before the sealing and delivering of these presents the receipt is hereby acknowledged hath bargained sold granted and conveyed and by these presents doth bargain, sell, and grant and convey unto the said Abraham E. Geiger for the use benefit advantage in trust for said Mary Ann Turner and the children she now has and those she may hereafter have by her present or future husband free from the disposure of her present or future husband all and singular the rights titles and interest of him the said Samuel Geiger of in and to the following named negroes slaves to wit **a man named Charles about thirty eight years old a woman named Mariah about forty years old, and a boy named John about two years old**. Also Thirty head of cattle. **Together with all and singular their increase and future issue,** said slaves and cattle being estimated to be worth Fifteen hundred dollars to have and to hold the above described property unto him the said Abraham E. Geiger trust for said Mary Ann Turner wife of said Johnathan Turner and all her children as aforesaid forever in fee simple free from the debts liabilities and contracts of her present or future husband to their only benefit and behoof."

November 23, 1857
From Alachua County Ancient Records
Bills of Sale A page 043

Samuel Geiger to heirs of deceased daughter Mary Harville (Abraham E. Geiger trustee): "This Indenture being made this Twenty third day of Novr A.D. Eighteen hundred & fifty seven Between Samuel Geiger of the County and State aforesaid of the one part and the Heirs of Mary Harville Deceased of Marion County State of Florida, of the other part. Witnesseth, that for and in consideration of the natural love and affection which the said Samuel Geiger has and bears to the heirs of his deceased daughter Mary Harville of the County of Marion State of Florida, wife of John E. Harville and for and in consideration of the sum of ten dollars in cash paid by Abraham E. Geiger at and before the sealing and delivering of these presents the receipt whereof is hereby acknowledged, hath bargained, sold, granted, and conveyed and by these presents doth bargain, sell, and grant and convey unto the said Abraham E. Geiger for the use benefit, and advantage in trust for said heirs of Mary Harville deceased free from the disposure of her said husband all and singular the rite, title and interest of him the said Samuel Geiger of and to the following named negroes Slaves to wit: **Bill a boy about seven years old and Lucy a girl about four years old and a boy about six years old**. Also Fifty head of cattle. **Together with all and singular their increase and further issue of said Slaves** being estimated to be worth Fifteen hundred dollars to have and to hold the above described property unto him the said Abraham E. Geiger in trust for said heirs of Mary Harville deceased forever in fee simple free from the debts liabilities and contracts of her said husband to their only benefit and behoof"

November 23, 1857
State of Florida, Alachua County
From Alachua County Ancient Records
Bills of Sale A page 046

Samuel Geiger to daughter Sarah Ann Geiger (William E. Sharp trustee): "This Indenture made this Twenty third of Nov A.D. 1857 Eighteen hundred & fifty-seven. Between Samuel Geiger of the County and State aforesaid of the one part, Sarah Ann Geiger of Marion County Florida of the other part. Witnesseth that for and in consideration of the natural love and and affection which he the said Samuel Geiger has and bears to his daughter Sarah A. Geiger of the County of Marion State of Florida, wife of Abraham E. Geiger and for and in consideration of the sum of Five dollars cash in hand paid by William E. Sharp at and before the sealing and delivering of these presents the receipt whereto is hereby acknowledged hath bargained sold granted and conveyed and by these presents doth bargain sell and grant and convey unto the said William E. Sharp for the use benefit and advantage in trust for said Sarah E. Geiger and the child she now has and others she may hereafter have by her present or future husband free from the displeasure of her present or future husband all and Singular the rites titles and interest of him the said Samuel Geiger of in and to the following named negroes slaves to wit **a boy named Elias about Thirteen years old and a girl named Rose about nine years old. Together with all and singular their increase and future issue** said slaves and cattle being estimated to be worth Fifteen hundred dollars. To have and to hold the above described property unto him the said William E. Sharp in trust for said Sarah Ann Geiger wife of said Abraham E. Geiger and all her children as aforesaid forever in fee simple from the debts liabilities and contracts of her present or future husband, to their only benefit and behoof."

November 23, 1857
State of Florida, Alachua County
From Alachua County Ancient Records
Bills of Sale A page 041

Washington W. Geiger Last Will and Testament: "In the name of God, Amen; I Washington W. Geiger of Alachua County and State of Florida, being of sound mind do make and declare this instrument my last Will and Testament.

In the first place, I desire to be plainly buried and with Masonic ceremonies if the same be convenient I desire my Executors to pay all my just debts-this they are to do out of any money that may be on hand at my decease, also out of the crop and likewise out of the debts due to me.

Having two places at this time I desire my Executors to sell one of them, either the one where I now live, or the one at the Levy or OkaWilla

Prarie in Putnam County of their own discretion, and to apply the money acuring therefore to the payment of my debts to the purchase of slaves or to invest-it in any way they be happy for the best interest of My Estate I desire that my executors keep together the remainer of all my estate, namely one of My places **My Negroes**, Stock of all kind, and every thing else, and that they have the same properly worked from year to year, under a first rate overseer, until My youngest child becomes of age, unless they first is to be a very unprofitable or impractable business, and in that event, they will dispose of my estate according to their best judgment, for the best interest of my children, either by dividing the same among them or selling it for distribution.

I desire that my Executors educate clothe and support my children out of the proceeds of Farm, this worked from year to year.

I desire that my Executor also pay out of the proceeds of the Farm, the annuity to be hereafter mentioned for the support of my beloved wife Sarah E. Geiger - This annuity or support of my Wife Sarah E. Geiger is thus to be provided for so long as my Estate shall be kept Together.

It is my desire that at any of my children getting married or becoming of age, that my Executors give them only a reasonable amount of the property if it can be spared from the support and education of the remaining children-as one or two negroes a horse a few cows and a little money to begin housekeeping with - but said child to share alike and the same to be accounted for according to its value when given at the final distribution of my Estate.

My beloved wife Sarah E. Geiger having expressed a desire to relinquish all claim for Dower on My Estate with a sum of obtaining an annuity in lieu thereof and feeling desirous to afford her every satisfaction I do hereby give and bequeath unto my said Dear Wife Sarah E. Geiger the sum of three hundred dollars ($300.00) per annum during her natural life, for her comfortable support, so long as she lives But if after my decease my said Dear Wife Sarah E. Geiger or any person or persons on her account Should prefer a claim for Dower on my estate, then and in that case, the bequest is null and void and the payment of the annuity shall cease.

I desire that on My youngest child becoming of age all my estate be equally divided among all my children, share and share alike, except what May be reasonable to provide for the annuity on support of my wife - Sarah E. Geiger should She be then living My executors can either divide the estate - or sell it - as they deem best for a more equal and just distribution among my children.

Should my beloved wife Sarah E. Geiger be living at the time My Youngest child become of age or whenever My estate be divided, My Executors will reserve out of the estate previous to the division a part or property sufficient to pay her said annuity - so long as she lives, and on her demise said fund or property will be equally divided among my children, Share and share alike.

It is my desire that should any of My negroes become unmanageable or very wicked that my Executors sell such negroes and purchase better ones in their stead.

It is my desire that my library of Books be equally divided between My sons

And it is My earnest desire that my executors educate my children in the best manner possible according to the means of my Estate - And I pray them all to use their influence to have the best of principals instilled unto them."

June 27, 1855
From Alachua County Ancient Records
Will Book A pages 073-077

Allen Gibson to daughter Mary A. Ellis: "This Indenture made and entered into this 29th day of August in the year AD 1857 Witnesseth I Allen Gibson of Marion County in the state aforesaid for and in consideration of the natural love and affection which I bear for my well beloved daughter Mary A. Ellis of Alachua County I have this day given unto her and the heirs of her body the following property to wit the **negro Woman named Eliza, aged twenty-two years and her child John aged six months also a negro girl named Martha aged ten years** to have and to hold the above described property to her and their only proper use benefit and behoof for and during her natural life and then to her heirs if any she may have but in default of such heirs for doth the said property or **the increase** is to revert to me as fully as if it had never been given to my said daughter and to become a part of my estate as it was previous to the execution of this instrument of writing"

August 29, 1857
State of Florida
From Alachua County Ancient Records
Bills of Sale A page 047

Henry Gradock to wife Mary M. Gradock: "Know all men by these presents that for and in consideration of the natural love and affection which I Henry Gradock have and bear for my wife Mary M. Gradock as well as for the purposes making a suitable provision for the support and maintenance of my said wife have given granted, bargained sold and conveyed & by these presents do so give bargain sell and convey unto my said wife her heirs and assigns the following mentioned and described property, Viz, Nine hundred and Twenty two acres of land more or less situate in Alachua County and State aforesaid & known and described as follows, To wit That parcel of land lying in section twenty five in Township ten of range twenty one commencing two chains East of the Half mile Stake and running north to the northern boundary line, all that land in said section lying west of said line & containing Three hundred and thirty five acres being the land hereby conveyed, Also Section Thirty six of Township Ten of Range Twenty one containing Six hundred and thirty seven & Sixty eight hundredths of an acre, Also the following Negro Slaves, to wit, **Briller about thirty five years old, Mary about twenty eight, Ed about twenty five, Daniel about twenty, Sophy about twenty one Shack about twenty five, Jeff about eighteen Ann about ten, Harriat about nine, George about three, Wilson about one year old, and Charles an infant born in January last**. Also four horses & two mules, one wagon & one buggy together with all and singular my household & kitchen furniture, and all and singular the plantation & farming utensils together with five hundred bushels of corn & about ten thousand pounds of hay & fodder and all the cotton on the plantation whether picked or unpicked. Also ten head of cattle branded H.G. and marked with a smooth crop and two splits in the right ears, Also fifty hogs of the same mark, Also the Gin head on said plantation and each & every article of value on said plantation of which I am lawfully possessed, To have and to hold all and singular the property above mentioned & described unto my said wife her heirs & assigns forever in fee simple together with the buildings out buildings improvements, & appurtenances to the said plantation belonging or in any way appertaining **and the issue & future increase of the female portion of the slaves above named and described** & also the increase of the cattle hogs &c above described. The said property herein conveyed to my said wife I hereby give to her absolutely & in fee simple forever with full power for her to dispose of it in such manner & at such time as she shall think fit & expedient, Nor shall any of the property herein conveyed be responsible for any future debts which I may contract without the will & consent of my said wife, Nor shall the issue & increase of said property, the rent proffits produce & gain thereof be subject for my debts hereafter contracted."

November 19, 1855
State of Florida, Alachua County
From Alachua County Ancient Records
Deed Record D pages 196-197

Edgwin S. Gunnell indicted for assault and battery. Enslaved people were used as a part of collateral to ensure he showed up for Court: "State of Florida vs Edgwin S. Gunnell - Assault & Battery - Continued to next term of the Court and the Defendant recognized in the Sum of four hundred dollars for his appearance at the next term of the Court, two hundred dollars for the principle and one hundred for each of the Securities

Edgwin S. Gunnell, Samuel W. Burnett and Lewelling Williams appeared in open court and acknowledged themselves to owe and Stand indebted to the State of Florida in the Sum of four hundred dollars, that is to Say, Edgwin S. Gunnell in the Sum of two hundred dollars, Samuel W. Burnett in the Sum of one hundred dollars, and Lewelling Williams in the Sum of one hundred dollars to be levied of their respective goods and chattles, Slaves, lands and tenements, if default be made in the following condition, that is to Say, if the Said Edgwin S. Gunnell Shall and appear at the next term of this court to answer an indictment for assault and Battery, and not depart to the Same without the leave thereof, then this obligation to be null and void otherwise to remain in full force and virtue."

December 14, 1854
From Alachua County Ancient Records
Judgment Record A* page 214

Gideon J. Hagood's 1/7 portion of the Estate of Levi Hickson deceased: "Know all men, That I Gideon J. Hagood of Marion County Florida a lawful heir of the Estate of Levi Hickson deceased the fifth of February One thousand Eight hundred and fifty Seven, in Consideration of the facts that Susan Hickson surviving widow of the said Levi Hickson deceased released her dower and total interest in the estate of the Said Levi Hickson deceased except the boy **Adam** reserved for her use during her life time and then reverts back to the heirs of the said Estate and upon the further Consideration of receiving one Seventh of the Estate of the said Levi Hickson and also the Negroes **Sandy, Mary, Jane, Benjamin, July, and Albert** as his Seventh of the Negroes of said Estate to have and to hold all and Singular the said property unto the said Gideon J. Hagood am firmly bound unto the said Susan Hickson Surviving widow of the said Levi Hickson deceased to pay annually during her life time the said Susan Hickson the full and Just sum of two hundred fifty dollars or her Certain attorney to which payment well and truly to be made and done, I bind myself and each and every of my heirs, Executors and administrators Jointly & Severally by these presents

Provided Nevertheless that the said Susan Hickson reserve and retain to herself a lien upon the said Negroes Sandy, Mary, Jane, Benjamin July, and Albert Junr. above enumerated as Security for the Annual payment of the said Sum of two hundred & fifty dollars then this Conveyance Shall be void, otherwise to remain in full force and effect

And provided also, that untill default by the said Gideon J. Hagood in the performance of the said Condition aforesaid, it may may be lawful for him to Keep and retain possession of said property, and to use and enjoy the same but if the same or any part thereof Shall be attatched at any time before payment &c by any other Creditor or Creditors of the said Gideon J. Hagood then it Shall be lawful for the said Susan Hickson to take immediate possession of the whole of said above named negroes or so much thereof as will be sufficient to pay the said sum during her lifetime to her own use and disposal"

January 1, 1858
State of Florida, Alachua County
From Alachua County Ancient Records
Deed Record C pages 332-333

Archelaus Hague indicted for assault with intent to kill; enslaved people were used as a part of collateral to ensure he showed up for Court: "State of Florida vs Archelaus Hague - Assault with intent to Kill - Continued to the next term of the Court and the Defendant recognized in the Sum of twelve hundred and fifty dollars for his appearance at the next term of the Court, five hundred for the principle, and two hundred and fifty for each of the Securities

Archelaus Hague, Thomas J. Prevatt, Stephen Fagan and Lemuel Wilson, appeared in open court, and acknowledged themselves to owe and Stand indebted to the State of Florida in the Sum of twelve hundred and fifty dollars, that is to say Archelaus Hague in the Sum of five hundred dollars, Thomas J. Prevatt in the Sum of two hundred and fifty dollars, Stephen Fagan in the Sum of two hundred and fifty dollars, to be levied of their respective goods and chattels Slaves, lands and tenements if default be made in the following condition, that is to Say if the Said Archelaus Hague Shall be and appear at the next term of this court to answer to an indictment for an assault with intent to kill, and Shall not thence depart the court without the leave thereof then this obligation to be null and void otherwise to remain in full force and virtue."

December 14, 1854
From Alachua County Ancient Records
Judgment Record A* page 213

James Hague to Hannah Eugenia Galpin for $800: "This Indenture made this fifteenth day of January eighteen hundred and fifty five, Between James Hague of Alachua County Florida, party of the

first part, and Hannah Eugenia Galpin of Duval County County Florida wife of George M. Galpin Witnesseth that Said party of the first part, in consideration of the Sum of eight hundred dollars, to him in hand paid by the said party of the Second part, the receipt whereof is hereby acknowledged, hath bargained and sold, and by these presents doth bargain and sell unto the said Hannah Eugenia, to her Sole and only use, and behoof for ever, her heirs and assigns, quite free and separate from all control, liability, and indebtedness of her said Husband, that certain **Negro woman Phillis of black complection and about forty five years of age, Slave for life** To have and to hold the Said woman Slave Phillis **her issue and increase** to the Said Hannah Eugenia Galpin her sole and only use as aforesaid, and to her heirs and assigns for ever, and said Slave Shall not be liable for the debts of her Said Husband, which may have been heretofore, or shall be hereafter contracted, and the Said grantor hereby warrants and covenants, that he has full right and title to the Said woman Slave, and to make absolute sale and delivery thereof"

January 15, 1855
From Alachua County Ancient Records
Deed Record D page 032

James Hague to Joseph Warren to pay back the $10,000 James owes him: "Know all men by these presents that I James Hague of the County and State aforesaid for and in Consideration of the sum of ten thousand dollars that I am Justly indebted in to Joseph Warren for work and labour done at my instance and request during the period of the last two years past, and in the further consideration of the sum of two hundred dollars to me in hand paid at and before the Sealing and delivery of these presents, by the said Joseph Warren of the same place the receipt whereof is hereby acknowledged, have bargained and sold, and by these presents do grant and Convey unto the said Joseph

Warren the following described personal property to wit **Penna a negro slave aged about twenty years and her two children Mary and Julia and Benjamin or Ben about twelve or fourteen years of age**, belonging to me free of all incumbrances title absolute. To have and to hold the above described negro property unto the said Joseph Warren his Executors administrators and assigns forever."

January 5, 1859
State of Florida, Alachua County
From Alachua County Ancient Records
Bills of Sale A pages 058-059

James Hague to Joseph J. Warren for $3,000: "Know all men that I James Hague of the County & State aforesaid for & in consideration of the sum of Three thousand Dollars, to me in hand paid by Joseph J. Warren, of the same County and State the receipt whereof is hereby acknowledged, do bargain, sell, transfer, assign and deliver unto the said Joseph J. Warren the following personal property to wit,

First all the crop of cotton, corn & potatoes, now growing on the farm where I am now living

Second all of the horses and mules on said farm, consisting of one mare & Colt, two horses and one Mule

Third all the Stock of Hogs, at present owned by me, and having my mark which said mark is a crop & half Crop in one ear and in the other ear a Crop & half crop & Split

Fourth, all of the Cattle now owned by me, and having my mark & brand, which said mark is the Same as that on the hogs and the brand this JH3.

Fifth all the forage and provisions of whatever nature on said farm

Sixth, all the Carts, Waggons, ploughs, and all other farming or planta-tion implements on the Said farm

Seventh, the following **Negroes Slaves, for life Called & Known as follows: Adam aged about Fifty five years Dorcas aged about Forty five years of age, Windzor aged about Thirty five years of age and Martha aged about Seven years** together with all my right, title, interest, Claim or demand of, in and to the said described and aforementioned property above bargained and Sold or intened So to be, to the Said Joseph J. Warren his Executors, administrators and assigns forever"

April 27, 1859
State of Florida, County of Alachua
From Alachua County Ancient Records
Deed Record E
Pages 079-080

Edward Haile to Catherine A. Sadler widow of Henry N. Sadler as collateral for $4,500 in loans: "This Indenture made this twenty third day of September in the year of our Lord one thousand eight hundred and fifty four Between Edward Haile of the State of South Carolina, party of the first part, and Catherine A. Sadler widow of Henry N. Sadler, late of said County Deceased party of the Second part Witnesseth, whereas the said Edward Haile party of the first part, in and by his certain three promissory notes in writing, bearing even date with these presents, has promised to pay to the said Catherine A. Sadler or four thousand five hundred Dollars for value received […] with interest upon the said Several Sums of money at the rate of Six per cent per annum from the first day of January in the year of our

Lord one thousand eight hundred and fifty four, as in and by said promissory notes relation thereunto being had will fully appear

Now this Indenture Witnesseth that the said Edward Haile party of the first part as well for and in consideration of the aforesaid debt or Sum of four thousand five hundred dollars, and for the better securing the payment thereof with the interest thereupon as aforesaid unto the said Catherine A. Sadler her heirs Executors, Administrators, and assigns, in discharge of the said recite promissory notes as of the further Sum of one dollar to her in hand paid by the Said Edward Haile at and before the Sealing and delivery hereof, (the receipt whereof is hereby acknowledged), hath Granted, bargained, Sold, released, aliened, remised transfered conveyed and confirmed, and by these presents doth grant, bargain, Sell, release alien, remise, transfer, convey, and confirm unto the said Catherine A. Sadler her heirs, Executors, administrators and assigns, all that certain tract or parcel of land lying and being in the County of Alachua, in the Said State of Florida upon and adjacent to Paynes Prairie, and known as Rocky Point or the McIntosh tract containing about fifteen hundred acres originally granted to George I. F. Clark being part of a grant of twenty Six thousand acres made to the said George I. F. Clark in the year Anno Domini eighteen hundred and Seventeen, which Said tract of land was conveyed by the Said George I.F. Clark to one Belton A. Copp in the year Anno Domini eighteen hundred and twenty three, and Subsequently conveyed by the Said Belton A. Copp to John H. McIntosh Senior Deceased, being within the Arredondo Grant, and bound on the North by land around at the date of this Indenture, or recently by the Estate of Duncan L. Clinch and John Y. Garay, on the East by Section twenty nine, on the South by Section thirty one, in the Arredondo Grant owned by B.A. Putnam and also by Section thirty six in the Said last mentioned Grant, owners name unknown and in the west by Land at the date of this indenture or recently owned by George I.F. Clark, the Said tract or parcel of land lying and being in Township Ten, South of Range nineteen, and twenty, together with all and Singular the buildings, improvements, ways, woods, waters water courses, rights liberties, privileges, hereditaments and appurtenances whatsoever hereunto belonging, or in any wise appertaining, and the remainder and remainders, reversion and reversions, rents, issues, and profits thereof, and also the following named Negro Slaves, to wit: **Jess, Martin, Ishmael, Glasgow, Jack, Stephen, John, Mose, Levy (Little Joe), Sarah, Bitsey, Patsey, Cherry, Abby, Nancy, Edward, William, July and Everett and the issue and increase of the said female Slaves**. To have and to hold the said tract or parcel of land hereinbefore mentioned and described, with tenements hereditaments and appurtenances, aforesaid, together with the negro Slaves aforesaid, and the issue and increase of the said female Slaves unto her the said Catherine A. Sadler her heirs, Executors, Administrators and assigns, to her and their only proper use, benefit and behoof for ever provided always nevertheless that if the said Edward Haile his heirs Executors, Administrators or assigns, Shall and do well and truly pay or cause or procure to be paid unto the said Catherine A. Sadler her heirs, Executors, administrators or assigns, the aforesaid sum of four thousand five hundred dollars on the days and times hereinbefore mentioned and appointed for payment thereof, with interest thereupon as hereinbefore specified without fraud or delay, and without any defalcation in the payment of the said promissory notes, as they become severally due and payable, then and from thenceforth this present Indenture, and the estate hereby granted, as also the said recited obligation, shall cause determine and become absolutely null and void to all intents and purposes, any thing herein before contained to the contrary in any wise notwithstanding."

September 23, 1854
State of Florida, Duval County
From Alachua County Ancient Records
Deed Record B pages 442-444

Edward Haile to Jacob Waldburg and Benj A. Putnam Administrators of the will of John H. McIntosh Junior as collateral for a

$4,500 loan: "This Indenture made this twenty third day of September in the year of our Lord one thousand eight hundred and fifty four. Between Haile of the State of South Carolina party of the first part, and Jacob Waldburg and Benj A. Putnam Administrators with the will annexed of all and Singular the lands, and tenements, goods and chattles, rights credits and effects that were of John H. McIntosh Junior late of said County Deceased, parties of the Second part

Witnesseth, Whereas the said Edward Haile party of the first part, in and by his three certain promissory notes bearing even date with these presents, has promised to pay to the said parties of the second part, administrators as aforesaid, or to their order, four thousand five hundred Dollars […] at the rate of Six per cent per annum from the first day of January in the year of our Lord one thousand eight hundred and fifty four, as in and by said promissory notes relation thereunto being had will fully appear,

Now this Indenture Witnesseth that the said Edward Haile party of the first part, as well for and in consideration of the aforesaid debt or Sum of four thousand five hundred dollars, and for the better Securing the payment thereof, with the interest thereupon as aforesaid, unto the Said parties of the Second part, their Executors, Administrators, and assigns, in discharge of the Said promissory notes as of the further Sum of one dollar to him in hand paid at and before the Sealing and delivery of these presents, by the Said parties of the Second part, (the receipt whereof is hereby acknowledged, hath granted, bargained, Sold, aliened remised, released, transfered, assigned, conveyed and confirmed, and by these presents doth grant, bargain, Sell, alien, remise, release, transfer, assign, convey, and confirm unto the Said parties of the Second part, their Executors, Administrators and assigns, all that certain tract or parcel of land lying and being in the County of Alachua in the Said State of Florida, upon and adjacent to Paynes Prairie, and known as Rocky Point, or the McIntosh Tract, containing about fifteen hundred acres originally granted to George I. F. Clark being part of a grant of twenty Six thousand acres made to the Said George I. F. Clark in the year Anno Domini eighteen hundred and Seventeen, which Said tract of land was conveyed by the Said George I.F. Clark to one Belton A. Copp, and subsequently conveyed by the Said Belton A. Copp to John H. McIntosh Senior deceased, being within the Arredondo Grant, and bounded on the North by land owned at the date of this Indenture, or recently by the Estates of Duncan L. Clinch and John Y. Gary, on the East by Section twenty nine, on the South by Section thirty one, in the Said Arredondo Grant owned by B.A. Putnam, and also by Section thirty Six in the Said last mentioned grant owners name unknown, and on the west by land at the date of of this Indenture, or recently owned by George I.F. Clark, the said tract or parcel of land lying and being in Township ten South of Range nineteen and twenty, together with all and Singular the buildings, improvements, ways, woods, waters, water courses, rights, liberties, privileges, hereditaments and appurtenances whatsoever thereunto belonging, or in any wise appertaining, and the remainder and remainders, reversion and reversions, rents, issues, and profits thereof and also the following named Negro Slaves, to wit, **Jess, Martin, Ishmael, Glasgow, Jack, Stephen, John, Mose, Levy, Little Joe, Sarah, Betsey, Patsey, Cherry, Abby, Nancy, Edward, William, July, and Everett, and the issue and increase of the Said female Slaves,** to have and to hold the Said tract or parcel of land hereinbefore mentioned and described, with the tenements, hereditaments, and appurtenances aforesaid together with the Negro Slaves aforesaid, and the issue and increase of the Said female Slaves, unto them the said parties of the second part, their and each of their Executors, administrators, and assigns, to them and their only proper use, benefit and behoof for ever, provided always nevertheless, that if the Edward Haile, his heirs, Executors, Administrators or assigns, Shall and do well and truly, pay or cause, or procure to be paid unto the Said parties of the Second part, their Executors, Administrators, or assigns, the aforesaid Sum of four thousand five hundred dollars on the days and times hereinbefore mentioned and appointed for payment thereof, with interest thereupon as hereinbefore Specified, without fraud or delay, and without any defalcation in the payment of the said promissory notes as they become Severally due and payable, there and from thenceforth this present Indenture, and the estate hereby granted, as also the Said recited obligations Shall cease, determine, and become absolutely null and void to all intents and purposes, anything hereinbefore contained to the contrary in any wise not withstanding."

September 23, 1854
State of Florida, Duval County
From Alachua County Ancient Records
Deed Record B pages 444-446

Thomas E. Haile to Edward Haile Guardian of Janet Matheson and Catherine Matheson minors as collateral for an $8,672.30 loan: "This Indenture made the twenty fourth day of March in the year of our Lord one thousand eight hundred and fifty four, Between Thomas E. Haile of the County and State aforesaid, and Edward Haile of South Carolina, Guardian of Janet Matheson and Catherine Matheson Minors.

Witnesseth, whereas the said Thomas E. Haile in and by a certain obligation or writing obligatory under his name and seal having even date herewith, Stands bound unto the said Edward Hale Guardian as aforesaid, in the sum of Eight thousand Six hundred and seventy two dollars, thirty cents (8672 30/100) conditioned for the payment of four thousand three hundred and thirty six dollars and fifteen cents, on the first day of January in the year of our Lord one thousand eight hundred and fifty five, with interest upon the said last sum of money at the rate of seven per cent per annum, as in and by the said recited obligation and condition thereof relation being thereunto had more fully and at large appears.

Now this Indenture Witnesseth, that the said Thomas E. Haile, as well for and in consideration of the aforesaid debt or sum of four thousand three hundred and thirty six dollars and fifteen cents, and for the better securing the payment thereof, with its interest unto the said Edward Haile Guardian as aforesaid, his Executors, Administrators and assigns, in discharge of the said recited obligation, as of the further sum of one dollar to him in hand paid by the said Edward Haile Guardian as aforesaid, at and before the sealing and delivery thereof the receipt whereof is hereby acknowledged, hath bargained, sold, released, conveyed and confirmed, and by these presents doth bargain, sell, release, convey and confirm unto the said Edward Haile Guardian as aforesaid, his heirs, Executors, Administrators and assigns, all and every the Negro Slaves herein after named, to wit **Ephraim Hetty, Haily, Fortune, Rainy, Ephraim Jr, Ned, Aggy, Allen, Nanny, Gus, Amos, Tom, Morris, Old Buck, Sarah Kitty, Emma, Abraham, and Hannah, together with the future issue of said female Slaves**. To have and to hold the said Negro Slaves and every of them, and the future issue of the said female Slaves, unto him the said Edward Haile Guardian as aforesaid, his Executors, Administrators and assigns, to his and their only proper use benefit and behalf forever,

provided always nevertheless, that if the said Thomas E. Haile his heirs, Executors, Administrators or assigns, Shall and do well and truly pay or cause or procure to be paid to the said Edward Haile, Guardian as aforesaid, his Executors, Administrators or assigns, the aforesaid debt, or sum of four thousand three hundred and thirty six dollars and fifteen cents, on the day and time herein before mentioned, and appointed for payment thereof, with the interest there upon, at the rate aforesaid according to the condition of the said recited obligation without any fraud or further duly then and from thenceforth as well this present indenture and the interest and Estate hereby conveyed, as the said recited obligation shall cease, determine, and become absolutely null and void to all intents and purposes any thing herein before contained to the contrary in any wise notwithstanding"

March 24, 1854
State of Florida, Alachua County
From Alachua County Ancient Records
Deed Record B pages 337-338

Thomas E. Haile to Edward Haile as collateral for a $4,237.17 loan: "This Indenture made this thirtieth day of March in the year of our Lord one thousand eight hundred and fifty four Between Thomas E. Haile of the County and State aforesaid, and Edward Haile of the State of South Carolina, Witnesseth note bearing date the eighteenth day of March in the year of our Lord one thousand eight hundred and fifty four, hath promised to pay Messrs I. and J.D. Kirkpatrick or order the sum of four thousand two hundred and thirty seven 17/100 dollars for value received, and which said promissory note has at the request and for the only accomodation of the said Thomas E. Haile been endorsed by the said Edward Haile being desirous to save, keep harmless and indemnified the said Edward Haile of and from all responsibility as endorser as aforesaid, Now this Indenture Witnesseth that the said Thomas E. Haile as well for and in consideration of securing the said Edward Haile from the payment of the note aforesaid as the sum of one dollar to him in hand paid by the said Edward Haile, at and before the sealing and delivery of these presents & the receipt whereof is hereby acknowledged, hath bargained, sold, released, conveyed and confirmed, and by these presents doth bargain, sell, release, convey and confirm unto the said Edward Haile his heirs, Executors, Administrators, and assigns, and all and every the Negro Slaves herein after named, to wit, **Ephraim, Hetty, Haily, Fortune, Rainy, Ephraim Jr, Ned, Aggy, Allen, Nancy, Guss, Amos, Tom, Morris, Old Buck, Sarah Kitty, Emma, Abraham, and Hannah, together with the future issue of the said female Slaves, to have and to hold the said Negro Slaves aforesaid, with the issue of the said female Slaves** to him the said Edward Haile his heirs, Executors, Administrators and assigns, to his and their only proper use benefit and behoof forever, provided always nevertheless that if the said Thomas E. Haile, his heirs, Executors or Administrators shall and do well and truly pay, or cause or procure to be paid unto the said Messrs I. and J.D. Kirkpatrick the aforesaid promissory note for four thousand two hundred and thirty seven 17/100 dollars, with the interest thereupon on the day and time herein before mentioned and appointed for payment thereof, or by other lawful means, save keep harmless, and indemnified the said Edward Haile, his heirs, Executors, and Administrators from the payment of the said note, and all costs damages or charges as endorser as aforesaid, then and from thenceforth, as well this payment Indenture, and the interest and Estate hereby granted as the said recited obligation, Shall cease, determine and become absolutely null and void, any thing herein contained to the contrary notwithstanding"

March 30, 1854
State of Florida, Alachua County
From Alachua County Ancient Records
Deed Record B
Pages 338-339

William Harn to daughter Mary C. Dell: "Know all men by these presents that I, William Harn of Hillsborough, State of Florida, for and in consideration of the natural love and affection which I bear unto my daughter Mary C., Spouse of Doctor James G. Dell of Alachua County aforesaid, and also for divers other good causes and considerations we thereunto moving, have given, granted and conferred, and by these presents doth give, grant and conferin unto the said Mary C. Dell all and singular the following negro slaves that is to say: **Elsy aged about thirty five years, Ceasar aged about thirty six years, Grace aged about eighteen years, Elsy aged about six years, Alice aged about three years, and Ceasar aged about two years**: To have and to hold the above mentioned and described negro slaves, unto the said Mary C. Dell, the heirs of her body and her assigns forever, and to her and their only proper use and behoof. And I the said William Harn the above mentioned and described negro slaves unto the said Mary C. Dell and her heirs and assignees as aforesaid against me my executors and administrators and all and every person and persons whatsoever shall and will warrant and defend forever by these presents"

December 12, 1850
State of Florida, Alachua County
From Alachua County Ancient Records
Deed Record A pages 282-283

Daniel C. Hart to Ingram & Babcock as collateral for a $447.70 loan: "Whereas I Daniel C. Hart of the State of Florida and County of Alachua am indebted to Ingram & Babcock of the county of Alachua and State of Florida in the full and just sum of four hundred & forty Seven 70/100 Dollars for which amt I have given my promisory note bearing date February 5th 1859 one thousand Eight hundred & fifty nine payable on the first day of January 1860 with Interest from date at the rate of Eight per cents Now Know all men by these presents that for and in Consideration of Said indebtedness and for the better Securing the payment of the Same to the said Ingram & Babcock their heirs Executors administrators and assigns I the said Daniel C. Hart have given granted bargained Sold Aliened remised released Conveyed and Confirmed and by these presents do give grant bargain, Sell, alien, remise give grant release, Convey and Confirm unto the Said Ingram & Babcock the following **negro Slave John about two years old** To have and to hold the above described negro Slave with all and Singular the rights, ways hereditaments unto issues profits reversion and reversions remainder and remainders whatsoever to the same belonging or in anywise appertaining to have and to hold unto the said Ingram & Babcock their heirs Executors, administrators and assigns forever, Provided nevertheless it is the true meaning and intent of these presents that if the Said Danl C. Hart shall and does well and truly pay or cause to be paid unto the said Ingram & Babcock there heirs Executors and assigns the said debt or Sum of Money aforesaid with interest thereon according to the true intent and meaning of Said rates then this deed of bargain and sale Shall Cease determine and become utterly null and void otherwise it Shall remain in full force and virtue"

February 5, 1859
State of Florida, Alachua County
From Alachua County Ancient Records
Mortgage Record A pages 161-162

Isaiah D. Hart, trustee for Maryann Hart, wife of William B. Hart appoints William B. Hart as attorney and trustee: "Know all men by these presents that I Isaiah D. Hart of the town of Jacksonville Duval County and State of Florida and trustee for Maryann Hart, wife of William B. Hart of Alachua County and State aforesaid - Have this day nominated constituted and appointed and by these present do nominate constitute and appoint William B. Hart of Alachua County aforesaid my true and lawful attorney for me and in my name as trustee as aforesaid to bargain sell transfer and convey **any and all of negroes named in the deed of trust;** The same to be sold with the concent and approbation of the said Mary Ann Hart and the proceeds to be applied to her use and benefit and in such manner as she may direct. Hereby ratifying and confirming all and whatsoever my said attorney shall carefully do or cause to be done in and about the premises aforesaid as fully as I might or could do if I were personally present."

March 19, 1850
From Alachua County Ancient Records
Deed Record A page 250

Mathew B. Hawkins indicted for assault with intent to kill; enslaved people used as a part of collateral to ensure he showed up for Court: "State of Florida vs Mathew B. Hawkins - Assault with intent to Kill - Continued to the next term of the Court and the defendant recognized in the Sum of five hundred dollars for his appearance at the next term of the Court, five hundred dollars for the principle two hundred and fifty dollars for each one of the Securities, Mathew B. Hawkins Giles U. Ellis and Philip Dell appeared in open Court and acknowledged themselves to owe and Stand indebted to the State of Florida in the Sum of five hundred dollars, that is to say Mathew B. Hawkins in the Sum of five Hundred dollars, Giles U. Ellis in the Sum of two Hundred and fifty dollars and Philip Dell in the Sum of two hundred and fifty dollars to be levied of their goods and chattles Slaves lands and tenements if default be made in the following condition, that is to say if the Said Mathew B. Hawkins Shall be and appear at the next term of the Court to answer an indictment against him for an assault with intent to kill, and not depart the Same without the leave thereof, then this obligation to be null and void, otherwise to remain in full force and virtue"

May 17, 1855
From Alachua County Ancient Records
Judgment Record A* page 239

James M. Hawthorn, Anderson Philpot, & Samuel Swindle were indicted for riots. Enslaved people were used as a part of collateral to ensure that they showed up for Court: "State of Florida vs James M. Hawthorn, Anderson Philpot, & Samuel Swindle - Riots: Continued to the next term of the Court and the defendant recognized in the sum of five hundred dollars for his appearance at the next term of the Court two hundred & fifty dollars for the principle and one hundred & twenty five for each Security James M. Hawthorn,

Anderson Philpot, Samuel Swindle Robert Hines & Jefferson Baisden, appeared in open Court and acknowledged themselves to stand
indebted to the State of Florida in the sum of five hundred dollars
that is to say James M. Hawthorn, Anderson Philpot, Samuel Swindle
in the sum of two hundred & fifty dollars Robert R. Hines & Jefferson
Baisden the sum of One hundred & twenty five dollars each to be
levied of their respective goods & chattels, Slaves, lands & tenements
if default be made in the following Condition, that is to say if the said
James M. Hawthorn Samuel Swindle, Anderson Philpot Shall well and
truly be and appear at the next term of this Court to answer to an
indictment for Riot and Shall not thence depart the Court without lien
thereof then this obligation to be null and void other wise to remain
in full force and virtue"

May 13, 1858
From Alachua County Ancient Records
Judgment Record B page 052

**Prisoners Donald Hemingway, Jacin Hemingway, Edwin Hem-
ingway, and Levena Hemingway indicted for trading with
enslaved people:** "State of Florida vs Donald Hemingway, Jacin
Hemingway, Edwin Hemingway, and Levena Hemingway - Trading with Slaves - On this day came the Solicitor J. B. Dawkins who
Prosecutes the Pleas of the State in this behalf as well as also as the
Prisoners in Person who having entered a Pleas of not guilty thereupon came a Jury [...] Who having being duly Sworn well and truly
to try and true deliverance make between the State of Florida and the
Prisoners at the Bar after having heard the testimony of Witnesses the
arguments of Council and the charge of the Court Retired in charge
of a Bailiff to consider of their verdict and afterwards to wit on the
same day returned into Court and rendered the following verdict We
the Jury find the defendant Jacin Hemingway guilty and assessed the

fine of five dollars and imprisonment One *** We the Jury find the defendants Donald Hemingway Edward Hemingway and Levena Hemingway not guilty thereupon it is therefore ordered considered and adjudged by the Court that the said Jacin Hemingway do Pay a fine of five dollars"

December 15, 1858
From Alachua County Ancient Records
Judgment Record B page 081

E. A. Hickson receives 1/7 share of the estate of Levi Hickson:

"Know all men, That I E. A. Hickson of Micanopy Florida a lawful heir of the Estate of Levi Hickson deceased the fifth of February One thousand Eight hundred & fifty Seven in Consideration of the facts that Susan Hickson Surviving widow of the said Levi Hickson deceased released her dower and total interest in the estate of the said Levi Hickson deceased except the boy **Adam** reserved for her use during her life time and then reverts back to the heirs of the said Estate and upon the further Consideration of receiving one Seventh of the Estate of the said Levi Hickson and also the **Negroes Pompey, Nelly, George, John Alick, Harry, Hannah, Abram, Winny & Child** as his Seventh of the Negroes of said Estate to have and to hold all and Singular the said property unto the said E.A. Hickson am firmly bound unto the said Susan Hickson Surviving widow of the said Levi Hickson to pay annually during her life time the said Susan Hickson the full and Just sum of two hundred & fifty or her Certain attorney to which payment well and truly to be made and done, I bind myself and each and every of my heirs Executors and administrators Jointly and severally by these presents

Provided Nevertheless that the said Susan Hickson reserve and retain to her Self a lien upon the said Negroes Pompey Nelly, George, John, Alick, Harry, Hannah, Abram Winny & Child above enumerated as Security for the annual payment of the said sum of two hundred & fifty dollars then this Conveyance Shall be void otherwise to remain in full force and effect,

And provided, also, that until default by the said E.A. Hickson in performance of the said Condition aforesaid it may be lawful for her to keep and retain possession of said property and to use and enjoy the same but if the same or any part thereof Shall be attatched at any time before payment &c by any other Creditor or Creditors of the said E.A. Hickson then it Shall be lawfull for the said Susan Hickson to take immediate possession of the whole of said above named Negroes or So much thereof as will be sufficient to pay the said sum during her life time to her own use and disposal"

January 1, 1858
State of Florida, Alachua County
From Alachua County Ancient Records
Deed Record C pages 335-336

E. P. Hickson receives 1/7 share of the estate of Levi Hickson: "Know all men by these presents that I E.P. Hickson of Micanopy Florida a lawful heir of the Estate of Levi Hickson deceased the fifth of February One thousand Eight hundred & fifty Seven in Consideration of the facts that Susan Hickson Surviving widow of the said Levi Hickson deceased released her dower and total interest in the Estate of the said Levi Hickson deceased Except the boy **Adam** reserved for her use during her life time and then reverts back to the heirs of the said estate, And upon the further Consideration of receiving one Seventh of the Estate of the said Levi Hickson and also the **Negroes**

Albert, Mary Sarah Jane, Claracy, Andrew, Cyrus, Reuben, Littleton, Piano, Mary, Arthur, as his Seventh of the Negroes of said Estate to have and to hold all and Singular the said property unto the said E.P. Hickson, am firmly bound unto the said Susan Hickson Surviving widow of the said Levi Hickson to pay annually during her life time the said Susan Hickson the full & Just sum of two hundred and fifty dollars or her Certain attorney to which payment well and truly to be made and done, I bind myself and each and every of my heirs, Executors and Administrators Jointly and Severally by these presents,

Provided Nevertheless that the said Susan Hickson reserve and retain to herself a lien upon the said Negroes Albert, Mary Sarah Jane, Andrew, Claracy, Cyrus, Reuben Littleton, Piano, Mary Arthur above enumerated as Security for the annual payment of the said Sum of two hundred & fifty dollars then this Conveyance Shall be void otherwise to remain in full force and effect,

And provided, also, that untill default by the said E.P. Hickson in performance of the said Condition aforesaid it may be lawful for him to Keep and retain possession of said property and to use and enjoy the same but if the same or any part thereof Shall be attatched at any time before payment &c by any other Creditor or Creditors of the said E. P. Hickson then it Shall be lawful for the said Susan Hickson to take immediate possession of the whole thereof as will be sufficient to pay the said sum during her lifetime to her own use and disposal"

January 1, 1858
State of Florida, Alachua County
From Alachua County Ancient Records
Deed Record C pages 333-334

William Hickson receives 1/7 share of the estate of Levi Hickson: "Know all men, That I William Hickson of Aiken South Carolina a lawful heir of the Estate of Levi Hickson deceased the Fifth of February One thousand Eight hundred and fifty Seven in Consideration of the facts that Susan Hickson Surviving widow of the said Levi Hickson deceased released her dower and total interest in the Estate of the said Levi Hickson deceased, Except the boy **Adam** reserved for her use during her life time and then revert back to the heirs of the said Estate and upon the further Consideration of receiving one Seventh of the Estate of the said Levi Hickson and also the **Negroes Dafney & Child Barbary, Adam, Mary, Robert Mariah Minas Junr and Lucy** as his Seventh of the Negroes of said Estate to have and to hold all and Singular the said property unto the said William Hickson am firmly bound unto the said Susan Hickson Surviving widow of the said Levi Hickson to pay annually during her life time the said Susan Hickson the full and Just sum of two hundred & fifty dollars or her Certain attorney to which payment well and truly to be made and done, I bind myself and each and every of my heirs, Executors and administrators Jointly and Severally by these presents

Provided Nevertheless that the said Susan Hickson reserve and retain to herself a lien upon the said Negroes Dafny, & Child, Barbary, Adam, Mary, Robert, Mariah, Minas, Albert, Mary, Junr, & Lucy above enumerated as Security for the annual payment of the said Sum of two hundred & fifty dollars, then this Conveyance Shall be void otherwise to remain in full force and effect,

And provided, also, that untill default by the said William Hickson in performance of the said Condition aforesaid, it may may be lawful for him to Keep and retain possession of said property, and to use and enjoy the same, but if the same or any part thereof Shall be attatched at any time before payment &c by any other Creditor or Creditors of the said William Hickson then it shall be lawful for the said Susan Hickson to take immediate possession of the whole of said above named Negroes or so much thereof as will be sufficient to pay the said sum during her lifetime to her own use and disposal"

January 1, 1858
State of Florida, Alachua County
From Alachua County Ancient Records
Deed Record C pages 330-331

Ezekiel P. Hickson to J. M. Croxton, W. J. Means, and J. A. Emmerson Commissioners for the Sale of the real estate of Levi Hickson deceased as collateral for $3,920 in loans: "This Indenture made on the twenty Seventh day of February in the year of our Lord One thousand Eight hundred & fifty nine, between Ezekiel P. Hickson of the first part; and J.M. Croxton W.J. Means and J.A. Emmerson Commissioners for the Sale of the real Estate of Levi Hickson deceased by the appointment of the Eastern Circuit Court of Florida of the Second part Witnesseth That whereas the said party of the first part on the 10th day of January A.D. 1859 made his two Certain promisory notes for the Sum of One thousand Nine hundred Sixty dollars Each and Signed and delivered the Same to the Said parties of the Second part, Whereby he promised to pay the said Sums of One Thousand Nine hundred & Sixty dollars respectively on one & two years with Eight per Cent interest from date and whereas the Said party of the first part is desirous of securing to the parties of the Second part the prompt and faithful payment of the said two promisory notes, and has already Executed and delivered to the said parties of the second part his indenture of Mortgage Now therefore the foregoing Consideration as well as for the further Sum of Five dollars to them in hand paid at and before the Sealing and delivery hereof the receipt whereof is hereby acknowledged the said party of the first part has given granted bargained Sold & Conveyed & by these presents does So give, grant bargain Sell and Convey unto the said parties of the Second part the following named and described Negro Slaves, To wit **Albert about forty five years of age Mary about Thirty Eight years of age Sarah about Eighteen years of age Clarissa about Sixteen years old Cyrus about twelve years old & Reuben about Six years old** To have and to hold the said Slaves **together with their future increase of the female portion thereof** unto the said parties of the Second part their heirs Executors or administrators and assigns forever for the use and benefit of the Estate of the said Levi Hickson deceased Provided always Nevertheless and these presents are upon the Express Conditions that if the said party of the first part Shall well and truly pay to the Said parties of the Second part or to their order the aforesaid sums of money according to the tenor and effect of the two promissory notes aforesaid when the same shall become due & payable then these presents to be null and void otherwise to remain in full force & virtue."

February 27, 1859
From Alachua County Ancient Records
Mortgage Record A pages 174-175

Levi Hickson to daughter Caroline Johnson: "To all persons to whom these presents shall come, Levi Hickson of Barnwell District in the State aforesaid, Send Greeting. Whereas the Said Levi Hickson is now the lawful owner in his own right of **a Certain female Slave named Polly aged about thirty years, and her four Children (to wit) Flora about two years, Sidney about Eight years, Van aged about Seven years, and Laura aged about one year** which he is desirous on account of his affection for Caroline Johnson, his daughter to give and assure in trust to the said Caroline Johnson and her Children as is herein after Expressed -- Now therefore Know Ye that the said Levi Hickson in Consideration of the love, and affection he hath and beareth unto the said Caroline Johnson and also for and in Consideration of divers other good and valuable Causes and Considerations him thereunto moving doth by these presents Acknowledge, testify and declare that the said Slaves Polly & her Children, Flora Sidney, Van, and Laura, **And the future issue and increase of the females** is hereby given and assured by the Said Levi Hickson, and Shall be held by him during his natural life, and after his death by William T. Hickson his Executors and administrators Subject to the following uses and trust and to and for no other use Trust or purpose whatsoever; That is to Say in trust for the Sole and Separate use benefit and behoof of the Said Caroline Johnson during her natural life, and in such manner that the Said Slaves, and their future issue and increase and the wages, income and profits thereof Shall not be subject to the Control, disposal, debts, Contracts of Engagements of the present or any future husband of the Said Caroline Johnson and after her death, then in trust to and for the use and behoof of such child or children of the said Caroline Johnson, as shall then be living, and the heirs of Such Child or Children. The issue of any deceased child to Stand in the parents Stead, and take in like manner the parents Share. And for default of issue of the said Caroline Johnson living at the same time of her death then to the use and behoof of right heirs of the Said Levi Hickson Forever Provided always that it shall and may be lawful for the Said William T. Hickson, at the request of the Said Caroline Johnson during her life, and of her Children after death to Sell or otherwise dispose of the Said Slaves, and their issues and increase or any part thereof, and invest the proceeds in other property real or personal which Substituted property Shall be Subject to all the trusts limitations and provisions herein Expressed and declared -- And provided always Nevertheless that it Shall and may be lawful for the Said Levi Hickson at anytime or time hereafter as often as he Shall think fit by deed or writing under his hand & Seal or by his last will duly made and subscribed to appoint any other person or persons to be a trustee or Trustees in the place of the trustee herein before named, and Such new trustee or trustees Shall and may have and Exercise the Same powers and authorities to all intents and purposes whatsoever as if he or they had been originally appointed by these presents - And provided lastly that the Said Slaves and their future issue and increase Shall be deemed and held on advancement of One

305

thousand five hundred dollars of the Share or portion of the Said Caroline Johnson in and out of the Estate of the Said Levi Hickson"

August 16, 1852 and in the Seventy Seventh year of the Independence of the United States of America
The State of South Carolina
From Alachua County Ancient Records
Deed Record E pages 312-314

Martin Hires indicted for Assault & Battery; enslaved people were used as part of collateral to ensure he showed up for Court: "State of Florida vs Martin Hirers - Assault & Battery - Continued to the next term of the Court, and the Defendant recognized in the Sum of two hundred Dollars for his appearance at the next term of the Court, two hundred Dollars for the principal and one hundred Dollars for each of the Securities

Martin Hirers Isaac Johns and Jonas Driggers appeared in open Court and acknowledged themselves to owe and Stand indebted to the State of Florida in the Sum of four hundred Dollars, that is to say Martin Hires in the Sum of two hundred dollars Isaac Johns in the Sum of one hundred dollars, and Jonas Driggers in the Sum of one hundred dollars, to be levied of goods and chattels, Slaves, lands and tenements, if default be made in the following condition, that is to say that if the said Martin Hires Shall be and appear at the next term of the Court to answer an indictment against him for disturbing Religious worship and not depart the same without leave thereof then this obligation to be null and void, otherwise to remain in full force and virtue"

May 17, 1855
From Alachua County Ancient Records
Judgment Record A* page 238

Joseph Holder to Thomas Tullis for $3,000: "Received of Thomas Tullis three thousand dollars, it being in full for the purchase of Seven Negroes, Slaves **Willy about thirty seven years old, Sally about fifteen years old, Joe about nine years old, Safa about eight years old, Margarit about six years old, Julier about five years old, Caroline about two years old**. The rights and title I warrant and defend against my self my heirs, Executors and assigns, and against all persons whatsoever lawfully claiming the seven, also warrant these sound and healthy.."

March 21, 1855
Alachua County Florida
From Alachua County Ancient Records
Bills of Sale A page 020

The State of Florida vs. Joseph Holder Senior. Charge: Adultery with a Negro female. "The defendant having been arrested and brought before the Court It is ordered that he Enter into recognizance with good and sufficient security in the sum of One Thousand Dollars conditioned for his appearance at the next Term of the Court, Whereupon the defendant produced one Thomas Tillis as his Said Security and being accepted by the Court the said defendant and the said Tillis were severally bound in the sum of one Thousand Dollars Each to the Governor of Florida upon condition aforesaid, and the case was continued until the next Term"

Friday, May 16, 1856
From Alachua County Ancient Records
Judgment Record A* page 385

Mary R. Holder has Stephen P. Bevill hold in trust real and personal property she's bringing into her impending marriage to Crawford Wadkins: "This Indenture of three parts be made this the Sixth day of February A.D. One thousand Eight hundred and fifty eight by and between Mary R. Holder of the State of Florida Alachua County of the first part and Stephen P. Bevill of the State and County aforesaid party of the Second part and Crawford Wadkins of the State and County aforesaid party of the third part. Witnesseth that whereas a marriage is intended to be had and Solemnized between the Said parties of the first part and third parts, and the said Mary R. Holder is possessed of Certain real and personal Estate, To wit a certain piece or parcel of land, situate lying and being in the County of Alachua and State of Florida known and described as follows To wit the South East quarter of the North West quarter and of the North East quarter of the North quarter of Section Twenty five Township Eight South Range Nineteen East Containing in all Eighty acres more or less also One hundred head of Cattle more or less, also two head of horses. Also **two negro Slaves to wit Milly a woman aged about twenty three years and Sarah her child about six weeks old**, also one hundred head of hogs more or less, also plantation tools, household and kitchen furniture. all of which the said Mary R. Holder with the Consent of the said Crawford Wadkins party of the third part is minded and disposed to transfer to Stephen P. Bevill party of the Second part, in trust for her own proper use and benefit.

Now therefore in Consideration of the promises and of One dollar paid by the said Stephen P. Bevill to the said Mary R. Holder, the receipt whereof is hereby acknowledged, the said Mary R. Holder doth hereby assign, transfer and set over to the said Stephen P. Bevill and his Executors and administrators all the lands, property, and effects above mentioned to hold the same to him the said Stephen P. Bevill and his Executors and administrators upon the Special trust, and for the uses and purposes following and none others namely,

First, that until the Solemnization of the marriage the said Stephen P. Bevill shall pay over to the said Mary R. Holder or shall empower her to receive for her own use all the income benefits and interest arising from the said lands, property, and effects and from any other Estate which may be substituted therefor as is hereinafter provided.

Second That from and after the Solemnization of the said marriage and during the Coverture of the said Mary R. Holder the said Stephen P. Bevill shall receive and collect the income profits and dividends of the said trust monies and effects or of any other substituted estate so often and whenever the same shall be payable, and after deduction of all incidental expences shall pay over the same or so much thereof as she shall not direct to be added to the principle for the purposes of accumulation to the said Mary R. Holder upon her Sole and Separate receipt therefor, and free from the Control or interference of her said husband or any other person whomsoever.

Third That in case of the decease of the said Mary R. Holder after the Solemnization of the said marriage and during the life of her said husband the said monies and effects shall be transferred and paid over by the said trustee to such person or persons as she the said Mary R. Holder by any instrument or note in writing subscribed by her in the presents of one Competent witness shall order and appoint to take and receive the same and in default of her mak-ing such appointment the same shall be transferred and paid to the Said Crawford Wadkins, being then her husband, and in case of his decease before the said property shall be actually transferred and paid over to him, then to such person or persons as would be the legal representatives of the said Mary R. Holder by the Statutes for the distribution of intestate Estate.

Fourth, That in the event of the said decease of the said Crawford Wadkins leaving the said Mary R. Holder all the property then held in trust under this Indenture Shall be transferred and Conveyed by to the said Mary R. Holder and until so transferred, the trustee shall pay over to her or Empower her to receive the income profits and dividends of the same for her own uses.

Fifth That the said trustee shall have power with the approbation or at the request of the said Mary R. Holder expressed in writing to sell and dispose of the said trust Estate or any part of it and the proceeds to invest in any other personal or real Estate according to the written direction of the said Mary R. Holder and the Estate so purchased shall be had and held by the trustee for the same uses and purposes, and upon the same trusts as are declared in and by this Indenture of and Concerning the property and Estate first above mentioned, and may be Sold and the proceeds reinvested from time, in trust in manner aforesaid, and it is hereby declared that the purchaser of any estate held in trust as aforesaid shall not be bound to see to the application of the Said purchase money.

Sixth, That in case of the decease of the party of Second part or of his resignation of the said trust he or his Executors or administrators shall convey transfer and pay over the whole of the trust Estate then held by him to such person or persons as may be appointed in writing by the said party of the first part, to be trustee entrusted under this Indenture, and Such new trustee or trustees Shall have power and shall hold the trust Estate Subject to all the provisions herein set forth and expressed and the receipt of such new trustee or trustees for the trust property shall be a complete acquitance and discharge, to the Said party of the Second part his Executor or administrators. And in like manner new trustees may be appointed from time to time as occasions may require, and the said party of the Second part doth hereby signify his acceptance of the said monies and effects and doth engage to hold and manage the same upon the trusts and for the uses hereinafter mentioned, and the said party of the third part doth hereby signify his assent to the provisions of this Indenture and doth Covenant to and with the said party of the Second part and his successors in the said trusts, to permit the said party of the first part, after the Solemnization of the said intended marriage to receive the aforesaid income and profit to her Sole and Separate uses and freely to dispose of the trust

Estate by her will or by her testamentary appointment to such person or persons as she may bequeath the same to, and not to interfere with the said trust Estate otherwise than in Conformity to the provisions of this Indenture."

February 6, 1858
State of Florida, Alachua
From Alachua County Ancient Records
Bills of Sale A pages 053-056

Benjamin Hopkins to M. S. Perry - land for enslaved people and $400: "This Indenture made this the 28th day of July in the year of our Lord 1853 Between Benjamin Hopkins of the County and State aforesaid of the first part and M. S. Perry of Alachua County State of Florida of the second Part Witnesseth for that whereas in consideration of the relinquishment of said Perry unto the said Benjamin Hopkins of his entire interest in the following Negroes formerly the property of Thomas Cherry Dec'd of the County of Alachua State of Florida, to wit: **Jack, August, January, Molly, Viny & her child, Lucinda and her child Louisa Susan & Nancy** and for the further consideration of four Hundred (400) Dollars to be paid in good and lawful money by said Perry to said Hopkins on the first day of January (1855) in the year of our Lord one thousand eight hundred and fifty five. The aforesaid Benjamin Hopkins has remised released and conveyed & quit claimed to the said party of the second part and to his Heirs and assigns forever all that certain tract or parcel of land lying and being Situated in Alachua County known as the Clerry tract & lot No (5) containing Sixteen hundred and Sixty six & two third (1666 2/3) acres being a part of Moses E. Levy Grant and Situated within the Arredondo Grant State of Florida & County of Alachua and adjoining lands now or recently owned by Moses E. Levy J.M. Croxton John White M.S. Perry and others together with all and singular the tenements hereditaments & appurtenances thereunto belonging or in anywise appertaining & the remainder or remainders reversion or reversions rents issues & profits thereof. To have & to hold all and singular the above premises mentioned & described unto the said party of the second part his heirs & assigns forever and to this I also bind my Heirs & assigns forever. This agreement made between the parties aforesaid is such that the said party of the second part will well & truly perform his part according to the premises hereinbefore Stated, if the said Hopkins of the first part shall make this his title to the above described Land a good and Sufficient Title thereto and it defend against all claims whatsoever. This being a part & parcel of the above quit claim given by the said Perry of the second part to the said Hopkins of the First part of certain Negroes hereinafter mentioned otherwise this said deed of quit claim to be void with all the conditions herein stated In Witness whereof the said party of the First part has hereunto set his hand & Seal the day & year above written"

July 28, 1853
State of Florida, Putnam County
From Alachua County Ancient Records
Deed Record T pages 455-456

Tillman Ingram and E. E. Adamson release right, title, and claim to 3 people they enslaved: "Whereas Alexander Matheson of the State of Florida and County of Alachua did execute and deliver to us Tillman Ingram and E. E. Adamson on the Twelfth day of June A.D. Eighteen hundred & fifty seven a mortgage of certain negroes amongst them were **Betsey & her children Henrietta & Edmund** beside others for the secure payment of the sum of Fifteen Thousand Dollars which said mortgage of Record with Clerk Office in the County of Alachua and State aforesaid in Book of Mortgages upon Page 114 & 5 and whereas the said Alexander Matheson has this day sold and delivered to Matthew Cheves the said Slaves Betsey & her children Henrietta Edmund or Edward Now Know all men by these presents that we Tillman Ingram and E. E. Adamson of the County of Alachua and State of Florida for and in Consideration of Five dollars to us in hand paid by Alexander Matheson the receipt whereof is hereby acknowledged have renounced and released and do hereby renounce and release all our right title or claim whatsoever both in law and equity to or upon the said negroes slaves Betsey Henrietta and Edward her children, under or by virtue of said mortgage given as aforesaid by the said Alexander Matheson to us as aforesaid"

February 13, 1858
State of Florida, Alachua Co.
From Alachua County Ancient Records
Mortgage Record A page 129

Inventory of Caroline Johnson: "The following is an inventory of the Separate Personal property belonging to Caroline Johnson wife of Francis C. Johnson now residing at Micanopy Alachua County Florida Viz **Amos a male Slave about fifty years old, Molly a female Slave about Eighteen years old & Hamp a male Slave about sixteen years old**"

October 11, 1859
From Alachua County Ancient Records
Deed Record E page 096

Samuel R. Johnson to Giles U. Ellis as collateral for a $50 loan:
"This Indenture made this Ninth day of March, in the year of our
Lord one thousand eight hundred and fifty three; between Samuel R.
Johnson of the County of Alachua and State of Florida of the first
part, and Giles U. Ellis of said county and State of the second part:
Witnesseth that whereas the said Samuel R. Johnson has this day made
executed and delivered to the said Giles U. Ellis his certain promissory
note, bearing such date with these presents, by which said promissory
note the said Samual R. Johnson promises to pay to the said Giles U.
Ellis or bearer on or before the first day of January in the year Eighteen hundred and fifty four the sum of Fifty dollars, with interest at
eighteen per cent on said sum of money from the date of said promissory note, until the said sum of money is paid,

Now Know all men by these presents that the said Samuel R. Johnson as well for the better securing of the payment of the said sum of
money in the said promissory note specified, and the interest thereon,
as well as for the sum of five dollars to him in hand paid by the said
Giles U. Ellis, the receipt whereof at and before the sealing and delivery of these presents is hereby acknowledged, hath granted, bargained
sold and conveyed and doth by these presents grant bargain sell and
convey unto the said Giles U. Ellis, and to his heirs and assigns a certain **negro man Slave named Ned aged about Eighteen years**; and
to have and to hold the said negro slave to the said Giles U. Ellis his
heirs and assigns forever to his and theirs only proper use and benefit
and behoof. And the said Samuel R. Johnson doth covenant grant and
agree to and with the said Giles U. Ellis his heirs and assigns, that he
the said Samuel R. Johnson will, and his heirs, executors and administrators shall warrant and defend to the said Giles U. Ellis, his heirs
and assigns the right and title to said negro slave against the claim of
himself the said Samuel R. Johnson and against the claim of all persons claiming by them or under him, and against the of all persons
whatsoever Provided Nevertheless and these presents are upon this
express consideration; that if the said Samuel R. Johnson his heirs or
assigns shall pay or cause to be paid to the said Giles U. Ellis, his heirs
executors administrators or assigns: the said sum of Fifty dollars, in

said promissory note mentioned together with all interest that may be due and owing thereon, at the time mentioned and appointed in the promissory note for the payment thereof; then and from thenceforth, as well this Indenture, and the note hereby created, and the said promissory note, shall cease, determine and be of no effect"

March 9, 1853
From Alachua County Ancient Records
Mortgage Record A pages 074-075

F. C. Johnson receives 1/7 share of the estate of Levi Hickson:
"Know all men that I F.C. Johnson of Micanopy Florida, a lawful heir of the Estate of Levi Hickson deceased the fifth of February one thousand Eight hundred and fifty Seven in Consideration of the facts, that Susan Hickson Surviving widow of the Said Levi Hickson deceased, release her dower and total interest in the Estate of the said Levi Hickson deceased. Except the boy **Adam**, reserved for her use during her lifetime, and then reverts back to the heirs of the said Estate, and upon the further Consideration of receiving one Seventh of the Estate of the said Levi Hickson and also the Negroes **Amos, Amy, Mary, Ann, Hampton, Polly, Flora Sidney, Vanda, and Laura**, as his Seventh of the Negroes of said estate to have and to hold all and Singular the said property unto the said F.C. Johnson are firmly bound unto the said Susan Hickson Surviving widow of the said Levi Hickson, to pay annually during her lifetime, the said Susan Hickson the full and just sum of two hundred and fifty dollars, or her Certain attorney, to which payment well and truly to be made and done I bind myself and each and every of my heirs Executors and administrators Jointly and Severally by these presents

Provided Nevertheless that the Said Susan Hickson reserve and retain to herself a lien upon the said Negroes Amos, Amy, Mary, Ann,

315

Hampton, Polly, Flora, Sidney, Vanda, Laura, above Enumerated as Security for the annual payment of the said sum of two hundred & fifty dollars then their Conveyance Shall be void otherwise to remain in full force and effect

And provided Also, that until default, by the said F.C. Johnson in performance of the said Conditions aforesaid it may be lawful for her to Keep and retain possession of Said property and to use and enjoy the same but if the same or any part thereof shall be attached at any time before payment &c by any other Creditor or Creditors of the said F.C. Johnson then it Shall be lawful for the said Susan Hickson to take immediate possession of the whole said above named negroes or so much thereof as will be sufficient to pay the said sum during her lifetime to her own use and disposal"

January 1, 1858
State of Florida, Alachua County
From Alachua County Ancient Records
Deed Record C pages 328-329

Francis C. Johnson to William Hickson in trust for Francis's wife Caroline Johnson: "This Indenture made and entered into this the fourteenth day of December in the year of our Lord one thousand eight hundred and fifty nine between Francis C. Johnson and William Hickson Witnesseth that I, the said F. C. Johnson for and in consideration of the Sum of five dollars to him in hand paid and also in consideration of the fact that the property hereinafter mentioned came in part to my wife Caroline Johnson from the Estate of her late father and in part from funds derived from the said Estate have granted, bargained, sold and conveyed and by these presents do grant, bargain, sell and convey to the said William Hickson the following described property to wit, the lot or tract of land in and adjoining the town of Mickanopy of the County and State aforesaid, and bounded as follows; Beginning at the North West corner of the lot owned by Dr. J.P. Stewart and running West 6.32 chains to the middle of the street in front of the house of Mrs. P.A. Smith, thence South 50.2 chains to a post thence West 5 chains thence South 14.91 chains to a set post thence East 4.40 chains to a set post, thence to the Section line 9.11 chains thence East to the South West corner of the land of Dr. J.A. Stewart, thence North 26.52 chains to the place of Beginning, Containing twenty five acres more or less, Also the following negroes to wit, **Amos, Amy and her child Ellen, Mary Ann and Hampton** to have and to hold the said land and negroes to the Said William Hickson in Trust nevertheless for the use of my Said wife Caroline and her heirs, and the Said Caroline to take possession, control and management of the Said Property and to use the rents, hire and profits arising therefrom as to her may seem best, I, further give to the said William Hickson the power to sell or otherwise dispose of the said Lands and negroes provided the Same is done with the consent of the said Caroline and with her consent to invest the proceeds of such sale as aforesaid in other property or Stocks which is to be held in the Same manner and for the Same uses and purposes as the Said Land and negroes, and the property acquired by the proceeds of sale of the Said land and negroes, as aforesaid to be Sold or otherwise disposed of and its proceeds to be invested in the manner and with the consent aforesaid and the Same power is given infinitive - to the Said Trustee with the consent aforesaid over any property which may be attained by the proceeds from the Sale or other disposition of property which may be acquired from the Sale or other disposition of any property obtained from the proceeds of the Sale of Said land and negroes."

December 14, 1859
From Alachua County Ancient Records
Deed Record E page 100

Jerome N. Jones to Mary C. Russell for $2,500: "Know all men by these presents that I Jerome N. Jones of the County of Alachua and State of Florida, for and in consideration of the sum of two thousand five hundred dollars to me in hand paid by Mary C. Russell of said County and State the receipt whereof is hereby acknowledged at and before the sealing and delivery of these presents, have granted bargained, sold, and delivered, and by these presents, do grant, bargain, sell and deliver unto the said Mary C. Russell, seven negro Slaves of the following description, to wit, **Silva about fifty five years old, Rebecca sixteen years old, Malinda seven years old - Sarah six years old - Gabriel five years old - Edward five years old and Elvira three years old**. To have and to hold said described slaves, unto her own, and only proper use, benefit and behoof forever. and I warrant said slaves to be sound of body and mind, and slaves for life."

October 7, 1854
State of Florida, Alachua County
From Alachua County Ancient Records
Bills of Sale A page 024

Osman S. Jones to Osman M. Kennedy for $3,000 for the use and benefit of Catharine J. Jones and the heirs of her body: "This Indenture made of agreement made and entered this the fourth day of December One thousand Eight hundred & fifty Eight Between Osman S. Jones of the County of Alachua and State of Florida party of the first part, Osman M. Kennedy of the State and County aforesaid party of the Second part <u>Witnesseth</u> that the said party of the first part for and in Consideration of the Sum of Three thousand dollars good and lawfull Money of the United States of America to him in hand paid at and before the Sealing and delivery of these presents the receipt whereof, is hereby acknowledged hath given, granted bargained, Sold, and doth so give grant bargain, Sell, deliver, and Convey unto the said party of the Second part, the following described property to wit **Two Negroes One named Sam about thirty Seven years of age of Black or dark Complection, the other by the name of Joe about twenty years Old of a light or Copper Color,** also five head of Horses, One Road waggon, and one two Horse Carriage To have and to hold the above described property under his own Sole Control for the use and benefit of Catharine J. Jones and the heirs of her body, and if the said Osman M. Kennedy Shall die before the said Catharine J. Jones or before the heirs of her body shall become of age, then the said Osman M. Kennedy, But, Provided all the parties Shall live until Coming of age of the heirs of Catharine J. Jones aforesaid, then at her death this property to be transferred to the use and benefit of the heirs aforesaid immediately, at the death of the said Catharine aforesaid, or if the said Osman M. Kennedy and the said Catharine Shall live until the coming of age of the heirs of the said Catharine J. Jones then the said property to be Conveyed and transferred unto the said heirs"

December 4, 1858
State of Florida, Alachua Cty
From Alachua County Ancient Records
Deed Record C pages 311-312

William Jones Last Will and Testament: "I William Jones of the District of Fairfield and state aforesaid do make and proclaim this my last Will and Testament

1st I will and direct, when I am dead that my body be decently Committed to its mother earth, and as soon Thereafter as possible that all My Just debts be paid after the manner hereafter directed

2 I will and bequeath to my wife Sarah Jones for and during the time of her natural life, the plantation on which I now live, also for the

same time I give her **my Negro boy Starke**, I also give to her and her heirs forever the following Negro slaves to Wit **Sally, Alford and Adeline**, also one horse four Cows & Calves Necessary house hold & Kitchen furniture and provisions for one year

3rd At the death of my wife the plantation next above given to her for life I will and bequeath to the Children of my Son Osmund to have and to hold the same Share and Share alike to them and their heirs forever

4th I give will and bequeath to my son Elisha H. Jones **My Negro man Eli**, to him and his heirs forever.

5 I give will and bequeath a **Negro Girl named Betsey** to my daughter Cynthia Kennedy to have and to hold the same for and during the term of her natural life to her sole and Seperate use behoof and benefit after her death it is my will that said Negro girl return to my estate and be divided among my children equally. It is also my will and desire that the boy Starke given to my wife for life, at her death return to my estate and be divided as is above provided in the Case of the girl Betsey

6th My Stock in the Charlotte and South Carolina R. Road I give and bequeath Share and Share alike to William Harrison Jones son of Osmond Jones and to the present infant son of Elisha H. Jones

7th **My Negro boys Joe and Jim** I give will and bequeath to the Children of Osmond Jones & **my two Negro girls Amy and Caroline** I give and bequeath to the Children of Elisha H. Jones to Them and Their heirs forever

8th It is my earnest wish and desire that my Executors hereinafter named shall if it is possible (unless a Contrury Course should be Manifestly more to the benifit of the parties in Interest) Keep together all my property until my debts are paid, then pay the Specified legacies herein made and then make division of the residue of my estate as is next below directed

9th After The payment of my debts and Specified legacies it is my will and I direct that the residue of my Estate be divided among my son Elisha H. Jones the Children of Osmond S. Jones taken as a Class Suereties *******, Nancy Kennedy and Muhaloth Davis, care being taken first to charge all advancements heretofore made to either sure and except those made to my son Elisha H. Jones, No advancement herein or heretofore made to him nor any Money I May have heretofore paid laid out & enfundid to and for his use and benifit, Nor shall my plantation or tract of lands Known as the old and the Small place Contigeuous thereto which by parcels I have given to my said son Elisha H. Jones, and mean to Convey by deed shall be Charged against him as advancements in said division but he shall take a full and agreed share with the rest, entitled under this clause in my will (these shares being Charges with Advancements over and above any gift herein or heretofore made to him, and the tracts of land above Specified, and any moneys I may have heretofore paid fir him which said Moneys I hereby renounce all right to claim or receive

10th And I do further will and direct that the shares out of the said residue of my estate falling to my three daughters Lucretia Wylie, Nancy Kennedy, and Mahacoth Davis, be held by them severally for and during the terms of their several lives, to their sole and seperate use behoof and benifit, and in no event to be liable or subject to the debts liabilities, or Contracts of their present or any future husband or husbands, and after the death of either one of my said daughters or of all of them, the share of the daughter so dead, shall go to the child or Children of the daughter so living; but should either one of said daughters, die leaving no heirs or Children or die bearing Them, and such Child or children should die before attaining The age of twenty one Years and leave no issue living at The Time of his her or Their death, Then and in that case The share of such daughter is to return to my estate and be divided as in case of Intestates estate

11th I do hereby nominate and appoint My friend Osmond Woodward & my son Elisha H. Jones Executors of this my last Will and testament, In testimony of all which I have this day The 19th of February 1852 set my hand

Codicil

It is my will and desire that the part of my will above mentioned and dated this 19th day of Febry 1852 in a part of the 7th Item thereof giving willing and bequeathing **My Negro boy Joe** to the children of Osmond Jones be revoked and of no effect, and I do hereby will and direct that the said boy Joe, be sold and The proceeds of said sale equally divided according to the division mentioned in the 9th Item of my last Will & testament above this Codicil to be taken and Considered as a part of my last Will & testament

Codicil

This Codicil is intended to be a part of my last Will and testament made on The 19th February 1852 and Witnessed by M.A.M. Leggs C.H. Durham and J.F. Durham,

1st I give and bequeath to my wife Sarah Jones **my Negro boy Starke** to her and her heirs forever, and I revoke so much of my said Will as leaves her only a life estate in said boy Starke. I also give and bequeath to my said wife and her heirs, my Negro Woman **Serasy**.

2nd I give and bequeath to the Children of my son Osmond L. Jones **my Negro boy Bill**, as well as the **negro boys Joe and Jim** bequeathed to them by the 7th clause of my will and I hereby revoke the Codicil to my Will in the fourth page Thereof, and confirm and republish the said Seventh Clause, with the additional bequeath being of Bill to O.L. Jones' children.

4th I give and bequeath my negro girl **Maria and her future increase** to Polly Mickle Kennedy to her sole and seperate use for life not subject to the debts Contracts or of any future husband and after her death to such issue as she may leave living at the time of her death, and in default of such issue so surviving I give and bequeath said slave and her increase to Polly Kennedy Sister Sarah Kennedy

5th I give and bequeath to my daughter Cynthia Kennedy the sum of Fifty dollars

In Witness whereof I have hereunto affixed my hand and Seal This Fifth of February A.D. 1853"

February 19, 1852 and February 5, 1853
State of South Carolina
From Alachua County Ancient Records
Will Book A pages 094-098

Thos. F. King to Elizabeth Hickson in consideration of their impending marriage: "Know all men by these presents that I Thos F. King for and in consideration of the sum of five dollars to me paid by Elizabeth A. Hickson and also in consideration of a marriage about to be solumnized between the said Elizabeth and myself and also for the purpose that the said Elizabeth may own and have the title to the following mentioned property do hereby sell and convey and relinquish to the said Elizabeth all the right and title which may accrue to one by reason of said marriage in any property real or property which may now be owned by the said Elizabeth or which she may hereafter acquire and particularly the property derived by her as heir from her late father's estate, to wit **the negro Slaves Pompey, George, John, Alick, Harry, Abe, Nelly, Hannah, Winney and her two children Barton & another a babe, together with the increase of the females of said negroes** and all the real property whatsoever which the said Elizabeth has derived or which or which she may hereafter receive as an heir from her said fathers estate; and the proceeds of the Sales of any personal or real property of said estate which the said the said Elizabeth has received or may receive or to which she may be entitled from a sale by the representatives of said Estate or by an order of sale from any Court."

August 1, 1858
From Alachua County Ancient Records
Deed Record E Pages 103-104

James J. Kennard indicted for stealing enslaved people: "The State of Florida vs James J. Kennard - Indicted for Stealing Slaves - "James J. Kennard late of the County of Alachua who stands indicted for stealing slaves was led to the bar &c and on motion of the Solicitor for the State and for reasons appearing to the Court the trial of the said indictment is deferred until the next term, and thereupon said James J. Kennard is remanded to the custody of the Sheriff and Jailer of this Court, and it appearing that there is not a sufficient jail or place of safe keeping of said James J. Kennard indicted as aforesaid in said County of Alachua

It is ordered that the Sheriff of Alachua do convey the said James J. Kennard to the jail of the County of Columbia Florida, ad deliver him into the custody of the Jailer of said County, and that the jailer and Sheriff of said County of Columbia, do receive the said James J. Kennard unto the said County jail, and Keep him the said James J. Kennard to answer the said Indictment, until the further order of this Court

December 11, 1856
From Alachua County Ancient Records
Judgment Record A* page 465

James J. Kinnard indicted for stealing enslaved people and escaped from jail: "State of Florida vs James J. Kinnard - Stealing Slaves - It appearing that said James J. Kennard has escaped from the jail of Columbia County where he was committed It is ordered by the Court that a capias do issue to the Sheriff of Alachua County to arrest him"

May 15, 1857
From Alachua County Ancient Records
Judgment Record A* page 520

George Leitner to Daniel Scott and Daniel D. Fenly as collateral for $28,000 in loans: "Know all men by these presents that George Leitner of the State of South Carolina and District of Fairfield, in the consideration of the Sum of twenty eight thousand dollars with interest from date herein after mentioned to him in hand paid, hath bargained, Sold and delivered, and by these presents doth bargain, Sell and in plain and a free market, deliver unto Daniel Scott and Daniel D. Fenly the following property, to wit: **one Negro man Slave named George about forty years of age, and Mary his wife about 25 years of age, and her child about two years old, little George nine years, and Nance Seven years old, Pressly twenty nine years, Mary his wife twenty years and Anderson her child two years old, Jane about five years old, Wentward about forty six years old, and Fanny his wife about forty years old, Daniel forty, and Maria his wife about forty years old, and her child Fanny three years old, little Daniel fifteen years, Sam nine, and Tery five years old, and Charlotte about nineteen, Harriet twenty eight, and her infant, and Eliza three years old, Cupid Sixty, John twenty and, Amos nineteen, Martha Seventeen, Isaac fifteen years old, Simon about forty Eight, and Rebecca his wife thirty years old, Lewis forty, and Sallie his wife thirty eight years old, Dave twenty two, Ned twenty, and John Sixteen years old, and Amanda nine years**

old, **Ellen twenty Six, Nelson eight, and Henry five years old, Dick three years old, Peter forty five, Caroline his wife thirty five years old, Safa forty years old, Nathan twenty three, Turner twenty one, and Wessly eighteen years old, Adeline fifteen years old, Mary and her child Seven months old, Antony forty five, Jad twenty eight, Bob twenty four, and Telda eighteen years old Alick forty four Andrew twenty two, and Tom twenty three years old**, To have and to hold all and Singular, the Said Negroes; **together with their future issue and increase** unto the Said Daniel Scott and Daniel D. Fenly of the State of South Carolina Fairfield District, their Executors, Administrators and assigns forever, provided nevertheless, and it is expressly agreed between the parties, that if the Said Georg Leitner, his Executors, Administrators or assigns, Shall well and truly pay or cause to be paid unto the aforesaid Daniel Scott and Daniel D. Fenly their certain Attornies, Executors, administrators or assigns, the following notes, Executions &c for the payment of which Said Daniel Scott and Daniel D. Fenly are bound as Sureties of Said George Leitner to wit, and payment for two thousand dollars in favor of the Commercial Bank - Columbia confession given in August or Sept 1854 with a credit $3000 or $3500 also Judgment in favor of the Branch Bank of the State at Columbia for three thousand two hundred dollars confession given in August or Sept 1854, and a note due the Bank of the State Charleston for about five thousand dollars date not precisely recollected also a note and Christian Entzminger for ten thousand dollars and transferred by will to Dr. Samuel Beakhart dated in Sept 1852, and a note given Adams & Frost for eight thousand dollars dated in Februa or march 1855, and Such Sum or Sums as the said Daniel Scott and Daniel D. Fenly may hereafter become bound for the payment of or Endorsers or otherwise for Said George Leitner then the above bill of Sale and every article and thing therein contained Shall cease and be utterly void, or else remain in full force and virtue"

August 9, 1855
State of Florida, Alachua County
From Alachua County Ancient Records
Deed Record D pages 162-163

George Leitner to John W. Anderson of Savannah as collateral for $16,990.55 in loans: "This Indenture made on the Seventh day of November in the year of our Lord one thousand Eight hundred and fifty six between George Leitner of the State and County aforesaid of the first part, and John W. Anderson of the City of Savannah and State of Georgia of the second part Witnesseth That whereas on the second day of June in the year of our Lord One thousand eight hundred and fifty six the said party of the first part did make in writing sign and deliver to the said party of the second part three several promissory notes bearing the date last above mentioned, and for value received, the amounts of the said notes and the time of there payment being as follows: To wit: One of the said notes to become due on the first day of December in the year of our Lord One thousand eight hundred and fifty six and for the Sum of Five thousand six hundred and thirty one dollars and fifty six cents, One of the said notes to become due on the first day of January in the year of our Lord One thousand eight hundred and fifty seven and for the sum of Five thousand - six hundred and Sixty three dollars and fifty one cents, and one of the said notes to become due on the first day of February in the year of our Lord One thousand eight hundred and fifty seven, and for the Sum of Five thousand six hundred and ninety five dollars and forty eight cents, making in all the Sum of Sixteen thousand nine hundred and ninety Dollars and fifty five Cents, owing to the said party of the second part by the said party of the first part on the three several promissory notes aforesaid And whereas the said notes may be discounted at some bank in the City of Savannah for my accommodation and may be received from time to time. And Whereas the said party of the second part has agreed to advance other sums of money to the said party of the first part, or by endorsing for him, enable the said party of the first part to realize other monies, as well as to furnish him in the course of business with plantation supplies, with the express understanding that the said party of the second part is by these presents to have the payment of all sums of money thus advanced as well as for all supplies, thus furnished secured to him by the said party of the first part And Whereas the said party of the first part is desirous of securing to the said party of the second part the prompt and safe payment of the three notes of hand as above said also to secure the payment of all sums of money which may hereafter be advanced on account of the said party of the first part, Now Know Ye therefore that for and on account of the foregoing considerations as well as for the further consideration of Five dollars to him in hand paid before the sealing and delivery hereof, the said party of the first part has given, granted, bargained sold and conveyed and by these presents does so give grant bargain sell and convey unto the said party of the second part his heirs and assign the following mentioned and described property: That is to say: All those two certain parcels of land or plantation known and described as lots Nos Eight and Nine (8 & 9) of the Arredondo Grant bounded on the North by Paine's Prairie, on the East by lands belonging to the estate of W.W. Geiger decd and lands now owned by Moses Freyermouth, On the south by lands belonging to the Estate of W.W. Geiger decd and on the west by Levy prairie and the lands of Dr. Harrison, containing three thousand three hundred and thirty three and one third acres, situated in the County of Alachua and State aforesaid, Also the following mentioned and described negro slaves To Wit: **George aged about thirty years, his wife Mary about twenty eight years old, their son George about Eleven years old, their son Nace about seven years old, their daughter Lizzie about three years old, and their son Simon about six months old. Pressley about thirty years old, his wife Mary about twenty five years old, their daughter Jane about seven years old, their son Anderson about three years old, and their daughter Emeline about eight months old, Nestard about forty five years old, his wife Fanny about forty years old, their son Isaac about Twenty one years old, and their son Ned about fourteen years old, Daniel about forty years old, his wife Mariah about thirty six years old, Charlotte their daughter about twenty one years old, their son Daniel about fifteen years old, their son Sampson about Eleven years old, their son Toney about seven years old and their daughter Fenny four years old, Harriet about** twenty eight years old, her son Lige about five years old and her son Gibbs about eighteen months old, Cupid about fifty six years old, his son John about twenty two years old, his son Amos about twenty years old, his daughter Martha about eighteen years old and his son Isaac about fifteen years old, Simon about forty nine years old, his wife Beck about thirty two years old, Lewis about forty two years old, his wife Sally about forty two years old, Davi their son about twenty two years old their son Ned about twenty years old, their son John about eighteen years old, and their daughter Amanda about Eleven years old, Ellen about twenty eight years old, her son Nelson about nine years old, her son Henry about seven years old her son Dick about five years old and her son Jefferson about five months old, Peter about forty four years old Ellick about forty four years old, his wife Sophy about forty four years old, their son Nathan about twenty three years old, their son Turner about twenty one years old, their son Wesley about nineteen years old, Mary Ann about eighteen years old and her son William about eighteen months old, Antony about forty four years old, his son Joe about twenty eight years old his son Bob about twenty five years old, his daughter Tildy about Twenty years old, Adeline about sixteen years old, **and Andrew about twenty two years old.** To Have and to Hold all and singular the aforegranted and described and conveyed plantation or parcels of land, together with all and singular the improvements buildings and appurtenances to the same belonging or in any wise appertaining, and the said negro slaves above named and described and herein conveyed, **together with the future issue and increase of the female portion thereof** unto the said party of the second part his heirs executors, administrators and assigns to his and their own proper use and behoof forever: Provided nevertheless and these presents are on the conditions following: That is to say if the said party of the first part shall well and truly pay to the said party of the second part, his heirs or assigns the amount of the three several notes (herein above described) together with the interest monies thereon, when the same shall become due and payable, provided further the said party of the first part shall well and truly pay any and every such note or notes as may be given in renewal of the same, or in renewal of any part thereof or in renewal of each other: Provided further the said party of the first part shall pay unto the said party of the second part his heirs and assigns, each and every sum of money which he may receive from the said party of the second part hereafter when the same shall become due and payable And provided further of the said party of the first part shall also save the said party of the second part harmless for the payment of which he may become responsible by endorsement or otherwise on account of the said party of the first part, then these presents to be null and void, else to remain in full force"

November 7, 1856
State of Florida, Alachua County
From Alachua County Ancient Records
Deed Record D pages 411-414

George Leitner (Planter) to John W. Anderson (Cotton merchant) as collateral for monies owed: "To all whom these presents may concern I George Leitner (Planter) of the County of Alachua & State of Florida Send Greeting

Whereas I the said George Leitner am indebted to John W. Anderson (Cotton Factor and commissioner merchant) of the City of Savannah & State of Georgia for advancement in money made to me from time to time upon my Cotton Crops and whereas I expect to receive of him future advancements upon the faith of my Cotton Crops, Now Know all men that I the said George Leitner of the County & State aforesaid in consideration of the said several advancements to me made and to be made as aforesaid mentioned and for the better security the payment thereof to the said John W. Anderson and also for and in consideration of the further sum of ten dollars to me in hand paid by the said John W. Anderson at and before the sealing and delivering of

330

these presents the receipt whereof is hereby acknowledged have bargained and Sold and by these presents do bargain and Sell and in plan and open market deliver unto the said John W. Anderson the following named and described Negro Slaves To Wit **Anderson about thirty three years old, his wife Kitty about twenty five years old their daughter Sicily about Eight years old, their Son Hampton about Twelve years old, their daughter Vicy about six years old, their Son Amos about four years old, their Son Frank about two years old & their Son Ralph about nine months old & also Lidia a girl about Twelve years old to have & to hold the said Negro Slaves above named and described together with the future increase of the female portion thereof** unto the said John W. Anderson his heirs and assigns forever Provided always nevertheless and it is the true intent and meaning of these parties that if the said George Leitner, his heirs & assigns Shall well and truly pay unto the said John W. Anderson his heirs and assigns the full and just sum of money ascertained by final Settlement after balancing accounts between them which said settlement Shall be made whenever the said George Leitner desires as to be actually due by the said George Leitner to the said John W. Anderson in the Shape of said advancement made by him as aforesaid mentioned, with interest upon the same at seven per Cent per annum, then these presents to be null and void otherwise to remain in full force and virtue"

September 8, 1857
State of Florida, Alachua County
From Alachua County Ancient Records
Mortgage Record A pages 118-119

Nancy R. Lewis inventory of separate property: "Inventory of the Separate property of Mrs. Nancy R. Lewis wife of John Lewis of Alachua County and State of Florida, To wit, one mare called Fashion 11

years old, **one Negro man named Robert 22 years old, A woman named Mary Ann 30 years old, and Adaline 10 years old, James 8 years old, Lord 6 years old, and one Infant named Isea, A woman named Eady 20 years old**, The Clerk of the Circuit Court for said County will please record the above inventory & oblige."

December 3, 1855
From Alachua County Ancient Records
Deed Record D page 193

Nancy R. Lewis Last Will and Testament: "I Nancy R. Lewis, wife of John Lewis of Alachua County late of Florida do make this my last will and testament, hereby revoking and making said all former wills by me at any time heretofore made; and first - I direct that my body be decently interred, and that funeral be conducted in a manner corresponding with my Estate and situation in life; and as to such worldly property as it has pleased God to invest me with, I dispose of the same as follows first I direct that **my slaves Robert, age about 22 years- Edy age about 21 years, Mary Ann age about 30 years and her children Adaline, age 10 years Jane age 8 years, Laura age 6 years, & Ida an infant** be retained in the possession of my Husband John Lewis, during the term of his natural life, said slaves to be used by him as his other Servants, but not to be liable or subject in any way to any debts that he may contract.

I first here direct that at the death of my said Husband, the above named slaves **with any natural increase**, that may be allotted to the same, be divided among my children share and share alike dispose as practicable - The names of my children are as follows - William B. Lewis, Charles W. Lewis, Francis R. Canicaid**, Wilber G. Lewis, Agnes E. Lewis Mary R. Lewis, Martha C. Lewis; And I so hereby make and ordain my Son, William B. Lewis, my Trustee, to act, and carry out the provisions of this my last will and testament"

February 24, 1856
From Alachua County Ancient Records
Will Book A pages 078-079

William R. Lewis to his son William Dixon Lewis: "Know all men by these presents that I William R. Lewis of the State of Florida and County of Alachua for and in Consideration of the love and affection which I have and bear for my Son William Dixon Lewis of the Same County & State as well as in Consideration by him of one dollar to me paid the receipt whereof is hereby acknowledged hath granted given Conveyed and Confirmed and by these presents doth grant give Convey and Confirm unto my Son the Said William Dixon Lewis the following negro Slaves to wit **Rina aged about thirty nine years, Amelia aged about Eighteen years Sylla aged about Sixteen years, John aged about Fourteen years, Thomas aged about thirteen years, Harriet aged about Eleven years Sam aged about nine years Isaac aged about Seven years** Provided nevertheless and upon this Express Condition that I am Still to Enjoy during my natural life the use and occupation of said Negroes Slaves and to have the right So long as I live to Control manage and govern the Same free of all Charge therefor and this gift is made upon the further limitation and restriction that if my Son the Said William Dixon Lewis Should not Survive me leaving no issue then the Said Negroes Slaves **together with their increase** to revert back absolutely to me but if the Said William Dixon Lewis Should Survive me and then die without issue of legal marriage then the Said Negro Slaves and their increase to be divided Equally between the half Brother & Sister of him the Said William Dixon Lewis if any living at his death and if none then between the uncles of him the Said William Dixon Lewis to wit John

H. Lewis, Green Lewis, Thomas W. Lewis and John B. Tillman Share and Share alike"

July 13, 1859
State of Florida, Alachua County
From Alachua County Ancient Records
Deed Record E page 046

John C. Ley to Samuel R. Pyles as collateral for a $600 loan: "This Indenture made this April 29th 1858 between John C. Ley of Micanopy of the one part and Samuel R. Pyles of this County of the other part, Witnesseth that for the faithful payment of a note given this date by the said Ley of the first part for the amount of Six hundred dollars due January 1st 1859 with interest from date to the said Pyles of the Second part, The said Ley by these presents bargains and mortgages **One Negro named Aaron aged about fifty years & one woman named Lavina about the Same age**"

April 29, 1858
Alachua County, State of Florida
From Alachua County Ancient Records
Deed Record C page 252

Thomas C. Love to Geo. L. Brown as collateral for a $364.39 loan: "This Indenture made this twenty eighth day of January in the year One Thousand Eight Hundred fifty between Geo. L. Brown of the County of Alachua and State of Florida and Thomas C. Love of the County of Levy in said State […] Now this indenture witnesseth that the said Thomas C. Love as for and in Consideration of the aforesaid sum Three Hundred and Sixty four Dollars and Thirty nine Cents, the same mentioned in said promissory notes, and for the better securing the payment thereof with the lawful interest thereon to the said Geo L. Brown his executors administrators and assigns, as well as Certain Advancement of many goods wares and merchandise to be made in future by the said Geo L. Brown to the said Thomas C. Love *** as also of the further sum of one Hundred Dollars in hand paid by Geo L. Brown to said Thomas C. Love, at and before the signing and sealing hereof which is hereby acknowledged, hath bargained and sold and doth hereby bargain and sell unto the said Geo L. Brown two Negro men Slaves named and described as follows to wit **Dan aged about Eighteen years, Dick aged about Twenty years**. To have and to hold the said Negro men Slaves to the said Geo L. Brown and to his heirs and assigns forever, provided all ways never the less, that if the said Thos C. Love his heirs Executors or administrators shall well and truly pay or cause to be paid unto the said Geo L. Brown His Executors administrators or assigns the aforesaid sum of Three Hundred Sixty four Dollars and thirty nine cents the same sum mentioned and described in said promissory notes together with the lawful interest thereon as due or hereafter to become due on or before the first day of January One Thousand Eight Hundred and Fifty one as well as all such further sum or sums money as shall be hereafter be acknowledged by the said Thomas C. Love by endorsement on this mortgage to be due by endorsement from the said Geo L. Brown to the said Thomas C. Love, then the foregoing mortgaged deed to be absolutely null and void other wise to remain in full force and virtue."

January 28, 1850
From Alachua County Ancient Records
Mortgage Record A pages 036-038

Thomas C. Love to Mathew W. Smith as collateral for a $1,000 loan: "This Indenture made this Sixteenth day of February A.D. 1855. Between Thomas C. Love, of Said State and County, and Mathew W. Smith of the Same place, Witnesseth that the said Thomas C. Love, for and in Consideration of five dollars to him in hand paid by the Said Smith, the receipt whereof is hereby acknowledged, as well for the better Securing the payment of a certain promissory note for the Sum of one thousand dollars, bearing even date with these presents, given and Signed by the Said Thomas C. Love to the Said Mathew W. Smith, and due and payable by the first day of January next, have granted, bargained, Sold, and delivered, and by these presents do grant, bargain, Sell and deliver to the Said Mathew W. Smith, three Negro Slaves, to wit: **Clarissa a woman, thirty Six years of age, Nancy Seven years of age, and Cyrus one year and Six months of age, the two last being Children of the Said first named Clarissa**; To have and to hold the Said Slaves to him the Said Mathew W. Smith, his Executors, Administrators and assigns for ever, and to his and their only benefit use and behoof, and I the Said Thomas C. Love, my heirs, Executors and Administrators, Shall and will warrant the Said Slaves to be Sound of body and mind, and to be Slaves for life and the title thereof to the Said Mathew W. Smith, Shall and will warrant, and for ever defend, by these presents Now the condition of this Indenture is Such, that if the Said Thomas C. Love Shall well and truly pay, or cause to be paid the Said promissory note, according to the tenor and effect of Said note, then, as well the Said note as this Indenture Shall cease, and be null and void else to remain in full force and virtue, both in law and Equity"

February 16, 1855
State of Florida, Alachua County
From Alachua County Ancient Records
Deed Record D page 044

Thomas C. Love to Mathew W. Smith as collateral for a $307.59 loan: "This indenture made this Sixteenth day of February A.D. 1855 between Thomas C. Love of said State and County, and Mathew W. Smith of the Same place, Witnesseth that the Said Thomas C. Love, for and in consideration of Five dollars to him in hand paid by the said Smith the receipt Whereof is hereby acknowledged, as well for the better securing the payment of a certain promissory note, for the Sum of three hundred and Seven 59/100 Dollars, given and Signed by the Said Thomas C. Love, to the said Matthew W. Smith, and due and payable on or before the first day of January next, ensuing, have granted bargained Sold and delivered and by these presents do grant bargain Sell and deliver, unto the Said Mathew W. Smith his heirs and assigns one certain Negro Slave, to wit, **Tom a boy thirteen years of age**, to have and to hold the said Slave unto him the said Smith his heirs and assigns forever, And the Said Thomas C. Love his heirs and assigns shall and will warrant the said Slave to be sound of Body & mind and a Slave for life. The condition of this indenture is such that if the Said Thomas C. Love his Executors or administrators shall well & Truly pay or cause to be paid the said promissory note according to the Tenor, and effect thereof, then the said note as well this indenture Shall cease and be null and void, Else to remain in full force and both in law and Equity"

February 16, 1855
State of Florida, Alachua County
From Alachua County Ancient Records
Deed Record D page 045

Samuel Lowman acknowledging property of wife Susan E. Lowman: "Be it Remembered that whereas my wife Susan E. Lowman is justly owner in her own right by gift from her Brother John Thorp to certain slaves to wit **Harry Bettie Mariah John Elisa Martha Tom**

Lalina Andrew Presley and June together with their increase and also by gift one horse by purchase three colts four mules and one Piano to which I have no Legal Claim or right nevertheless for the purposes of fully settling the question that I may or might Set up to said property above described and fully confirm and establish her title to the same and also for and in consideration of the natural love and affection which I bear her by Law Wife I do hereby give grant and convey unto her all my right title and interest to said property decried in full to use manage or dispose of as to her may seem *** and right free from all debts contracts or liabilities that I may contract or incur to the only proper use benefit and behoof to her and her heirs forever"

April 23, 1859
State of Florida, County of Alachua
From Alachua County Ancient Records
Deed Record E page 013

J. C. Massey to his daughters Charlotte E. Heath and Rosa M. Heath: "For and in consideration of the love and respect that I have for my two Daughters Charlotte E. Heath and Rosa M. Heath I give to them **one female Slave named Violet about fifty years old** to the Said Charlotte E. Heath and Rosa M. Heath their heirs executors or administrators, or assigns free of all claims or demands." - J. C. Massey

September 5, 1857
State of Florida, Alachua County
From Alachua County Ancient Records
Deed Record D page 492

John P. C. Massey to Mrs. Rosa M. Heath as collateral for $4,109.55 in loans: "Whereas I John P. C. Massey of the County of Alachua & State of Florida am indebted to Mrs. Rosa M. Heath of the County of Alachua and State of Florida – Administratrix of the Estate of Washington R. Heath dec'd in the full and Just Sum of Four Thousand one hundred & nine dollars & fifty five cents ($4109.55/100) for which amount I have given my promissory notes bearing date May 4th to wit: Lot No (1) one: Range (3) three: Block (2) Two: and Lot No (3) three: Block (2) Two: Range (3) Three: and No (4) Block (2) Two: Range (3) Three: and Lot No. (1) One: Block (4) four: Range (3) three: and Block No Two Range (5) Together with all and Singular the rights, members, hereditaments and appurtenances as to the premises belonging or in any wise appertaining, Also the following named Negro Slaves to wit: **A Negro Woman and her two children Viz: Charlotte a negro Woman about (24) Twenty four years old, Julia a girl about (6) Six years old; and Frank a Boy (3) three years old** to have and to hold the above described premises, together with the above described Negroes, unto the said Rosa M. Heath her heirs, Executors, Administrators and assigns forever, Provided nevertheless that it is the true interest and meaning of these presents, That if the said John P. C. Massey does and shall well and truly pay or caused to be paid, unto the said Rosa M. Heath her heirs, Executors, Administrators or assigns the said debt or Sum of Money aforesaid with the interest thereon according to the true interest and meaning of the said note; Then this deed of bargain and Sale Shall cease determine and be utterly null & void, otherwise it Shall remain in full force and virtue."

May 4, 1857
State of Florida, Alachua County
From Alachua County Ancient Records
Mortgage Record A pages 100-101

S. C. Massey to son Thomas D. Massey: "For and in consid-eration of the Love and natural respect which I have to my son Thomas D. Massey I give to him a certain **Negro boy named Toney, about ten years old.**"

September 5, 1856
State of Florida, Alachua County
From Alachua County Ancient Records
Deed Record D page 509

Alexander Matheson to his wife Harriet Mary Matheson: "This Indenture made on the tenth day of November in the year of our Lord one thousand eight hundred and fifty six between Alexander Matheson of the first part & his wife Harriet Mary Matheson of the second part both of the County and State aforesaid Witnesseth, That Whereas the said party of the first part is lawfully seized and pos-sessed of the property hereinafter described and whereas also he is desirous of securing to his wife the said party of the second part a competency out of his property; Know yea therefore, that I the said party of the first part, for and in consideration of the natural love and affection which I have and bear for and to my said wife as well as for the consideration above mentioned have bargained, sold, and con-veyed and delivered and by these presents do so bargain, sell, convey and deliver to my said wife the party of the second part aforesaid, the following named and described Negro Slaves, Viz; **Lewis about forty years old, his wife Dolly about forty five years old and his son Jim about fourteen years old, her daughter Mary about eleven years old, her daughter Sill about nine years old, her daughter Belly about seven years old, and her son Lewis about five years old; Bill about forty years old Aaron about thirty years old, Hes-ekiah about fifty years old, Rachel about forty years old, Betsy about twenty five years old, her daughter Henryetta about nine**

years old and her son Edward about five years old, Nanny about eighteen years old. To have and to hold the above described and conveyed Negro Slaves, unto the said party of the second part and the heirs of her body, lawfully begotten by the said party of the first part forever, free from all control of the said party of the first part and in no wise subject to any contract, or debts which the said party of the first part may enter into or contract or be liable for

The said negro slaves **together with the further issue and increase of the female portion thereof** as well as the profits arising from their labors and service to belong & exclusively to the said party of the second part during her covesture with the said party of the first part to be held by the said party of the second part for the use and benefit of such child or children as the said party of the first part may leave lawfully begotten of the said party of the second part.

And should the said party of the second part die leaving no lawful issue the slaves above mentioned and described together with their future issue and increase are to become part and parcel of the estate of the said party of the first part but should she die leaving lawful issue before the said party of the first part then the said party of the first part shall have the controle of the property aforesaid for the use and benefit of such child or children as the said party of the second part may leave at her decease to be divided between them, share and share alike."

November 10, 1856
State of Florida, Alachua County
From Alachua County Ancient Records
Deed Record D pages 377-378

Alexander Matheson to Tillman Ingram and E. E. Adamson as collateral for a $15,000 loan: "Whereas I Alexander Matheson of the State of Florida and Alachua County of Alachua am indebted to Tillman Ingram of the County of Alachua and State of Florida and E. E. Adamson of the State of South Carolina Kershaw District in the full and just Sum of Fifteen Thousand dollars for which amount I have given my promissory note, bearing date June twelfth one thousand Eight hundred and fifty Seven payable on demand with Interest from date at the rate of Seven per cent the Interest to be computed as principal, annually until paid. Now know all Men by these presents, that for and in Consideration of said Indebtedness, and for the better Securing the payment of the same to said Tillman Ingram & Edward E. Adamson their heirs, Executors, administrators and assigns I, the said Alexander Matheson have given granted bargained Sold, aliened remised released, conveyed and confirmed, and by these presents do give grant bargain Sell alien remise release convey and confirm unto the said Tillman Ingram and Edward E. Adamson the following tracts or parcels of land Situate lying and being in the County of Alachua and State of Florida Known and described as follows to Wit: Beginning at a Stake on the Eastern Boundary of the Town of Gainesville and running East two hundred and twenty yards to a Stake, thence north Four hundred and forty four yards to a Stake, thence west to the said boundary of the Town of Gainesville to a Stake then South along said Eastern boundary to the point of beginning containing Ten acres more or less lying and being in Section four Township Ten Range twenty Arredondo Grant Known as Lots two and Three East Gainesville, Together with as and Singular the rights ways members hereditaments, issues and profits, reversion and reversions remainder and remainders, whatsoever to the same belonging or in any wise appertaining also the following named personal property Negro Slaves To Wit **Billy aged about forty years, Aaron aged about thirty five years, Hezekiah aged about fifty years and his wife Rachel aged about forty-five; Lewis aged about forty years, and his wife Dolly aged about thirty five old, and their children Jim aged fifteen years, Mary aged Twelve years Celin aged Ten years Betsey aged twenty five years, and her Children**

– Henneretta aged nine years and Edmond aged five years, Shen aged thirty years and his wife Amelia aged twenty-five years and their children, Simon aged Seven years Sue four years and Infant: Violet twenty years old and her Infant, Charlotte and her Infant. **Patsey twenty five years old and her Infant** To Have and to Hold the above described premises together with the named personal property Negro Slaves with and Singular the rights ways, members hereditaments, rents issues and profits, reversion and reversions, remainder and remainders whatsoever to the same belonging or in any wise Appertaining to have and to hold unto the said Tillman Ingram and Edward E. Adamson their heirs Executors Administrators and assigns forever Provided nevertheless it is the true meaning and interest of these presents that if the said Alexander Matheson shall and does well and truly pay or cause to be paid unto the said Tillman Ingram and E. E. Adamson their heirs Executors and assigns the said debt or sum of money aforesaid with the interest thereon according to the true intent and meaning of said note then this deed bargain and sale shall cease determining and become utterly null and void otherwise it shall remain in full force and virtue"

June 12, 1857
State of Florida, Alachua County
From Alachua County Ancient Records
Mortgage Record A pages 104-106

Alexander Matheson gave enslaved people to Tillman Ingram and E. E. Adamson as collateral for a $15,000 loan. Tillman Ingram and E. E. Adamson renounce and release claim to several of the enslaved named in the original document. "Whereas Alexander Matheson of the State of Florida and County of Alachua did execute and deliver to us Tillman Ingram and E. E. Adamson on the Twelfth day of June A. D. Eighteen hundred & fifty seven a mortgage of certain negroes amongst them were **Betsey & her children Henrietta & Edmund** beside others for the secure payment of the sum of Fifteen Thousand Dollars which said mortgage of Record with Clerk Office in the County of Alachua and State aforesaid in Book of Mortgages upon Page 114 & 115 and whereas the said Alexander Matheson has this day sold and delivered to Matthew Cheves the said Slaves Betsey & her children Henrietta Edmund or Edward

Now know all men by these presents that we Tillman Ingram and E. E. Adamson of the County of Alachua and State of Florida for and in Consideration of Five dollars to us in hand paid by Alexander Matheson the receipt whereof is hereby acknowledged have renounced and released and do hereby renounce and release all our right title or claim whatsoever both in law and equity to or upon the said negroes slaves Betsey Henrietta and Edward her children, under or by virtue of said mortgage given as aforesaid by the said Alexander Matheson to us as aforesaid"

February 13, 1858
State of Florida, Alachua Co.
From Alachua County Ancient Records
Mortgage Record A page 129

Christopher Matheson to Alexander Matheson, held in trust for Christopher's daughter Mary C. McCaa: "Know all men by these presents that I, Christopher Matheson of the Town of Camden in the District and State aforesaid In consideration of Natural Love and affection for my daughter Mary C. McCaa wife of Dr Thomas W. McCaa and also in further consideration of Five dollars to me paid by Alexander Matheson all these being likewise of the District and State aforesaid have given bargained sold and delivered and by these presents do give bargain sell and deliver unto the said Alexander

Matheson a certain **Negro Woman Slave named Margaret about Eighteen years of age** To Have and to hold the said Negro woman Slave named Margaret, **Together with the future issue and increase** unto the said Alexander Matheson his Executors and administrators In trust and upon this Special confidence that he the said Alexander Matheson his Executors and Administrators Shall and do suffer and permit the said Mary C. McCaa to retain the possession of the said Slave Margaret with her issue and increase and to receive use and enjoy the hire profits and labor thereof to her sole and seperate use free from the control contracts debts and disposals of her present or any future husband for and during the term of the natural life of the said Mary C. McCaa. And upon this further Special trust and confidence that after and immediately upon the death of the said Mary C. McCaa he the said Alexander Matheson his Exors or Admrs shall hold the said Negro Slave Margaret Together with her future issue and increase for the benefit of the heirs of the body of the said Mary C. McCaa who may be living at the time of her death Share and Share alike to them their Executors administrators and assigns forever, But in case the said Mary C. McCaa should die leaving no heirs of her body alive at the time of her death them and in that case for the benefit of the said Christopher Matheson his Executors administrators or assigns forever"

April 24, 1852
South Carolina, Kershaw District
From Alachua County Ancient Records
Deed Record D pages 403-405

Christopher Matheson to Thomas R. Taylor as collateral for a $4,340 loan: "To all whom these presents Shall come Christopher Matheson of Camden in the State aforesaid Send Greetings Whereas the Said Christopher Mathison am indebted to Thomas R. Taylor,

Commissioner in Equity for Kershaw District by my Bond conditioned for the payment of Four Thousand Three hundred and forty dollars in two equal annual Instalments from the Second day of February A.D. 1857[…] Now Know ye that I the Said Christopher Mathison for the better Securing the payment of the Said Sum of money above mentioned unto the Said Thomas R. Taylor, his Successors in office his or their Certain Attorney or assigns together with the lawful Interest for the Same according to the consideration of Said Bond, have bargained and Sold and by these presents do bargain Sell and in plain and open market deliver unto the Said Thomas R. Taylor Commissioner as aforesaid the following named Negro Slaves. To Wit; **Rachael and her four Children, Viz, Little Rachael, John Frank Pinder, Mariah and her Child Harriet**, To have and to hold the Said Negro Slaves above named unto the Said Thomas R. Taylor, Commissioner as aforesaid his Successors in office, his or their certain Attorney, and assigns forever, Provided always nevertheless, That if the Said Christopher Mathison his executors or Administrators Shall & do well and truly pay or cause to be paid unto The Said Thomas R. Taylor Commissioner as aforesaid, his Successors in office his or their certain Attorney or assigns the full and just Sum above mentioned according to the true intent & meaning of the Bond aforesaid and of these presents, then this deed of Bargain and Sale to all and every clause article and thing therein contained Shall cease determine and be utterly void and none effect anything hereinbefore contained to the contrary thereof in anywise notwithstanding […] if default happen to be made of or in payment of the Said Sum above mentioned according to the true intent and meaning of the Said Bond that then and in Such case, it shall and may be lawful to and for the Said Thomas R. Taylor his Successors in office, his or their Certain assigns attorneys or agents from time to time and at any time hereafter peaceably and quietly to enter into any or all of the Messuage lands or tenements of the Said Christopher Mathison and to take the Negro Slaves above named into his or their custody and possession and the Same to hold and retain to his or their own use and behoof as his or their own proper goods and Chattels from henceforth and forever or the Same to Sell and dispose of at his or their Will and pleasure returning the overplus if any their

Should happen to be after paying the sum above mentioned unto the Said Christopher Mathison his Executors Administrators or assigns"

February 2, 1857 and in the Eighty first year of the American Independence
The State of South Carolina
From Alachua County Ancient Records
Mortgage Record A pages 098-100

John T. Matthews to Thomas M. Boulware as collateral for a $3,500 loan: "This Indenture made this the twenty Sixth day of March A. D. One thousand Eight hundred & fifty Nine, Between John T. Matthews of the County of Alachua & State of Florida party of the first part and Thomas M. Boulware of Chester District South Carolina party of the Second part Whereas the Said party of the Second part, has become Surety for the Said party of the first part, on a Certain note made by the Said party of the first part, made payable at the Commercial Bank of Columbia South Carolina for the Sum of Thirty five hundred dollars made about the first of October A.D. One thousand Eight hundred & fifty Eight, and four Months after date, together with the interest that may accrue after due untill paid In Consideration Whereof as well as for the further Consideration of One dollar to the Said party of the first part in hand paid at and before the Sealing and delivery of these presents by the Said party of the Second part, the receipt whereof is hereby acknowledged, the Said party of the first part hath given granted bargained, Sold, Conveyed & Confirmed, and by these presents doth So give grant bargain Sell and Convey unto the Said party of the Second part his heirs and assigns the following described property to wit lands Known and described as follows To wit Section Twenty Seven (27) Twenty Eight and Thirty Four Range twenty Township Nine together with all and Singular the appurtinances heriditaments thereunto belonging or in any ways appurtaining, Also the following described Negroes To wit **Charles a Negro Man Slave**

about Twenty five years Old Nelson a Negro Man Slave about twenty two years old Also a Negro Woman Slave about Thirty one years old Tina a Negro girl Slave about Twenty years old together with their future increase to have and to hold unto the said party of the Second part his heirs and assigns forever Provided Nevertheless that it is the true intent and meaning of these presents that if the said party of the first part Shall well and truly pay or cause to be paid the Said note on or before the Twenty first of January A.D. One thousand Eight hundred and Sixty then this Indenture of Mortgage to become null and void else to remain in full force & virtue"

March 26, 1859
State of Florida, Alachua Cty
From Alachua County Ancient Records
Mortgage Record A page 230

John H. May indicted for stealing an enslaved person: "State of Florida vs. John H May - Stealing a Slave: On this cause being called the prisoner was arraigned and plead not guilty. There not being time to try the cause at this term of the Court and it appearing that the prisoner is in delicate health by consent of Solicitor It is ordered by the Court that the prisoner do enter into a recognizance at Ten thousand dollars for his appearance at the next term of the Court: Whereupon the principal John H. May, and his sureties William May, Samuel R. Johnson and Harry Graddock appeared in open Court and acknowledged themselves indebted to the State of Florida in the said Sum of Ten Thousand dollars: That is to Say, the principal John H. May in the Sum of Ten Thousand Dollars, and his Sureties William May, Samuel R. Johnson and Henry Graddock in the Sum of Three Thousand three hundred and thirty three dollars each, to be levied upon of their respective goods & chattels, lands, tenements and Slaves if default be made on the following condition,

That is to say, if the said John H. May shall be and appear at the next term of this Court to answer to an indictment for stealing a Slave, and shall not thence depart the Court without leave thereof then this obligation to be null and void, else to remain in full force and virtue

And now on this day also appeared Andrew J. Wall a witness in behalf of the State in the above cause, and acknowledged himself indebted to the State of Florida in the sum of Two hundred dollars, to be levied upon of his goods and chattels, slaves lands and tenements, in default of his appearing at the next term of this Court, as a witness in the above cause"

December 15, 1855
From Alachua County Ancient Records
Judgment Record A* pages 339-340

John H. May charged with stealing an enslaved person: "The State of Florida vs John H. May - Stealing a Slave - On motion of the Solicitor It is ordered by the Court that this cause be continued and that the defendant be discharged upon his recognizance Entered unto last Term"

May 16, 1856
From Alachua County Ancient Records
Judgment Record A* page 384

Prisoner John H. May indicted for stealing an enslaved person and found not guilty: "The State of Florida vs John H. May - Stealing a Slave - And now on this day came the Solicitor J. B. Dawkins

Esq. who prosecutes the pleas of the State in this behalf as well also the defendant in his own proper person and by his attorneys and the prisoner being formally arraigned pleaded "not guilty" and put himself upon the Country and thereupon came a jury...who being duly selected and sworn well and truly to try and true deliverance make between the State of Florida and the prisoner at the bar, after having heard the testimony of witnesses the argument of Counsel and charge of the Court retired to consider of their verdict rendered the following to wit, We the Jury find the Prisoner Not Guilty

Whereupon it is ordered considered and adjudged by the Court that the defendant do have and recover of and from the State of Florida his costs in this behalf Expended Taxed at Dollars and cents and the plaintiff in mercy &c"

May 14, 1857
From Alachua County Ancient Records
Judgment Record A* page 519

T. W. McCaa (married to Christopher Matheson's daughter) received from Christopher Matheson 7 enslaved people as a loan: "I hereby acknowledge that I have this day received from Mr. Christopher Matheson of the State and District aforesaid the following named negroes to wit **Old Tom, Boston, Docter, Craton, little Tom, Limas, and Dicy** as a loan the use of the same being allowed to me by him as advancement of his daughter now my wife and I hereby promise to hold the Said negroes as his property Claiming only the labor of the same during his will and pleasure

I also acknowledge that the Interest of the Said C. Matheson in the said negroes is for and during the natural life of John Fraser, the same being derived by John Fraser from the will of his Father John Baxter

Fraser and purchased by C. Matheson for such Term at the Sale by the Sheriff of the property of John Fraser in case I retain the Said negroes during the Term of John Frasers life by consent of C. Matheson I hereby obligate myself to render up the same and the Increase thereof to such person or persons as may be lawfully intitled to them as remainderman"

February 12, 1852
State of South Carolina, Kershaw District
From Alachua County Ancient Records
Deed Record D page 405

John McCrory Last Will and Testament: "I, John McCrory of the District of Fairfield in the State aforesaid being weak of body, but of sound and disposing mind and memory, do make and declare as and for my last will and testament the following:

1. I will and direct that the whole of my estate real and personal shall be sold by my executors, the time and terms of such sale to be fixed by them according to their discretion, so as best to promote the interest of my estate

2. I direct my executors to have **all of my negroes** now in the State of Florida, brought back to the State of South Carolina to be sold, as I believe the purchase money therefrom can be better secured in this State - If however my executors should think it advantageous to sell any of them in Florida, they are hereby authorized to do so.

3. I hereby invest my executors as either of them with full power and authority to sell and dispose of the whole of my estate, both in this State and in the State of Florida, and to execute good and sufficient title deeds to all of my real estate.

351

4. I will and direct my executors to apply their proceeds of the sales made by them as last collected towards satisfaction of my debts according to law and after paying all of my debts out of my estate then balance thereof I direct, to be equally divided, share and share alike between my wife and children."

August 27, 1859
The State of South Carolina
From Alachua County Ancient Records
Will Records 2 pages 415-416

John McKinlay to Charles L. Wilson for $1,600: "Know all men by these presents that I, John McKinlay of said State and County for and in consideration of the Sum of Sixteen hundred dollars, to me in hand paid by Charles L. Wilson of said County the receipt whereof at and before the sealing and delivery of these presents is hereby acknowledged, have given, granted, bargained, sold, and conveyed, and do by these presents give, grant, bargain, sell, and convey unto the said Charles L. Wilson the following described property, to wit, **Emily a negro female slave, and her two children namely Cuffee a boy aged about seven years, and Henry a boy aged about Eighteen months and also Tena a negro female slave, aged about twenty three years Together with all the future issue and increase of said slaves.**" To Have and to hold the above described property to him the said Charles L. Wilson his heirs and assigns forever [...]"

January 4, 1851
State of Florida, Alachua County
From Alachua County Ancient Records
Deed Record A page 356

George W. Means, Samuel C. Means, & William J. Means to L. G. Holloway as collateral for $6,528 in loans: "This Indenture made this tenth day of May in the year one thousand Eight hundred and fifty six between George W. Means, Samuel C. Means & William J. Means of the first part and L.G. Holloway of the second part Witnesseth That whereas the said parties of the first part are indebted to the said party of the second part for the purchase of some negroes in the same negroes in the Sum of Six Thousand five hundred twenty eight dollars […] without interest […] for the purpose of making the payments of the above Sums of money Secure and punctual the said parties of the first part for the consideration of five dollars to them in hand paid at & before the sealing and delivery hereof, the receipt whereof is hereby acknowledged have bargained and Sold and do by these presents bargain & Sell unto the said party of the Second part his heirs and assigns the following mentioned negro Slaves: To Wit **Jack a boy aged about thirty three years and generally Known as Jack Sullivan; Jack aged about thirty years & Known as Jack Ervin; Jeff aged about thirty years, Lewis aged about twenty seven years, Anderson aged about twenty years, Wallace aged about sixteen years, Ellen aged about twenty one years & her child Sarah aged about two years, Jim aged about Seven years & Henry aged about five years**, To Have & to hold the negro Slaves unto him the said party of the second part, his heirs and assigns forever, Provided always nevertheless & these presents are on the express condition That if the said parties of the first part shall well and truly pay or cause to be paid to the said party of the second part or his assigns the said promissory notes herein above described that is to say: the sum of Three hundred and fifty seven dollars on the first day of January eighteen hundred and fifty seven The like sum of Money on the first day of January 1858. The same sum of money again on the first day of January 1859. and the sum of Five thousand four hundred and fifty seven dollars on the first day of January 1860, then these presents to be null and void and of non effect. otherwise to be and remain in full force and virtue"

May 10, 1856
State of Florida, Marion County
From Alachua County Ancient Records
Mortgage Record A pages 087-089

Horace Merry to William H. Hickman as collateral for a $8,424.72 loan: "Known all men by these presents that I Horace Merry of the county and State aforesaid in consideration of the sum of Eight Thousand four hundred and Twenty four dollars and seventy two cents to me in hand paid by William H. Hickman of Marion County and the State aforesaid the receipt whereof I do hereby acknowledge, do hereby give grant bargain sell and convey unto the said William H. Hickman his heirs and assigns forever The following tract or parcel of land together with certain negros whose names are handwritten within That is to say The North East quarter of Section No Thirty in township No twelve South of Range No Twenty one and containing one hundred and sixty three acres and forty eight hundreths of an acre and entered in the Receivers Office at Newnansville on the sixteenth day of August in the year one thousand eight hundred and forty seven. Also the west quarter of section twenty nine in Township twelve south of Range Twenty one East containing Eighty acres and eight hundreths of an acre. Entered in the Land Office at Newnansville by land warrant No. 5572 and patented at the city of Washington on the tenth day of November in the year one thousand eight hundred and fifty one, all of which will more fully appear reference being had to the United States General Land Office Also the certain parcel of lands known as lot No one of fractional section No nineteen in Township number Twelve south of Range No Twenty one East containing forty four acres and eighty five hundreths of an acre and recorded at

354

the records office at Newnansville on the fourth day of April in the year one thousand eight hundred and fifty as will more fully appear recours being had to said Office And also four Hundred and Sixty Six acres in section Twenty five of Township No Eleven of Range No 20 being and situate in the county of Alachua, commencing at the north west corner of said section and running along the northern boundary line, such a distance and to such a point as will make the number of four hundred and sixty six acres when said point is connected by a line running parallel with the western boundary of said section and intersecting the southern boundary line of the same section at a point equally distant from the southwestern corner, with the point on the northern boundary from the northwestern corner As well as the south half of section No Thirty six of Township No Eleven and Range No twenty-containing Three hundred and twenty five acres more or less being and situate in the county of Alachua as well as the following slaves "That is to Say" **Ben aged about forty - Lucy also forty - Diannah nineteen Flora seventeen. March Thirty five. Dolly Twenty-nine Chloey nine Incy about five years** To have and to hold the aforegranted premises and slaves above named to the said William H. Hickman, his heirs and assigns to his and their use & behoof forever [...] Provided nevertheless that if the said Horace Merry his heirs executors or administrators shall pay unto the said W. H. Hickman his executors administrators or assigns the said sum of Eight thousand four hundred and twenty-four dollars and seventy-two cents on or before the first day of January which shall be in the year of our Lord one thousand Eight hundred and fifty five; then this deed shall be void otherwise shall remain absolute."

February 19, 1853
State of Florida, Alachua County
From Alachua County Ancient Records
Mortgage Record A pages 071-073

Horace Merry to Jones McCarthy as collateral for a $4,000 loan:
"This indenture made on the twenty ninth day of August in the year
one thousand eight hundred and fifty five between Horace Merry of
the first part and Jones McCarthy of the second part witnesseth that for
and in consideration of the sum of four thousand dollars ($4000.00)
to the said party of the first part paid (the receipt whereof is hereby
acknowledged) by the said party of the second part, the said party of
this first part hath bargained, sold, given, granted and conveyed and by
these present does so bargain, sell, give, grant and convey unto the said
party of the second part, the following mentioned and described lands,
and negro slaves, to wit: four hundred and sixty acres of land in section
twenty five of township eleven, of Range twenty situate in the county
of Alachua & state aforesaid, commencing at the north west corner
of said section running along the northern boundary line such a distance and to such a point as will make the number of four hundred and
sixty acres, when said point is connected by a line running parallel with
the western boundary line of said section, and intersecting the southern boundary line of the same section at a point equally distant from
the south western corner with the point on the northern boundary line
from the north western corner of said section, comprising the entire
interest of the said party of the first part in said section, also the south
half of section thirty six, of township eleven, of Range Twenty in the
said county and state aforesaid, containing three hundred and twenty
five acres, together with all and singular the improvements & appurtenances to the same belonging or in any wise appertaining, as well as
the following Negro Slaves, to wit: **Ben aged about forty five years,
Dianna aged about twenty years, Flora aged about nineteen years,
Mariah aged about thirty five years, Chloe aged about twelve
years, Lucy aged about seven years, Sally aged about thirty years,
Mary aged about two years, and Betsy aged about two years**. To
have and to hold the aforegranted & described premises together with
the improvments thereon, and the Slaves above mentioned under the
said party of the second part, his heirs and assigns forever, to his & to
their own proper use and behoof, provided always nevertheless that if
the said party of the first part, shall on or before the first day of January
in the year one thousand eight hundred and fifty seven, pay or cause to

be paid to the said party of the second part, his heirs, Executors administrators or assigns, the sum of four thousand dollars with interest at eight percent per annum, from the twenty fourth day of August in the year one thousand eight hundred and fifty five then these presents as well as a certain note of hand given by the said party of the first part, to the said party of the second part, for the sum of four thousand dollars, and bearing date the twenty fourth day of August in the year one thousand eight hundred and fifty five, to be void and of no effect in law or otherwise to be and remain in full force and virtue."

August 29, 1855
State of Florida, Alachua County
From Alachua County Ancient Records
Mortgage Record A pages 081-082 and
Mortgage Record A pages 201-203

Horace Merry to James McCarthy as collateral for a $6,170 loan:
"This Indenture made on the twentieth day of April in the year of our Lord one thousand eight hundred and fifty nine Between Horrace Merry of the first part and James McCarthy of the second part Witnesseth That for and in consideration of the sum of Six Thousand one Hundred and seventy dollars to him in hand paid at and before the sealing and delivery hereof the receipt whereof is hereby acknowledged the said party of the first part has bargained sold given granted & conveyed and by these presents doth so bargain sell give grant & convey to the said party of the second part his heirs and assigns forever the following mentioned and described plantation or parcel of land and negro Slaves That is to say Four Hundred and sixty six acres of land in Section twenty five of Township Eleven Range twenty situated in the County of Alachua & the State aforesaid commencing at the North west corner of said section and running along the northern boundary line such a distance and to such a point as will make of four hundred

and sixty acres above said point is connected by a line running parallel with the western boundary line of said section of a point equally distant from the South Western Corner with the point on the northern boundary line from the North Western corner of Said Section comprising the entire interest of the Said party of the first part in Said section Also the South half of section thirty Six of Township Eleven of Range twenty in the County and State aforesaid containing three hundred and twenty five acres more or less together with all the appurtenances and improvements to the Same belonging & appertaining as well as the following mentioned and described negroes Slaves To wit **Diana aged about twenty four years Flora aged about twenty three years March aged about thirty nine years Chloe aged about Sixteen years Lucy aged about Eleven years Sally aged about thirty four years Mary aged about Six years Betsey aged about Six years Easter about one year old and Sarah about two years old,** To have and to hold the parcels of land above described and conveyed together with all and Singular the houses building & improvements & appurtenances to the Same belonging or in anywise appertaining & the Said Negro slaves **together with the future issue and increase thereof** unto the Said party of the second part his heirs heirs executors administrators and assigns in fee forever to his & to their proper uses benefit and behoof Provided always nevertheless and these presents are upon the express condition that when the Said party of the first part Shall pay to the said party of the second part heirs or assigns his certain promisory note bearing even date with these presents and made payable one day after the date thereof to the said party of the Second part or order with eight per cent interest from date together with all the interest which may accrue thereon before the payment of the Same the Said promisory note being under Seal and for the Sum of Six Thousand one hundred and Seventy dollars Then these presents to be null and void and of non effect either in Law or equity otherwise to remain in full force and virtue"

April 20, 1859
State of Florida, County of Alachua
From Alachua County Ancient Records
Deed Record E pages 025-026

John M. Miller to Frances A. Shannon for $6,000: "Know all men by these presents that I John M. Miller of the County of Alachua and State of Florida of the first part for and in consideration of the sum of Six thousand dollars to me in hand paid at or before the ensealing and delivering of these presents by Frances A. Shannon of the same place of the second part the receipts whereof is hereby acknowledged have bargained and sold and by these presents do grant and convey unto the said party of the second part his executors administrators and assigns, **Ten negroes named Tom Mary, Charles, George Sam Jessee Letty Marion Elizabeth and William,** also five mules, one sorrel mare, two Wagons one Buggy fifteen head of hogs, and five head of Cattle - Household and Kitchen furniture together with Cotton contained in house and field on plantation of party of the first, To have and to hold the same unto the said party of the second part his executors administrators and assigns forever."

December 1, 1856
From Alachua County Ancient Records
Deed Record D page 393

John Mizell to Joshua Mizell for $4,000: "Know all men by these presents that I John Mizell of the State and County aforesaid, have this day bargained unto Joshua Mizell of the County and State aforesaid, for the Sum of four thousand dollars, to me in hand paid, the receipt of which is hereby acknowledged, certain property viz, **one Negro girl named Rebecca, one Negro boy named Emanuel,** two horses, and my interest in a certain tract of land won in Suit against Paul McCormack, Situated on Orange Lake, in Marion County Florida, and I do hereby warrant and defend the right and title of Said property, unto the Said Joshua Mizell, and his legal representatives, against all and person or persons lawfully Claiming the Same."

March 15, 1855
State of Florida, Alachua County
From Alachua County Ancient Records
Deed Record D pages 083-084

David W. Mizell Trustee & wife vs John H. May regarding who owns enslaved people: "David W. Mizell Trustee &c & wife vs John H. May - Replevin - And now on this day came the parties by their respective attorneys and Issue being Joined, thereupon came a Jury [...] who being duly sworn well and truly to try the issue Joined between the parties, after hearing the Testimony of Witnesses, the argument of counsel and the charge of the Court, retired to consider of their Verdict and thereafter and upon the same day said Jurors returned into Court and rendered the following Verdict to wit: We the Jury do find the said slaves in said plaintiffs' declaration mentioned to be the property of said plaintiffs and do assess their damages at our cost,

Whereupon It is ordered considered and adjudged by the Court that the plaintiffs do have and retain the possession of the said slaves in said declaration mentioned, and do have and recover of and from said defendant the said sum of our cost, for their damages together with their costs in this behalf expended..."

May 12, 1856
From Alachua County Ancient Records
Judgment Record A* page 372

Abraham Mott Last Will and Testament: "In the name of God Amen. I, Abraham Mott of Alachua County State of Florida being of Sound mind disposing mind and memory, do make declare and publish this my last Will and Testament Imprimes;

I bequeath to my son Benjamin Mott and to the heirs of his body **my Negro boy named George age about Fifteen Years**.

2nd Item; I bequeath to my Son Mathew Mott **my Negro boy Jacob age about Twelve years** forever

3rd Item; I bequeath to my Daughter Jane Mott forever **a Negro Girl Named Margaret now about fourteen years of age**

4th Item; I bequeath to my Daughter Catharine Mott forever **a Negro boy named Aleck now about Ten years of age**

5th Item; I bequeath unto my Daughter Frances Mott forever **a Negro Girl named Lenee age now about nine years**

6th Item; I bequeath unto my Daughter Ann Eliza Mott **a Negro boy named Sam aged about Eight Years** forever

7th Item; I bequeath to my Daughter Adaline Mott forever **a Negro boy named Parish, aged now about five years**

8th Item; I bequeath unto my Daughter Sarah Mott **a Negro man named Wash aged about Thirty five**, and should no division of my estate be had until my daughter Sarah is of age and said Negro Wash Should be of less value than the property bequeath to any of the other heirs I devise that She be made equal with them in every respect

9th Item; I bequeath unto my beloved wife Eliza Ann Mott **my Negro Woman Martha and Tener** to be held and Enjoyed by her during her Natural life, should She remain unmarried so long after my death.

361

10th Item; It is my will and pleasure that my Stock of Horses, Cattle and Hogs, Should be used Jointly by my family until my Children Shall respectively become of the age of Twenty one years and be married and that each Shall respectively receive his or her Share at such period

11th Item; I desire all of my lands to my Said Children to be equally divided among them Share and Share alike and to the heirs of Their body forever Respective when they shall become of the age of Twenty one years and be married.

12th Item; It is my Will and pleasure that upon The Marriage or death of my said Wife Eliza Ann Mott The Negro Woman Martha and Lener herein before bequeathed to her shall be equally divided in manner and form, as provided for the distribution of the other property Mentioned in this Will

13th Item; It is also my Will and pleasure that the Several Negroes hereinbefore bequeathed to my Children respectively shall not be given to them until they shall respectively reach the age of Twenty one Year and be married"

September 18, 1858
State of Florida, Alachua County
From Alachua County Ancient Records
Will Book B pages 012-014

Mrs. S. E. Myers loaned 2 enslaved people to T. I. Myers: "I acknowledge that the following negroes **Joseph and Sawney** are the property of Mrs. S. E. Myers, that she has loaned them to me until she shall choose to demand them back and then I agree to deliver them to her on her order."

February 11, 1858
From Alachua County Ancient Records
Bills of Sale A page 048

Mrs. S. E. Myers loaned 2 enslaved people to J. G. Jinkins: "I acknowledge **Patsy and increase, Bella** the property of Mrs. S. E. Myers and I bind myself to deliver them to the said S. E. Myers when-ever demanded"

February 11, 1858
From Alachua County Ancient Records
Bills of Sale A page 048

James T. Oneil & W. H. Clark Executors of Samuel Clark estate to James G. Cooper Trustee to the Children of John C. Pelot by his present wife Jane Ann Pelot for $1,920: "Know all men by these presents that we James T. Oneil & W. H. Clark Executors of Samuel Clark late of Nassau County deceased for and in Consideration of the Sum of Nineteen hundred & Twenty Dollars, to us in hand paid, at and before the Sealing and delivery of these presents, by James G. Cooper Trustee to the Children of John C. Pelot by his present wife Jane Ann Pelot "to wit" Alice Jane Pelot and other that may be born unto them the receipt whereof we do hereby acknowledge have bargained and Sold, and by these presents do bargain, Sell and deliver unto the Said James G. Cooper Trustee as aforesaid, Two Certain Slaves, to wit, **One man named Cain aged about 30 years and his daughter Rachael aged about 13 years with her future increase**, to have and to hold the Said property or Slaves In trust for the Sale and Separate use benefit and behoof of the Said Children of the said John C. and Jane A. Pelot with this Condition the Said James G. Cooper Trustee as aforesaid is hereby empowered to Sell, or otherwise dispose of Said Negroes, by and with the Consent of John C. Pelot, or in case of his death with the Consent of Jane A. Pelot, and to invest the proceeds in other property provided no loss shall be sustained by said Children unto the said James G. Cooper Trustee as aforesaid for said Children their heirs, Executors, Administrators and assigns, to have and to hold said Negroes for their only proper use and behoof forever"

February 17, 1859
State of Florida
From Alachua County Ancient Records
Deed Record C pages 389-390

Margaret W. Paisly to brothers William R. Paisly and Stephen S. Paisly: "Know all men by these presents that I Margaret W. Paisly of the State and County aforesaid in consideration of the natural love and affection which I have and bear for my two brothers, to wit William R. Paisly and Stephen S. Paisly and also for Diverse other good causes and considerations Me the Margaret W. Paisly hereunto moving, have given granted and confirmed and by these presents Do give grant and confirm unto the William R. Paisly and Stephen S. Paisly all and singular my rights title and interest in and to the following Negro slaves. To wit **one negro woman named Judy aged about forty five years and one negro girl named Dinah aged about sixteen years**

to have and to hold, all and singular the said negro slaves, **and their increase** unto the said William R. Paisly and Stephen S. Paisly , their heirs and assigns, to the only proper use and behoof of the William R. Paisly and Stephen S. Paisly their heirs Executors and administrators and assigns forever and I the said Margaret W. Paisly all and singular the said negro property to the said William R. Paisly and Stephen S. Paisly against me the said Margaret W. Paisly my executors and administrator, and all and every other person and persons, Whatsoever shall and will warrant and forever defend by these present, of and singular Which said negros I the said Margaret W. Paisly have put the said William R. Paisly and Stephen S. Paisly in full possession by delivery to them the said William R. Paisly and Stephen S. Paisly the forgoing negroes have at the time of sealing and delivery of these presents, in the name of the whole present hereby granted provided neverless, that the said negro slaves shall be held by the said William R. Paisly for the use and benefit of my father and Mother, to wit Thomas Paisly and Elizebeth Paisly during their natural lives and after their death of the said Thomas Paisly and Elizebeth Paisly then the said William R. Paisly and Stephen S. Paisly to agree to pay to Elizabeth C. Boals the sum of two hundred dollars for her own use and and the heirs of her body and not to be subject to the debts of her husband and provided that the said negroes shall be living at the death of the said Thomas Paisly and Elizabeth and then the said William R. Paisly and Stephen S. Paisly are to divide the aforesaid property and the increase of same equally"

June 16, 1853
State of Florida, Alachua County
From Alachua County Ancient Records
Deed Record B page 196

Margaret W. Paisly to Elizabeth Paisly for $50: "Know all men by these presents that I Margaret W. Paisly for and in consideration of the sum of Fifty Dollars to me in hand paid by Elizabeth Paisly of the County and State aforesaid the receipt whereof is hereby acknowledged have granted bargained and sold unto the said Elizabeth Paisly **a certain Negro girl slave named Letty aged thirteen years** to have and to hold the said Negro slave to the said Elizabeth Paisly for and during the natural life of the said Elizabeth Paisly and no longer. And provided and it is expressly understood that upon the decease of the said Elizabeth Paisly it shall be the duty of the heirs Administrators or Legal representatives of the said Elizabeth Paisly to return and deliver the said Negro slave to the said Margrett W. Paisly her heirs or Assigns

September 8, 1853
State of Florida, Alachua County
From Alachua County Ancient Records
Deed Record B page 220

Richard H. Parker to William Dell as Trustee for Richard's wife Hannah Parker: "Know all men by these presents that I, Richard H. Parker of the County and State aforesaid for and in consideration of the natural love and affection which I bear towards my wife Hannah Parker as well for divers other divers and good causes me thereunto moving have given granted sold and conveyed, and do by these presents give, grant sell and convey unto William Dell of said County and State, and in case of his death to such other person as by law shall be appointed as Trustee of my said wife Hannah Parker, the following described property and estate to wit, one tract or parcel of land containing forty acres, being the South East Qr of the North East qr of Section No. one Township No. Eight South of Range No. nineteen E. also one tract of land containing forty (40) acres being the North East Qr of the North west Qr of Section No. one (1) in Township No. Eight (8) South of Range No. Nineteen (19) East Also the named negroes, to wit, **Anny aged thirty years, Jane aged ten**

years, Jenny aged eight years, Jack aged twenty four years, Calvin aged twenty years, Charlton aged sixteen years, Sarah aged twelve years, Till aged ten years, York aged eight, Also seventy five head Stock Cattle, marked crop and split in one ear, swallow fork and underbit in the other, branded thus IB also fifty head of hogs, marked split and underbit in on ear, underbit in the other, and three horses, To Have and to Hold to the said William Dell as Trustee as aforesaid his heirs and assigns to and for the uses following to wit, to the use and for the benefit of the said Hannah Parker during her natural life, and provided also and the said above mentioned property is conveyed upon this express stipulation, that the said William Dell Trustee as aforesaid shall pay over to the said Hannah Parker all the rents, issues and profits of the above conveyed property and in case of her death that he shall deliver the same to the heirs of her body by her present marriage"

January 24, 1851
State of Florida, Alachua County
From Alachua County Ancient Records
Deed Record A page 368

Documenting property of Sarah A. Paulling that she's bringing into her impending marriage to John Lewis (Benjamin Boulware & Musco Boulware, Trustees): "This Indenture made and entered into this Seventh day of February A. D. One thousand Eight hundred & fifty nine between Sarah A. Paulling of the first part of the County of Alachua & Benjamin P Boulware and Musco Boulware of the State and County aforesaid party of the Second part and John Lewis also of the State and County aforesaid party of the third part

Witnesseth That Whereas a Marriage is intended to be had and Solemnized, between the said parties of the third and first part, and the

Said party of the first part is Seized and possessed in her own right of Certain property both real & personal, as follows To Wit, an interest of one fourth in all the lands Situate lying and being in the County aforesaid Known and described as follows The South East quarter of the North East quarter of Section twenty Eight of Township Nine of Range twenty two (28-9-22) Containing Thirty nine & half acres more or less Also the West half of the South west quarter of the South East quarter of Section twenty two in Township nine of Range Twenty two East (22-9-22) Containing One hundred and ninety nine acres, Also One hundred & Seventy Nine acres in Section Twenty Seven of Township Nine of Range twenty two East (27-9-22) Situated in the North half of said Section Twenty Seven and not including the North East quarter of the north East quarter of Said Section Land being bounded by the Section line except on the South and where it joins with the north East quarter of the North quarter of Said Section Also the North East quarter of the South West quarter of Section twenty two Township Nine South of Range Twenty Two East (22-9-22), Containing Thirty nine acres and 80/100 of an acre, Also the North east quarter of Section Twenty Two in Township Nine South of Range Twenty two East (22-9-22), in the district of land subject to sale at Newnansville Florida Containing one hundred & fifty nine acres & 26/100 of an acre Also the North East quarter of the North East quarter of Section Twenty Eight (28) & the North West quarter of the North West quarter of Section Twenty Seven in Township Nine South of Range twenty two (27-9-22) Containing Seventy Nine 46/100 of an acres, And the South East quarter Section Twenty one in Township Nine South of Range twenty two (21-9-22) Containing One hundred & fifty nine acres & 12/100 of an acre Also Together with the following described personal property to wit, **Prince, a Negro man Slave about fifty years old, Eliza a Negro woman Slave about the age of fifty, Lewis a Negro Slave about Twenty two years old, Jane a Negro Slave about Eighteen years old, Sarah a Negro Slave about Sixteen years old, Rueben a Negro Slave about Thirteen years old, Charles a Negro Slave about Eleven years old, John a Negro Slave about Nine years old, Mary a Negro Slave about Seven years old, Henry a Negro Slave about three years old,** Also two

Mules one Waggon Together with all the house hold & Kitchen furniture Also an interest in one Sixth in a Cotton gin Mill &c Situate on the lands above described (all of which the said party of the first part with the Knowledge and consent of the said party of the Third part is minded and disposed to transfer assign and Set over to the said party of the Second part interest for the purposes hereinafter mentioned

Now therefore in Consideration of the premises and the Sum of one dollar by the Said party of the Second part to the Said party of the first part in hand paid at and before the Sealing and delivery of these presents the receipt whereof is hereby acknowledged the Said party of the first part hath Sold assigned transferred & Set over all the property both real and personal above described to hold in trust for the use and benefit of the said party of the first part during the time of her natural life and at her death to be equally proportioned and divided among the heirs of her body as well the issue that She may bear as those that are now living this property in no wise to be subject or liable to the debts or demands against the party of the third part either those that have been Contracted or those that may be contracted and in the case of the death or resignation of the Said trustees or either of them then and in that case they their heirs Executors or administrators shall transfer convey & pay over the whole of the property above described together with the increase thereof to such person or persons as may be appointed by the said party of the first part as such Trustee or Trustees under this indenture and in case of the death of the said party of the first part then the person or persons acting as trustee or trustees to pay over the property to such person or persons as may be appointed by the person of the first part in her last will and testament and in absence of the will then to such person or persons as may be appointed Guardian of said heirs or if the heirs are of age then to them in their own persons"

February 7, 1859
State of Florida, Alachua County
From Alachua County Ancient Records
Deed Record C pages 365-367

Eliza D. Payne sets out what she is leaving to Geo B. Payne:
"Whereas Geo B. Payne is the only surviving Child of my Husband,
Geo Morton Payne by a first marriage and whereas my said Husband,
Since my intermarriage with him has applied a portion of the property
received with his first wife Susan M. Lewis to the uses of the family
and whereas I have been pleased by Providence in the relation of a
mother to the said Geo B. Payne since his Infancy and while I have
diligently and conscienciously endeavored to perform the duties and
borne to him and still bear to him the affection of One And whereas
the said Geo B. Payne has been visited with heavy pecuniary misfor-
tunes, Now I the undersigned in consideration of the premises and
with a view to make some just provision as far as providence may
enable me for the children of the said Geo B. Payne do hereby appoint
& agree that the Children of said Geo B. Payne shall constitute in the
aggregate and be considered law parents as my own and as such shall
receive in the final distribution of my estate for equal division among
them survivor or survivors of them at the date of such distribution
one childs part that is such childs part as would be the share of the
said Geo B. Payne as one of my children at the time of my death upon
the conditions following to wit should either of my daughters Celia
Becky Susan Harrison or Bettice Morton Payne die after attaining at
the age of twenty one years they shall have respectively the right and
power to dispose of by will or other appointments such portions of
my estate as would belong to them respectively at the date of said
distribution, this distribution made in favour of my daughters is not
intended to extend to my sons in the event of the death of either of
them not leaving heirs of their body

2nd The amount which has been advanced to the said George B. Payne
for the benefit of his family, viz **two Slaves Frank at the price or
sum of three hundred dollars and Susan at the price of three
hundred & fifty dollars** and such other advancements in money or
property as may be made to the said George B. Payne for the benefit

of his Children or to either of my other children to be taken into account at the date of final distribution of my Estate and while no interest on him is to be charged on account of said Slaves, Frank & Susan future advances shall be on terms prescribed at the time such advances shall be made

3rd To remove and prevent all grounds of misunderstanding and Controversy above all things to be deprecated and prevented the provisions thus made for the children of the said George B. Payne will and is intended to cover and annul all private claims and transaction between the said George B. Payne and my said husband George M. Payne, except such as shall be situated between them before the death of either and whereas the said George B. Payne has received his academical and professional Education from the funds of the family and three of the younger children are now being & to be educated nothing herein contained shall bar my right in the event of my death to set apart such part or sum for their Education as shall be necessary to give them respectively such Education as I may deem advisable and without demenution of their respective shares on a final division of the Estate or to appoint a time at which such division shall take place or to allot to said children of said George B. Payne their respective shares in property or money or to convey the same in trust for their benefit or to hinder the said George B. Payne to whom the power is hereby given if not exercised by myself of conveying said shares of his said children or any one or more of them in trust for their benefit on such terms as he may deem prudent and suitable"

August 30, 1852
From Alachua County Ancient Records
Deed Record C pages 197-198

George B. Payne of Jno M. Payne & Co. to assorted creditors as collateral for $5,276.64 in loans: "This Indenture made on the Eight day of May in the year of One Thousand Eight hundred and Between George B. Payne of the first part and Edward Tatnall Payne & John Charles Bickley merchants using the name Style and Firm of Payne & Bickley, and Charles V. Chamberlain, David Miller, Alexander Isaacs, merchants using the name Style & Firm of Chamberlain, Miller & Co. and Ezekiel B. Stoddard & Caleb Fromberger merchants using the name, Style & Firm of E. B. Stoddard & Co. and William H. Gilliland, Sidney S. Howell, James Gilliland, & James H. Nichols merchants using the name Style & firm of Gilliland, Howell & Co. and William H. Farley, and Hiram Roberts and Roosevelt Hyde & Clark, parties of the second part.

Witnesseth That Whereas the said party of the first part is a member of the Firm of Jno M. Payne & Co. and also of the Firm of Payne, Brown & Co., and whereas the said party of the first part is responsible for the debts of said Firm, and Whereas the said Payne & Bickley hold just claims and demands against the said Firm of John M. Payne & Co. to the amount of One Thousand Dollars now past due with a considerable Sum of Interest money thereon and whereas the said Firm of Chamberlain Miller & Co. holds just Claims and demands against the said John M. Payne & Co. for the Sum of Six hundred and Seventy Seven 48/100 dollars now past due with a considerable amount of Interest money thereon, And also on the said Payne Brown & Co. to the amount of Eight hundred & Sixty 39/100 dollars past due with Interest thereon, and whereas also the said Gilliland Howell & Co. holds just claims and demands against the said Jno M. Payne & Co. to the amount of Twelve hundred and ninety Eight 77/100 dollars, now past due, with Interest thereon and whereas the said party of the first part is indebted individually to the said William Farley in the Sum of Three Hundred and Forty dollars, and to the said Hiram Roberts in the sum of Five Hundred dollars both of which last mentioned Claims are past due with a considerable amount of Interest thereon. And Whereas the said Jno M Payne & Co. are indebted to the said Roosevelt, Hyde & Clark in the sum of Six hundred dollars now past due with a considerable amount of Interest thereon, and whereas it is the desire of the said party of the first part as far as lies in his power to secure to the said parties of the Second part, the faithfull payment of the said sums of money Aforesaid respectively together with all the Interest Invoices which has accrued or may yet accrue thereon

Now therefore for the foregoing consideration as well as for the further consideration of the Sum of Ten dollars to him in hand paid by the said parties of the second part at and before the Sealing and delivery hereof the receipt whereof is hereby acknowledged the said party of the first part has given granted bargained sold & delivered & by these presents does give grant bargain Sell & deliver unto the said parties of the second part the Following mentioned & described Property, That is to Say **A Negro Girl Slave named Matilda aged about Twenty five years A Negro Man Reuben a diseased Slave aged about Twenty Five,** Two horses & a Buggy now in the possession of the said party of the First part & also all the Household & Kitchen Furniture valued at One Thousand dollars & now in the possession of the said party of the first part To have & to hold the said described & mentioned Property, And the said parties of the Second part in proportion to their respective Claims and demands as aforesaid and to their heirs and assigns Forever. Provided always nevertheless & these presents are upon the Express condition following, Viz, That if the said party of the first part shall well and truly pay or cause to be paid to the said parties of the Second part or their heirs or assigns the respective amounts of money due to them as hereinbefore stated together with the Interest thereon on or before the first day of January Eighteen & Sixty one, then these presents to be Null & Void otherwise to remain in full force & virtue"

May 8, 1858
State of Florida, Alachua County
From Alachua County Ancient Records
Mortgage Record A pages 135-137

Isham W. Peacock indicted for larceny; enslaved people were used as a part of collateral to ensure he showed up for Court: "State of Florida vs Isham Peacock - Larceny - Continued on the affidavit of the Defendant, recognized in one thousand dollars, Five Hundred Dollars for principal two hundred and fifty for the Securities, Daniel Lynn and John M. Hires.

Isham Peacock Daniel Lynn and John M. Hires appeared in open Court and acknowledged themselves to owe and stand indebted to the State of Florida in manner following that is to say the said Isham Peacock in the sum of Five hundred dollars and the said Daniel Lynn in the sum of Two hundred and fifty dollars and the said John M. Hires in the sum of Two hundred and fifty dollars to be levied of their respective goods and chattles Slaves Lands and Tenements if default be made in the following Conditions that is to say if the said Isham Peacock Shall be and appear at the next Term of this Court to answer an Indictment for Larceny and shall not thence depart from the Court without leave then this obligation to be null and void Else to remain in full force and virtue"

December 15, 1853
From Alachua County Ancient Records
Judgment Record A* page 154

Inventory of the Separate property of Jane Ann Pelot Recorded according to act March 6th 1845 Thomsens Digest 221: "1 Plantation and appurtenances defined by U. States Survey as South West Quarter of North East Quarter of Section thirty four Township Seven South Range eighteen East, the East half of South East Quarter of

Section twenty Seven Township Seven South Range eighteen East West half of South West Quarter Section twenty Six Township Seven South Range eighteen East North West Quarter of North East Quarter Section thirty four Township Seven South Range eighteen East West half of the East half of the North East Quarter of Section thirty four Township Seven South Range East the West half of the South East Quarter of Section thirty four Township South Range eighteen East Containing in all three Hundred and Sixty acres lying being and Situate in the County of Alachua State of Florida Also, Household and Kitchen furniture, also forty Head of Stock Cattle, Mark Smooth Crop in one ear and under Square in the other Branded (symbols) also **four Negroes to wit three Negro men Slaves Eleven, Frank, Bobb and one Negro woman Ann**"

February 19, 1855
From Alachua County Ancient Records
Deed Record D page 054

Sarah A. Pelot wife of John C. Pelot to James G. Cooper as trustee for her children: "Know all men by these presents that I Sarah A. Pelot wife of John C. Pelot of said County and State for and in consideration of the love and affection I have for my sons James Cooper John Crews Charles Edmund & George Gustavus and my daughters Marian Stewart wife of Charles C. Stewart - Mary Elizabeth Strobath, Sarah Ann Adaline Jane Julia Frances Christiana Rebecca and infant son Abram William as well as for the further consideration of the sum of five dollars to me in hand paid by James G. Cooper of Nassau County the receipt whereof is hereby acknowledged have granted, bargained and sold and by these presents do grant, bargain and sell unto the said James G. Cooper the following described property to wit **a negro man slave named John aged forty four years one named Stephen aged thirty five years, a negro girl Slave named Caroline**

aged thirty years and one named Henrietta aged forty four years negro boy named Jim aged seventeen years negro boy named Charles aged fourteen years one bay horse four mules, one wagon, one pleasure carriage one Piano Forte, Fifty head of stock cattle under square and under bit in each ear and branded letter (P). To have and to hold the said described property to him the said James G. Cooper his heirs & assigns in trust nevertheless and upon the express condition that the property **with the future increase, profit & labor thereof** be held in trust for the sole use benefit and enjoyment of my said Sons James Cooper John Crews Charles Edmund, George Gustavus & Abram William and my Said daughters Marian Stewart, Mary Elizabeth Strobhar, Sarah Ann Adaline Jane, Julia Frances & Christiana Rebecca and their heirs and assigns forever"

November 10, 1853
State of Florida, Columbia County
From Alachua County Ancient Records
Deed Record E pages 142-143

Patrick Philips to William Andrews for $2,500: "Know All men by these presents that I Patrick Philips of the State of Florida and County of Duval, of the first part, for and in consideration of the Sum of Twenty Five hundred Dollars lawful money of the United States of America to me in hand by William Andrews of the State and County aforesaid of the Second part well and truly paid at and before the ensealing and delivery of these presents the receipt whereby is hereby acknowledged. Have bargained sold and conveyed and by these presents do bargain sell and convey unto the said party of the second part all the following described Negro Slaves, to wit: **Sylva female, Black, aged about forty years, Hanah female, Black aged about Eighteen years, Peter male Black, aged about Sixteen years, Lydia female black aged about twelve years, Printer, male, black aged**

**about Eighteen years, all the last named four Slaves being the
children of the Said Lydia and all Slaves for life. Together with
all the future issue and increase of the females of Said Slaves.** To
have and to hold all the above named and described Slaves with all and
singular the future issue and increase of the females thereof unto the
Said party of the Second part, his heirs and Executors and Administrators and assigns to his and their own proper use and behoof forever."

October 7, 1856
From Alachua County Ancient Records
Bills of Sale A pages 033-034

William H. Poole to B. F. Young as collateral for $2,500 in loans:
"Know all men by these presents that I William H. Poole of the
County of Lounds and state of Alabama for and in consideration
of the sum of Two Thousand five hundred dollars to me in hand
paid by B. F. Young of the County and State aforesaid the receipt
whereof I do hereby acknowledge have granted, bargained, and sold
and by these presents do grant, bargain, and sell, unto the said B. F.
Young his executors, administrators and assigns the following negro
slaves to wit, **Frederick a boy about 20 years of age, Phileimon
a boy about 12 years old, Betsy a woman about 50 years of age
and her child Lidia about 8 years old Clara a woman 25 years
of age and Liah a girl about 8 years old** now remaining and being
in the possession of the said William H. Poole to have and to hold
all and singular the said negroes before mentioned unto the said B.
F. Young his executors administrators and assigns forever. And I the
said William H. Poole myself my heirs administrators and executors
all and singular the said negroes before mentioned unto the said B.
F. Young his executors administrators and assigns forever. And I the
said William H. Poole myself my heirs administrators and executors
all and singular the said negroes beforementioned unto the said B. F.

377

Young his executors administrators and assigns against me the said William H. Poole my administrators and executors and against every other person whatsoever shall and will forever warrant and defend by these presents Provided always and it is hereby agreed between the parties to these presents that if I the said William H. Poole my heirs executors or administrator or any of us do and shall well and truly pay or cause to be paid unto the said B. F. Young his executors administrators or assigns the sum of twelve hundred and fifty dollars on or before the 1st day of January in the year 1858 with interest at 8 per cent per annum from and after the 1st day of January next insuing the date hereof according to the condition of a certain Bond bearing even date herewith given by me the said William H. Poole to the said B. F. Young then these presents and every thing contained herein shall cease and be void [...] in case default shall be made in the payment if the said sum of $1250 at the time limited for the payment thereof it shall and may be lawful for the said B. F. Young his executors administrators or assigns to take possession of all or any of the negroes hereinbefore mentioned **and their issue or increase if any** and to sell and dispose of the same for the best price he can obtain and out of the money to arise from such sale thereof to pay and retain to him and themselves the said sum of $1250 and all charges toucthing the same he and they rendering to me the said William H. Poole my executors &c the surplus monies (if any there shall be) anything herein to the contrary notwithstanding. And until the default be made in the payment of the said sum of money at the time fixed for the payment thereof I the said William H. Poole to remain and continue in quiet and peaceable possession of the said negroes"

May 1, 1856
State of Florida, Alachua County
From Alachua County Ancient Records
Bills of Sale A pages 029-031

John T. Prevatt indicted for playing and betting at cards; enslaved people were used as a part of collateral to ensure he showed up for Court: "State of Florida vs John T. Prevatt - Playing and betting at cards - John T. Prevatt, and John B. Standley appeared in open Court and acknowledged themselves to owe and stand indebted to the State of Florida in manner following that is to say, the said John T. Prevatt in the Sum of Fifteen hundred dollars, and the said John B. Standley in the Sum of Fifteen hundred dollars, to be levied of their respective goods and chattels, Slaves, lands and tenements if default be made in the following conditions, that is to say if the said John T. Prevatt shall be and appear at the next Term of this Court to answer to an Indictment for playing and betting at cards, and shall not thence depart without leave, then this obligation to be null and void, else to remain in full force and virtue"

May 6, 1853
From Alachua County Ancient Records
Judgment Record A* page 129

W. J. Pringle's 1/7 share of the Estate of Levi Hickson: "Know all men, That I W.J. Pringle of Sumpter South Carolina a lawful heir of the Estate of Levi Hickson deceased the fifth of February One thousand Eight hundred & fifty seven in Consideration of the facts that Susan Hickson Surviving widow of the said Levi Hickson deceased released her dower and total Interest in the estate of the said Levi Hickson deceased except the boy **Adam** reserved for her use during her lifetime and then reverts back to the heirs of the said estate and upon the further Consideration of receiving one Seventh of the Estate of the said Levi Hickson and also the Negroes **Henry Junr Betsey, Littleton George, Lucinda, Soloman, Edward, Littleton Junr Lindy, Mausice, Eliza, Jane, Allen, Philip, Abbie,** as his Seventh of the Negroes of said Estate to have and to hold all and Singular the said property unto the said W.J. Pringle, Am firmly bound unto the said Susan Hickson Surviving widow of said Levi Hickson to pay annually during her life time the said Susan Hickson the full and Just sum of two hundred & fifty dollars as her Certain attorney to which payment well &truly to be made and done, I bind myself and each and every of my heirs, Executors and administrators Jointly and Severally by these presents,

Provided Nevertheless that the said Susan Hickson reserve and retain to her self a lien upon the said Negroes Henry Junr Betsey Catharine George Jr Lucinda Edward Jane Jr Allen Phillip Abbie Above enumerated as security for the annual payment of the said sum of two hundred & fifty dollars then this Conveyance Shall be void otherwise to remain in full force and effect,

And provided also that untill default by the said W. J. Pringle in performance of the said Condition aforesaid it may may be lawful for him to Keep and retain possession of Said property and to use and enjoy the same but if the same or any part thereof Shall be attatched at any time before payment &c by any other Creditor or Creditors of the said W.J. Pringle then it shall be lawfull for the said Susan Hickson to take immediate possession of the whole said above named Negroes or so much thereof as will be sufficient to pay the said sum during her lifetime to her own use and disposal"

January 1, 1850
State of Florida, Alachua County
From Alachua County Ancient Records
Deed Record C pages 329-330

W. C. H. Rainy and wife Mary R. Rainy (formerly Mary R. Henderson) recording the property Mary possessed before their

marriage: "I W. C. H. Rainy and Mary R. Rainy (formerly Mary R. Henderson) his wife both citizens Of the State aforesaid who were married within the period of six months from the date hereof. Do hereby agree to record in the Office of the Clerk of the Circuit Court for the County of Alachua State aforesaid all the separate property of the said Mary R. Rainy of which she was seized and possessed before the *** aforesaid. An inventory of which is hereunto annexed and that the said property shall remain beyond the Control of the said William C. H. Rainy. And shall not be taken in execution for his debts according to the statute law in such cases made and provided.

Inventory of property belonging to Mary R. Rainy, wife of William C. H. Rainy **Louisa - a slave about Eighteen years of age, Sarah, a slave about fourteen years of age**"

November 4, 1859
State of Florida, Alachua Co.
From Alachua County Ancient Records
Bills of Sale A page 065

C. A. Ramsey and Moses Ramsey to H. L. Hart as collateral for $4,500 in loans: "This Indenture made this first day of July in the year of our Lord One thousand Eight hundred & fifty nine between C. A. Ramsey and Moses Ramsey of the County of Alachua State of Florida and H. L. Hart of the Town of Palatka County of Putnam State aforesaid Witnesseth that for and in Consideration of the Sum of four thousand five hundred dollars to them the Said C.A. Ramsey and Moses Ramsey paid by the said H.L. Hart the receipt whereof is hereby acknowledged by the said C.A. Ramsey and Moses Ramsey have given granted Sold and Conveyed and by these presents do give grant Sell and Convey unto the said H. L. Hart his heirs and assigns all that tract and parcel of land Known and described as follows to wit, Section twenty one (21) Township Ten (10) Range Nineteen (19) Whereon Moses Ramsey now lives, and lot number ten (10) Block two (2) in the Town of Gainesville together with all the improvements and appurtinances thereto belonging or in any wise appertaining Also the following Negro Slaves belonging to the said C. A. Ramsey and Moses Ramsey **Wiley Harry Alexander and Sam** To Have and To Hold the above granted premises and their appurtinances with the said named Negro Slaves unto the said H. L. Hart his heirs and assigned to his and their only proper use and behoof forever [...] these presents are upon the express Condition that if the said C.A. Ramsey and Moses Ramsey their heirs Executors or administrators or any of them do and shall well and truly pay or cause to be paid their Certain promisory notes [...] then these Shall become null and void otherwise to remain in full force and virtue"

July 1, 1859
From Alachua County Ancient Records
Mortgage Record A pages 194-195

John G. Rawls and wife Martha Rawls to Solomon Warren the younger for $700: "Know all men by these presents that we John G. Rawls and Martha Rawls, wife of said John G. Rawls of the said County and State, for and in consideration of the sum of seven hundred dollars to us in hand paid by Solomon Warren the younger of said County and State have granted, bargained, sold and confirmed and, by these presents do grant, bargain, sell and confirm unto the said Solomon Warren the younger his heirs and assigns **a negro woman named Martha of yellow complexion and about twenty-eight years of age**. And we do covenant with the said Solomon Warren the younger, his heirs and assigns for ourselves, our heirs, Executors and administrators that the said negro woman Martha is a slave born, that she is in sound health bodily and mentally, and we will and our heirs,

Executors and administrators shall the said property to the said Solomon Warren the younger his heirs and assigns forever warrant and defend."

December 13, 1856
Florida, Alachua County
From Alachua County Ancient Records
Bills of Sale A page 067

Malinda Richard to daughter Susan C. Clark: "Know all men by these presents, that I, Malinda Richard of the County of Alachua and State of Florida, in consideration of the Maternal love and affection which I have and bear for my Daughter Susan C. Clark, of the County and State aforesaid, and also for divers other good causes and considerations [...] have given, granted, and confirmed, and by these presents, do give, grant, and confirm unto the Said Susan C. Clark and the heirs of her body begotten, the following described personal property, to wit; **a Negro girl named Affy aged fourteen years**, to the only proper use and behoof of the said Susan C. Clark, during her natural life, and to the heirs of her body only afterwards. If the said Susan C. Clark Shall die without Issue born, then the above described property to revert back to the grantor, her heirs, Executors, Administrators and assigns forever, and if an attempt Shall be made by any person or persons, to Sell or dispose of the above described property without the consent of the grantor, her husband John C. Richard Sr. or the consent of her Executors, Administrators and assigns, then and in that case, the Said above described property to revert back at once and immediately to the grantor, her heirs and assigns."

May 25, 1854
From Alachua County Ancient Records
Deed Record B pages 384-385

Thomas Roach to Samuel C. Youngblood in trust for Nancy Elizabeth Garison: "Know all men by these presents that I Thomas Roach of the District and State aforesaid, in consideration of the good will, and affection that I have and bear to the objects as hereinafter Stated, and for divers other good reasons me thereunto me moving, have given conveyed and delivered, and by these presents do give grant and convey, and in plain and open market deliver to Samuel C. Youngblood of Said District, **a Negro girl named Louisa about thirteen years of age,** to have and to hold the said negro girl **together with her Issue** to the said Samuel C. Youngblood, his heirs, Executors, and administrators, upon the special trust and confidence however for the said Samuel C. Youngblood to Stand Seized and possessed of the said Negro girl together with her future increase if any, for the above and separate use and benefit of Nancy Elizabeth Garison wife of I. P. Garison, for and during her natural life, and from and immediately after her death, Said Negro girl Louisa and her Issue, to belong absolutely and discharged of all trust, to such Issue of said Nancy E. Garrison, as may be living at her death, and in default of her leaving such Issue, then to such children of mine by my present wife Mary Roach as may be living at the death of said Nancy E. Garrison and in default of such Issue then being alive to my right and proper heirs, and distributes, Said Trustee if he sees proper may suffer and permit Said Negro girl to go into the actual possession of Said Nancy E. Garrison and may also, permit said Nancy E. Garrison to have and enjoy the labor and services of Said Negro girl for her Sole use, but such possession is confer no right whatever upon the Husband of said Nancy either to Negro or her Services"

March 10, 1852
South Carolina, York District
From Alachua County Ancient Records
Deed Record B page 417

Andrew Robb named as Trustee for his wife Martha Robb; also discussing the $12,000 that Andrew Robb Tillman Ingram, and Philip Dell owe to the Governor of Florida: "In the matter of the petition of Andrew Robb & his wife Martha Robb - On filing and reading the Said petition and it appearing to the Satisfaction of the Court that the said Martha Robb is without a trustee, and it further appearing that said Andrew Robb have given made and executed to the Governor of the State of Florida & to his Successors in office in the penal Sum of twelve thousand dollars, for the use & benefit of those who may be interested therein; Conditional that the said Andrew Robb as trustee Shall well & faithfully discharge his duties as such trustee for the said Martha Robb for Certain property in such petition Specified as also as enumerated on the Condition of said bond; It is ordered and decreed that Said Andrew Robb be & he is hereby appointed trustee for the said Martha Robb for the purposes aforesaid

Decr 27th 1858
B.A. Putnam - Judge

Know all Men by these presents that we Andrew Robb, Tillman Ingram, and Philip Dell, of the County of Alachua in the State of Florida are held and firmly bound unto the Governor of the State of Florida and his successors in Office in the penal Sum of twelve thousand dollars to be paid to said Governor or to his Successors in Office for the use and benefit of those persons who Shall be Entitled thereto as named in the Condition of this bond hereunder written, Suit for recovery of which to be instituted on Said bond for the use of Said persons as often as there may be a breach of said Bond in the name of the Said Governor or his Successors in Office, and for the payment of which said Sum of Twelve thousand dollars well and truly to be made, we Jointly and Severally bind our selves our heirs and Executors & administrators firmly by these presents, Sealed with our Seals and dated this Twenty Seventh day of December AD 1858

Whereas by the decree of the Circuit Court of the County of Glynn in the State of Georgia Certain property, that is to say, a **Negro man named Fortune valued at One thousand dollars: One negro man named Isaac, valued at Seven hundred and fifty dollars; One negro woman named Eve, valued at three hundred dollars One negro woman named Mary valued at three hundred dollars, a Negro girl named Sarah valued at three hundred dollars and a negro woman very old of no value** muniments of title for Eleven hundred acres of land in the said County of Glynn worth one thousand dollars and notes and accounts valued at five hundred dollars, has been awarded and decreed to Martha Turner, now Martha Robb and wife of said Andrew Robb for and during the period of her natural life and after her death to go to and be distributed to and among her Children: And whereas the said Andrew Robb has been appointed Trustee for said Martha Robb and her Children to take after her death, to take possession and have the Charge, Control and management of said property as such trustee

Now the Condition of the foregoing obligation as such that if the said Andrew Robb shall well and faithfully discharge his duties as such trustee and if he Shall survive his said wife thereof after her death he shall when lawfully required to do So, he shall well and truly and faithfully distribute the said Enumirated property, or so much thereof as Shall then be existing in specie such as may hereafter be required by sale or Exchange of any Existing property, and such as may be purchased with the funds of sale or investing from Monies arising from any of said notes or accounts, and Shall especially fairly and faithfully divide and distribute to the said Children of his said wife and to those who may be Entitled thereby, the said Enumerated Negroes or the survivors of them at the time when distribution Shall be made: and the issue or such issue thereof as Shall also be surviving at said period of distribution, then the foregoing bond to be null and void, otherwise to be and remain in full force and effect In testimony whereof the Said Andrew Robb and Tillman Ingram and Philip Dell have hereunto affixed their names and seals the day and year first above written"

December 27, 1858
In the Circuit Court, Eastern Circuit of Florida
In Chancery, Alachua Circuit
From Alachua County Ancient Records
Chancery Order Book A pages 143-145

Martha Robb wife of Andrew Robb - inventory of her separate property: "Inventory of the separate property of Mrs. Martha Robb wife of Andrew Robb of Alachua County & State of Florida. To Wit: **One Negro Boy - slave named Issac about 14 or 15 years of age.**"

November 5, 1857
From Alachua County Ancient Records
Deed Record C page 099

Jacob E. Robinson to George L. Brown as collateral for $600 in loans: "This Indenture made this thirtieth day of January one thousand eight hundred and fifty five, Between George L. Brown of the County of Alachua and State of Florida, and Jacob E. Robinson of the same County and State, Whereas the said Jacob E. Robinson […] Stands indebted to the said George L. Brown in the sum of six hundred dollars, the same sum mentioned in said promissory notes together with lawful interest for the same as in and by the said recited notes […] Now this indenture Witnesseth, that the said Jacob E. Robinson as well for and in consideration of the aforesaid Sum of six hundred Dollars, the same mentioned in said promissory notes, and for the better securing the payment thereof, with the lawful interest thereon to the said George L. Brown, his executors, administrators and assigns as well as certain advancements of money goods and merchandise to be made in future by the said George L. Brown to the said Jacob E. Robinson, as also for the further sum of one dollar in hand paid to said Jacob E. Robinson at and before the signing and sealing hereof, which is hereby acknowledged, hath bargained, and sold and doth hereby bargain and sell, unto the said George L. Brown, Two negro women slaves, named and described as follows, to wit; **Sarah aged about forty five years and Rose aged about thirteen years,** To have and to hold the said negro women slaves to the said George L. Brown, and to his heirs and assigns for ever, provided always nevertheless that if the said Jacob E. Robinson his heirs Executors or administrators shall well and truly pay, or cause to be paid unto the said George L. Brown, his executors, administrators, or assigns the aforesaid sum of Six hundred dollars [...] on or before the first day of January one thousand eight hundred and fifty six, as well as all such further sum or sums of money, or merchandize as shall be hereafter acknowledged by the said Jacob E. Robinson's endorsement on this mortgage to be duly advancement from the said George L. Brown to the said Jacob E. Robinson, then the foregoing mortgage Deed to be absolutely null and void, otherwise to remain in full force and virtue."

January 30, 1855
From Alachua County Ancient Records
Deed Record D pages 029-030

Mary Rollins to niece Celie T. Cothran: "Know all men by these presents that I Mary Rollins of the State of Florida and County of Alachua for the natural love and affection that I have of and for Celie T. Cothran my niece as well as for the further consideration of the Sum of five dollars good and lawful money to me in hand paid at and before the ensealing and delivering of these presents the receipt whereof is hereby acknowledged have given granted bargained Sold and by these presents doth So give grant bargain and sell unto the said Celia T. Cothran the following described property To wit **One Negro woman and named Pheby about eighteen years old and her two Children One about two years old named Emeline the other about four months old named Sarah Together with all and Singular her and their future issue and increase** To have and to hold the above described property with the future increase thereof upon the following consideration to wit that the title thereof Shall rest and remain in the Said Celie T. Cothran from and after the date of these presents nevertheless the said Mary Rollins to have the possession of as well as the use and benefit of the above described personal property together with the future increase thereof during the term of the natural life of her the Said Mary Rollins and at her death to go into the possession of the Said Celie T. Cothran for the use of her and the heirs of her body during the term of the natural life of her the Said Celie T. Cothran and at her death to be equally divided between and among the heirs of the body of her the said Celie T. Cothran

This property not to be subject to Sale for any debts that may be contracted by Mary Rollins from and after the date hereof whilst it may remain in the possession of the said Mary Rollins neither for any debt that may be contracted during the life of her the Said Celie Cothran by themselves her husband or husbands agents or attorneys nor any other person whatsoever but to remain free from all incumbrances or liabilities during the life of the Said Celie T. Cothran and at her death to be equally divided among the heirs of her body

And in case the Said Celie T. Cothran Should die leaving no heirs then and in that case the above described property together with the future increase thereof to go to James M. Tilman and his heirs and after his death to be equally divided among the heirs of his body"

May 10, 1859
State of Florida, County of Alachua
From Alachua County Ancient Records
Deed Record E pages 027-028

Mary C. Russell to Charles L. Wilson to make provision for all minor children of Charles L Wilson & Lydia Wilson: "This indenture made the twenty sixth day December A.D. one thousand eight-hundred and fifty-four Between Mary C. Russell of the County of Alachua and State of Florida, Party of the first part and Charles L. Wilson of the County and State aforesaid party of the Second part, Whereas the said party of the first part is desirous to make provision for Susan, Martha, Matilda J. & Frances E. the children of Charles L & Lydia Wilson, all of whom are minors against future consequences, and for their maintenances and support. Now therefore this Indenture witnesseth that this said party of the first part for and in consideration of the sum of five dollars lawful money of the United States, to her in hand paid by the said party of the Second part, before the ensealing and delivery of there presents, the receipt whereof is hereby acknowledged, have granted bargained and sold, and delivered and by these presents do grant, bargain, sell and deliver unto the said party, the Second part Seven Negro Slaves of the following description, to wit; **Silva Fifty five years old, Rebecca Sixteen years old Malinda eleven years old, Sarah Six years old, Gabriel five years old, Edward five years old, and Elvira three years old**, to have and to hold the said described Slaves to the said party of the second part his successors and assigns. In Trust, to and for the several uses, intents and purposes hereinafter mentioned namely,

First--In trust to hire out said slaves, or employ them in such manner as to him may best, and to take collect and receive the income and profits thereof, and out of the same to pay all taxes assessments and charges, that may be imposed thereon.

Second In Trust, to appropriate the residue of such profits, and income to the support & maintenance, and education of Susan, Martha Matilda J. & Frances E. the children of Charles L. and Lydia Wilson.

Third. In Trust, to convey to each one of above named Children one fourth part of the above described personal property, upon their marrying, or attaining the age of twenty one

Fourth, In Trust, Should one or more of the above named children die before marrying or attaining the age of twenty one, then the above described Slaves shall be divided between the survivors Share and share alike.

And the said party of the second part, doth hereby signify his acceptance of this trust and doth hereby covenant and agree, to and with the said party of the first part, faithfully to discharge, and execute this same, according to the true intent and meaning of these presents."

December 26, 1854
From Alachua County Ancient Records
Deed Record D page 013

John Jos. Sanchez & William Dell trustees to Caroline Gieger:
"Know all men by these presents that we John Jos. Sanchez & William Dell Trustees named in the annexed deed for and in consideration of the Stipulations made entered into in this Land deed by the said Caroline Gieger, and in pursuance and in Consideration of the premises, and of the aforesaid trust, and also of the for the Sum one dollar to us paid by Caroline Gieger the receipt of which is hereby acknowledged have bargained, Sold and delivered and do by these presents do bargain Sell and deliver to the Said Caroline Gieger the following property named deed discribed in Said deed to Wit; **One negro woman named Ferebe aged about Twenty Years One negro Child named Nancy aged about Two Years, One negro Child named Ellen aged about One Year.** One Sorrel mare & Colt ten cows & Calves marked Swallow fork and underbit in one ear over Slope the other branded S.G.

also ten Head of Sheep also all the household and Kitchen furniture now in the possession of the Said Samuel Gieger To have & to hold the aforesaid Slaves and other personal property to the said Caroline Geiger and to her executors administrators and assigns forever"

January 13, 1850
State of Florida, Alachua County
From Alachua County Ancient Records
Deed Record A page 228

George W. Sanchez & Thomas C. Love vs. George B. Ellis Sheriff of Alachua County regarding disposition of the Wilson negroes - "Bill for Injunction & Relief - Motion of Injunction: The injunction prayed for Can not be granted for the following reasons

1ˢᵗ George B. Ellis the only defendant to the Bill is but Sheriff and the ministerial officer to execute the writ of execution placed in his hands - therefore it is necessary that the Bill should include as defendants the plaintiffs in the execution against which relief is sought The Bill does not even Set forth who the plaintiffs in execution are

2ⁿᵈ Were the proper parties Embraced in the Bill, under our statute no injunction to Stay proceedings at law after judgement Can be granted, until notice given, and bond &c See Digest page 456 & 453

But suppose these defects cured, and the application made for injunction I am not aware of any power this Court has to take away vested rights of a party on a judgment which they have regularly procured

This Court has no power to release and cancel a bond unless its terms and Conditions have been Complied with and upon a proper case requiring the interference of a Court of Chancery

If the judgement on the Claim, bond was erroneously entered that is to say If the parties to the Bond did not neglect refuse to deliver the property to the Sheriff or other officer having said execution according to the terms, and Conditions of this bond as is alledged by the sheriff on his return to the claim bond, then the execution is illegally issued and our statutes points out the remedy See Digest page (360)

Again - If the Wilson negroes levied upon are in Consiquence of the trust upon them assessed by the sheriff exceeding the market value - then the statute Dec 14th 1855 points out a remedy in that particular If however the Condition of the Bond was broken I do not think this Court has, the Power on the tender of the property, after judgement on the bond to vacate the judgement or release the property of the defendants from liability for the payment of the debt or to cancel the bond

But as the defendants in all executions have the right to direct what property of theirs shall first be sold to satisfy an execution against them these defendants therefore have the right to require of the sheriff that the Wilson negroes embraced in the claim bond do be first sold

Of the course the defendants Sanchez & Love, are materially interested in seeing that they are sold for the full value at any rate for Enough to pay the Judgement against them the proceeds of the sale of said negroes should of course be credited on the judgement rendered in the claim bond"

February 18, 1857
From Alachua County Ancient Records
Chancery Order Book A pages 119-120

Simeon J. Sanchez indicted for gambling; enslaved people used as part of collateral to ensure he showed up for Court: "State of Florida vs Simeon J. Sanchez - Gambling - Continued by consent of parties, and the Defendant recognized in the Sum of one thousand dollars, for his appearance at the next Term of this Court, five hundred dollars, for principal and five hundred dollars for the security

Simeon J. Sanchez, and William D. Clark appeared in open Court, and acknowledged themselves to owe and Stand indebted to the State of Florida in the Sum of one Thousand dollars, That is to say Simeon J. Sanchez in the sum of five hundred dollars, and William D. Clark in the Sum of five hundred dollars, to be levied of their respective goods and chattels Slaves, land tenements, If Default be made in the following condition. That is to say, If the said Simeon J. Sanchez Shall to and appear at the next Term of this Court, to answer an Indictment for gambling, and shall not thence depart from the Court without leave, then this obligation to be null and void, else to remain in full force and virtue"

December 16, 1853
From Alachua County Ancient Records
Judgment Record A* page 156

Francis Shannon and Sarah E. Shannon his wife to Serena E. Miller: "This Indenture made the 29th day of December A.D. One thousand Eight hundred & fifty between Francis Shannon and Sarah E. Shannon his wife of the County of Alachua State of Florida parties of the first part and Serena E. Miller party of the Second part Witnesseth that the Said Francis Shannon and Sarah E. Shannon his wife for and in Consideration of the natural love and affection which they have and bear Serena E. Miller and also for and in Consideration of the Sum of Five dollars to him in hand paid by the said Serena E.

Miller at and before the Sealing and delivery of these presents, the receipt whereof is hereby acknowledged, Have given, granted, aliened enfeoffed and Confirmed and by these presents, do give grant aliened enfeoffed and Confirm unto the Said Serena E. Miller, her heirs and assigns all that Certain tract or parcel of land lying and being in the County of Alachua and State of Florida and Known as Section thirty five (35) in Township number (9) Range number twenty one (21) Containing Six hundred & forty acres more or less together with **ten Negroes named Tom, Mary, Charles, George, Sam, Jessie, Letty, Marion, Elizabeth & William**, also five mules one Sorrel Horse and the Cotton contained in House and field on the aforesaid tract of land together with all and Singular the tenements hereditaments and appurtenances thereunto belonging or in any wise appertaining and also all the estate, right title, interest, property possession Claim and demand whatsoever of the said parties of the first part of in or to the above described premises and every part and parcel thereof with the appurtenances To Have and to Hold all and Singular the above mentioned premises together with the above described personal property unto the Serena E. Miller her Successors and assigns forever"

December 29, 1850
From Alachua County Ancient Records
Deed Record E page 632

William Shedd to Samuel G. Barkly in trust for William's daughter Catharine E. Jones wife of Osmand S. Jones: "Know all men by these presents that I William Shedd of the district of Fairfield in the State aforesaid in Consideration of the natural love and affection I have and bear for and towards my daughter Catharine E. wife of Osmand S. Jones and of Five dollars to me in hand paid at and before the sealing of these present by Samuel G. Barkly of the District of Fairfield and State aforesaid have given bargained, Sold, and delivered, and by these presents do give bargain Sell and deliver unto the said Samuel G. Barkly his heirs and assigns forever, **The nine following Negro Slaves, namely, Maria a woman about Twenty Seven years old and her four children Nelly, Wade, Beckey and an infant not named, a woman Beckey about twenty one years of age and her two children Jim & Bob** In trust nevertheless for the following uses and purposes and none other,

First in Trust to allow my said daughter Catharine Jones to have the use and Services or the annual hire of said Slaves to her Sole and Separate use for and during the term of her natural life, and at and after the death of my said daughter, then in trust, to divide said Slaves and their future increase among such issue as my said daughter Catharine shall have living at the time of her death."

March 10, 1856
The State of South Carolina, Fairfield District
From Alachua County Ancient Records
Deed Record C pages 388-389

Enslaved man name Simon indicted of an assault with intent to kill a white man: "The State of Florida vs Simon a Slave - Indictment for an assault with intent to kill - Now on this day Simon a Slave late of the County of Alachua who stands indicted of an assault with intent to Kill, was led to the bar in custody of the Sheriff and jailer of this court and James B. Dawkins the Solicitor prosecuting for the State by consent of the court saith that he will not prosecute further on behalf of the State vs. Simon a slave, who stands accused of an Assault with intent to Kill and thereupon the Solicitor informing the court that he intended to prosecute said Simon a slave for an Assault and Battery upon a white man with intent to Kill, he the said Simon a slave, was remanded to jail in the county of Marion to answer offence there being no sufficient jail or place of safe Keeping in the county of Alachua

It is therefore ordered that the Sheriff of Alachua County do convey the said Simon a slave to the jail of Marion County and deliver him unto the custody of the jailer of said County and that the jailer of said county of Marion do receive said Simon a slave unto said County jail and Keep him until the further order of this court"

December 12, 1856
From Alachua County Ancient Records
Judgment Record A* pages 472-473

Enslaved man named Simon convicted of assault & battery with intent to kill a white man, to be executed by hanging: "The State of Florida vs Simon a Slave - convicted of Assault & Battery with intent to Kill a white man - Simon a slave who stands convicted of an assault & Battery with intent to Kill a white man was again led to the bar in custody of the Jailor of this court and thereupon it being demanded of him if anything he had for himself or Know to say why the Court here to Judgment and Execution against him of and upon the premises should not proceed replied that he had nothing to say, whereupon the Court proceeded to pass the following sentence

"The sentence of the court is that you Simon a slave whereof you stand convicted be therefore hanged by the neck until you are dead that the Sheriff of Alachua County as his deputy do on peril of what may fall thereon cause execution to be done in the premises upon you on Friday the Twenty ninth day of May now next ensuing being the Twenty ninth day of May in the year of our Lord one Thousand Eight hundred and fifty seven at or near the town of Gainesville in the said County of Alachua between the hours of nine oclock in the forenoon and Twelve oclock at noon of the same day; and that you now be taken from hence to the jail at Ocala in Marion County from whence you came there or in some other convenient jail within the Eastern Circuit of Florida to be closely kept until the day of Execution appointed as aforesaid you are to be taken to the place of Execution there to be hanged as aforesaid until you are dead"

May 15, 1857
From Alachua County Ancient Records
Judgment Record A page 532

John J. Smallwood to Andrew Ormand for $925: "Know all men by these presents that I John J. Smallwood of Waldo County of Alachua and State of Florida for and in consideration of the sum of Nine hundred twenty five Dollars lawfull Money of the United States to me in hand paid at and before the ensealing and delivery of these presents by Andrew Ormand of the County and State aforesaid, the receipt whereof is hereby acknowledged have bargained and Sold and by these presents do grant and convey unto the said Andrew Ormand his heirs Executors administrators and assigns **One Negro Slave named "Andrew" about twenty seven years old and about five feet nine Inches high**. To have and to hold the same unto the said Andrew Ormand his Executors administrators and assigns forever"

May 7, 1859
From Alachua County Ancient Records
Bills of Sale A page 066

James H. Smith and wife Mary Smith to George L. Brown as collateral for a $152.25 loan: "This Indenture made this Second day of February One Thousand Eight Hundred & fifty between George L. Brown of the County of Alachua and State of Florida on the one part, and James H. Smith & Mary Smith his wife of the other part both of said County and State Whereas the said James H. Smith and Mary his wife […] Stands indebted to the said George L. Brown in the sum of One Hundred and fifty two Dollars and Twenty five cents the said sum mentioned in said promissory note together with Lawful interest for the same to wit Eight per cent as interest by the said receipted note relation being had hereto more fully and at Law appears Now this Indenture Witnesseth that the said James H. Smith and Mary his wife for and in consideration of the aforesaid Sum One Hundred and fifty two Dollars and twenty five cents, the sum mentioned in Said promissory note, and for the better securing the payment thereof with the Interest at 8 per cent more due thereon or hereafter to become due to the said Geo L. Brown his Executors administrators and assigns as of the further sum of One Dollar in hand paid to the said James H. Smith & Mary his wife by the said George L Brown at and before the Sealing and delivery hereof the receipt of which is hereby acknowledged, Hath bargained & Sold and do hereby bargain & sell unto the said George L. Brown a certain **Negro Woman Slave aged about Twenty Four years of a yellow Complexion named Lizzie and her two Children named Eileen & William aged respectively four years & one year old**, said Negroes now in the possession of the said James H. Smith & Mary Smith to have and to hold the said Negro Slaves to George L. Brown and to his heirs and assigns forever provided never the less that if the said James H. Smith and Mary his wife or either of them or either of their heirs executors Administrators shall & do well and truly pay or cause to be paid unto the said George L. Brown his Executors Administrators or assigns the aforesaid sum of One Hundred & fifty two Dollars and Twenty Five cents, Together with the Interest due thereon or here after to become due on or before the first day of January One Thousand Eight Hundred and fifty one, as well as all such further sum or sums of money as shall here after be acknowledged by the same James H. Smith & Mary his wife to be due by further advancement from the said George L. Brown to the said James H. Smith & Mary his wife, Then This deed of Mortgage as well as the promissory note mentioned and described herein to be void other wise to be & remain in full force and virtue"

February 2, 1850
From Alachua County Ancient Records
Mortgage Record A pages 038-040

Sarah Smith, Mary Clements, and Tappington Singletary, sisters and heirs at law (Complainants) vs John G. Tyner (Defendant)- Dispute over division of assets of Henry Lindsay who died intestate: "This cause came on to be heard, and was argued by counsel, viz. E. Bissell and McQueen McIntosh Esqrs for complainants, and M. Whit Smith and J.J. Sanderson, Esqrs for Defendant, and therefore, upon consideration thereof, it was ordered, adjudged and decreed, as follows, Viz

First That the Said Sarah S. Smith, Mary Clements and Tappington Singletary and the Sisters and only legal heirs and distributes of the assets which were of Said Henry Lindsay deceased, and as Such, are entitled to a distributive Share of one third, each, of Said estate.

Secondly That Said Henry Lindsay died intestate, in the County of Alachua, Florida, in the Spring of AD 1841: That one Thomas Colding, duly administered upon the assets which were of said Henry Lindsay Deceased.

Thirdly That on the 29th day of November AD 1841: the Said John G. Tyner, then and Still a resident of the State of Florida, went unto the State of Georgia and purchased of the Said Tappington Singletary, who then resided in the State of Georgia, all her right, title, interest, claim and demand to her deceased Brother Henry Lindsays estate, of which Thomas Colding of Alachua County was administrater, being one third part thereof, after the debts of Same were paid, for the Sum of Sixty Six dollars and Sixty Six cents, and procured to be Signed and delivered to him from her an assignment bearing date on that day in writing, embracing a power of Attorney to him the Said Jesse G. Tyner, authorising him in her name, and for his use, to Sue for and collect the Same.

Fourthly That on the 30th day of November AD 1841 the Said John G. Tyner, then a resident of said Alachua County, went from Florida to the State of Georgia, and then and there purchased of the Said Sarah Smith, who then resided in State of Georgia, all her interest, right, title, Claim and demand to her Deceased Brothers (Henry Lindsays) estate, of which Thomas Colding of Alachua County was administrator, being one third part thereof after the Same were paid, for the Sum of $66 66/100, and on that day procured a written assignment from her of the Same, which Said assignment in writing was on that day Signed and delivered to him, and embraced also a power of Attorney to him the Said John G. Tyner, authorising him in her name, and for his use, to Sue for and collect the Same.

Fifthly That on the 27th day of November AD 1841, the Said John G. Tyner then a resident of Alachua County, went from the State of Florida unto the State of Georgia, and then and there purchased of the Said Mary Clements who then resided in the State of Georgia, all her interest, right, title, claim and demand to her deceased Brothers (Henry Lindsays) estate of which Thomas Colding of Alachua County was administrator being one third part thereof, after the debts of the Same were paid, for the Sum of $66 66/100, and on that day procured a written assignment from her of the Same, which was on that day Signed by her, and delivered to him, and embraced also a Power of Attorney to him the Said John G. Tyner, authorising him in her name and for his use, to Sue for and collect the Same

Sixthly That after the purchasing of Said interest of Said Tapping Singletary, Sarah Smith, and Mary Clements in Said estate, he the Said John G. Tyner Sued the Said Administrator for the Same, by filing a Bill in Chancery in this Court, in Said County of Alachua against the Said Administrator, and on the 8th day of May AD 1846, obtained a decree of Said Court in his favor, wherein the Said Thomas Colding as administrator of the estate which was of Said Henry Lindsay deceased, was ordered to pay within 30 days thereafter to Said Tyner the Sum of $392.97 3/4 being the full amount of the money of said estate in his hands as Such administrator, after paying all the debts and expenses of Said estate, and to deliver to the Said John G. Tyner the following property and debts constituting the balance of the assets of said estate, and which where then and there delivered to him Viz

A negro man named Ruetey, valued by the Master in Chancery at $200.00
A negro woman named Mary and her child 400.00
2 Mares 107.00
Thos J. Smith's note on hand 50.00
Judgment vs Curry 60.00
Demand against Enoch Daniels 30.00

Seventhly That Said Tappington Singletary, Sarah Smith and Mary Clements, were Severally induced thus to Sell their Said interests in Said estate of said Henry Lindsay deed, to the Said John G. Tyner for an inadequate price as consideration, and to execute and deliver Said written assignments thereof to the Said John G. Tyner from misrepresentation then and there made to them by the Said John G. Tyner as to the extent and value of Said estate.

Eighthly And it further ordered, adjudged, and decreed, that the Said written assignment or conveyance of the interest of the Said Tapping Singletary in Said estate of said Henry Lindsay decd, bearing date the 29th day of November AD 1841, and attached to the answer of Said John G. Tyner in this cause, be, and the Same is hereby declared null and void as against the Said Tapping Singletary, her heirs, Executors administrators or assigns. And that the Said of written assignment or conveyance of the interests of Said Sarah Smith in Said estate of Said Henry Lindsay deceased, bearing date the 30th day of November AD 1841, and attached to the answer of Said John G. Tyner in this cause be and the Same is hereby declared null and void as against the Said Sarah Smith, her heirs Executors, administrators and assigns. And that the Said written assignment or conveyance of the interests of said Mary Clements in Said estate of Said Henry Lindsay decd bearing date the 27th day of November AD 1841, and attached to the answer of Said John G. Tyner in this cause, be and the Same is hereby declared null and void as against the Said Mary Clements, her heirs, Executors, administrators and assigns

Ninthly And it is further ordered, adjudged, and decreed, that the Said John G. Tyner do pay to the Said Tapping Singletary, Sarah Smith, and Mary Clements, or their respective Attorney or Attornies, Executors, administrators or assigns, within 60 days from the entering of this decree, the Sum of nine hundred and eighty nine dollars and ninety Seven cents ($989.97) with interest thereon at the rate of six per cent from the 8th day of May AD 1846, and the costs of this Suit to be taxed by the Clerk and that execution do issue for the Same.

Lastly And it is further ordered, adjudged, and decreed, that the Said John G. Tyner do have leave within Said 60 days, and after notice thereof to the Solicitor of the complainants, to make application, accompanied with proofs, for the reduction of said amount, on the Showing that in truth he has not collected and received, and could not in exercise of due dilligence, have collected and received the said debts due and owing Said estate, and turned over to him or any of them, and if upon Such Showing it Shall appear reasonable and Just that a reduction Should be made by this Court, then that the amount thus decreed to be deducted, Shall by Supplemental decree be allowed as a credit."

September 3, 1855
From Alachua County Ancient Records
Chancery Order Book A pages 102-106

Maria Sourbray to John C. Hague for $350: "Know all men by these presents that I Maria Sourbray of the Town of Newnansville, in the County of Alachua, and State of Florida, of the first part, for and in consideration of the Sum of three hundred and fifty dollars, lawful money of the United States, to me in hand paid at or before the ensealing and delivery of these presents by John C. Hague of the Same place, of the Second part, the receipt whereof is hereby acknowledged, that the said party of the first part, have bargained, and Sold, and by these presents, do grant and convey unto the Said party of the Second part, his Executors, Administrators and assigns, **one Negro boy named Joe about three years old**, to have and to hold the same unto the said party of the Second part, his Executors, Administrators, and assigns forever."

August 28, 1854
From Alachua County Ancient Records
Deed Record B page 416

Maria Sourbray to daughters Sarah Hague and Amanda Hague: "Be it known to all whom there may concern, that I Maria Sourbray widow of the first part, and Sarah Hague and Amanda Hague of the Second part all of the Town of Newnansville, and County and State aforesaid, Witnesseth, that the Said Maria Sourbray for and in consideration of the natural affection She the Said Maria Sourbray has between her two Daughters the Said Sarah and Amanda Hague, formerly Sarah Lipsy and Amanda Lipsy, and also the further consideration of the Sum of five dollars lawful money of the United States to me in hand paid at or before the delivery of these presents the receipt whereof is hereby acknowledged, that the Said party of the first part, hath given, granted, bargained, and Sold, and by these presents do give, grant, bargain and Sell unto the Said Sarah and Amanda Hague a certain **Negro woman known by the name of Amelia, and her child about four months old named Nancy, and her further increase which She the Said Amelia may bear**. To have and to hold the Said bargained property to their and each of their own proper use benefit and behoof forever. And it is on these conditions, that the Said Maria Sourbray Shall have the benefit of the labor and use of the said bargained property during her natural life, the same as if this transfer had not been made, but immediately after the death of the Said Maria Sourbray, to be the property of the Said Sarah Hague and Amanda Hague, and I do, for myself, my heirs, Executors, Administrators and assigns, agree to warrant and defend the Sale of the said property hereby sold, forever against all and every person and persons whomsoever."

December 19, 1854
State of Florida, Alachua County
From Alachua County Ancient Records
Deed Record D page 144

John B. Standley Last Will and Testament: "Will of John B. Standley deceased

In the name of God Amen. I, John B. Standley of Alachua Co. Fl., being of sound and disposing mind, but feeble in body, do make and publish this my last Will and Testament.

First, I give my body to the grave, and my spirit to the God who gave it.

Secondly, it is my will that all my just debts be paid.

Thirdly, I will and bequeath the residue of my property, real and personal, after the payment of my debts to my beloved wife Penelopy Standley, my son James Standley, and my daughter Laura Standley, to be equally divided between them share and share alike.

Fourthly, it is my will that the property, real and personal, hereby bequeathed to my beloved wife Penelopy Standley, my son James Standley, my daughter Laura Standley, be kept together and made subject to the full control and management of my wife Penelopy Standley during the minority of James Standley and Laura Standley.

Fifthly, **it is my will that an overseer be employed by my wife to take charge of the Negroes,** carry on the plantation subject to the supervision and advice of my wife Penelopy Standley.

Sixthly, it is my will that James Standley live with, protect and comfort his mother Penelopy Standley, and hold and enjoy his portion of the property hereby bequeathed subject to the management and control of his mother Penelopy Standley during the term of her natural life

Seventhly, it is my will that the property hereby bequeathed to my daughter Laura Standley be deeded (on her marriage) by my wife Penelopy Standley in trust to some suitable person and discreet, selected by my wife, for the use and benefit of my said daughter Laura Standley free from the debts and liabilities of her husband.

Eighthly, it is my will that no division of the property take place during the minority of my children James Standley and Laura Standley.

Ninthly, it is my will and I do hereby appoint Penelopy Standley and Samuel R. Pyles to carry into effect this my last Will and Testament."

December 22, 1859
From Alachua County Ancient Records
Will Book B pages 003-005

John B. Standley to John H. Ellis Guardian of Thomas S. Ellis for $6,000: "Know all men these presents that I John B. Standley of the State and County aforesaid am held and firmly bound unto John H. Ellis Guardian of Thomas S. Ellis in the Sum of Six thousand dollars […] John B. Ellis has this day for himself and as Guardian for Thomas S. Ellis Sold their entire equal and undivided interest; Sold unto the above bounded John B. Stanley the following Negros Slaves to wit; **Negro woman Mary aged about forty five years and her Children Jim Martha John Andrew, Elsey, Alfred, Sam Job and Bill of the ages of nineteen Seven five and three years respectfully** for the Sum of Six Thousand of which amount the Sum of three Thousand Dollars is this day paid And the remaining Three Thousand Dollars to be paid on 1st January AD 1858 with 6 (Six) per cent interest from date […] if the Said Thomas S. Ellis on his attaining the age of twenty one years Shall ratify Said contract by consenting to Said Sale as transfer of his interest therein then the above bound John B. Stanly is to pay the Said Sum of Three Thousand Dollars with interest as aforesaid; And if Said Thomas S.

Ellis Should fail to ratify his interest as aforesaid then this obligation to be void and of no affect"

February 5, 1857
State of Florida, Alachua County
From Alachua County Ancient Records
Deed Record D pages 420-421

Claudius C. Stewart to Mary J. Halliday for $1,000: "Know all men by these presents that I Claudius C. Stewart of the Town of Newnansville, in the County of Alachua and State of Florida, of the first part, for and in consideration of the sum of one thousand dollars, lawful money of the United States to me in hand paid by Mary J. Halliday, wife of S. F. Halliday of the place aforesaid, have bargained and sold, and by these presents do grant and convey unto the said party of the second part, her Executors, Administrators, and assigns **one negro boy named Saunders**, to have and to hold the same unto the said party of the second part, her Executors, Administrators, and assigns for ever"

January 19, 1854
From Alachua County Ancient Records
Bills of Sale A pages 019-020

E. M. Stewart to George L. Brown, trustee to the children of John C. Pelot by his first wife Sarah Pelot (deceased) for $1,500: "Received of George L. Brown as trustee to the children of John C. Pelot, by his first wife Sarah A. Pelot deceased, fifteen hundred Dollars, for Two Negroes -- to wit **Lucy, woman aged, thirty eight years dark complection and her son Samuel aged twenty one -- mulatto.** The two Negroes above mentioned and sold as above stated to George L. Brown as trustee for the children of John C. Pelot and Sarah A. Pelot I warrant to be healthy and sound, slaves for life and the titles I hereby warrant to defend against the claims of all any person whatsoever."

October 20, 1855
From Alachua County Ancient Records
Deed Record D page 388
See also Alachua County Ancient Records
Bills of Sale A page 032

William H. Stringfellow to Sallie A. Stringfellow: "Know all men by these presents that I William H. Stringfellow of the State and County & County aforesaid have conveyed granted and given & released unto my beloved Sallie A. Stringfellow, and in the event of her dieing intestate to the heir or heirs of her body, all my right, title claim and interest in the following Negroes to wit, **the man Burrel, woman Julia & her Children Sarah William Josh Stephen Andrew, Caroline & Nancy, & the woman, Lavinia & her Children Hester & Lizzy together with all increase born hereafter** to them and by these presence do warrant, and defend the same to her and in event of her dieing intestate against myself and all others on my account, lawfully claiming or to claim the same, to the heirs of her body."

January 5, 1857
State of Florida, Alachua County
From Alachua County Ancient Records
Deed Record D page 451

Henry J. Strobhar to Noble A. Strobhar for $500: "Know all men by these presents that Henry J. Strobhar, of the County and State aforesaid for and in consideration of the Sum of Five hundred dollars to me in hand paid at and before the Sealing and delivery of these presents by Noble A. Strobhar of Alachua County in the State of Florida. The receipt whereof is hereby acknowledged, have bargained and sold and by these presents do bargain Sell and deliver unto the Said Noble A. Strobhar all my rights title and Interests in and to the following Slaves to wit: **a negro woman named Pleasant, about Twenty Seven years of age and a girl named Charlotte about four years of age, and a girl named Patsy about Seven years of**

age, to have and to hold, all my interest and right in and to the Said Slaves to wit: Pleasant, Patsy, and Charlotte unto the Said Noble A. Strobhar his heirs Executors Administrators and assigns to his and their only proper use and behoof forever."

July 18, 1855 and in the Eightieth year of the Independence of the United States of America
State of Georgia, Effingham County
From Alachua County Ancient Records
Bills of Sale A page 034

Noble A. Strobhar to Samuel R. Pyles as collateral for $2,650.57 in loans: "This Indenture made this the nineteenth day of November in the year of our Lord one thousand Eight hundred & fifty Eight Between Noble A. Strobhar of the County of Alachua and State of Florida of the first part and Samuel R. Pyles of the same place of the Second part Witnesseth that the said Noble A. Strobhar for and in Consideration of the Sum of One dollar to him in hand paid by the said Samuel R. Pyles and for the forbearance to Sue by the said Samuel R. Pyles as well as for the Securing the payment of the notes hereinafter described has granted bargained Sold aliened transferred and Conveyed and by these presents doth grant, bargain, Sell, Alien, transfer and Convey unto the Said Samuel R. Pyles his heirs and assigns all those Certain portions and tracts of land Situate lying and being in the said County of Alachua more particularly Known and described according to the Maps and plats in the United States Land office as the West half of the North East quarter, East half of the North West quarter and East half of the South West quarter of Section Eleven Township Seven Range Eighteen S&E and the West Half of Lots Number two & three in Section Two and lot Number Two in Section Three Township Seven South Range Eighteen East and the West half North West quarter Section Eleven, Township Seven Range

Eighteen South & East and the East half of North West quarter of Section Eleven Township Seven South Range Eighteen East Containing Five hundred & forty five and forty two hundredths more or less, together with all the rights tenements appurtenances and hereditaments thereunto in anywise appertaining or belonging, And the Said Noble A. Strobhar doth also bargain, Sell and Convey unto the said Samuel R. Pyles his heirs and assigns **a Negro man named Adam of dark Complexion about thirty years of age, and a Negro woman named Alginora of Yellow Complexion about Twenty Seven years of age and her child about two years of age named Cyrus** To have and to hold the said tracts of land above described, and the Negroes above named to the said Samuel R. Pyles his heirs and assigns forever And the said Noble A. Strobhar will and his heirs and administrators Shall the afore granted premises to the said Samuel R. Pyles his heirs Executors and administrators forever warrant and defend by virtue of these presents and the said Noble A. Strobhar covenants with the said Samuel R. Pyles his heirs Executors and administrators that the said Negroes Adam Alginora and Cyrus are Slaves born and in sound health & body and mind and that he the said Noble A Strobhar his heirs Executors and administrators Shall the said Negroes to the Said Samuel R. Pyles his heirs Executors and administrators forever warrant and defend Provided Nevertheless that if the said Noble A. Strobhar his heirs Executors or administrators shall pay unto the said Samuel R. Pyles his Executors administrators or assigns the amount of a Certain promisory note made by the said Noble A. Strobhar payable to the said Samuel R. Pyles or bearer bearing even date with these presents and due one day after for the sum of Four hundred and forty two Dollars and Ninety Six Cents with interest thereon at Eight per Cent, And also another Certain promisory note by the said Noble A. Strobhar payable to Philip Dell or bearer bearing even date with these presents due one day after date for the Sum of One thousand and Seventy one Dollars and twenty four Cents with Eight per Cent interest thereon and also a Certain other and third promisory note made by the said Noble A. Strobhar payable to the Edward Remington or bearer bearing even date with these presents, and due One day after date for the Sum of Eleven hundred and thirty Six dollars and thirty

Seven Cents with interest at Eight per Cent thereon Now if the said Noble A. Strobhar his heirs Executors or administrators shall pay unto the said Samuel R. Pyles his Executors administrators and assigns the three promisory notes above mentioned and described on or before the nineteenth day of December which will be in the year of our Lord Eighteen hundred & fifty nine with all legal interest which may be due upon the same according to the tenor of the same and all expences incurred by the said Samuel R. Pyles in Collecting the same then as well this deed as the above described promissory note to be utterly void otherwise to remain in full force"

November 19, 1858
From Alachua County Ancient Records
Mortgage Record A pages 151-153

Lorenzo Suggs indicted for receiving grain from an enslaved person: "The State of Florida vs Lorenzo Suggs - On motion of the Solicitor it is ordered by the Court that an alias Capias do issue in this cause"

May 12, 1856
From Alachua County Ancient Records
Judgment Record A* page 360

M. J. Tharp to Susan E. Louman for $1,650: "Received of Susan E. Louman by Cash and Note Sixteen hundred and Fifty dollars for **a Family of Four Negroes. Namely, Mariah aged Twenty years and Sabina aged seven years, ***da aged Four years, Preston**

aged two years and which Negroes I warrant the title, Elsmore & to be Slaves for life."

August 15, 1856
State of South Carolina, Richland District
From Alachua County Ancient Records
Bills of Sale A page 039

Elizabeth Townsend, Sarah Townsend, and Margaret Townsend vs. Joseph G. Bell regarding ownership of an enslaved man: "Plaintiffs Elizabeth Townsend, Sarah Townsend and Margaret Townsend, Infants within the age of Twenty one years who sue by their next friend William Townsend, Guardian of said Infants, Plaintiffs vs. Joseph G. Bell Defendant

And now on this Thirteenth of December in the year of our Lord one Thousand eight hundred and fifty two come the said Plaintiffs by their Attorney John P. Sanderson and the said Defendant came by his attorney James M. Baker and on the calling of the above cause on the trial Docket at this Term of this Court, there appearing to be no plea demurrer or motion filed therein

It is on motion of the said plaintiffs attorney, considered that the said plaintiffs do have judgement by Nil, Dicit and forasmuch as this Court is ***advised as to the amount of damages sustained by the said plaintiffs, by reason of the removal of the Negros in said plaintiff declaration mentioned and discribed and also to whom the said negro Tom does of right belong, and of the truth of said matters alleged as set forth in said declaration, it is on motion of said plaintiffs attorney ordered that a writ of Enquiry be awarded to enquire of the said damages and also to whom the said **Negro Tom** does belong and thereupon to wit: on the Fourteenth day of December in the year of our Lord one Thousand eight hundred and fifty two came a Jury [...] who being duly elected tried and sworn to determine of the truth of the said matters alleged in said plaintiffs declaration and of the damages sustained by said plaintiffs, after hearing the evidence, retired to deliberate upon their verdict, and thereupon and on the same day the same Jury returned into Court and rendered the following verdict to wit,

We the Jury find the Negro Man Tom to be the property of the plaintiffs and we assess the plaintiffs damages at Eighteen Hundred dollars [...]

It is therefore considered adjudged and ordered by this Court that the said plaintiffs do have and recover of and from the said Defendant the sum of Eighteen hundred dollars, and his costs by him in and about his said action in this behalf expended, and the defendant in mercy &c, and that the title interest and claim to the said Negro man Tom of the said Defendant is forfeited and that the said Negro man Tom is the property of the said plaintiffs"

December 14, 1852
From Alachua County Ancient Records
Judgment Record A* pages 100-101

Elizabeth Townsend et al (Complainants) vs. Joseph G. Bell and his wife (Defendants) - to get Elizabeth's enslaved people back who were willed to her: "This cause coming on for a further hearing on this the fifteenth day of December AD Eighteen hundred and fifty two before the Honorable Thomas Douglas Sitting in Chancery for the Eastern Circuit of Florida,

And it appearing to the Court, that at the last May Term of this Court the Exceptions herein heretofore filed to the Defendants Answer in this Cause, were argued and adjudged by the Court, and the Defendants answer was to be decreed to be insufficient in certain particulars more specially set forth in said Decretal order of May last, and the said Defendants were ordered to put in a better answer within three months from the date of said Decretal order And it further appearing to the Court that said better Answer has not been put in,

It is considered ordered and adjudged and Decreed by the Court that the said Bill of Complaint be taken Pro Confesso in so far as the Answer to the same has been adjudged to be insufficient, that is to say,

That it is confessed by the defendants that the said James L. Townsend did depart this life about the Month of December AD Eighteen hundred and forty two, in the County of Alachua and State of Florida, That he left real and personal Estate in said County amounting to between eight and nine thousand Dollars,

That the said Elizabeth Townsend filed a petition before the Judge of the County Court for the County of Alachua on the Eighteenth day of February AD Eighteen hundred and forty four and that Exhibit B, is a true Copy of said petition,

That one of the Children of the **Negro Woman Nancy** was named **Phebe**, That a life Estate in the **Negro boy Tom** was assigned to the said Elizabeth, That the **Negro Boy Ansel** was also assigned to the said Elizabeth as Dower, and that the Exhibit C.C. does contain a full exhibit of all the property in which a life Estate was assessed to the said Elizabeth as Dower,

That the slave sold to the said Arthur Floyed is still in the possession of said Floyed.

That a life estate in the Girl Phoebe was assigned as a part of Dower to the said Elizabeth,

That the said Negro Woman Nancy has been born to her since the said assignment of Dower three children that they are still alive that none of them are now in possession of the said defendants or their agents, but have all been sold by them, that the said Negro Man Tom was offered for sale in Savannah,

That the infant child spoken of is the child of the said Negro Woman Nancy born since the assignment of dower to the said Elizabeth,

That the said Negro Woman Nancy and her Child have been sold by the said defendants, and that the said Negroes Tom and Nancy are a portion of the Slaves referred to in the Exhibit marked C.C. in which a life estate was assigned to the said Elizabeth as her dower,

And that the said Children Margaret Elizabeth Townsend and Sarah Townsend are justly entitled to reversionary interest in said property, and upon final hearing of this cause the said complainants shall not be required to prove any of the foregoing allegations contained in their said Bill of Complaint but the same shall be in all respects held deemed and considered as fully proven admitted and confessed by the said defendants."

December 15, 1852
Alachua Circuit Court, Alachua County
From Alachua County Ancient Records
Chancery Order Book A pages 072-074

Concerning distribution of the estate of James L. Townsend: "Estate of James L. Townsend, late of Alachua County and State of Florida deceased, for the purpose of a more equal division of said Estate, between the heirs of said deceased Beg leave to report The real estate consisting of Five hundred and Seventy three acres and thirty one hundredths of an acre, was offered for sale at Auction before the Court house door of Newnansville, County and State aforesaid on the second Monday in May last, after having been advertised for sale in the newspaper published at Alligator, and notice of the sale posted in three public places in the Town of Newnansville

The Said real Estate was Sold for cash One hundred and Sixty acres was Struck off to Oliver Bryant who was the highest bidder at Seven dollars and fifty cents per acre amounting to the Sum of One thousand two hundred dollars, which Sum was Five hundred and twenty Six and 33/100 dollars less than the Said Oliver Bryant's Share in said Estate

Four hundred and thirteen and 33/100 acres was sold to William B. Wimberly who was the highest bidder for the Sum of seven dollars and fifty cents per acre, amounting to the Sum of Three thousand one hundred dollars

The personal property to wit: **Negro Slave Phebe and her infant** was sold at the Same time and place, the Same notice of the Sale having been given, as was given of the sale of the real Estate.

The terms of the sale of said Slaves were as follows, One half cash and the balance to be paid on the first day of January AD 1856 the last note to be secured by a note with approved personal Security

The said Slaves were Sold to William B. Wimberly, who was the highest bidder for the sum of Eight hundred and Seventy nine dollars, which two purchases of the land and Slaves by William B. Wimberly amount to the Sum of Three Thousand Nine hundred and Seventy nine dollars, which amount exceeds his interest in said Estate in the Sum of Two Thousand two hundred and fifty dollars and sixty seven cents

The Land bought by the Oliver Bryant are Known and described as follows" The East half of the North East 1/4 of Section 9, and the West half of the South West 1/4 of section 10 Township 7 South of Range 18 East, Containing 160 acres as aforesaid

And the lands bought by the said William B. Wimberly are Known and described as so much of the east half of the South East 1/4 of Section 21 and the West half of the North West 1/4 and the West half of the South East 1/4 of Section 22, and of the North East 1/4 of Section 28 and of the West half of the North West 1/4 of Section 27 in Township 7 South of Range 18 East, as lies East of a certain Stream, Known as the Townsend Branch And the West 1/2 of the 1/2 of the North West 1/4 & the West 1/2 of the South East 1/4 of Section 27 in the Same Township and Range and containing by estimation 413 33/100 acres as aforesaid

And they further report that the aforesaid purchasers have fully complied with the terms of the said Sale, and that they the said Commissioners are ready to make such distribution of the proceeds, and execute titles to said real and personal property as your Honor may direct.

Dec 10th AD 1855

And there being no exceptions filed, on motion of Messrs Smith & Bradford, Solicitors, for Complainant, It is ordered, adjudged_and decreed, that the said report and all things therein contained, do stand ratified and confirmed and that the sale so made is approved of by this Court, and be firm and effectual forever

And it appearing by said report among other things that the said William B. Wimberly in right of his wife, being claimant therein, became purchaser of lands and said negro slaves, at said sale, and purchased over and above the sum he was entitled to receive, the Sum of Two thousand two hundred and fifty two dollars and Sixty Seven cents ($2252.67) which sum is due from him to be paid to such claimants herein as have not as yet received that proportion

And It is further adjudged and decreed that the said Commissioners do execute to said Oliver Bryant & wife in right of his wife, purchaser as aforesaid deed of the lands purchased by them, and that they do also execute to Said William B. Wimberly purchaser as aforesaid deed of the lands and Slaves purchased by him, at any time upon his paying of the full amount of his contracts

And it is further ordered adjudged and decreed by and with Consent of parties that there be allowed to said Commissioners Prevatt Bradford & Dell a Commission of five per cent upon the gross amount of the sales of said land and slaves being five per cent upon the Sum of $5,179 amounting to $258.95 being the Sum of $86.31 for each one and that the said Commissioners be allowed to retain the same out of any monies in their hands or hereafter to come into their hands liable to be appropriated for that purpose and report the same to this Court.

And It is further ordered adjudged and decreed that the said Commissioners do ascertain and procure bill of all the taxable costs and charges in this Suit including their commission herein allowed and distribute the Same equally among the said claimants herein, and retain the Same out of any monies due therein, if there is so much due them, and of not then they are respectively required to pay into the hands of said Commissioners their respective proportions, and the Said Commissioners will report the same to this Court with Vouchers"

December 10, 1855 and March 1856
From Alachua County Ancient Records
Chancery Order Book A pages 115-118

John H. Townsend indicted for Larceny and used enslaved people as part of collateral to ensure he showed up for Court: "State of Florida vs John H. Townsend - Larceny - Continued on the affidavit of Defendant Recognized in One Thousand Dollars Five hundred dollars for principal Two hundred and fifty Each for the Securities William Townsend and Zachariah Kittler

John H. Townsend William Townsend and Zachariah Kittler appeared in open Court and acknowledged them selves to owe and stand in debted to the State of Florida in manner following that is to say the said John H. Townsend in the Sum of Five hundred dollars and the said William Townsend in the sum of two hundred and fifty dollars and the said Zachariah Kittler in the Sum of two hundred and fifty dollars to be levied of their respective goods and chattels Slaves lands and tenements if default be made in the following Conditions that is to Say If the said John H. Townsend shall be and appear at the next term of the Court to answer an Indictment for Larceny and shall not thence depart without leave then this obligation to be null and void else to remain in full force and virtue"

December 14, 1853
From Alachua County Ancient Records
Judgment Record A* page 152

Jonathan Turner & Maryann Turner to Thomas Foleston & William Bloodgood as collateral for a $400 loan: "This Indenture made this the ninth day of May A. D. 1850, between Jonathan Turner & Maryann Turner, his wife of Alachua County Florida. Witnesseth that the said parties of the first part being indebted to Thomas Foleston & William Bloodgood of the City of New York partys of the 2d part, for the purchase money of Sec 30 T9 P19 of the Arredondo Grant and in order to secure a part of the purchase of the same do hereby in consideration of the Sum of Four Hundred Dollars to them in hand paid the receipt Whereof is hereby acknowledged grant bargain & sell unto the said Thomas Fileston & William Bloodgood parties of the second part their heirs and assigns, a certain **negro male slave named Peter aged about ten years** now being on the plantation of said Jonathon Turner - to have and to hold to said parties of the second part forever [...] if the said Jonathon Turner & his wife Mary Ann

Turner her either of them or their heirs a legal shall well & truly pay or came to be paid to the said parties of the second part the sum of Four Hundred Dollars, upon the first day of January 1851 with interest, then this conveyance shall be void and of no effect."

May 9, 1850
From Alachua County Ancient Records
Deed Record A page 256

John D. Weimer indicted for selling spiritous liquor to an enslaved person: "State of Florida vs John D. Weimer - Selling Spiritous liquor to a Negro: On this day came as well the Solicitor who prosecutes the pleas of the State in this behalf, and the Defendant in person and his Council M. McIntosh Esqr. and the said Defendant pleaded not guilty, Thereupon came a Jury […] Who were duly Elected, tried and Sworn, a True Verdict to render, James J. Kennard and John T. Prevatt were examined as witnesses in behalf of the State. And the Said Jury having the evidence, and the argument of Council, and the Charge of the Court, retired to consider of their verdict, and thereafter and upon the same day the said Jury returned into Court and rendered the following verdict, We the Jury find the Defendant guilty. Whereupon the Court assessed the punishment at a fine of fifty dollars. It is therefore considered by the Court that the State of Florida do have and recover of and from the said Defendant the Sum of fifty dollars, and the costs of this prosecution"

December 15, 1853
From Alachua County Ancient Records
Judgment Record A* page 162

John D. A. Weimer to John Glisentyner for $950: "Know all men by these presents that I John D. A. Weimer of Alachua County State of Florida, for and in consideration of the sum of nine hundred and fifty dollars to me in hand paid at and before the sealing and delivery of these presents by John Glisentyner, the receipt whereof I do hereby acknowledge, Have bargained, sold, and delivered, and by these presents do bargain, sell, and deliver, unto the said John Glisentyner a certain Negro Slave named **Liza, aged fifteen years**, to have and to hold the said Slave Liza unto the said John Glisentyner his heirs and assigns, to his and their only proper use and benefit forever."

February 11, 1854
From Alachua County Ancient Records
Bills of Sale A page 018

John Whitaker and Margaret Whitaker et al. against Isabella Scota McRa and James Chesnut Whitaker et al. regarding substitution of enslaved people: "Whereas I the undersigned John Whitaker with my wife Margaret Whitaker and others did on the eighteenth day of April Eighteen hundred and fifty five, file our bill in the Court of equity for the district and State aforesaid, against Isabella Scota McRa, James Chesnut Whitaker and others, praying among other things for reciprocal substitution of certain negro slaves respectively set out in schedules A & B exhibited with said bill

And whereas further such proceedings were had under said bill, that the Honorable Court of Equity aforesaid on the fifteenth day of November Eighteen hundred and fifty five, did order and decree among other things "that the negro slaves set forth in "schedule B as the negro slaves of complainant John "Whitaker be substituted for the negro slaves mentioned "in Schedule A as derived by Mrs. Margaret Whitaker "under the will of her father the late Duncan McRa that the said John Whitaker do by proper deed convey the said negro slaves to Lawrence Whitaker in trust for the use and benefit of Margaret Whitaker during the term of her natural life upon the same "terms, conditions, restrictions and limitations over "as are mentioned in the will of the late Duncan McRa "of and concerning the thirty slaves bequeathed to "his daughters"

Now Know all men by these presents that I John Whitaker in pursuance of the said order and in consideration of a substitution of negro slaves therein ordered to be made to me, have bargained sold and delivered and by these presents do bargain sell and deliver unto the said Lawrence Whitaker the following named negro slaves, being those mentioned in Schedule B filed with said bill, viz: **Flora, Mary, Grace, Beck, Sarah Flora, Flora Molly, Emma Mack, Bennett, Miles, Simon, Tod, Terra, Hilliard William & Joe** Eighteen in number

To Have and to Hold the said negro slaves **with their future issue and increase** unto the said Lawrence Whitaker his Exes and admins forever but upon this special trust and confidence, that he shall hold the said negro slaves for the use and benefit of Mrs. Margaret Whitaker during the term of her natural life, to her sole and separate use, without being in any manner subject to the debts contract or control of her husband, and from and immediately after her death to the heirs of her body who may be then living, or to the issue of such heirs then living & according to the terms conditions, restrictions and limitations mentioned in the will of the late Duncan McRa of and concerning the thirty slaves bequeathed to his daughters, And I do hereby warrant the said slaves and their issue unto the said Lawrence Whitaker trustee as aforesaid his Exrs & admrs forever

In witness whereof I have hereunto subscribed my hand and seal this second day of June 1856

In obedience to orders of the Court I hereby **substitute negro woman Hannah with her two children Daphne and Rose with their future issue and increase instead of man Joe named in the**

423

foregoing deed, and I do hereby convey them to the said L. Lawrence Whitaker upon the same terms, conditions, and limitations as are above expressed. Witness my hand and seal this ninth day of Sept 1856"

June 2, 1856 and September 9, 1856
South Carolina, Kershaw District
From Alachua County Ancient Records
Deed Record D pages 389-390

Thomas Whitaker Executor of estate of Ellen Chesnut to Mary W. Haile and Edward Haile: "Received from Thomas Whitaker Executor of Ellen Chesnut deceased the following named Negroes to wit **Joe, Buck, Mary, Rhacheal, Biddy, Daphny, Anthony Joe, Mama Jane, Ben, and Philip** which Negro Slaves **we have received and hold until the future issue and increase of them**, Subject to the provisions contained in the first Clause of the will and Testament of Ellen Chesnut deceased in relation to the bequest, therein made to each of her daughters, and having received the full Share of all the personal Estate of said Ellen Chesnut, to which Mary W. Haile, her daughter is entitled under the last will and Testament of her mother, the Said Ellen Chesnut, we the Said Mary W. and her husband Edward Haile do hereby acknowledge the Same and do hereby forever acquit and discharge the Said Thomas Whitaker forever all present and future liability to us, or either of us as Executors as aforesaid"

February 9, 1852
From Alachua County Ancient Records
Bills of Sale A page 064

John Wiggins to his children: "Know all men by these presents that I John Wiggins of the county of Alachua and State of Florida in consideration of the natural love and affection which I have and bear for my children James Sherouse, Caroline Wiggins, Perry Wiggins, George Wiggins, Burrell Wiggins, Oscar Wiggins, and Benjamin Wiggins, and also for various other good Causes and consideration Me the said John Wiggins hereunto moving have given, granted and confirmed and by these presents do give, grant and confirm unto the said James Sherouse, Caroline Wiggins, Perry Wiggins, George Wiggins, Burrell Wiggins, Oscar Wiggins and Benjanin Wiggins all and singular my goods, chattles, leases and personal Estate whatsoever in whose hands, custody or possession soever they be consisting in part of **Negro woman Lucy** Horses, Hogs &c &c To have, hold and enjoy, all singular the goods, chattles and personal Estate aforesaid unto the said James Sherouse, Caroline, Perry, George, Burrell, Oscar & Benjamin Wiggins their executors, administrators and assigns to their only proper use and benefit and behoof of the said James Sherouse, Caroline, Perry, George, Burrell, Oscar & Benjanin Wiggins their executors and assigns forever.

And I the said John Wiggins all and singular the said goods and chattles, personal Estate and other premises to the said John Wiggins their executors, administrators and assigns against me the said James Sherouse Caroline, Perry, George, Burrell, Oscar & Benjamin Wiggins My executors and administrators and all and every other persons and persons whatsoever shall and will warrant and forever defend by these presents of all and singular which said goods, chattles, personal Estate and other premises, I, the said John Wiggins have put the said James Sherouse, Caroline, Perry, George, Burrell, Oscar, and Benjanin Wiggins in full possession by delivering to them the Negro Woman Lucy at the time of the Sealing and delivery of these presents in the name of the whole premises hereby granted."

August 16, 1851
State of Florida, County of Alachua
From Alachua County Ancient Records
Deed Record B page 061

Charles L. Wilson and Samuel Russell are indebted to John McKinlay for $2,200 for four enslaved people: "Know all men by these presents that we, Charles L. Wilson and Samuel Russell are held and firmly bound unto John McKinlay in the sum of Two thousand two hundred dollars for the payment whereof well and truly to be made we bind ourselves our heirs, executors and Administrators jointly and severally, firmly by these presents signed and sealed this 29th day of January A.D. 1851.

The conditions of the above obligation is such that whereas the above bounded Charles L. Wilson is indebted to the said John McKinlay in the sum of Eleven hundred dollars being the balance of the price of four negro slaves purchased by the said Charles L. Wilson from the said John McKinlay, and to secure the payment of which a deed of Mortgage has this day been executed by the said Charles L. Wilson to the said John McKinlay Now if the above bounded Charles L. Wilson shall pay to the said John McKinlay his heirs or assigns the sum of Eleven hundred dollars in three annual commencing on the first day of January A.D. 1853 Then that obligation as said at the above mentioned Deed of Mortgage to be null and void else to remain in full force and virtue"

January 29, 1851
From Alachua County Ancient Records
Mortgage Record A pages 061-062

Charles L. Wilson to John McKinlay as collateral for an $1,100 loan: "This Indenture made this Twenty ninth day of January in the year of our Lord one thousand eight hundred and fifty one between Charles L. Wilson of said State and County on the one part, and John McKinlay of said State and County on the other part Witnesseth That whereas the said Charles L. Wilson is indebted to the said John McKinlay in the sum of Eleven hundred dollars being the balance of the purchase money or price of four negro slaves purchased by said Wilson from Charles McKinlay which said amount of money is to be paid by the said Wilson to the said McKinlay in three equal annual installments commencing on the first day of January in the year of our Lord Eighteen hundred and fifty two. Now Know all men by these presents that I the said Charles L. Wilson in consideration of the foregoing agreement as well as in consideration of the sum of Five dollars to me in hand paid by the said McKinlay at and before the sealing and delivery of these presents the receipt whereof is hereby acknowledged; have granted bargained, sold and conveyed, and do by these presents grant, bargain, sell and convey unto the said John McKinlay his heirs and assigns the following described property, to wit, **Emily a female negro slave and her two children namely, Cuffee a boy aged about seven years, and Henry a boy aged about eighteen months. Also Tena a female negro slave aged about Twenty three years Together with all the future issue and increase of said Slaves.** To Have and to hold the said Negro slaves to him the said John McKinlay his heirs and assigns forever And I the said Charles L. Wilson for myself, my heirs, executors and administrators, will forever warrant and defend to the said John McKinlay his heirs and assign the right and title to the above conveyed negro slaves Provided Nevertheless that if the said Charles L. Wilson shall pay to the said John McKinlay the said sum of Eleven hundred dollars in manner following, to wit, Three hundred and sixty six dollars and sixty six cents ($366 66/100) on the first day of January in the year of our Lord Eighteen hundred and fifty two, Three hundred and sixty six dollars and sixty six cents ($366 66/100) on the first day of January in the year Eighteen hundred and fifty three, and also the sum of Three hundred and sixty six dollars and sixty six cents ($366 66/100) on the first day of January in the year Eighteen hundred and fifty four, then and in that case the above sale and conveyance to be null and void, else to remain in full force and effect And provided also that until default be made by the said Charles L. Wilson in the payment of the said sums of money as above expressed and witness the above granted property into remain in the possession and subject to the control of the said Charles L. Wilson It is to be understood that the foregoing mortgage deed is to take effect from the 4th day of January A.D. 1851"

January 29, 1851
State of Florida, Alachua County
From Alachua County Ancient Records
Mortgage Record A pages 060-061

Charles L. Wilson to Geo R. Fairbanks as collateral for a $500 loan: "Know all men by these presents that whereas I Charles L. Wilson of Alachua County Florida am justly indebted to Geo R. Fairbanks of the City of St. Augustine in the Sum of five hundred dollars or thereabouts by virtue of a certain bond given by me to said Fairbanks on the 11th May 1849 for the purchase of a tract of land in said County

Now therefore in consideration of the premises, and of a release this day executed by said Fairbanks of a portion of said land to one James Sikes, and for the better securing to said Fairbanks the said sum of money I do hereby sell, assign, transfer, and convey to said Fairbanks his heirs and assigns **a certain Mulatto boy named William aged about 28 years** and now on my plantation in said County, to have and to hold the said slave to him the said Fairbanks his heirs and assigns forever Provided Nevertheless and this Indenture is upon the express condition that the said Wilson shall faithfully and truly, and according to the tenor of said bond in writing obligatory hereinbefore refered to pay to the said Fairbanks the said sums of money thereby secured to be paid, this that obligation and indenture shall be void, and of none effect, otherwise to be and remain in full force and virtue"

February 26, 1851
From Alachua County Ancient Records
Deed Record A pages 354 and 354A

Charles L. Wilson to Lydia Wilson on behalf of his four children: "Know all men by these presents that I Charles L. Wilson, of the County and State aforesaid for and in consideration of five dollars to me in hand paid by Lydia Wilson, as well for the love and affection which I have and bear unto my four children Susan, Martha Matilda Jane, and Francis Elizabeth, have granted, bargained, Sold conveyed and delivered, and by these presents do grant, bargain, Sell, convey and deliver unto the said Lydia Wilson and my four children, the following described Slaves, to wit: **Emily a woman about twenty four years old, and her three Children, Hendry, John and Eliza**, to have and to hold the Said described Slaves, and every and all of them unto the Said Lydia Wilson for and during the term of her natural life, and at her death to revert to and be equally divided amongst my Said four children above named, and none other, and if either or any of my Said four Children die before the Said Lydia Wilson then the Share of Such deceased child or children to go to and be divided Equally amongst those of my said four Children above named that remained and are alive at the death of the Said Lydia Wilson and none others, **and also the increase of the Said described Slaves** are to be used and disposed of in the Same manner and for the Same purposes and objects, as the present described Slave are and in no other manner.

December 15, 1854
State of Florida, Alachua County
From Alachua County Ancient Records
Deed Record B page 441

Charles L. Wilson and Samuel Russell to John McKinlay as collateral for a $2,200 loan: "Know all men by these presents that we, Charles L. Wilson and Samuel Russell are held and firmly bound unto John McKinlay in the sum of Two thousand two hundred dollars for the payment whereof well and truly to be made we bind ourselves our heirs, executors and Administrators jointly and severally, firmly by the presents signed and sealed this 29th day of January A.D. 1851 The conditions of the above obligation is such that whereas the above bounded Charles L. Wilson is indebted to the said John McKinlay in the sum of Eleven hundred dollars being the balance of the price of **four negro slaves** purchased by the said Charles L. Wilson from the said John McKinlay, and to secure the payment of which a deed of Mortgage has this day been executed by the said Charles L. Wilson to the said John McKinlay Now if the above bounded Charles L. Wilson shall pay to the said John McKinlay his heirs or assigns the sum of Eleven hundred dollars in three annual commencing on the first day of January A.D. 1853 Then that obligation as said at the above mentioned Deed of Mortgage to be null and void else to remain in full force and virtue"

January 29, 1851
State of Florida, Alachua County
From Alachua County Ancient Records
Mortgage Record A pages 061-062

Sheriff Charles L. Wilson to William B. Wimberly Guardian of Sarah Townsend and Margaret Townsend Minors, and Elizabeth Wimberly his wife: "This Indenture made this the seventh day of May in the year of our Lord One thousand eight hundred and fifty three between Charles L. Wilson Sheriff in and for the County and State aforesaid of the first part, and William B. Wimberly Guardian of Sarah Townsend and Margaret Townsend, Minors and Elizabeth Wimberly, wife of the said Wimberly of the said County and State of the second part;

Witnesseth, that where the said Charles L. Wilson Sheriff as aforesaid under a fieri facias issued from the office of the Clerk of the Circuit Court of the County aforesaid under the signature of the Clerk and seal of said Court dated the Twenty eight day of January in the year of our Lord One thousand Eight hundred and fifty three and came to the hand of said Sheriff the day and date last aforesaid, on the fifth day of February in the year of our Lord One thousand eight hundred and fifty three, levied upon and seized the following property, to wit, Three head of horses and **two negro slaves Pheoby and infant** to satisfy said fieri facias issued under a Judgement against Joseph G. Bell for the sum of Eighteen hundred dollars ($1800) recovered on the four-teenth day of December in the year of our lord One thousand eight hundred and fifty two in the Circuit Court of the Eastern Circuit of Floria held at the Court House in Newnansville in and for the County of Alachua in favor of Willaim B. Wimberly, Elizabeth Wimberly his wife, Sarah Townsend and Margaret Townsend, Minors, who sued by their next friend William B. Wimberly and the said Charles L. Wilson Sheriff as aforesaid after due and legal notice thereof, on the second day of May in the year of our Lord one thousand eight hundred and fifty three offered for sale to the highest bidder the above named and described property, levied upon as aforesaid, and on the day and date last aforesaid struck off and sold the same to John P. Sanderson Agent and Attorney for William B. Wimberly Guardian of Sarah Townsend and Margaret Townsend Minors, and Elizabeth Wimberly wife of the said William B. Wimberly for the sum of fifty dollars, the said John P. Sanderson being the highest bidder and the said sum of fifty dollars for the negro women and infant, and ten dollars for each of said horses being the highest amount bid therefor. […] Charles L. Wilson Sheriff as aforesaid under the authority vested in him by law for and in consideration of the premises, and the sum of fifty dollars to him in hand paid by the said parties of the second part, at and before the ensealing and delivery of these presents the receipt whereof is hereby acknowledged hath bargained, granted and sold, and by these presents doth grant bargain and sell unto the said parties of the second part, all the right, title interest claim and demand of the said James G. Bell and his wife, and of the said Charles L. Wilson Sheriff as aforesaid under and virtue of levy aforesaid whatsoever in and to the following described property, to wit, Three head of horses, and two negro slaves to wit, Pheoby a negro girl and an infant child of the said Slave Pheoby, to have and to hold the above mentioned and described property unto them the Parties of the second part their heirs and assigns to the only proper use and behoof of the said parties of the second part, their executors, administrators and assigns forever,

And the said Charles L. Wilson Sheriff aforesaid doth hereby covenant and agree to and with the said parties of the second part, their executors administrators, heirs and assigns, that he the said party of the first part the title to the above mentioned and described property, as herein conveyed against himself, and against all persons whomsoever shall and will by these presents forever warrant and defend."

May 7, 1853
State of Florida, Alachua County
From Alachua County Ancient Records
Deed Record B pages 168-169

Charles L. Wilson indicted for assault with intent to kill; and enslaved people were used as part of collateral to ensure he showed up for Court: "State of Florida vs Charles L. Wilson - Assault with intent to kill - On this cause being called it was ordered to be continued, and the defendant required to enter unto a recognizance of Five hundred dollars for his appearance at the next term of this

Court, Whereupon came the defendant Charles L. Wilson principal and his Securities George L. Brown and Elias Earle in open Court and acknowledged themselves indebted to the State of Florida in the Sum of Five hundred dollars, That is to Say the principal Charles L. Wilson in the sum of Five hundred dollars, and his Securities George L. Brown and Elias Earle in the Sum of Two hundred and fifty each to be levied upon of their respective goods & chattels, slaves, lands and tenements if default be made, on the following condition, That is to say: If the said Charles L. Wilson shall be and appear at the next term of this Court to answer to an indictment for "Assault with intent to Kill" and not depart thence without the leave of the Court, then this obligation to be null and void else to remain in full force and virtue"

December 15, 1855
From Alachua County Ancient Records
Judgment Record A* page 341

Charles L. Wilson & James J. Kennard indictment for stealing enslaved people: "The State of Florida vs Charles L. Wilson & James J. Kennard - Indictment Stealing Slaves - A True Bill"

December 10, 1856
From Alachua County Ancient Records
Judgment Record A* page 462

Charles L. Wilson & James J. Kinard indicted for stealing enslaved people: "The State of Florida vs Charles L. Wilson & James J. Kinard - Stealing Slaves - The death of Charles L. Wilson being suggested

On motion of Mr. Dawkins, It is ordered by the Court that the Sheriff of Alachua County bring the body of James J. Kinard from the County Jail of Columbia County Said Kinard having been there imprisoned by order of Court at the last term"

May 11, 1857
From Alachua County Ancient Records
Judgment Record A* page 504

Lemuel Wilson and Rafaila Wilson to James Pendarvis as collateral for an $83 loan: "Know all men by these presents that we Lemuel Wilson and Rafaila Wilson his wife for and in Consideration of Eighty three Dollars to us in hand paid the receipt whereof is hereby acknowledged have bargained sold and Conveyed And by these presents do bargain sell and convey unto James Pendarvis his heirs and assigns all our right title and interest in the following described property to wit: Thirty five head of cattle more or less marked with a pail Handle in one ear and crop in the other and Branded with a Spur The condition of the above obligation is such, that if the said Lemuel Wilson or his wife Rafaila Shall pay or cause to be paid unto Asa Clark Administrator on the Estate of Elizabeth Harrison a certain note for the amount of Eighty Three Dollars made payable at January 1851 for the hire of **negro woman Mily** for the present year then this obligation to be null and void else to remain in full force and effect"

January 1, 1850
State of Florida, Alachua County
From Alachua County Ancient Records
Mortgage Record A page 041

Lemuel Wilson to George L. Brown as collateral for a $1,651.96 loan: "This Indenture made and entered into this Seventh day of April in the year one thousand eight hundred and fifty five, Between Lemuel Wilson of Alachua County State of Florida, of the first part, and George L. Brown of the Same County and State of the Second part, Witnesseth, Whereas the Said party of the first is justly indebted to the Said party of the Second part in the Sum of Sixteen hundred and fifty one 96/100 Dollars lawful money of the United States,, conditioned for the payment of eight hundred and twenty five and 98/100 Dollars, with interest thereon at eight per cent per annum, on or before the first day of January next ensuing, the date hereof as appears by his certain Bond or writing obligatory bearing even date with these present. Now for the better Securing of the said party of the Second part the payment of the Said Bond, or writing obligatory, according to the true intent and meaning thereof, as also in consideration of the Sum of Ten Dollars, by the Said party of the Second part to me in hand paid at and before the ensealing and delivery of these presents, the receipt whereof is hereby acknowledged The Said party of the first part, hath bargained, Sold and delivered, and by these presents doth bargain, Sell and deliver unto the Said party of the Second part, the following real estate and personal property of and belonging to the Said party of the first part, to wit, **one Negro Man named Latimore Black complextion, aged about thirty two years**, and one certain tract of land containing about one hundred and Sixty acres situate in the County State of Florida, and known and described in the land office at Newnansville Fla as the East half of south west Quarter of section twelve, and the North East of the North West Quarter, and the North West Quarter of the North East Quarter of Section thirteen in Township eight of Range eighteen East, also one other certain tract situate within County and State aforesaid known as the South West Quarter of the the South East Quarter of Section thirteen, Township eight. south of Range eighteen East containing forty acres more or less, together all and singular the hereditaments and appartenances thereunto belonging or and anywise appertaining, and the reversion and reversions, remainder and remainders, rents, Issues and profits thereof and also all the estate, right, title, interest, claim and demand after the said party of the first part of, in and to the same, and every part and parcel thereof. with the appurtenances,

TO HAVE AND TO HOLD the said hereby granted premises and property unto the said George L. Brown party of the second part and to his heirs and assigns for ever, provided always, Nevertheless and these presents are upon this express condition, That if said party of the first part, his Executors and administrators, or any of of them shall well and truly pay, or cause to be paid unto the said party of the second part, his certain Attorney, Executors, Administrators, or assigns, the Said sum of money mentioned in the condition of the said Bond or writing obligatory, with the interest thereon, and at the time therein mentioned, and according to the true intent and meaning of the said Bond and the condition thereof, then as well this present indenture as the estate herein conveyed, shall cease and determine, and be null and void, Else to remain in full force and virtue."

April 7, 1855
From Alachua County Ancient Records
Deed Record D pages 125-126

Lemuel Wilson and Rafaela Wilson to George L. Brown as collateral for an $818.95 loan: "This Indenture made this the first day of January A.D. One thousand Eight hundred and fifty Seven between Lemuel Wilson of the County and State aforesaid of the first part and his wife Rafaela, And George L. Brown of the same place of the second part, Witnesseth: That the said party of the first part for and in consideration of the sum of Eight hundred and Eighteen Dollars and 95/100 to them in hand paid by George L. Brown party of the second part at and before the sealing and delivery of these presents, the receipt whereof is hereby acknowledged, have bargained sold aliened remised released Conveyed and confirmed and by these presents do grant bargain sell alien remise release convey and confirm unto the said George L. Brown and to his heirs and assigns forever the following property. To Wit: A **negro man slave named Latimore, black Complexion aged about thirty two years**: and also the following described parcels or lots of land viz: the East half of South West Quarter of section Twelve and North half of North East quarter and North half of the North West Quarter of section thirteen all in Township No Eight South of Range No Eighteen East in the district of land subject to sale at the land office at Newnansville Fla To Have and to Hold all and singular the foregoing property with the appurtenances thereunto belonging unto him the said George L. Brown his heirs and assigns forever. The condition of the foregoing obligetion or Indenture is such that whereas party of the first part Lemuel Wilson is justly indebted to the party of the second part in the sum of Eight hundred and eighteen & 95/100 Dollars for goods wares and merchandize, heretofore delivered to him the said party of the first part and whereas the said party of the first part has this day made and delivered to the said George L. Brown his certain promissory note bearing even date herewith for the said sum of Eight hundred and Eighteen and 95/100 Dollars, in settlement of his account with the said party of the second part: Now if the said party of the first part, his Executors or administrators shall and do well and truly pay to the said George L. Brown, his Executors administrators or assigns the amount due on said note including interest thereon, on or before the first day of January A.D. 1858, then this obligation to be null and void else to remain in full force and virtue."

January 1, 1857
State of Florida, County of Alachua
From Alachua County Ancient Records
Deed Record C pages 044-045

William B. Wimberly in right of his wife Elizabeth Wimberly, Margaret Townsend by Soloman F. Halliday her guardian ad litem; and Oliver Bryant in right of his wife Sarah Bryant - splitting up the estate of James L. Townsend: "In the Circuit Court of the Eastern Circuit of Florida in Chancery Between William B. Wimberly and Elizabeth Wimberly his wife, Margaret Townsend by Solomon F. Halliday her guardian ad litem, and Oliver Bryant and Sarah Bryant his wife Defendants,

This cause came on to be heard on the Bill, answers and proofs, and was argued by Counsel, and thereupon before consideration thereof, it was ordered, adjudged and decreed as follows, viz. That the Said complainant William B. Wimberly in right of his wife Elizabeth Wimberly, Margaret Townsend, and Oliver Bryant in right of his wife Sarah Bryant, are the Sole heirs at law of James L. Townsend deceased, and as Such heirs at law are entitled to an undivided equal distribution Share or portion equal to one third each, of the following real and personal estate, belonging to Said Estate of Said James L. Townsend, to wit: The East half of the North East quarter of Section nine (9), and the west half of the South West quarter of Section ten (10) Township Seven (7) South of Range eighteen (18) East, and So much of the East half of the South East Quarter of Section twenty one (21) and of the West half of the North West quarter, and of the West half of the South West quarter, of Section twenty two (22) and of the North East quarter of Section twenty eight (28) and of the West half of the North west quarter of Section twenty Seven (27) in Township Seven (7) of Range eighteen (18) as lies East of a certain Stream known as the Townsend Branch, and the west half of the East half of the North West Quarter and the west half of the South East Quarter of Section twenty Seven (27) in the Same Township and Range, together with the tenements, hereditaments, and appurtenances thereunto belonging or in any wise appertaining the above described premises lying and being Situate in the County of Alachua and State of Florida, and also an undivided Share or portion in the following described personal property, to wit, **one Negro woman Named Johebes and her infant**.

And it is further ordered, adjudged and decreed, that partition be made of the lands, Slaves and premises mentioned in the pleadings in this cause, that is to Say: the lands and Slaves hereinbefore described and Set forth, among the Said parties, according to their respective rights and interests therein, and that Thomas J. Prevatt, Bennett M. Dell and Thomas A. Bradford, Suitable and competant persons to act as Commissioners, Selected and agreed upon by the parties, be, and they are hereby appointed Commissioners, for the purpose of making Such partition in pursuance of the Statute in Such case made and provided. That Said Commissioners Shall be Sworn before entering upon their duties by the Clerk of this Court, or by any Justice of the Peace in this Circuit, faithfully and impartially to execute the trust reposed in them, and Shall have power to imploy a Surveyor if necessary for the purpose of making such,

And it is further ordered, that they Shall be allowed for their Services as Commissioners as aforesaid, not exceeding three dollars per day, for every day actually employed as Commissioners, and who Shall proceed thereafter, to make partition of the property in question, according to this order, and according to the Statute, and having made such partition, Shall report the Same in writing, to this Court, without delay, under their hands or the hands of any two of them, Specifying therein, the manner of executing this decree, and describing the land divided, and the part or Shares, allowed to each party, with the quality, corners, and distances of each Share, and a description of the parts, Stones, or other monuments thereof, deed the items of their charges in the premises.

And it is further ordered, adjudged, and decreed, that the costs of this suit, including all costs, charges and expenses of dividing and partitioning the premises, to be taxed and allowed by this Court, Shall be paid rateably, and proportionable by the Defendants, and Complainant,

And it is further ordered, adjudged and decreed, that all further questions arising in this cause, be reserved for further order and decree, until the coming of the report of the Commissioners"

December 23, 1854
From Alachua County Ancient Records
Chancery Order Book A pages 085-086

William B. Wimberly and his wife Elizabeth Wimberly, vs Margaret Townsend and Oliver Bryant and his wife Sarah Bryant regarding sale of enslaved people and lands: "In Chancery Between William B. Wimberly and Elizabeth Wimberly his wife Complainants and Margaret Townsend by Solomon F. Halliday her guardian ad litem and Oliver Bryant and Sarah Bryant his wife Defendants - This cause having been brought on to be heard upon the report of Thomas J. Prevatt, Bennett M. Dell and Thomas A. Bradford, Commissioners appointed therein under and by virtue of a Commission out of, and under the Seal of this Court, and on reading and filing Said report, which bears date, 1st day of January 1855, by which it appears that the Said Commissioners certify and report, that the Said lands cannot be divided and partitioned to the Said devisees without great injustice. And there being no objection filed to Said report, It is on Motion of M. Whit Smith of Counsel for complainants Ordered Adjudged and decreed, and this Court by virtue of the authority therein vested, doth order, adjudge and decree that the Said report and all things therein contained Stand ratified and confirmed. And it appearing to the Satisfaction of the Court, that the Said Bennett M. Dell hath departed this life Since Said report, it is further ordered that Phillip Dell be appointed a Commissioner in place of Said B. M. Dell deceased, And the Court being Satisfied that Said report of Thomas J. Prevatt, Bennett M. Dell and Thomas A. Bradford, Commissioners as aforesaid is Just and correct, doth hereby order, adjudge and decree that the Said land and Slaves be Sold at public Auction by and under the direction of the Said Thomas J. Prevatt, Bennett M. Dell and Thomas A. Bradford Commissioners as aforesaid, of the Town of Newnansville in the Said County of Alachua, on the Second Monday in May next, and to continue from day to day until the Same is completed, and that Said Commissioners do cause Notice of Said Sale to be immediately published until the day of Sale, in the Newspaper published at Alligator Florida, and that they post up Notices, thereof in three public places in the Town of Newnansville, And that the Said Commissioners may in the Sale of Said lands, Sell the Same in Such quantities and upon Such terms as they may deem proper and best calculated for the interest of the parties, and may **Sell the Slaves together or Separate**, and upon Such terms as they may also deem best, And it is further ordered, Adjudged and decreed, that the Claimants may Severally purchase to the extent of their interest in Said lands and Slaves, but Should they purchase over and above the amount of their interest, then for any Such excess, they Shall comply with conditions imposed upon other purchasers. And it is further ordered, that the Said Commissioners make a full and ample report to this Court, after Said Sale, of their proceedings in this behalf.

And it is further ordered, adjudged and decreed, that Said Commissioners Shall be allowed as remuneration for their Services, Such a commission on the amount realized from the Sale of Said lands and Slaves, as this Court in its discretion may hereafter direct, together all incidental expences to be hereafter taxed by this Court,

And it is further ordered, that Said Commissioners do not execute title to Said purchasers, or deliver any of Said property until directed So to do by this Court"

March 14, 1855
From Alachua County Ancient Records
Chancery Order Book A pages 087-088

William B. Wimberly Complainant vs. Oliver Bryant et al. concerning division of the Estate of James L. Townsend: "This cause having been brought on to be heard upon the report of Thomas J. Prevatt, Thomas A. Bradford and Philip Dell Commissioners appointed therein to sell the premises described in the bill of Complaint in this cause, and according to the decree of this Court herein heretofore made, and on reading and filing said report which bears date the 24th day of December AD 1855 in the words and figures following to wit:

"To the Hon William A. Forward, Judge of the Eastern Judicial Circuit of Florida, Thomas J. Prevatt, Thomas A. Bradford and Philip Dell, Commissioners appointed by your Honor to sell the real estate and personal property belonging to the Estate of James L. Townsend, late of Alachua County and State of Florida deceased, for the purpose of a more equal division of said Estate, between the heirs of said deceased Beg leave to report The real estate consisting of Five hundred and Seventy three acres and thirty one hundredths of an acre, was offered for sale at Auction before the Court house door of Newnansville, County and State aforesaid on the second Monday in May last, after having been advertised for sale in the newspaper published at Alligator, and notice of the sale posted in three public places in the Town of Newnansville

The Said real Estate was Sold for cash

One hundred and Sixty acres was Struck off to Oliver Bryant who was the highest bidder at Seven dollars and fifty cents per acre amounting to the Sum of One thousand two hundred dollars, which Sum was Five hundred and twenty Six and 33/100 dollars less than the Said Oliver Bryant's Share in said Estate

Four hundred and thirteen and 33/100 acres was sold to William B. Wimberly who was the highest bidder for the Sum of seven dollars and fifty cents per acre, amounting to the Sum of Three thousand one hundred dollars

The personal property to wit: **Negro Slave Phebe and her infant** was sold at the Same time and place, the Same notice of the Sale having been given, as was given of the sale of the real Estate.

The terms of the sale of said Slaves were as follows, One half cash and the balance to be paid on the first day of January AD 1856 the last note to be secured by a note with approved personal Security

The said Slaves were Sold to William B. Wimberly, who was the highest bidder for the sum of Eight hundred and Seventy nine dollars, which two purchases of the land and Slaves by William B. Wimberly amount to the Sum of Three Thousand Nine hundred and Seventy nine dollars, which amount exceeds his interest in said Estate in the Sum of Two Thousand two hundred and fifty dollars and sixty seven cents

The Land bought by the Oliver Bryant are Known and described as follows "The East half of the North East 1/4 of Section 9, and the West half of the South West 1/4 of section 10 Township 7 South of Range 18 East, Containing 160 acres as aforesaid

And the lands bought by the said William B. Wimberly are Known and described as so much of the east half of the South East 1/4 of Section 21 and the West half of the North West 1/4 of and the West half of the South East 1/4 of Section 22, and of the North East 1/4 of Section 28 and of the West half of the North West 1/4 of Section 27 in Township 7 South of Range 18 East, as lies East of a certain Stream, Known as the Townsend Branch And the West 1/2 of the 1/2 of the North West 1/4 & the West 1/2 of the South East 1/4 of Section 27 in the Same Township and Range and containing by estimation 413 33/100 acres as aforesaid

And they further report that the aforesaid purchasers have fully complied with the terms of the said Sale, and that they the said

Commissioners are ready to make such distribution of the proceeds, and execute titles to said real and personal property as your Honor may direct. - Dec 10th 1855 AD

And there being no exceptions filed, on motion of Messrs Smith & Bradford, Solicitors, for Complainant, It is ordered, adjudged and decreed, that the said report and all things therein contained, do stand ratified and confirmed and that the sale so made is approved of by this Court, and be firm and effectual forever

And it appearing by said report among other things that the said William B. Wimberly in right of his wife, being claimant therein, became purchaser of lands and said negro slaves, at said sale, and purchased over and above the sum he was entitled to receive, the Sum of Two thousand two hundred and fifty two dollars and Sixty Seven cents ($2252.67) which sum is due from him to be paid to such claimants herein as have not as yet received that proportion

And It is further adjudged and decreed that the said Commissioners do execute to said Oliver Bryant & wife in right of his wife, purchaser as aforesaid deed of the lands purchased by them, and that they do also execute to Said William B. Wimberly purchaser as aforesaid deed of the lands and Slaves purchased by him, at any time upon his paying of the full amount of his contracts

And it is further ordered adjudged and decreed by and with Consent of parties that there be allowed to said Commissioners Prevatt Bradford & Dell a Commission of five per cent upon the gross amount of the sales of said land and ~~negroes~~ slaves being five per cent upon the Sum of $5,179 amounting to $258.95 being the Sum of $86.31 for each one and that the said Commissioners be allowed to retain the same out of any monies in their hands or hereafter to come into their hands liable to be appropriated for that purpose and report the same to this Court.

And It is further ordered adjudged and decreed that the said Commissioners do ascertain and procure bill of all the taxable costs and charges in this Suit including their commission herein allowed and distribute the Same equally among the said claimants herein, and retain the Same out of any monies due therein, if there is so much due them, and of not then they are respectively required to pay into the hands of said Commissioners their respective proportions, and the Said Commissioners will report the same to this Court with Vouchers"

March 1856
From Alachua County Ancient Records
Chancery Order Book A pages 114-118

John Wymer charged with receiving bacon from enslaved people without a permit: "State of Florida v John Wymer - Receiving Bacon from Slaves without permit" - On this day came as well the Solicitor of the State of Florida, John P. Sanderson Esqr. who prosecutes the pleas of the State in this behalf, and the defendant in person and George W. Cato Esqr. his attorney, and the said defendant plead not guilty; thereupon came a jury […] who were duly elected, tried and sworn a true verdict to render

Daniel Holder was examined as a witness on behalf of the prosecutor, And the said Jury having heard the evidence and the arguments of counsel and the charge of the Court, were sent out of Court to consider of their verdict, and thereafter, and upon the same day the said Jury returned into Court, and rendered the following verdict, We, the Jury, find the defendant not Guilty, Thereupon he is discharged from custody"

May 6, 1853
From Alachua County Ancient Records
Judgment Record A* page 126

1860's

E. E. Adamson to Catharine F. Fordenburg for $800: "For and in consideration of the sum of Eight hundred dollars secured to be paid to me by A. Fordenburg and C. Fordenburg I have this day Sold and delivered unto Catharine F. Fordenburg and by these presents do sell and deliver unto her **a certain negro boy named John a Shoemaker by trade maimed in one leg**. The title to which Boy John I warrant in me and hereby guarantee to be good but make no other warrantee whatever except as to title and Sound in bodily health."

January 26, 1860
From Alachua County Ancient Records
Bills of Sale A page 068

Inventory of property received by Nathan H. Bauknight by his wife Martha E. Bauknight: "The schedule herein after written is an inventory of the property Received by Nathan H. Bauknight by his wife Martha E. Bauknight which is to be recorded in the Clerk's Office of Alachua County for the purpose of creating a Separate and independant Estate for the said Martha E. Bauknight, not subject to any debts or incumbrance of the said Nathan H. Bauknight husband of the said Martha E. Bauknight according to the Statute Law of the State of Florida in Such Case made and provided **One Negro f=girl Slave for life aged Eleven or twelve years, dark Complexion**, Two

Beds & Bedsteads, One Cooking Stove One Lot Crockery ware, one Set chairs, one lot Tables, one Buggy, All of which came into the possession of the said Nathan H. Bauknight Subsequent to the first of October AD One thousand Eight hundred & Sixty"

October 1, 1860
State of Florida, Alachua County
From Alachua County Ancient Records
Deed Record E page 224

Mary Bethune to Mrs. Johannah H. Burgheim for $2,400: "Know all Men by these presents that I Mary Bethune of Duval County Florida for and in consideration of the sum of Two thousand four hundred Dollars to me in hand paid at and before the Sealing and delivery of these presents by Mrs. Johannah H. Burgheim Alachua County Florida the receipt whereof I do hereby acknowledge have bargained and Sold, and by these presents do bargain sell and deliver unto the said Johannah H. Burgheim her heirs Executors administrators and assigns **the three following Negro boys to wit, James aged about Sixteen years Alec aged about fourteen years and Anderson aged about nine years warranted Sound in limb and body** to have and to hold the negro boys to wit James, Alec and Anderson, unto the said Johannah H. Burgheim her heirs Executors, Administrators, and assigns, to her and her only proper use and behoof forever."

November 12, 1862
State of Georgia, Chatham County
From Alachua County Ancient Records
Bills of Sale A page 070

Johanna Burgheim vs. Abraham Fredenburg & C. Fredenburg his wife - Bill for Foreclosure regarding mortgage on an enslaved man to secure payment of a note: "It being made to appear to the Satisfaction of the Court that Service by publication has been perfected on Said defendant according to the terms of the Statutes in Such case made and provided and that Said defendant have not appeared to answer, plead, or demurer to Said Bill of Complaint - It is therefore ordered that the same be taken as Confessed against them. It is further ordered, adjudged, and decreed, that the mortgage on the **Negro Slave John**, to Secure the payment of a note made payable to the order of Edward E. Adamson, be and the Same is hereby foreclosed in favour of Said Complainant, as the assignee of said note and Mortgage and all interest under the same is ["hereby foreclosed" struck through]- and that Said defendants, and all persons claiming or to claim by through or under them, be and the Same are hereby forever foreclosed, and barred of and from their rights, or Equity of redemption on the Said Mortgaged property. It is further ordered, adjudged and decreed that the Said Complainant recover from the Said defendants the Sum of One thousand and ten dollars, good and lawful Money, with interest on the same until paid in Satisfaction of said note and Mortgage - and that execution be issued for the same and levied first on said negro Slave John and Shall be had, after publication in terms of the Statutes, And should the proceeds arising from the Sale of said Negro Slave John be insufficient to satisfy said debt, with interest and Costs, then any balance remaining due and unpaid to be satisfied by levy on and Sale of the goods and chattels lands and tenements generally of said defendant, or so much thereof as may be necessary to satisfy such balance of principle and interest herein decreed Complainants, together with her reasonable Costs in this behalf laid out and expended"

April 11th 1865
In Circuit Court for Alachua County April Term 1865
From Alachua County Ancient Records
Chancery Order Book A pages 186-187

Edward Cale and Lydia Cale to Philip Dell as collateral for $1,800 in loans: "This Indenture made the 10th day of February in the year of our Lord one thousand Eight hundred and Sixty one between Edward Cale, Lydia Cale the wife of Said Edward Cale of said County of the first part and Philip Dell of the same place of the second part Witnesseth that the said party of the first part in consideration of the sum of one Dollar to them duly paid hath sold and by these presents do grant and convey to the said party of the second part and his assigns the following chattel and property namely **a Negro male Slave named Washington of Black complexion and aged about twenty five years** now in their possession at the County aforesaid together with all the Estate title and interest of the said party of the first part therein [...] if the said party of the first part Shall well and truly pay unto the party of the second part or his assigns at maturity the full amount principal and interest of five certain promisory notes Executed by the said party of the first part Each for the Sum of Three hundred and twenty dollars each bearing date the tenth day of February ano Domini Eighteen hundred and fifty nine the first come due and payable on the first day of January A. D. 1860. The second payable on the first day of January A. D. 1861 the third payable the first day January A. D. 1862 and the fourth payable on the first day of January A. D. 1863 and the fifth payable on the first day of January A. D. 1864 and also and the certain promisory note Executed by the said party of the first part for the sum of Two hundred dollars bearing date the 16th day of February A. D. 1861 payable one day after date all of Said notes bearing held said party of the second part then this conveyance shall be void otherwise to remain in full force and Efect The said Philip Dell is hereby authorized for further Secureting to take the said Negro Slave Washington above conveyed or entitled so to be unto his immediate possession or at any time the said Philip Dell or his heirs and or his assigns may think proper"

February 10, 1861
State of Florida, Alachua County
From Alachua County Ancient Records
Mortgage Record A pages 287-288

John L. Cameron to his wife Margaret N. Cameron: "This Indenture made this the Ninth day of December in the year of our Lord One thousand Eight hundred & Sixty, Between John L. Cameron of the County and State aforesaid of the first part, and Margaret N. Cameron wife of the Said John L. Cameron of the Said County & State Witnesseth that the said John L. Cameron for the natural love and affection which he bears his wife, the Said Margaret M. Cameron, and also for the further Consideration of one dollar to him in hand paid by the Said Margaret M. Cameron the receipt whereof is hereby acknowledged, hath bargained, Sold, Granted, given, and delivered to the said Margaret M. Cameron: and does by these presents bargain Sell grant give and deliver to Said party of the Second part to her use and only her use and the issues of her body forever the following property (to wit) 1 Bed and furniture 1 Do two matrasses, 1 looking glass, one double barrel shot gun Gold watch & chain 1 lot Books 2 Trunks 1 lot Crockery 1 lot Potware 1 lot Cooperware, 2 Jars, 2 Smoothing Irons, 1 lot tools, 1 **Negro girl named Charlotte aged about fourteen years** twenty Six head Cattle To Have and to Hold the Said property to her and the heirs of her body to them and their use benefit and behoof forever"

December 9, 1860
State of Florida, Alachua County
From Alachua County Ancient Records
Deed Record E page 301

Asia Minor Caston Last Will and Testament: "In the name of god Amen I Asia Minor Caston citizen of the county and state aforesaid being sensible of my enfeebled condition and Knowing the uncertainty of life and being of a sound mind and disposing memory do make And constitute this my last will and testament

1ˢᵗ I will and bequeath to my beloved wife Milly Caston my bay Horse and buggy my Rocking chair, the large mat that I bought at Bradfords sale all the property now on her place in New River County which I have a right or claim to all my corn at the frank Kennedy place excepting five bushels which I have sold them being all about fourty bushels the same being in the S*** house in a heap to itself (the corn which I have sold to Coln Bryant is measured out in **** if he refused to take it, I, desire the same to be sold by my Executor, or Executors provided my wife relinguish her dower in the place I sold to W. Wash Scott and delivers to my Executor J. J. Barnards receipt for D.A. Friars note and two other notes and D.A. Friar one for twenty one dollars principal and the other Seventeen dollars and Some cents which were to be paid in Hauling and Wade H. Bryants note for ten dollars

2 I authorise my Executor to Execute titles to W. Wash Scott for the land which I sold him, to be in all respects as valid as though I had executed the same in my proper writing the said Scott was to pay me one hundred and twenty five dollars for the above mentioned land

3 I will and bequeath to my two sons, Samuel Napolean Caston and Alson Bolivar Caston **my two Negroes Lewis and Sene**, if the wish to take one a piece they can appoint commissioners who may appraise the said Negro slaves, and the one who takes the most valuable slave can pay to the other the excess of vallue so as to equalize the bequest between them my said two Sons, my two feather beds and matresses, bedstead and whatever other Household furniture I have with me all my Books and my clothing I may have provided they execute titles to W. Wash Scott for the lot in the town of Newnansville upon which I formerly lived, for which he the said Scott was to pay to me one hundred dollars

4th I desire all the property which I possess in Alachua County not disposed of above to be sold my negroes to be hired out and the proceeds applied to the payment of my debts until all my Just debts are paid, except that I wish my Wife Milly Caston to have fourty dollars annualy for five years out of the Hire of my Negroes, provided she complies with the requisition in the first clause of this my last will and Testament, I do not wish my Negroes to be hired out of this county, now if my above named Sons Samuel Napolean and Alston Bolivar Caston are able to pay off and do settle my debts and also pay to my Wife Milly Caston the above instalments of fourty dollars for five years, then and in that case they may take full possession of my said two Negroes Lewis and Sene and all the property I have bequeathed to them

5th I appoint and constitute Stephen Fagan my Executor to this my last will and testament, I desire him to take charge of the property I have bequeathed to my sons immediately after my decease and to take care of the same until my said Sons come to this place, if the desire to sell the articles bequeathed to them above in order to apply the proceeds to the payment of my debts they are at liberty to dispose of the same for that purpose by authorising my Executor to sell the same for the payment of my debts"

November 6, 1862
State of Florida, Alachua County
From Alachua County Ancient Records
Will Book B pages 025-027

D. B. Chappleman to Mary C. McDermott for $915: "Received of Mary C. McDermott Nine hundred and fifteen dollars in full value of **a Negro Boy named Primus** which I warrant to be Sound in body and mind and the title I will defend."

January 5, 1863
State of Florida, Alachua County
From Alachua County Ancient Records
Bills of Sale A page 069

William D. Clark indicted for murder. Enslaved people were used as part of collateral to ensure he showed up for Court: "State of Florida vs William D. Clark - Murder - Continued to the Next term of the Court and the defendant Recognized in the Sum of Ten thousand dollars for his appearance at the next term of the Court Charles Haile Thomas E. Haile Alexander Matheson Thomas W. McCaa Lewis F. Roux Samuel K. Ring & James B. Bailey appeared in open Court & acknowledged themselves to Stand indebted to the State of Florida in the Sum of Thirteen hundred & fifty dollars each to be levied of their respective goods & chattels Slaves lands & tenements if default be made in the following conditions that is to say of the said William D. Clark Shall be and appear at the next term of the Court to answer an Indictment for Murder and Shall not thence depart the Court without leave thereof then this obligation to be null & void other ends to remain in full force & virtue"

April 12, 1860
From Alachua County Ancient Records
Judgment Record B page 270

William D. Clark indicted for betting at cards; used enslaved people as part of collateral to ensure he showed up for Court: "State of Florida vs William D. Clark - Betting at Cards - Continued to next term of this Court and the defendant Recognized in the Sum of Five hundred Dollars for his appearance at the next term of the Court and acknowledged himself to Stand indebted to the State of Florida in the sum of Five hundred Dollars to be levied of his Respective goods & chattels, Slaves lands & tenements if default be made in the following Conditions that is to say if the said William D. Clark shall be and appear at the next term of the Court to answer an Indictment for Playing & Betting at Cards and Shall not depart thence without leave thereof then this Obligation to be null & void else to remain in full force & virtue"

April 11, 1864
From Alachua County Ancient Records
Judgment Record B page 516

L. D. Colding to Mary C. McDermott for $1,000: "Received Micanopy November 3rd 1862 of Mrs. Mary C. McDermott One thousand dollars in full for **a Slave named Kitty Ann about twenty one years of age.** Said girl I warrant Sound of Body and Mind also will defend the title and Claims against all person or persons."

November 3, 1862
State of Florida, Alachua County
From Alachua County Ancient Records
Bills of Sale A page 069

James G. Cooper to Mary E. Scott for $10,000: "Know all men by these presents that I James G. Cooper of the County of Alachua State of Florida party of the first part for and in Consideration of the sum of Ten Thousand Dollars to me in hand paid by Mary E. Scott of the same place party of the Second part, the receipt whereof is hereby acknowledged, have bargained and Sold and by these presents do grant and Convey unto the party of the Second part his Executors, administrators and assigns the following described personal property to wit **One Negro man named Abram Forty Eight years of age, One man Dave forty five years of age, One man Peter Twenty years of age One Man John Twenty years of age, one Boy Doctor fifteen years of age, One Boy Strong Fourteen years of age, One Boy Andrew Twelve years of age One Boy Wesley Eight years of age, One Boy Philip Eight years of age, One Boy Eight years of age, one Boy James three years of age One Boy Neil Eight years of age, One boy Jessie three years old, one Boy Henry thirteen years of age, One Woman Dianna forty two years of age, One Woman Ginney forty five years of age, One girl Georgianna, Seventeen years of age, One girl Martha Sixteen years of age, One girl Martha Ann Twelve years of age, One girl China One year old** To Have and to hold the above described Negroes Slaves unto the said party of the Second part her heirs executors administrators and assigns forever"

June 3, 1863
From Alachua County Ancient Records
Deed Record E pages 500-501

James G. Cooper to John C. Pelot for $15,000: "Know all men by these presents that I James G. Cooper of Nassau County in said State, having bargained, Sold and Conveyed unto John C. Pelot of Alachua County certain Negro Slaves to wit, **Clarissa, John, Mary, Philip,**

Harry, Miles, Ann, Betsey, Martin Adam, Plato, Mary and Matilda thirteen in number with the issue and increase of the females named for and in Consideration of the sum of Fifteen thousand dollars, to me in hand paid, at the time of the sale and delivery of said Negroes Slaves by said John C. Pelot, which said thirteen Negro Slaves mentioned were the Sole and Separate property of my wife Jane Pharaba Cooper, a portion being conveyed by deed and the remainder by will to her and her Children by the late John D. Vaughan of Nassau County the father of my said wife Jane Pharaba Cooper Therefore, to replace the said Negroes Slaves Sold, Conveyed and delivered as aforesaid and for and in Consideration of the sum of Fifteen Thousand dollars received by me for said Negroes Slaves as aforesaid, I have given, granted, bargained, Sold, Conveyed and delivered and by these presents do give, grant, bargain, Sell Convey and deliver unto the said Jane Pharaba Cooper, my wife, as aforesaid for he own Sole and Separate use benefit and behoof during her life time, and remainder to our children Mary Elizabeth Pelot wife of John Crews and Frances Marion Cooper, the following Negroes Slaves being thirteen in number, To wit: **Hester, Maria Rhacheal, Moses, Rinah, Charles, Bob, Clara, Joe, Dick, Patty Christianna and Lizzy** -- To Have and to hold the said Negroes Slaves **with the future increase of the females** unto the said Jane Pharaba Cooper and our said Children Mary E. Pelot and Frances Marion Cooper in the manner aforesaid to them their heirs Executors and administrators forever"

October 13, 1863
State of Florida, Alachua County
From Alachua County Ancient Records
Deed Record E pages 557-558

J. M. Geiger, J. M. Miller, and J. T. McIntosh assessed their taxes too low on land and property including people they enslaved:

"At a meeting of the Board of County Commissioners. Present C. Rain Mathew Hinson, Wm Strickland and E.H. Jordan President of the Board

1st Ordered that as D. A. Frier Tax Assessor and Collector has Reported the following persons as having assessed their Tax too low Viz, J. M. Geiger on Lands, Negroes House Furniture &c, J. M. Miller on Negroes, Robert Archer on lands and J. T. McIntosh on Negroes, that he now take the Oath and his Books be received [...]

10th Ordered that V. R. Prevat, B. Haynes and Wade H. Sparkman be Commissioners to inquire into the Correctness of the return of J. M. Geiger's Taxable property for the year 1860 and make their return to the County Commissioners under oath as soon as practible thereafter

11th Ordered that John Sparkman, John N. Orman and Col Edward Lewis be appointed Commissioners to inquire into the correctness of the return of J. M. Miller Taxes on Negroes for the year 1860 and make their return to the County Commissioners under oath as soon as practible thereafter [...]

13th Ordered that R. E. Johnson, A. W. Cook and R. S. Stoughton be appointed Commissioners to inquire into the Correctness of the tax return on the Negroes of John T. McIntosh and to make report to the County Commissioners under Oath as soon as practible thereafter"

March 4, 1861
County Commissioners Court
Alachua County, Gainesville
From Alachua County Ancient Records
County Commission Minutes Book 1 pages 135-137

The Tax for 1863 on different types of property: "At a meeting of the board of County Commissioners, met pursuant to adjournment, Present Mathew Hinson, Enoch T. Geiger, J.M. Sparkman C. Rain & E.H. Jordan President of the board […] Ordered that the Tax for 1863 on the following species of property be assessed as follows Viz on

Negroes at Six hundred & fifty (650$) per Head
Hammock land at Ten (10$) per acre
Pine land & Improvements four (4$) per acre
Horses and Mules Two Hundred (200$) per head, Stock Cattle Ten (10$) per head
Hogs Three (3$) per head,
Sheep Eight (8$) per head
Regular kept Stallions One Thousand (1000$) each"

June 1 1863
State of Florida, Alachua County, Gainesville
From Alachua County Ancient Records
County Commission Minutes Book 1 page 170

John B. Dell itemization of what his new wife Laura Standley brought into their marriage from the estate of her father John B. Standley: "Whereas there has been had and Solmnized a Marriage between myself and Laura Standley, daughter of the late John B. Standley deceased and Penelope L. Standley And whereas there was a certain portion of said property belonging to the Estate of the Said John B. Standley set apart and taken posesion of by me as the share to which my said wife Laura was Entitled

Now therefore this is to show that I received the following described property from said Estate the part set apart or her use and benefits to wit the following designated Negro Slaves; **Jim, Ellen, Richard,**

Allen, Lunn, Hannah, Rebecca, Stephen, Anne, JR, Hannah, Henrietta, Jack, Phillis, Tom, Caroline, Ammous, Phinas, Sizmore, Monkey, Simm, America, Bob, Jane, Dinah, Charlotte, Buckey, Mose, Alfred, Joe, Sam, Jody, Ike, Elsey, Burke, Victoria, Henry, Briney, George, Joe, Bice, George, Sarah, Cornelia, also the following described Lands Twenty hundred and Twenty 48/100 acres Known as the "Old Place", Nineteen Hundred and Thirty three 06/100 Acres Known as "Williams Hammock Land" Two hundred & Eighty three 08/100 Acres of Waters Pond Land and also the following Named Horses One Gray Horse Fan, Gray Mare "Bonnetts of Blue" Sorrel mare colt Betsey bay Horse Nancy Sorrell Horse Driver, gray mare Texas Sorrel Colt Buck Hill, gray mare colt Brundy, gray mare Bonnett, Also the following mules Dick, Haywood, Georgianna Big Black Dolby, Black Polly, Dandy Jack Taylor, Beggins Boggins, Dragins, and Hickman, Blacksmith Tools, two Sugar Boilers Cyrus Waggon, *** Waggon, and Six hundred & thirty Eight head of Cattle, and thirty head of sheep,, and the sum of three thousand & three hundred & nine dollars

There was an indebtedness of James W. Standley to my wife upon the division of said Estate of John B. Standley, bring her deficeincy of property upon said division by which has not been recurred by me"

January 1862
State of Florida, Alachua County
From Alachua County Ancient Records
Deed Record E pages 363-364

Philip Dell to Charles Gavin as collateral for a $500 loan: "This Indenture made this Fourteenth day of March A.D. One thousand Eight hundred & Sixty between Philip Dell of the County of Alachua and State of Florida party of the first part and Charles Gavin of the

Same place party of the Second part Witnesseth that the party of the first part for and in Consideration of the Sum of Five hundred Dollars to him in hand paid by the party of the Second part the receipt Whereof is hereby acknowledged hath bargained & Sold and by these presents do bargain and Sell the following described personal property to wit **Negro woman Lucy and her three children Julia Mary and Martha**, To have and to hold the said described personal property to the party of the Second part his heirs Executors administrators and assigns absolutely [...] these presents are upon this Condition that if the party of the first part Shall well and truly pay at Maturity his certain promisory note given to the party of the Second part for the Sum of Five hundred dollars and due January the first Eighteen and Sixty two bearing Eight per Cent Interest and having even date herewith with all costs and charges then these presents Shall become void and of no force virtue or effect otherwise to remain valid and binding"

March 14, 1860
From Alachua County Ancient Records
Mortgage Record A pages 231-232

Thomas Frasier Last Will and Testament: "I Thomas Frasier of Sumpter District in the said State do make and ordain this as my last will and testament.

First I desire that all my just debts be paid

2nd Item It is my will that the tract of land which I own near Bishopville, and in which is my residence with the house hold & Kitchen furniture and Plantation tools belonging to the same shall be Kept for the use of my wife Anne Fort Frasier for life and for the use of my unmarried daughters So long as they may continue Single and at the death of my wife and death of such of them as may continue unmarried I give the said tract of Land to my son Samuel Thomas Frasier for life and at his death to go to his children then living the issue of any deceased child to represent their parent and the Share to which such parent would have been entitled if living, and in case my said Son shall die leaving no child or children or issue of a decease child surviving then the said tract of land to return to my estate and be divided among my issue then living in the proportions they would take the Statutes distributions

3rd Item I give to my wife the following Negroes to wit, **John, Franky, Nancy, Amanda, Hester, and Matilda, for her life and at the death to go to my children as hereafter directed**

4th Item I give to my Son my Gold watch and Chain my wearing apparel and my Books

5th Item I give to each of my Grand Children the daughters of my daughter Amanda Whitworth Six hundred Dollars to be paid out of the sales hereafter to be directed with intrist from the day of my death the said sum to be in full of all claim against me on account of the value of a Negro named **Lydia** recovered in a suit against Martin Rhodes

6th Item It is my will that as Soon after my death as may be prudent my Executor Shall bring back all My Negroes, horses, Mules, and Waggons from Florida to South Carolina and hire out the Negrors untill all my debts are paid and then as soon as practable, the Negrors before Set apart for my wife shall be delivered to her and the remainder divided by three or more disinterested persons to be chosen by my executors Equally among all my children the Negrors put in the possession of any of my children to be brought on as part of My Estate

7th Item It is my will that the lot which I own in the Town of Gainesville Florida shall be Sold by My Executor when my Son arrives at the age of Twenty one years of age at public Auction to the highest bidder, that my plantation in Florida and South Carolina near Bishopville Shall be sold as soon as my executor shall be able to realize Ten dollars per acre for the same and if not Sold before my Son arrives at the age of twenty one years then to be Sold at public Auction to the highest bidder, that all my cattle Hogs Horses, Mules, Household & Kitchen furniture belonging to my Florida Settlement and all my property which I may have and which I may Give no Specific directions about in this Will Shall be Sold as soon after my death as may be advisable all of said Sales to be on such times as my executor shall direct

8th Item It is my will that my family have a comfortable Support out of my Estate untill a division of the Negroes be made

9th It is my will that whatever money may come to the hands of my executor from the sale above directed or from other sources as after paying all my debts and any sums provided for in the will Shall be equally divided between my wife Ann Fort Frasier and my Six Children Sarah E., Margaret L. B*****Omera wife of G. P. Thomas, Mary R., Martha Jane and Samuel Thomas Share and Share alike the share of Each to be invested by my Executor in a good Bond Bank Stock or negros and held by him as trustee for them the Share of my wife to be for her use for life and after her death for my children as hereafter to be directed

10th Item It is my will and desire that the share which each of my children shall take under the third (3) Sixth (6) and ninth (9) clauses of this my will Shall be for the use of such child for life and at his or death for such children as he or she may have alive at his or her death the issue of any deceased child to take the share to which their parent would have been entitled if living and in case either of my children shall die having no child or children or issue of a deceased child Surviving then the Share of such child to return to my Estate and be divided among my issue then living in the proportions they would take under the Statutes of distribution of this State

11th It is my will that the Share of such of my daughters as are now or hereafter may be married Shall be for their sole and Separate use and not to be in manner Subject to the debts contracts liabilities or control of their husband, and that my Executor hereafter named shall be their Trustee

12th Item I direct that the provisions heretofore named for my wife Shall be in lieu and bay of Dower

13th Item I direct that **the issue and increase of all my negrors** above given off Shall follow the condition in other *** as respects trustees and limitations"

April 18, 1860 and in the Independence of the United States of America Eighty fourth year
The State of South Carolina
From Alachua County Ancient Records
Will Book B pages 029-033

A. Fredenburg & C. F. Fredenburg to Edward E. Adamson as collateral for an $800 loan: "Whereas we A. Fredenburg & C. F. Fredenburg have this day purchased a Negro boy of Edward E. Adamson named **John** for the Sum of Eight hundred dollars for which we have given our joint and Several note bearing even date with these presents, Now Know all Men by these presents that for and in Consideration of the premises and to Secure the Said Edward E. Adamson in the payment of said note and for the further Consideration of one dollar by him to us paid before the Sealing and delivery of these presents, have bargained and Sold and by these presents do bargain & Sell unto the Said Edward E. Adamson his heirs Executors, Administrators and assigns the Said Negro boy John to have and to hold the Same upon this Express Provision and Condition however that if we or either of us pay or cause to be paid unto the said Edward E. Adamson the Said Sum of Eight hundred dollars together with Eight per Cent interest according to the legal effect of a note this day given and at the time therein Specified, then this obligation to be null and void else to remain in full force & virtue"

January 26, 1860
From Alachua County Ancient Records
Mortgage Record A page 223

Piercy Geiger widow and administrator of the Estate of Samuel Geiger vs. Simeon A. Edwards and his wife Louisa Edwards et al. - fighting over the Estate of Samuel Geiger: "Piercy Geiger widow & admrx of the Est Saml Geiger deceased vs Simeon A. Edwards & his wife Louisa Edwards etc., Abraham E. Geiger Guardian ad litem of the heirs of Mercy Harvel deceased, Henry Geiger & Martha Elizabeth Geiger his wife, Elijah Tucker and Margery Ann Tucker his wife, Johnathan Turner & Mary Ann Turner his wife, Enoch T. Geiger Guardian at litem of Louisanna Geiger and Enoch T. Geiger Guardian ad litem of Samuel Geiger Jr. an infant - Bill for Partition

This cause coming on to be heard on the twenty first day of November One thousand Eight Hundred & Sixty one, upon the bill answer & proofs Submitted and the Same having been taken under advisement, and on consideration had thereon, and the Court being of Opinion that the said Several deeds of the Twenty third day of November AD 1857 in said bill and answer mentioned are good and valid deeds, and did Convey to the respective doners a good title to the property in the Said deeds respectively mentioned it is ordered adjudged & Decreed That the Said Slaves named **Jane, Ned, & Henrietta** & the thirty head of Cattle **with the issue & increase** as mentioned in the said deed of the Twenty third of November AD 1857 so made by the said Samuel Geiger to Enoch T. Geiger in Trust for Louisa Jane Edwards wife of Simeon A. Edwards and the children of the said Louisa Jane as mentioned in Said deed, are not of the assets of the Estate of the said Samuel Geiger deceased, but belong to the said Enoch T. Geiger as trustee as aforesaid, and that the said Piercy Geiger administratrix as aforesaid do Surrender & deliver up the same to the said Enoch T. Geiger as such trustee for the uses and purposes in said deed mentioned

That the said Slaves named **Anderson, Charlotte & Ellen** & the Said thirty head of Cattle **with the issue and increase** of the same as mentioned in said deed of the Twenty third day of November AD 1857 So made by the Said Samuel Geiger deceased to the Said Enoch T. Geiger in Trust for Martha Elizabeth Geiger wife of Henry J. Geiger & the children of the said Martha Elizabeth as mentioned in said deed are not of the Estate of the said Samuel Geiger deceased but belong to the Said Enoch T. Geiger as trustee as aforesaid: And that the said Complainant, the Said Piercy Geiger administratrix do Surrender & deliver up the same to the said Enoch T. Geiger as such Trustee for the use and purposes in said deed mentioned

That the said Slaves **Vine, Ann, & Willis with their issue & increase** as mentioned in said deed of the twenty third of November AD 1857 So made by the said Samuel Geiger to the said Enoch T. Geiger in Trust for Margery Ann Tucker wife of Elijah Tucker and the Children of the said Margery Ann as mentioned in said deed, are not of the assets of the Estate of the said Samuel Geiger deceased, but belong to the said Enoch T. Geiger as Trustee as aforesaid and that the said Complainant the said Piercy Geiger administratrix as aforesaid do Surrender & deliver up the same to the said Enoch T. Geiger as such Trustee for the uses & purposes in said deed mentioned

That the Slaves named **Elias, Rose & Louis** & fifty head of Cattle **with their issue and increase** as mentioned in said deed of the twenty third of November AD 1857, So made by the said Samuel Geiger to the said William E. Sharp in trust for Sarah Ann Geiger wife of Abraham E. Geiger & the child & children of the said Sarah Ann as mentioned in said deed are not of the assets of the Estate of the said Samuel Geiger deceased but belong to the said William E. Sharp as trustee as aforesaid, and that the said Complainant Piercy Geiger &

the child & children of the said Sarah Ann as mentioned in said deed are not of the assets of the Estate of the said Samuel Geiger deceased but belong to the said William E. Sharp as trustee as aforesaid and that the Said Complainant Piercy Geiger administratrix as aforesaid do Surrender & deliver up the Same to the said William E. Sharp as such Trustee for the use and purposes in said deed mentioned

That the Slaves **Elick, Sopha, & Eliza** & the said fifty head **with the issue & increase** of the same: and the Kitchen & household furniture of the said Samuel Geiger as mentioned in said deed of the twenty third of November AD 1857 So made by the said Samuel Geiger to Enoch T. Geiger in Trust for Louisanna Geiger are not of the assets of the estate of the said Samuel Geiger deceased, but belong to the said Enoch T. Geiger as Trustee as aforesaid, and that the said Complainant the said Piercy Geiger administratrix as aforesaid do Surrender & deliver up the same to the said Enoch T. Geiger as such Trustee for the uses and purposes in said deed mentioned

That the said Slaves **Charles Mariah John** and the said Thirty head of Cattle, **with the issue & increase** of the Same, as mentioned in Said deed of the twenty third of November AD 1857 So made by the said Samuel Geiger to the Said Abraham E. Geiger in Trust for Mary Ann Turner wife of Johnathan Turner, and the Children of the Said Mary Ann as mentioned in said deed: are not of the assets of the Estate of the Said Samuel Geiger deceased, but belonging to the said Abraham E. Geiger as Trustee as aforesaid: and that the said Complainant the said Piercy Geiger administratrix as aforesaid do Surrender & deliver up the same to the said Abraham E. Geiger as such Trustee for the uses & purposes in said deed mentioned

That the said Slaves **Bill Lucy & Jim** & the said Fifty head of Cattle **and their issue and increase** as Mentioned in said deed of the Twenty third of November AD 1857 So made by the said Samuel Geiger to the said Abraham E. Geiger in Trust for the heirs of Mercy Harville deceased wife of John E. Harville as mentioned in said deed, are not of the assets of the Estate of the said Samuel Geiger deceased, but belong to the said Abraham E. Geiger as Trustee as aforesaid, and that the complainant the said Piercy Geiger administratrix as aforesaid do Surrender & deliver up the same to the said Abraham E. Geiger as such trustee for the uses & purposes in said deed mentioned

That the said Slaves **Edward Mary & Solomon** with the fifty head of Cattle **together with their increase of said Slaves** as mentioned in said deed of the Twenty third of November AD 1857 So made by the Said Samuel Geiger to Enoch T. Geiger are not of the assets of the Estate of the said Samuel Geiger deceased, but belong to the said Enoch T. Geiger and that the said Complainant the said Piercy Geiger administratrix as aforesaid do surrender and deliver up the same to the said Enoch T. Geiger as the owner thereof

And the Court being further of the opinion, that upon the death of the said Joseph Samuel Geiger under the age of twenty one years without issue, unmarried & intestate as set forth in Said bill & answer the intent of the said Joseph Saml Geiger in & to the Said Slaves **George & Nancy** & the said thirty head of Cattle **with their issue and increase** as mentioned in the said deed of the Twenty third of November AD 1857 So made by the said Samuel Geiger in his life time,

It is further Ordered adjudged & decreed that the same or such portion thereof as was not otherwise disposed of, are of the assets of the said Estate of the Said Samuel Geiger & Subject to distribution as such after the payment of debts

And it is further ordered - that it be referred to a Master in Chancery to ascertain & take an account of the issue and increase of the said Slaves & Cattle in the said Several deeds respectively mentioned & referred to and to make a report of the same to the Court with Convenient Certainty & dispatch: to the End that Such further & other proceedings may be had in the premises as to Justice may appertain

And the Court being further of Opinion that the said deed So made by the said Samuel Geiger & Executed by and between him and John

Jos Sanchez & William Dell & the said Caroline Geiger wife of the said Samuel Geiger of the nineteenth of January AD 1855, and the said deed of the said John Jos Sanchez & William Dell to the said Caroline Geiger of the Thirteenth of January AD 1855 purporting to convey **a Negro woman named Fereh a Negro child named Nancy and a Negro child named Ellen** & one Sorrel Mare & Colt Two Cows & Calves, Ten head of sheep and all the house hold & Kitchen furniture of the Said Samuel Geiger then in his possession were inoperative & void

It is further ordered, adjudged, & decreed that the said Complainant Piercy Geiger widow & administratrix as aforesaid of the said Samuel Geiger deceased do have and receive as her distributive Share of the said Estate after the payment of all debts, "a childs part" in Lieu of a dower as prayed for in said bill - and that the estate of the said Samuel Geiger deceased of which he died Seized & possessed & to which he was rightfully Entitled both real & personal after the payments of all debts, be Equally divided & distributed among the said Several distributes to wit: between the said Piercy Geiger widow as aforesaid and the Several Said Children of the said Samuel Geiger now living, including the heirs of the said Mercy Harville deceased who together by & through their Said Trustees are entitled to one Share and that be appointed Commissioner to distribute the said personal Estate & for that purpose to make Sale of such part or portion of the same as may be deemed necessary: & to partition the said real Estate accordingly

And it is further ordered that if the said real Estate cannot in the opinion of the Said Commissioner be partitioned amongst the said parties without manifest injury to any one or more of them, that then the said real Estate be rented or that the said Commissioner, report the facts to the Court with such recommendations in the premises as to them may seem Just and Equitable"

December 2, 1861
From Alachua County Ancient Records
Chancery Order Book A pages 174-178

T. B. Griffin, guardian of minor children, delivers enslaved people to Samuel Spencer that were the subject of a lawsuit: "By virtue of a decree this day made By his Honor James B. Dawkins, allowing to the Solicitors, employed in a Suit brought by William Downs and others against Thomas M. Braswell and others in which Said Suit Certain Negro Slaves there named have recovered and delivered to me as guardian of the Said Minor Children, duly appointed, I have in accordance with the Said decree assigned and delivered to Samuel Spencer one of the Solicitors in said Suit the following Negro Slaves Viz, **Priscilla, Charlotte, & Lizzie**, to have and to hold the said Negro Slaves in fee Simple to him the Said Samuel Spencer, his heirs, Executors administrators and assigns forever"

January 20, 1865
State of Florida, Alachua County
From Alachua County Ancient Records
Deed Record E page 613

John Grimes, James H. Johnson, & Eli Futch, Executors of the last will and testament of William Wright: "This Indenture made the fifth day of March, In the year of our Lord One Thousand Eight hundred & Sixty one, Between John Grimes of Said State & County of Bullock James H. Johnson, of Said County of Liberty, and Eli Futch of Said State & County of Bryan, Executors of the last will and Testament of William Wright late of the County and State first aforesaid, Deceased, of the first part and Dr. Peter Statesbury, of Scriven County in Said State of the Second part,

470

Whereas, Said William Wright deceased as aforesaid, made his last will and testament in writing, which was duly proved and admitted to record the December term thereof, in the year of our Lord One thousand Eight hundred & Sixty which among other provisions Contains the following

Item Seventh, I direct my executors herein after named, at Public Auction on the first Tuesday in the month of January after my death, if practicable, giving two months notice, in one gazette in each of the Cities of Savannah Macon, and Augusta; and **Negroes to be Sold** on twelve month credits for approved papers Secured by Mortgage at the discretion of My Executors

Item ninth I desire that all my Lands not herein otherwise disposed of Shall be advertised by my Executors, at Such time as they may think advisable and be Sold, Either at public outcry or private Sale if at public outcry, upon twelve months time for approved paper to be Secured by Mortgage on the property, after an advertisement of two months in Some public gazette.

Item Tenth - I give to my Executors full power and authority to Sell any portion of my Estate they may think proper Subject to the discretion hereinbefore given, as to the land and Stores, and invest them with all the powers necessary to carry into Effect this my will: as in and by said last will and testament remaining of record in Said Court of Ordinary reference being thereunto had, will fully appear.

And Whereas, Said parties of the first part, Executors as aforesaid, after publication and advertisement thereof according to the requirements of Said last will and testament on the first Tuesday in March, in the year of our Lord One thousand Eight hundred and Sixty one, before the Court House in the City of Savannah, between the legal hours of Sale Exposed for Sale at public out cry all the lands and Stores which were of said William Wright in his life time Except Such land and Stores as are under the terms of Said last will and testament reserved from Sale or from exposure at public outcry, when all that property herein after particularly described was Struck off to the Said party of the Second part, at and for the Sum of Four hundred & Eighty dollars, he being the highest and best bidder for the Same

Now this Indenture Witnesseth, That the said parties of the first part, Executors as aforesaid, for and in Consideration of the Sum of Four hundred and Eighty Dollars to them in hand paid by the Said Peter Statesberry at and before the Sealing and delivery of these presents the receipt whereof is hereby acknowledged, Have granted, bargained, Sold, Aliened remised, released, and Confirmed, and by these presents by force & virtue of said above recited will. Do grant bargain, Sell, alien, remise, release, and Confirm unto the Said Peter Statesberry and to his heirs and assigns all that lot or parcel of land Situate lying and being in the County of Alachua, in the State of Florida described and Bounded as follows: in Section Eleven (11) Township Ten (10) Range Nineteen (19) of the Arredondo Grant Containing Six hundred & forty acres, formerly Known as the property of James Rey - Together with all and Singular the houses, out houses, Edifices, buildings, Stables, yards, gardens liberties, privileges, easements, commodities hereditaments, rights Members and appurtinances whatsoever, thereunto belonging or in any wise appertaining: And the reversion and reversions remainder and remainders, rents, issues, and profits thereof And all the Estate, right, title, interest, and property or possession Claims and demand whatsoever, in law or Equity of the Said William Wright at and immediately before the time of his decease and which his said Executors have had since his death, as fully to all intents and purposes, as said Executors may or can convey the same, under the powers of said last will and testament of in or to the same, or any part or parcel thereof with the appurtinances. To Have And To Hold The said Lot or parcel of land above described, and all and singular other the premises hereby granted, bargained, sold, aliened and confirmed, with the heriditaments unto the said Peter Statesberry his heirs and assigns to the only proper use and behoof of the said Peter Statesberry his heirs and assigns forever and to and for no other use, intent or purpose whatsoever"

March 5, 1861
State of Georgia, Chatham County
From Alachua County Ancient Records
Deed Record E pages 316-318

Thomas E. Haile sells an enslaved man out of the trust of his wife Esther Serena Haile because of his "bad qualities" and replaces him with an enslaved boy: "Whereas there was a certain **Negro boy named Washington about the age of Twenty five years** held in Trust by L. L. Whitaker of South Carolina for the use benefit and behoof of my wife Esther Serena Haile and whereas I have Sold & assigned said boy Washington for reasons of his bad qualities, And whereas I am desirous of protecting and preserving said Trust Estate Now know ** all Men by these presents that I Thomas E. Haile in Consideration of the premises and for the Sum of One dollar in hand to me paid by L. L. Whitaker Trustee of my said wife Esther Serena Haile do bargain Sell and convey unto the said L. L. Whitaker Trustee as aforesaid a certain **Negro boy named Fortune about Seventeen years of age** to be held by him upon the same terms limitations and trusts as the said Negro boy Washington was Given under my hand and Seal this Twenty first day of May AD 1860"

May 21, 1860
From Alachua County Ancient Records
Deed Record E page 189

Robert H. Hardaway to daughter Manfredonia Richard (Husband Osciola W. Richard trustee): "Know all men by these presents that I Robert H. Hardaway of said County and State for and in Consideration of the natural love and affection which I have and bear to my daughter Manfredonia Richard, of the County of Alachua State of Florida and for and in Consideration of the sum of Five dollars Cash in hand paid by the said Manfredonia Richard, the Receipt whereof is hereby acknowledged do by these presents give and grant unto my said daughter Manfredonia Richard a Certain **Negro girl named Rose fourteen years old of dark Complexion**, To have and to hold the said Negro girl, **with the future increase of her** to her the said Manfredonia Richard and her heirs, free from her husband or husbands debt or debts of her present or future husband for her Sole use and benefit and behoof forever, and I do hereby Constitute and appoint her husband Osciola W. Richard her trustee, with full power to sell and good and legal title to Execute to the same, without recourse to the Courts of the Country and the proceeds to be invested in and for like purposes"

February 19, 1863
State of Georgia, Thomas County
From Alachua County Ancient Records
Deed Record E page 473

William Harn Last Will and Testament: "Know all men by these presents, that I, William Harn of the county of Alachua and State of Florida being in health and of sound and disposing mind and memory do make and publish this my last Will and testament hereby revoking any former Wills by me at any time made

And as to my real estate and all the property real and personal of which I shall die seized or possessed, or to which I Shall be entitled at the time of my decease I devise bequeath and dispose thereof in the manner following to wit;

First. - My Will is that all my just debts and funeral expenses shall by my Executors hereinafter named be paid out of my estate as soon after my decease as to him shall seem convenient.

Item - I give, devise and bequeath unto my beloved daughter Mary C. Stroble & the heirs of her body, all my real estate consisting of the lands and improvements embraced in the plantation Known as the "Harn Place", situated about three and a half miles from the town of Newnansville, all my cattle, horses, hogs and Stock of all Kinds; household and Kitchen furniture; farming implements and tools of all Kinds, and the following negro slaves, to wit; **Hannah Isaac, Jim, Bason, Lewis, Silvy Eliza, Margaret, Jim, Harry, Dick Frank, Agnes, Ann, Easter, Sim and Salina**, To have and to hold all of the above described property unto the said Mary C. Stroble, the heirs of her body, their Executors Administrators and assigns forever.

I give and bequeath unto my much beloved grand children James Livingston Harn, and Willie Harn, children of my deceased Son, William S. Harn, the following described negro Slaves to wit; **Betsy and her four children, Sampson, William Margaret, and Eliza, and Sam, a man** to have and to hold the said described slaves unto the said James Livingston and Willie Harn, their heirs Executors Administrators and assigns forever"

November 9, 1864
State of Florida, County of Alachua
From Alachua County Ancient Records
Will Book B pages 058-060

Daniel C. Hart to John E. Thompson as collateral for $1,000 in loans: "Know All Men by these presents that I Daniel C. Hart of the County and State aforesaid in Consideration of the Sum of one thousand Dollars to me in hand paid by John E. Thompson of the Same County and State (the receipt Whereof is hereby acknowledged) have granted bargained and Sold and by these presents do grant bargain and Sell unto the Said John E. Thompson the following personal property to wit **A Negro Woman named Sophy -- about twenty eight years old A Negro girl named Sarah about five years old And a Negro Girl named Susan about three years old** To have and to hold all and Singular the Said Negroes herein named unto the Said John E. Thompson his executors Administrators and assigns to his and their sole use forever And I the said Daniel C. Hart for myself, my executors and administrators do covenant to and with the said John E. Thompson his executors administrators and assigns That I am lawfully possessed of the said negroes as my own property that the same are free from all incumbrances and that I will and my executors and administrators shall warrant and defend the same to the said John E. Thompson his executors administrators and assigns against the Lawful claims and demands of all person Provided always and these presents are expressly upon this Condition Whereas the said Daniel C. Hart is indebted to the said John E. Thompson by his certain promissory note for the Sum of Seven hundred and fifty Dollars Dated at Gainesville on the 9th day of April 1860 and Due the 1st November year last aforesaid and drawing 8 percent Interest from the date thereof, and whereas also the said John E. Thompson has Signed for and with the said Daniel C. Hart as Security a certain promissory note for the sum of two hundred and fifty Dollars dated the 9th day of April 1860 and payable on the 1st November after Drawing 8 percent in favor of   — or Bearer Now if the said Daniel C. Hart Shall and do well and truly pay or cause to be paid unto the said John E. Thompson his promissory note first aforesaid when the same Shall become due and also pay the aforesaid promissory note for Two hundred and fifty Dollars on the day herein before mentioned and appointed for payment thereof or by other lawful means Save Keep harmless and indemnified the Said John E. Thompson from the payment of the said note first aforesaid and all costs Damages or charges as surety aforesaid then and from thence forth as will this present deed hereby made as the said recited obligation Shall cease determine and become absolutely null & void anything herein contained to the contrary notwithstanding"

April 9, 1860
State of Florida, County of Alachua
From Alachua County Ancient Records
Deed Record E pages 173-174

A. J. Hewlett Last Will and Testament: "Know all men by these presents that I, A. J. Hewlett do write this as my last Will and testament and that I do desire that this writing Stand in any Court of Justice, Should it ever be tested, which I hope will have no cause as I give my small amount of property out just as I wish, and should any defect be found, the meaning is right as below stated and as follows;

I wish first that my wife Maria J. Hewlett for her help in making me leave home in the year 1859, that she have the sum of ($5) five dollars in the old bank bills by my brother H. C. Hewlett who I leave as my Guardian for my daughter and others

I now desire that my daughter Viola Davis Hewlett have the house and lot together with all the furniture complete on fourth 4th St. between Hanover and Brunswick Sts. in the town of Wilmington and State of North Carolina, Lot No. 71 together with the following named negroes; **Mary, Jane, Fannie and Henry, and Margaret**,- All the above I leave in charge of my brother H. C. Hewlett, who will see that justice be done my daughter this I leave to her Viola D. Hewlett, and to her heirs; Should she die leaving no heirs the property all goes back to my family to be equally decided amongst them all

I now desire that my brother H. C. Hewlett, for his goodness to me have the other house and lot adjoining the above one between the same streets N,,70, together with the following named negroes; **Alston, Zilphy, Amelia and Harriett**, to him and his heirs forever

I now wish to prepare for Miss Kate L. Davis who has waited on me night and day for so long a time; My brother H. C. Hewlett will see that she is well taken care of. I desire that he take her into his house, as he promised me he would. I give to Miss Kate L. Davis, for her support the following named negroes; **Abby, Washington, Morse and Jim**. My brother Henry C. Hewlett to have the negroes in charge, and to support Miss Davis while she remains single. Should she marry the negroes will be hired out, and the proceeds divided amongst all my heirs, Should she die, the negroes to be divided as above or in case of marriage

I now wish, as I do not know how much money I may leave, that after the way is paid to Wilmington N.C. for all the negroes, and Henry C. Hewlett paid for his trouble that each of my brothers and sisters and the heirs of my deceased brother have the sum of fifty dollars ($50) and my mother have 1- one hundred and if not so much left they must be satisfied with ($25) twenty-five dollars and wait in property

My Banks Land I give to all my heirs with my fathers my 18 acres on the sound, I give to my brother W. S. Hewlett. Now I wish my brother H.C. Hewlett to attend to all the above and I appoint him Guardian for my daughter and her estate, and to Miss Kate L. Davis. All the above I do give in my good senses and wish this writing to Stand forever"

January 26, 1865
State of Florida, Alachua County
From Alachua County Ancient Records
Will Book B pages 061-063

Ezekiel P. Hickson and wife Anna P. Hickson to Benjamin W. Powell for $27,000: "This Indenture made on the Seventh day of April in the year One thousand eight hundred & Sixty three between Ezekiel P. Hickson and Anna P. Hickson his wife of the first part, and Benjamin W. Powell of the Second part Witnesseth That for and in Consideration of the sum of Twenty Seven thousand dollars to them in hand paid at and before the Sealing and delivery hereof the receipt whereof is hereby acknowledged, the Said parties of the first part are given, granted bargained Sold and delivered and by these presents do so give grant, bargain, sell and deliver to the said party of the second part the following named and described property "That is to say" the following Slaves to wit, **Albert about Forty five years of age Eliza about thirty Seven, Mary about thirty five Peano about twenty eight, Arthur twenty seven Litt Twenty Seven, Sarah twenty one, Clarissa twenty, Lang Sixteen Mary ten, Sir fourteen, Reuben Seven, Amos Five, Jim two, Selina nine, Kizzie five and John two years old, Also two Small infants names not known and the children of Clarissa and Sarah**, Also three Mules and five horses, Also the entire Stock of Cattle and hogs now owned by the parties of the first part, all the Seed Cotton on the plantation, two Cotton gins, two Waggons, all the Meat on the plantation, all the Corn fodder potatoes and provision generally all the plantation and farming tools and utensils

Also all the sugar and Syrup on the place and every thing appertaining to the plantation herein after named and Conveyed with the exception of the household and Kitchen furniture - The said parties of the first part have further given, granted, bargained, Sold, Conveyed and by these presents do so give grant bargain, Sell and Convey to the said party of the Second part the following plantation or parcel of land "Viz" The South East Quarter of the lot of land Known as Number Eleven of the twenty thousand acre grant formerly Known as the Moses Levy grant Containing four hundred & Nineteen 86/100 acres more or less Also two hundred & Sixty and 25/100 acres on the north west Quarter of the Same lot No Eleven - making in all Six hundred and Seventy Nine & 98/100 acres more or less Situate in the County of Alachua & State of Florida

To Have and to hold the Slaves, and other personal property above named to the Said party of the Second part & to his heirs and assigns, and the said parcels of land above named and Conveyed & described, together with all and Singular, the houses buildings improvements and appurtinances to the Same belonging or in anywise appertaining to the Said party of the Second part & to his heirs and assigns in fee Simple forever - And the said parties of the first part Covenant and agree with the Said party of the Second part that they are Seized in fee of the above granted and Conveyed premises lands and personal property, that they are free from all incumbrances that they have a good right to Sell and Convey the same to the said party of the Second part, And they their heirs Executors or administrators Shall warrant and defend the aforesaid property, to the said party of the Second part his heirs Executors or administrators and assigns.."

April 7, 1863
State of Florida, Alachua County
From Alachua County Ancient Records
Deed Record E pages 508-509

Robert R. Hines indicted for assault with intent to kill, used enslaved people as part of collateral to ensure he showed up for Court: "State of Florida vs Robert R. Hines - Assault with intent to Kill - Continued to next term of this Court and the defendant Recognized in the Sum of Two hundred & fifty dollars for his appearance at the next term of the Court Peter Sparkman & Joseph J. Mickle appeared in open Court & acknowledged themselves to stand indebted to the State of Florida in the Sum of One hundred & Twenty five dollars Each to be levied of their respective goods & chattles Slaves land

& Tenements if default be made in the following Condition that is to say if the Said Robert R. Hines Shall be and appear at the next term of the Court without leave thereof then this obligation to be null & void otherwise to remain in full force & virtue

April 12, 1860
From Alachua County Ancient Records
Judgment Record B page 271

Washington M. Ives to Jessie T. Bernard, trustee for Mary E. Scarborough for $640: "Know all men by these presents that I Washington M. Ives of the State and County aforesaid, for and in Consideration of the sum of Six hundred forty dollars to me in hand paid by Jessie T. Bernard trustee for Mary E. Scarborough wife of Lindley M. Scarborough the receipt whereof I do hereby acknowledge have bargained, Sold, and delivered, and by these presents do bargain sell, and deliver to the said Jessie T. Bernard trustee as aforesaid a certain **negro girl Slave named Melinda aged about Eleven years old**. To have and to hold the said Negro girl **and the increase of her body** to the said Jessie T. Bernard as trustee as aforesaid for the Sole use and benefit of the said Mary E. Scarborough and her heirs forever. And I the said Washington M. Ives do hereby warrant and defend the said girl Melinda to be sound in body and mind and a Slave for life."

September 12, 1862
State of Florida, Columbia County
From Alachua County Ancient Records
Bills of Sale A page 069

William B. Lewis to John Lewis after $10,000 in loans were paid back: "Know all men by these presents that William B. Lewis of said County and State for and in Consideration of the sum of Ten thousand dollars represented by certain promisory notes named and delivered by said William B. Lewis by being returned to him the said William B. Lewis and being thereby cancelled, and paid off, all of which is hereby acknowledged, hath bargained and Sold and delivered and by these presents doth bargain, sell and deliver unto the said John Lewis his heirs and assigns forever the following personal property heretofore bargained, Sold and delivered by the said John Lewis to the said William B. Lewis by deed of Indenture or Bill of Sale, Signed Sealed and delivered on the tenth day of December A. D. 1855 and thereby conveying the same property which is hereby conveyed and returned by the said William B. Lewis to the said John Lewis for the Same Consideration, to wit, the promisory notes above described Originally moving as the Consideration between said parties to said deed of the 10th December A. D. 1855 Twenty Negroes Slaves conveyed as above and now returned and recorded by the present deed together with Such increase and addition as have been born to and added by natural increase to the females of said Conveyed property Since the 10th of December A. D. 1855 the date as aforesaid of said first deed of Indenture - Said Original Twenty Negroes Slaves named as follows, **Old March Bill Washington, Ben, Aaron Will, little March George Alfred, Tim, Margaret, Marriah, Caroline, Lucy, Eliza, Betty Cela Effa and Emma**, It being understood that Aaron shall remain in possession of said William B. Lewis as an advancement as one of the heirs of said John Lewis to be accounted for to the Estate of said John Lewis and to be appraised as a portion of said Estate and Said William B. Lewis to retain said Slave Aaron at the appraised valuation of Aaron which valuation is to be deducted from the amount which may be due to said William B. Lewis as his Share or proportion of said Estate as One of the heirs of said John Lewis In addition to said twenty Slaves and their increase, the following personal property is also hereby reconveyed and returned, also included in said deed of December the 10th A. D. 1855 to wit two Mules, four horses, two old Waggons and wagon gear, one Set of plantation tools and utensils, consisting of plows, hoes, axes and grubbing hoes, and also One Cotton gin, To have and to hold all of the foregoing described property, to wit, said Slaves and their increase as aforesaid, and Said Mules, horses, wagons, and gear, and plantation tools, utensils and gin, to the only use & behoof of him the said John Lewis, his heirs administrators Executors or assigns forever"

April 23, 1863
State of Florida, Alachua County
From Alachua County Ancient Records
Deed Record E pages 485-486

Wm F. Mann to Elizabeth T. Fretwell for $400: "Recorded Silver Springs Fla. 12th April 1860 from Elizabeth T. Fretwell Four hundred dollars in full for a certain **Negro girl named Mary about Twenty one years old (unsound)** the right and title whereof I warrant to the Said Elizabeth T. Fretwell and his heirs and assigns together with the further issue and increase of the Said Mary against all claims whatsoever I also warrant her a Slave for life"

April 12, 1860
From Alachua County Ancient Records
Deed Record E pages 301-302

L. A. Mason to Adaline Gardner for $1,800: "Received of Adaline Gardner Eighteen hundred dollars in full payment for Certain **Negro Slave boy named Joe about fifteen years of age,** Title to which said negro Slave I will warrant. I also warrant said negro Slave boy to be Sound and healthy

April 13, 1863
Gainesville Florida
From Alachua County Ancient Records
Bills of Sale A page 070

John T. Matthews to James A. McCrorey & Edward Lewis as collateral for $1,825 in loans: "This Indenture made on the fourth day of August in the year of our Lord One thousand Eight hundred & Sixty Between John T. Matthews of the State & County aforesaid of the first part, and James A. McCrorey of the State of South Carolina & Edward Lewis of the State of Florida & County aforesaid of the Second part Witnesseth: That Whereas the Said party of the first part is indebted to the Said James A. McCrorey in the Sum of Eighteen Hundred & Twenty five dollar together with Seven per Cent interest thereon from the fifth day of March in the Year One thousand Eight hundred and fifty four, Which Said Sum of Money & interest is due on a certain Sealed note made by the Said party of the first part and delivered to the Said James A. McCrorey on the fifth day of March in the year Eighteen hundred & fifty four as aforesaid, which Said note was payable one day after date thereof; And whereas further the Said party of the first part desires to Secure to the Said James A. McCrorey the faithful payment of the Said promisory note together with the interest which has accumulated thereon: and Whereas further on the fifteenth day of March in the year of our Lord One Thousand Eight hundred & fifty nine the Said Edward Lewis Signed as security for

484

the Said party of the first part a Certain promisory note due on the
first day of January One thousand Eight hundred & Sixty in favour
George Gillett Admr of David Gillett deceased on which Said promisory note the Said Edward Lewis is now Sued and Whereas the Said
party of the first part desires & designs to Save the Said Edward
Lewis from any & all loss he may Sustain by reason of having Signed
the promisory note last aforesaid together with the Said party of the
first part Now therefore for the foregoing Consideration as well as
for the further Sum of Five dollars to him in hand paid at and before
the Sealing & delivery of these presents by the Said parties of the
Second part the receipt whereof is hereby acknowledged The Said
party of the first part has given granted bargained Sold & Conveyed
& by these presents does give grant bargain Sell and Convey unto
the Said parties of the Second part the following described property
Viz That Certain Town Lot in the Village of Gainesville now occupied by S. McCall and formerly owned by John Richard Containing
one acre of Land more or less & Situate about three hundred yards
North of the Court House & about two hundred yards East of the
boarding House now Kept by Mrs. Heath Also the whole of Sections
Twenty Seven & Eight & Thirty four of Township Nine of Range
twenty Containing Nineteen hundred acres more or less Situate in
Alachua County & State aforesaid Also the following named Negroes
Slaves To Wit **Phoby a female Slave about Thirty one years of
age Adam a Male Slave about fifteen years of age Robert a male
Slave about Ten years old & Judy a female Slave about Eight
Years old**, Also the following named & described mules, To wit Jack
a dark bay, Nance a Grey Mule Mike a Sorrel, big Jane a Sorrel &
little Jane a Sorrel Kit a Sorrel Punch a bay & Dick a Sorrel, Also
the Certain Steam Mill together with all its appurtenances Situate on
the parcel of Land herein above described To Have and to Hold the
above Mentioned and described property unto the Said parties of
the Second part and to their heirs Executors or administrators and
assigns forever, together with all and Singular the improvements,
houses, buildings Steam Engines & Mills & their appurtinances on
the real Estate herein above described and Conveyed Situated or in

any wise appurtaining and belonging [...] if the Said party of the first part Shall well and truly pay to the Said James A. McCrorey the amount of the promisory note & interest thereon as herein before Stated & Shall also Save harmless the Said Edward Lewis from any pecuniary loss he may Sustain in Consequence of being a Signer to the Said promisory note to Geo Gillett as administrator aforesaid, then these presents to be null & void & of non effect otherwise to be & remain in full force & virtue"

August 4, 1860
State of Florida, Alachua County
From Alachua County Ancient Records
Mortgage Record A pages 255-257

A. A. Maulden indicted for murder; enslaved people were used as a part of collateral to ensure he showed up for Court: "State of Florida vs A. A. Maulden - Murder - Continued to the next Term of the Court and the defendant Recognized in the Sum of Ten Thousand Dollars for his appearance at the next Term of the Court A. A. Maulden in the Sum of Ten Thousand dollars & Twelve hundred & fifty Dollars for the Security each A. A. Maulden, G. P. Thomas, John Little, T. W. McCaa, A. Matheson, Joseph A. Scott, Peter Sparkman, Mitchell Kirkland, John R. W. Grissom appeared in Open Court and acknowledged themselves to Stand indebted to the State of Florida in the Sum of Ten thousand Dollars that is to say A. A. Maulden in the sum of Ten Thousand Dollars

G. P. Thomas, John Little, T. W. McCaa, A. Matheson, Joseph A. Scott Peter Sparkman, Mitchell Kirkland, & John R. W. Grissom in the Sum of Twelve hundred & fifty Each to be levied of their Respective goods & chattels, Slaves lands & tenements if default be made in the following Condition, that is to say if the said A. A. Maulden shall

be and appear at the next term of the Court to answer to an Indictment for Murder, and shall not thence depart the Court without leave
thereof, then this Obligation to be null & void otherwise to remain in
full force & virtue"

October 17, 1861
From Alachua County Ancient Records
Judgment Record B page 473

**James A. McCrory to wife Lucretia McCrory to provide support
for her if his business fails:** "Know all men by these presents that
I James McCrory of the State & County aforesaid for and in Consideration of the natural love and affection which I have and bear
for and towards my wife Lucretia McCrory and for the purposes of
providing a Competent Support for my Said wife in the event of my
failure in business have given granted bargained Sold & Conveyed
and by these presents do So give grant bargain, Sell & Convey unto
my Said wife the following named and described property To wit,
**John a male Slave about thirty years of age of a black Com-
plexion, Jane a black female Slave about twelve years of age;**
Also the following named & described Mules, To wit Dick a Sorrel
Mare mule Nine years Old, Jane a Sorrel Mare mule ten Years Old,
Remus a bay mare mule Seven Years Old, Bill a black horse mule
nine Years Old, Tim black horse mule Six Years old & Molly a Black
mare mule Seven Years Old

To Have and Hold the above mentioned and described personal property unto my wife the Said Lucretia McCrory & to her heirs of her
body by me lawfully begotten forever, And these present are Executed
upon the Express Condition that I James McCrory Shall during the
lifetime of myself have the Management of Said property for the use
and benefit of my Said wife but that the Said property Shall in no

manner be liable to my debts or Subject to my Contracts Except with the free Consent of my Said wife"

July 10, 1860
State of Florida, Alachua County
From Alachua County Ancient Records
Deed Record E page 199

Inventory of personal property belonging to Susan J. McDonald: "An inventory of Personal property belonging to Susan J. McDonald wife of Thadius A. McDonald **Kitty a Negro woman aged about twenty two years and her child Linas aged about 14 months** Said property is now in the County aforesaid and the Clerk of the Circuit Court is hereby requested to record this Indenture in the proper Book Receipt for that purpose"

August 4, 1860
Recorded Feby 22th 1861
State of Florida, County of Alatchua
From Alachua County Public Records
Deed Record E page 265

Document by John C. Pelot and Jane A. Pelot outlining the property of Mrs. Julia McDonell: "The following is the property of Mrs. Julia McDonell wife of Samuel P. McDonell which Came from the Estate of her Father Thomas Pyles Viz **a Negro man named Dick aged 45 years his wife Elsy aged 40 years, a Negro boy named Henry aged 22 years, a Woman named Silla aged 55 years and a**

Negro girl named Elsy aged 12 years Also 1/3 interest in a Section of land lying in Alachua County bounded directly South by land of Mrs E. M. Stewart North East & West by other lands on the Arredondo Grant, Also **a Negro Boy named Robr. aged 10 years**"

June 15, 1864
From Alachua County Ancient Records
Deed Record E page 596

Inventory of the property belonging to Marion S. McDonell:
"Inventory of the property Real and personal of Marion S. McDonell wife of Donald R. McDonell Citizens residing in the County of Alachua State of Florida the property being in Said County

1st the undivided interest of One third of land, Known as Section Sixteen Township Nine Range Nineteen East being and lying in the County and State aforesaid

2nd **Edmund a Negro man aged about forty five years**

3rd **Frank a Negro man aged about Thirty five years**

4th **Betty a Negro woman aged about Thirty five years**

5th **Rose a Negro girl aged about fourteen years of age**"

May 26, 1863
From Alachua County Ancient Records
Deed Record E page 497

Thomas P. McHenry indicted for betting at cards; enslaved people were used as part of collateral to ensure he showed up for court: "State of Florida vs Thomas P. McHenry - Playing & Betting at Cards - Continued to next term of the Court and the defendant Recognized in the sum of Five hundred Dollars for his appearance at the next term of the Court and acknowledged himself to Stand indebted to the State of Florida in the Sum of Five hundred Dollars to be levied of his respective goods & chattels, Slaves lands & tenements if default be made on the following Conditions that is to say if the said Thomas P. McHenry shall be and appear at the next term of the Court to answer an Indictment for Playing & Betting at Cards and Shall not thence depart the Court without leave thereof then this obligation to be null & void else to remain in full force & virtue"

April 11, 1864
From Alachua County Ancient Records
Judgment Record B page 515

Determining assessed value of people enslaved by John T. McIntosh & J. M. Miller: "At a meeting of the Board of County Commissioners. Present Wm Strickland C. Rain J.M. Sparkman Mathew Hinson and E.H. Jordan President of the Board

1st Ordered that the report of R.E. Johnston A.W. Cook and R.L. Stoughton Commissioners appointed to view and assess the property of John T. McIntosh as per order made 11th day of March AD 1861 be rec'd which report is that said Negro property should be assessed at Two Thousand dollars said amt of Two Thousand dollars being the amt assessed by the said John T. McIntosh

2nd Ordered that the report of John Sparkman John N. Orman and Edward Lewis Commissioners appointed to view and assess the Negro property of J. M. Miller as per order made the 11th day of March AD 1861 be rec'd said Commissioners report that said Negro property should be assessed at Four Thousand Eight Hundred dollars when said J.M. Miller assessed same at Three thousand dollars

3rd Ordered that the Taxes for the year 1861 be assessed at Fifteen per cent (15 pr cent)"

April 22, 1861
County Commissioners Court - Gainesville
From Alachua County Ancient Records
County Commission Minutes Book 1 page 139

John T. McIntosh to Thomas G. F. Wells and James P. McIntosh in trust for his infant children in the State of South Carolina: "Know all men by these presents That I John T. McIntosh of the Town of Micanopy, County of Alachua and State of Florida for and in Consideration of the natural love and affection which I have and bear unto my infant Children Anna R. McIntosh, Sally May McIntosh and John Edgar McIntosh of the State of South Carolina, at and before the ensealing and delivery of these presents the receipt whereof is hereby acknowledged, have, given, granted, bargained, Sold, and delivered, and by these presents do give, grant, bargain Sell & deliver unto the Said Thomas G.F. Wells and James P. McIntosh all and Singular the following Slaves to wit **A Negro woman named Mary Jane aged twenty years or there abouts & a Mulatto girl named Margaret aged thirteen years or thereabouts** & which Said two Slaves are now in the Said State of South Carolina

Also **a mulatto woman named Martha aged Thirty Six years or thereabouts**
also **a mulatto boy named Sam aged fifteen years or thereabouts**

also **a mulatto Girl named Mary aged Ten years or thereabouts**
also **a mulatto boy named Alexander aged Eight years or thereabouts**
also **a mulatto girl named Isabella aged Six years or thereabouts**
also **a mulatto boy named William aged four years or thereabouts**
also **a mulatto boy named Adam aged three years or thereabouts**
and **a mulatto Girl named Sarah aged one year or thereabouts**

To have and to hold, the Said Slaves and every of them **together with their future increase of the said female Slaves** unto the Said Thomas G.F. Wells and James P. McIntosh, Nevertheless to and for the Sole Separate and only use benefit and behoof of my Said Children Anna R., Sally May, and John Edgar, untill they Shall respectively arrive at the age twenty one years

That is to Say that if Said Anna R. McIntosh upon arriving at the age of twenty one years Shall be entitled to a conveyance from the Sole Trustee of her distributive Share of the Said Slaves, and shall be entitled to receive and take the Same in possession, and So one of my other two said Children, Sally May & John Edgar So soon as they are each of them Shall respectively arrive at the age of twenty one years as aforesaid"

December 5, 1861
From Alachua County Ancient Records
Deed Record E pages 329-330

Henry Meinhard & Bro to Jessie T. Bernard Trustee for Mary E. Scarborough for $1,600: "Received from Jessie T. Bernard, Trustee for Mary E. Scarborough Sixteen hundred Dollars being in full for the purchase of **one Negro Slave named Ellick aged about twenty four years of age warranted Sound** unto the Said Jessie T. Bernard

Trustee for Mary E. Scarborough The right and title of said Slave we warrant and defend against the Claims of all persons whomsoever"

September 3, 1862
Savannah
From Alachua County Ancient Records
Deed Record E page 419

James M. Mills indicted for murder; enslaved people were used as a part of collateral to ensure he showed up for Court: "State of Florida vs James M. Mills - Murder - Continued to next term of the Court and the defendant Recognized in the Sum of Ten thousand dollars for his appearance at the next term of the Court James M. Mills in the Sum of Ten thousand dollars and Twenty five hundred dollars for each of the Security each James Mills Edward Sims Senr & James Kincaid in the sum of Twenty five hundred Dollars each to be levied of their Respective goods, & chattels, Slaves, lands, tenements if default be made in the following Condition that is to say if the said A. A. Maulden Shall be and appear at the next term of the Court to answer to an indictment for Murder, and shall not then depart the Court without leave thereof, then this obligation to be null & void, otherwise to Remain in full force & virtue"

October 17, 1861
From Alachua County Ancient Records
Judgment Record B page 474

John Mobley Sr. to daughter Lucretia McCrorey: "Know all men by these presents, that I John Mobley Senr of the State and district aforesaid in Consideration of the love which I have for my daughter Lucretia McCrorey the wife of James McCrorey of the Same State and district, have given, and granted and by these presents do give and Grant unto my Said daughter the following Negroes Slaves, and mules to wit, **a Negro boy Simon at Two thousand dollars, John at Fifteen hundred Dollars, Aleck at one thousand Dollars,** and Seven Mules and a Waggon and Harness at Eleven hundred and Ninety Dollars To Have and To Hold, the Said Negro Slaves and Mules and wagon, and Harness for the Sole and Separate use of the Said Lucretia McCrorey for and during the term of her natural life and at her death to her issue who may be then living according to the Statutes of distribution and in Case my Said daughter Should die without Children living at the time of her decease and in Case my Said daughter Shall die leaving children at the time of her death, and all of Said Children Shall die under the age of twenty one years of age without having Children living at the time of their death, then in either case the Said property Shall return to me if living and if dead Shall return to my estate and be equally divided among my heirs at law, and distribution according to the Stateuts of distribution."

February 17, 1860 and in the Eighty fourth year of the Independance of the United States of America
State of South Carolina, Fairfield District
From Alachua County Ancient Records
Deed Record E pages 217-218

Richard H. Parker Jr. & Hannah Parker to Wm. F. Smith as collateral for a $500 loan: "Know all men by these presence that we Richard H. Parker Jnr & Hannah Parker of the County and State aforesaid for the better security of the sum of five Hundred dolars by note without Interest from date Due Wm F. Smith or bearer dated 25th Feb 1860 do hear by grant bargain And Sell unto the said Wm F. Smith and his heirs and assigns the following property **1 negro Slave Viz Boy Jerry about sixteen years old** to have and to hold said negro in his possession for ever […] if the said note of Five hundred dolars be paid by us or by our hears or assignes there and in that event this Instrument of writing to be null and void and the negro to be returned to us or our heirs otherwise to be in full force and effect"

February 25, 1860
State of Florida, Alachua Co
From Alachua County Ancient Records
Mortgage Record A page 226

Benjamin W. Powell to Ezekiel P. Hickson as collateral for $23,000 in loans: "This Indenture made on the Seventh day of April in the year of our Lord One thousand Eight hundred & Sixty three between Benjamin W. Powell of the first part and Ezekiel P. Hickson of the Second part both of the County & State aforesaid, Witnesseth that for and in Consideration of the Sum of Twenty three Thousand Dollars to him in hand paid at and before the Sealing and delivery hereof the receipt whereof is hereby acknowledged the said party of the first part has given granted bargained Sold and delivered and by these presents does So give, bargain, Sell and deliver to the said party of the second part the following named and described property To wit **Albert a Negro Man about forty five years old Eliza thirty Seven, Mary thirty five Pianno twenty Eight, Archer twenty Eight, Lett twenty Seven, Sarah twenty one, Clarissa twenty, Larry Sixteen Mary ten, Lee fourteen, Reuben Seven, Amos five, June two, Selena nine, Kizza five, and John two years old, also two small infants names not Known and the Children of Clarissa & Sarah** Also the following described plantation or parcel of land To wit the

South East Quarter of the lot Known as number Eleven of the twenty thousand acre grant containing four hundred and nineteen 96/100 acres more or less, Also two hundred & Sixty two/100 acres in the North West Quarter of the Same Lot Number Eleven making in all Six hundred and Seventy nine & 98/100 acres more or less Situated in the County of Alachua and State of Florida To Have and to hold the afore Sold and Conveyed Slaves to the said party of the Second part & his heirs and assigns and to have and to hold the plantation or parcels of land above Sold and Conveyed together with all and Singular the houses building improvements and appurtinances to the same belonging or in any wise appertaining unto the said property of the Second part his heirs and assigns in fee forever [...] these presents are upon the Express Condition that if the said party of the first part Shall well and truly pay or cause to be paid to the said party of the Second part the following named promisory notes bearing even date with these presents, all bearing Eight Per cent interest from the third day of March A.D. 1863 To wit One note due on the Seventh day of April in the year One thousand Eight hundred & Sixty four One note due & payable on the Seventh day of April in the year One thousand Eight hundred & Sixty five One note due & payable on the Seventh day of April One thousand Eight hundred & Sixty Six, one note Due & payable on the Seventh day of April in the year One thousand Eight hundred & Sixty Seven - One note due and payable on the Seventh day of April One thousand Eight hundred & Sixty Eight, Each of the aforesaid five Several promisory notes being for the Sum of Four thousand Six hundred Dollars with interest as aforesaid Signed by the Said party of the first part & made payable; to the order of the said party of the Second part, Then these presents to be null and void and of none effect otherwise to be and remain in full force & virtue"

April 7, 1863
State of Florida, Alachua County
From Alachua County Ancient Records
Mortgage Record A pages 309-310

Samuel R. Pyles last will and testament: "This is the last will and testament of me Samuel R. Pyles for the due Execution whereof I hereby appoint my wife Ann Pyles, my brother Lewis G. Pyles and Samuel Tucker, my Executors, it being my intention that my wife shall have the whole management and direction of my Estate after my death and the appointment of the others above named, is for the purpose of assisting her, and it being also my intention and I do hereby declare that my wife Ann, shall continue in the possession and management of all my Estate during her natural life-

I direct that previous to all else in this will contained that all my Just debts be paid.

I further will and bequeath that after the death of my wife Ann, that the following distribution of my property shall be made-

To my Brother Lewis, and my Sisterinlaw Martha McCall, one Share cash,

to Samuel Tucker and William Tucker, Children of Jane Tucker, late Jane Pyles, one Share

To the children of Thomas W. Pyles one Share,

to my Sister Rebecca Harn wife of William Harn one Share,

to James Gadsden Dell and Mary Rebecca Dell children of Mary Catherine Dell daughter of William Harn and Rebecca Harn, one share

To Charlotte Helveston my sister one Share,

To James H. Piles and Francis S. Hope one Share each of the real Estate, notes and money, only, and no share of the **Negro property**

I also will and declare and charge all persons connected ***** my will and testament, that **my faithful Servant Harry** ************ of his fidelity shall at the death of my wife, Ann be free * far as the laws of the land permit and that *** shall ** him in securing to him the benefits of this provision, but I do wish and desire that he shall remain in the possession of my wife Ann, to assist her in the care and management of her property,

I also will and declare that **his wife, Dorcas, and her mother Easter** Shall have the benefits of the above provisions and stand and be placed in the same position as Harry

And the said Harry, Dorcas, and Easter, are hereby excepted out of any other provision of this my will"

April 8, 1862
From Alachua County Ancient Records
Will Book B pages 023-024

O. W. Richard indicted for betting at cards; enslaved people were used as part of collateral to ensure he showed up for court: "State of Florida vs O. W. Richard - Playing & Betting at Cards - Continued to next term of the Court and the defendant Recognized in the Sum of Five hundred Dollars for his appearance at the next term of the Court and acknowledged himself to Stand indebted to the State of Florida in the Sum of Five hundred to be levied of their respective goods & chattels Slaves lands & tenements if default be made on the following Condition that is to say if the said O. W. Richard Shall be and appear at the next term of the Court to answer an Indictment for

Playing & betting at Cards and Shall not thence depart the Court without leave thereof then this Obligation to be null & void else to remain in full force & virtue"

April 11, 1864
From Alachua County Ancient Records
Judgment Record B page 515

James M. Richardson to his children: "Know all men by these presents that I James M. Richardson the State and County aforesaid, for and in Consideration of the natural love and affection which I have and bear for and towards my Children herein after named & for the purpose of providing for their future Comfort and independance in life & for divers other good Consideration me moving thereunto, have given granted Sold & Conveyed & by these presents do So give grant Sell and Convey to my said Children herein after respectively named the following named Negro Slaves, "To wit"

To my son John G. Richardson **Frank aged about Eighteen years & Caroline One year old**

to my Son James P. Richardson **Andrew about twenty years old & Virginia One Year old**

to my daughter Mary E. Scott wife of William Scott, **Alick Eighteen years old & Sarah about Seventeen years Old**

to my Son William T. Richardson **Columbus about twelve years old & Amanda about nine years old**

to my Son Henry S. Richardson **Joseph about fourteen years Old & Tennessee about Six years Old,** to my daughter Martha C. Richardson **Daniel about Nine Years Old & Winnie about twenty three years Old;**

& to my Son John G. Richardson James P. Richardson William T. Richardson & Henry Richardson on trust for the use & benefit of my Children Samuel T. Woodward, E. Florence, E. Calhoun P. Willie M. Richardson the following named Slaves "Viz" **Norman about thirty nine years Old, Newton about four years Old Anny about twenty five years old, Robert about four years Old Valentine five years Old, Florida One year Old, June one year Old, Eli Six years Old, Jessie three years old, Ferdinan four years Old, Albert Eight years Old, Minerva forty years Old & Martha about thirteen years old & Jane three months old**

To Have and to Hold the Slaves above named and conveyed unto the Said John G., James P., William T., Henry S. Richardson & Martha C. Richardson & Mary E. Scott respectively during their natural lives free from any debts or Contracts which they may make, & on the condition, that they are not to Sell or dispose of the Said Slaves or their future increase without the consent of me the said James M. Richardson & that on the death of the said children last above named that the Said Slaves Norman, Newton, Anny, Robert, Valentine, Florida June, Eli Jessie, Ferdinan, Albert, Minerva & Martha unto the said John G, James P., William T., & Henry S. Richardson for the uses & trust following Viz to Keep the Said Slaves in common for the benefit & behoof of my children, Samuel T. Woodward E, Florence E., Calhoun P., & Willie M. Richardson during their minority & to convey the Same to the together with their issue & increase share and share alike as they attain the age of twenty one years or marry said conveyance to be so made that the said Shares shall not be liable for the debts or contracts, but shall remain to be divided at their respective deaths to their legal heirs - Provided nevertheless that during the life time of me the said James M. Richardson I shall have the control & management of the said shares last above named

And these presents are made with the express understanding that if any one child portion shall by death or in some other providential way be less than the portions of the others that at my decease such child or children's portion shall be made equal to that of the rest before a division share and share alike is had of my Estate"

May 26, 1862
State of Florida, Alachua County
From Alachua County Ancient Records
Deed Record E pages 406-407

Jessie T. Bernard Trustee for Mary E. Scarborough purchased one enslaved person for $1,600 from Henry Meinhard & Bro in Savannah: "Savannah September 3, 1862 - Received from Jessie T. Bernard Trustee for Mary E. Scarborough Sixteen hundred Dollars being in full for the purchase of **one Negro Slave named Ellick aged about twenty four years of age warranted Sound** unto the Said Jessie T. Bernard Trustee for Mary E. Scarborough The right and title of said Slave we warrant and defend against the Claims of all persons whomsoever"

Recorded Sept 12, 1862
Alachua County
From Alachua County Ancient Records
Deed Record E page 419

William W. Scott to Robert Erwin and Charles S. Hardee merchants as collateral for $10,000 in loans: "This Indenture made and entered into this the twentieth day of April A.D. one thousand eight hundred and Sixty between William W. Scott of the Town of Newnansville Alachua County State aforesaid Merchant party of the first part and Robert Erwin and Charles S. Hardee merchants and factors of Savannah Georgia Partners doing business under the firm name and Style of Erwin & Hardee parties of the Second part Witnesseth That for and in Consideration of the Sum of five Dollars to the party of the first part in hand paid by the parties of the Second part at the time of the executing and delivery of these presents the receipt whereof is hereby acknowledged and also in consideration of the fact that the Said party of the first part is wanting and desirous of obtaining a certain amt of ready money to Carry on his business in the State of Florida aforesaid and the Said parties of the Second part propose to furnish him with funds from time to time to him as he may require not to exceed at any time the Sum of ten thousand $10,000 Dollars in the aggregate therefore in the Consideration of the promises and for the better Securing any Sum or Sums of money So advanced from time to time to him by the Said parties of the Second part to the Said party of the first part which may be found to be due the Said parties of the Second part and which may remain unpaid at any time the Said party of the first part hath bargained Sold and Conveyed and by these presents doth bargain Sell and Convey unto the Said parties of the Second part and to their heirs executors administrators and assigns in fee Simple forever all that certain Tract or parcel of land lying and being Situate in the County of New River State of Florida and Known and Described upon the plat Books of the United States Land office at Newnansville Florida as the South half (S 1/2,) of the Southeast quarter (SE 1/4) Section Six (S.6) and the Northwest quarter of the North West quarter (NW 1/4) of NW 1/4) and the northeast quarter of the South west 1/4 (NE 1/4 of SW 1/4) and the north west quarter NW 1/4 of Section Seven and the South east quarter of the South west quarter (SE 1/4 of SW 1/4) of Section (6) Township Six (T6) Range 18 East (R.18,E,) Containing three hundred and Sixty (360) Acres more or less also all that certain

Tract or parcel of land lying and being Situate in the County of Alachua State of Florida and Known and described as the South East quarter and the South half of the North East quarter and the East half of the South West quarter of Section thirteen and the north half of the North East quarter Section twenty four and the North half of the North west quarter Section (24) Twenty four and the North west quarter of the South west quarter of Section thirteen Township Seven Range Eighteen also certain Town lots in the Town of Waldo County and State aforesaid and Known and described upon the plat of said Town as lots Numbered one and two (1 & 2) in Block number ten (10) And lots numbered one and two (1 & 2) in Block number Sixteen with Store house upon the Same with all the appurtenances Thereunto belonging or in any wise appertaining and all the right Title Interest of the party of the first part of in or to the Same with free egress and ingress to the Same at all times by the Said parties of the Second part, and also the following described Negro property to wit, **Abram thirty five years of age, John Nineteen years of age, Peter Nineteen years of age, Dave forty years of age, Dianna Thirty years of age, Georgian fifteen years of age, Marth Eleven years of age, Gilbert Six years of age, Jim two years, Betty a girl nineteen years of age, Neal Seven years of age, and Strong thirteen years of Age** Also the following described personal property One Six mule wagon and harness for the Same one black horse mule Jack one black mare mule Beck bay horse mule Mike Sorrel horse mule Sam and Grey mare mule Ginny one Sorrel mare Sally one Grey mare Polly one bay mare Doll one Sorrell horse Dav one Stallion horse Calhoun Seventy five head of Stock Cattle more or less And fifty head of hogs And also Certain Stocks of Goods Consisting of goods Wares & merchandise of whatever description in Store in the Town of Newnansville and in the Town of Waldo in Alachua County aforesaid also the books of accounts and Bills receivable arising from the Sales of goods in Store at this time or that may be purchased and placed in and Sold out of the Stores of the Said party of the first part during the time he may be indebted for any monies that may be advanced in accordance with this agreement by the Said parties of the second part We the party of the first part and Said party of the first part covenants and agrees to and with the Said parties of the Second part that he is seized in fee Simple of the above granted premises and that he is possessed absolutely of the personal property there conveyed and that he will and his heirs and assigns shall warrant, and defend the same to the parties of the second part against all claims Whatsoever Nevertheless, and these presents are upon this Condition if the party of the first part shall well and Truly pay or cause to be paid all monies found to be due the Said parties of the Second part for advances made during the current year, and from year to year as long as this agreement between the parties may continue Then and in that case This Indenture to be null and Void and of none effect against the Said party of the first part or any claiming or to claim by through or under him or them"

April 20, 1860
State of Florida, Alachua County
From Alachua County Ancient Records
Mortgage Record A pages 233-235

William W. Scott to Robert Erwin and Charles S. Hardee merchants as collateral for $5,000 in loans: "This Indenture made and entered into this the Twentyeth day of April A.D. 1860 Between William W. Scott of the Town of Newnansville Alachua County & State of Florida Merchant party of the first part and Robert Erwin and Charles S. Hardee Merchants and Factors the firm name & Style of Erwin & Hardee parties of the Second part Witnesseth that for and in Consideration of the Sum of Five dollars to the party of the first part in hand paid by the parties of the Second part at the time of the Execution and delivery of these presents, the receipt whereof is hereby acknowledged and also in Consideration of the fact that the Said party of the first part is wanting and desirous of obtaining a Certain amount of Money to Carry on his business in the State of Florida aforesaid and the Said parties of the Second part proposes to furnish him with funds from time to time to him as he may be given not to Exceed Five thousand dollars ($5000) in the aggregate therefore in Consideration of the premises and for the better Securing any Sum or Sums of Money So advanced from time to time to him by the Said parties of the Second part to the Said party of the first part, which may found to be due the Said parties of the Second part & which may remain unpaid at any time the Said party of the first part hath bargained, Sold and Conveyed and by these doth bargain, Sell and Convey unto the Said parties of the Second part and to their heirs Executors & administrators and assigns in fee Simple forever, all that certain tract or parcel of Land lying and being in the County of New River State of Florida and Known and described in the plat Book of the United States Land office at Newnansville Fla. as the E 1/2 of SE 1/4 of the SW 1/4 of Sc 4 only and the SE 1/4 of the SE 1/4 Section two 2 & the NE 1/4 of the NE 1/4 Section 11 and the N 1/2 of the NE 1/4 & the SE 1/4 of NW 1/4 and the S 1/2 of the NE 1/4 Section Twelve all lying and being in Township Six S Range 19 E Containing five hundred & twenty acres more or less, Also the following described Negroes to wit, **Ginny aged Thirty years old, Gabe Ten years old, Lewis two years old, Henry twelve years old, Doctor Fourteen years of age**, Also one Bay mare Fanny, One Bay Mare Flora & one open top Buggy & harness Nevertheless, and these presents are upon this Condition of the party of the first part Shall well and truly pay or Cause to be paid all monies found to be due the Said parties of the Second part for advances made the Current year, and from year to year as long as this agreement among the parties may continue then & in that Case this Indenture to be null & void and of no effect against the parties of the first part or Claiming or to Claim by through or under him or them"

April 20, 1860
State of Florida, Alachua County
From Alachua County Ancient Records
Mortgage Record A pages 257A-258

William W. Scott marrying Mary E. Strobhar, itemizing what Mary Strobhar is bringing into the marriage including enslaved people: "This Indenture made this 17th day of June A. D. One thousand eight hundred and Sixty two, between William W. Scott of the County & State aforesaid of the first part, and Mary E. Strobhar of the same place of the second part -- Witnesseth, That Whereas a Marriage intended to be Solemnized between the said parties of the first part & Second part and the said party of the Second part is possessed of Certain property Consisting of Slaves, monies, Chattels, Choices in action, rights & Credits accruing from the Estate of her deceased husband Noble H. Strobhar which She now holds and enjoys in her own right & title -- Now therefore, in Consideration of the premises it is hereby covenanted and agreed to, by the said party of the first part, that if after his marriage with the said party of the Second part, She Shall fail at her death, to have a child or children by him the said party of the first part, then and in that case, all of the aforesaid property, which She now holds and possesses, described in the annexed Schedule marked (A) together with all the increase arising therefrom shall go to, and be owned possessed and enjoyed by her son Noble James Strobhar for his full benefit & behoof -- And the said party of the first part, and the said party of the Second part mutually freely and voluntarily, agree to accept and abide the Covenants herein Enumerated, which shall take effect from and after the Solemnization of said Marriage"

June 17, 1862
State of Florida, County of Alachua
From Alachua County Ancient Records
Deed Record E pages 498-499

William W. Scott to James G. Cooper for $10,000: "Know all Men by these presents that William W. Scott of the County of Alachua

State of Florida party of the first part for and in Consideration of the Sum of Ten Thousand Dollars to me in hand paid by James G. Cooper of the Same place party of the Second part the receipt whereof is hereby acknowledged have bargained & Sold and by these presents do grant and Convey unto the party of the Second part his Executors administrators and assigns the following described property to wit **One Negro Man named Abram Forty Eight years Old, One man Dave Forty five years of age, One Man Peter Twenty years of age, One man John Twenty years of age, One Boy Doctor fifteen years of age, One boy String Fourteen years of age, One Boy Andrew Twelve years of age, One boy Wesley Eight years of age, One Boy Philip Eight years of age, One Boy Gibbut Eight years of age, One Boy James Three years of age, One Boy Jessie three years of age, One Boy Neal Eight years of age, One Boy Henry Thirteen years of age, One Woman Diannah Forty years of age, One woman Ginny Forty years of age, One Girl Georgeanna Seventeen years of age One Girl Martha Sixteen years of age, One Girl Martha ann Twelve years of age, One girl Clarissa One Year old** To Have and to hold the above described Negroes Slaves unto the said party of the Second part his heirs Executors administrators and assigns forever"

February 17, 1863
From Alachua County Ancient Records
Deed Record E page 466

William W. Scott and wife Mary E. Scott to Amelia C. Scott and Martha J. R. Scott for $2,500: "Know all men by these presents that I William W. Scott and Mary E. Scott of the County of Alachua and State of Florida parties of the first part for and in Consideration of the Sum of Two and Five thousand Dollars to us in hand paid by Amelia C. Scott and Martha J. R. Scott of the Same place parties of the Second part, the receipt whereof is hereby acknowledged have bargained and Sold and by these presents do grant and Convey unto the parties of the Second part their Executors administrators and assigns the following described personal property to wit **One Negro man named Abram Forty Eight years of age, One man named Dave Forty five years of age, One man named Peter Twenty years of age, One man John twenty years of age, One boy Doctor Fifteen years of age, One Boy Strong fourteen years of age, One Boy Andrew twelve years of age, One Boy Wesley, Eight years of age, One Boy Philip Eight years of age, One Boy Gilbert Eight years of age, One Boy James Three years of age, One Boy Jessie Three years of age, One Boy Henry thirteen years of age, One Woman Dianna Forty five years of age, One Woman Ginny Forty five years of age, One Girl Georgeann Seventeen years of age, One Girl Martha Sixteen years of age One Girl Marthann Twelve years of age One Girl Ten years old** To Have and to Hold the above described Negroes Slaves unto the Said parties of the Second part their heirs Executors and administrators and assigns forever"

December 9, 1863
From Alachua County Ancient Records
Deed Record E page 571

Laura Standley married John B. Dell. This is an itemization of what Laura Standley inherited from her father's estate: "Whereas there has been a marriage had and soluminized between John B. Dell of Alachua County Florida and Laura Standley daughter of the late John B. Standley decd. & Penelope L. Standley and whereas I Penelope Standley have been appointed Guardian for the said Laura and desirous that the estate which was received from John B. Standley Estate deceased and which she may be entitled to be settled upon her and was to her benefit under the statue of the state of Florida The folowing schedule of property is desirious by me as her Gardian to be inventored and recorded for the purpose therein expresed according to the statute in sutch case mode & provided viz the amount land as appraised $48,114.14, Negroes as apparaised $32,600.00

Names **Henry, Hannah, Milly, Simon, Hannah, Calley, Steve, Joe, Bill, Caroline, Robert, Bill senr, Harriat, Ame, Rebecca, Ammous, America, Carlina, Elcey, Alford, George, Simeon, Sarah, Mary, June George Tim Richard Sarah Davis Rhebin, Isaak, Joe Maria Tom Monky Jane William Harry Hettie Jake"**

April 10, 1861
From Alachua County Ancient Records
Deed Record E page 277

J. Murray Stewart Last Will and Testament: "In the name of God Amen. I, James Murray Stewart of Alachua County State of Florida, being in infirm health but of sound and disposing mind and memory do make publish, and declare this my last will and testament in the manner following that is to say - first I commend my soul to God who gave it; and my body to the earth to be decently interred

It is my will that all of my just debts and the charges of my funeral be paid and discharged by my executor hereinafter named and appointed, out of my estate, as soon as conveniently may be after my decease

I give, devise, bequeath and dispose of all my estate real and personal after the payment of my debts & funeral charges as aforesaid in the following manner;

One half of all my property both real and personal of which I may die seized and possessed, I give bequeath and devise to my loved wife Sarah Annis Stewart during her natural life if my said wife Sarah Annis does not marry again, but if she should contract matrimony then said property then bequeathed to her, to go in fee simple to my child James Murray Stewart Junior or if my said wife should not marry a second time and my said child should survive her then said property to be and remain to my said child, James Murray Stewart junior, in fee simple, and if my said child should not survive the marriage of his mother as aforesaid, or if she does not marry again if he should not out-live her, then my said property to be equally divided between my brother Thomas O. Stewart and my sisters Matilda S. Brown and Eliza Mary Stewart or their children pro stipes my said brother and sisters taking the place of my said child if he is not alive when the contingences occur, if they do occur which are sought to be provided for as above

The remaining half of all my property real and personal, I give and devise to my son James M. Stewart Junior in fee simple but should he die without marriage or having issue and his mother survives him without having married a second time, then said property herein bequeathed to my son to go to his mother my said wife, and then with remainder *** to my said brother and sisters or their children as aforesaid my said brother and sisters or their children as aforesaid to be the heirs and remainder now of and to my said son James M. Stewart Junior to all the property herein and hereby bequeathed and devised to him, except as hereinbefore expressed in every contingency wherein his mother my said wife cannot take in accordance with the provisions of this my will, as herein before set forth or in the event my said son does not leave a child or children, or a wife him surviving

It is my will that **my negro man slave Ben** as an acknowledgement of his faithful service rendered me, be set free or manumited if the same can be done consistent with the laws of Florida his freedom to take effect the first of January 1865 or if the laws of Florida do not sanction the setting free of slaves, I then desire that my executor endeavor to have a special act passed by the General Assembly of Florida, manumiting Ben

And if that cannot be done, I desire that he may be considered the property of my son (additional to his one half share of my property as aforesaid), and that in that event, Ben be permitted to have the benefit of all his labor for himself I hereby nominate, constitute and appoint my trusted friend Joseph M. Arnow to be the Executor of this my last Will and testament"

July 4, 1864
From Alachua County Ancient Records
Will Book B pages 054-057

Jacob G. Stroble to Philip Dell and William B. Wimberley as collateral for $2,500 in loans: "This Indenture made this the Second day of April in the Year of our Lord One thousand Eight hundred & Sixty between Jacob G. Stroble of the County of Alachua and State of Florida of the first part, and Philip Dell and William B. Wimberly of the Same County & State of the Second part Witnesseth that the Said party of the first part for and in Consideration of the Sum of Two Thousand five hundred Dollars to him in hand paid at and before the Sealing and delivery of these presents the receipt whereof is hereby acknowledged have bargained Sold Aliened remised released Conveyed and delivered and by these presents do bargain, Sell, remise release, Convey Confirm and deliver unto the Said parties of the Second part and to their heirs Executors administrators and assigns forever all and Singular the following described property: To wit one certain **Negro woman Slave named Mary, of Black Complexion and aged about Twenty years** Seven head of Horses, the Same which are now in my possession, Forty head of Cattle now in my mark and brand together with my entire Stock of hogs and also all my right, title interest and estate, claim and demand of in and to Certain lots in the town of Waldo in the County and State aforesaid, described in the plat or plan of said town as follows to wit: Lot No Three of Block No Sixteen, together with all my interest in the adjoining lots in Said Block, and any and all lots in Said town - To Have and to Hold all and Singular the Said granted and described premises with the appurtinances thereunto belonging or in anywise appertaining unto them the Said parties of the Second part their heirs Executors administrators and assigns forever Provided Nevertheless, and these presents are upon the Express Condition Whereas the Said party of the first part has for a valuable Consideration executed and delivered to the Said parties of the Second part his Certain promisory note for the Sum Two Thousand five hundred dollars bearing even date herewith with interest at the rate of eight per Cent, Now if the Said party of the first part, to this Indenture has Certain attorney, administrator or Executor Shall pay or Cause to be paid to the Said parties of the second part heirs Executors administrators or assigns the Said Sum of Money Mentioned in the said promissory note with the interest thereon according to the tenor thereof at maturity, and Shall further pay all necessary costs and charges for the foreclosure of this Instrument if the Same Shall be done, then this obligation to be null & void else to remain in full force & virtue"

April 2, 1860
From Alachua County Ancient Records
Mortgage Record A pages 247-249

Free man of color Joseph Valentine (about 22 years old) sold himself to Phillip Dell as an enslaved person: "Then came a free man of color aged about 22 years by Andrew Robb, Judge of probate for said County, who declares that he desires to sell himself to Phillip

Dell as a Slave, and desires the Court to Examine him whether the act is done of his own free will & accord or not

Andrew Robb Judge of probate for said County, Whereupon the Court ordered the said Joseph Valentine to be brought before it & appointed E. M. Graham Solicitor to represent said negro, & the said Joseph Valentine negro as aforesaid having been brought into Court & Examined, as to whether the act of selling himself to Phillip Dell was voluntarily or not declared that he did so without fear or compulsion & of his free will & accord, Whereupon it was declared by the Court that Joseph Valentine aged about 22 years is the property & slave of Phillip Dell & subject to his order & control & to the laws of the State of Florida governing Slaves he having made a judicious choice of a master […] Phillip Dell & Joseph Valentine for himself waives the four week notice requisite under the act to allow persons of african Descent to select their own master"

October 14, 1862
In the Circuit Court for the Suwannee
Circuit Alachua County Fall Term 1862
From Alachua County Ancient Records
Judgment Record B page 487

Joseph J. Warren to Mirome Hague: "Know all men, that Joseph J. Warren of the County & State aforesaid for and in Consideration of the Sum of One dollar to him in hand paid by Mirome Hague wife of James Hague of the same County & State, as well as for the esteem and affection of the Said Joseph J. Warren for the said Mirome Hague doth hereby Grant, bargain, Sell and deliver unto the said Mirome Hague her heirs and assigns forever all the personal and real property hereinafter described to wit Five head of Horses and One Mule now owned by the said Joseph J. Warren, and all the hogs and Cattle belonging to the said Joseph J. Warren having the following marks & brands which Said marks is a Crop and half Crop in one Ear and in the other Ear a Crop & half Crop and Split and the brand this "JH3" also all the waggons and farming utensils on the place now occupied by James Hague, Also **the following Negroes Slaves for life Negro Man Adam aged about Fifty Seven years of age Negro Woman named Dorcas aged about forty Seven years of age Negro Man named Windsor aged about Thirty Seven years Negro Girl Martha aged about Nine years,** also the following Real Estate, to wit S1/2 Lots 6 no and Two lots no Six N1/2 of Lot No. Seven of Section Thirty three and S1/2 Lot No three and Lot No Four of Section Thirty four T8 SR 19E Containing Three hundred & fifteen acres and Twenty Six hundreds of an acre as per returns made by US Survey to the land Office at Newnansville Florida together with all the privileges and appurtinances as to the same belonging, To Have and To Hold the above described personal and real Estate, **together with the increase** of the Said personal property to the said Mirome Hague her heirs and assigns forever. The grantor hereby Covenants with the granter her heirs and assigns that the title so conveyed is clear, free, and unencumbered, and that he will warrant and forever defend the same against all claims what Soever"

December 13, 1861
State of Florida, County of Alachua
From Alachua County Ancient Records
Deed Record E pages 334-335

John Whitaker to his sons Duncan Whitaker, Thomas Whitaker, and John Whitaker Jr. - Moved 103 enslaved people to his plantation in Alachua County Florida: "Whereas I John Whitaker of the district and State aforesaid have removed to my plantation in the State of Florida in Alachua County a large number of Negroes Slaves divided to my wife Margaret Whitaker from the last will & testament of her Father Duncan McRae and her mother the late Mary McRae to the said Margaret McRa and her mother the late Mary McRa to the said Margaret my wife for her life free from the debts Contracts and Interest of her husband to her Sole and Separate use and at and immediately upon her death to the issue of her body living at the time of her death, And Whereas I am advised by Competent legal authority in the State of Florida that in order to hold the said Negroes under the terms of the said wills which regarding as a duty I greatly desire to do it is necessary that I express the same by deed now in consideration of the above,

Know all men by these presents that I John Whitaker of the District and State aforesaid do hereby bargain Sell and deliver unto Duncan Whitaker Thomas Whitaker and John Whitaker my Sons their Executors & administrators the following Negroes Slaves with their issue & increase from the first of June last, So far as I have any right or Claim thereto, now numbering One hundred & three, Viz **Hamet, Jane Maggy and her two children Bennett Miles Green, Martha, Nancy, Judy, Lyddy, Lucy, Isaac, Simon, Tom, Abby, Becky, Emily, Lim, Isaac Aggy, Ned, Susannah, Paddy, Martha, Jacob, Amy, Bidy, IsMat, Phillis, Milly, Derry, Sylva, Forty, Adam, Forty Nancy, Nara, Venus, Nancy, Amy, Peggy, Blucher, Dick, Ballard, Cretia Doby, Harry, Ceasar, Hector, Benj, Frank, Julia, Dinah, Hector, Wili, Williams, Anber, Hannah, Hatcher, Margaret, Daniel, John, Amally & Child, Baltus, Anber, Hannah, Isaac, George, Dick, Walker, Bridget, Thomas Hetty & two children, Peggy & Frank, Jess, Preston, Bidy, Grace, Oliver, John Sandy, Maria, Job, Paul, Aleck, George, Unity, Patrick, Clarison, Fanny, Lane, Hannah Lane, Becky, Sip, Sandy, Brickan, Scipio, Cain, Hester, George with their issue and increase** to Have & to Hold the said Negroes Slaves to the said Duncan Whitaker, Thomas Whitaker, & John Whitaker, or the Survivors of them, their heirs Exors or admrs, when this special trust and Confidence that they hold the same to the Sole & Separate use of the said Margaret R. Whitaker for and during the term of her natural life only to be in no case Subject to her debts contracts liabilities or disposition of her husband, and from & immediately after her decease, to her children living at the time of her death share and Share alike to them, & their heirs forever and in all respects exactly as provided in the last will and testament of the said Duncan McRa and Mary McRa intending hereby, neither to make nor attempt any change whatsoever, but merely perfecting in Florida the tenor by which the said property has always been held by me"

July 27, 1862 & in the Eighty Seventh Year of her Security & Independance of
South Carolina & in the Second Year of the Confederacy
State of South Carolina, Kershaw District
From Alachua County Ancient Records
Deed Record E pages 454-456

James H. Williams to Florida A. Standley to solemnize their intended marriage and itemizing what Florida A. Standley is bringing into the marriage: "This Indenture made this Twenty Seventh day of April Anno Domini One thousand Eight hundred & Sixty one Between James H. Williams of the County & State aforesaid of the first part and Florida A. Standley of the Same place of the Second part Witnesseth That a marriage is intended to Solmnized between the said parties of the first & Second parts and the Said party of the Second part is posesed and Seized of Certain property consisting in lands Tenements - Negr Slaves, Monies *** in Active right & Credits- Which she now holds and posesses in her own right & title,

Now therefore in Considerating of the premises it is hereby covenanted and agreed by the said party of the first Part with the Said party of the Second part that from and after the Solumnization of Said Marriage the Said party of the Second part Shall continue To hold said property in the following manner to wit, All property real and personal, Slaves chases in Action, monies, rights, and credits which the Said party of the Second part is now Seized and posesed or which She may at any time hereafter become possessed after and during Coveanture with the Said party of the first part and all the increase arising from any of the Said property whatsover Shall continue to abide and rest in Said property as Separatly Solely absolutely and perfectly as if She were Sole and unmarried

And it is further agreed and Covenanted by the Said party of the first part with the Said Party of Second part that the Said party of the Second part Shall have the Sole and Exclusive Power after the Solmnizatin of said marriage and during Covanture to Sell Convey or transfer any of said property which She many hold, or which She may hereafter hold during Covanture with Said party having the Same power over Said property, as she had while a Single woman,

And it is further agreed and Covenanted by the Said Party of the first Part with the Said party of the Second Part, that he Shall not have power to dispose of, Sell transfer or convey any of said property which the Said property of the Second part now holds or which may hereafter come to her posesion or any of the increase of Said property at anytime after the Solemnization of said marriage and during coventure with Said party,

And the Said party of the First part and the Said party of the Second part hereby Mutually freely and voluntarily agree to Stand and abide the Several Covenants enumerated in this Indenture

Schedule of Negro property belonging to Florida A. Standley the Second party named in this Schedule **Charity aged twenty years, Mitchell aged fifteen years, Anderson age two years, Henritta age three years August age twenty nine years Eliza age twenty one Amy age four years Berrin age two years, Joe age twenty four years Metez age Sixteen years Bawby age forty nine years Anne aged thirty eight years Richard aged twenty years Francis age fifteen years Walter age Sixteen years, Matilda aged eight** years Mary Anne thirty fore years, Sophia age Sixteen years Jackson age twenty years Friday age twenty fore years"

April 27, 1861
State of Florida, County of Alachua
From Alachua County Ancient Records
Deed Record E pages 284-286

Theophilus Williams to Philip Dell as collateral for a $2,877 loan:
"This Indenture made the Thirteenth day of March in the year of our Lord One thousand Eight hundred and Sixty Between Theophilus Williams of the County of Alachua & State of Florida of the first part and Philip Dell of said County and State of the Second part, Whereas the said Theophilus Williams in and by a certain promissory note in writing under his hand bearing even date here with promised to pay unto the said Philip Dell or bearer the Sum of Twenty Eight hundred & Seventy Seven dollars One day after date thereof for value received with Eight per Cent interest thereon from date as in and by said note Specified being thereunto had more particularly appears, Now this Indenture Witnesseth that the said Theophilus Williams as well for and in Consideration of the aforesaid Sum of Twenty Eight hundred & Seventy Seven dollars and for better Securing the payment thereof with its interest unto the Said Philip Dell his heirs Executors administrators and assigns in discharge of the said mentioned and recited promissory note as of the further Sum of One dollar to him in hand paid by the Said Philip Dell at and before the Sealing and delivery hereof the Receipt Whereof is hereby acknowledged, hath granted bargained sold released and Confirmed and do by these presents grant bargain Sell release and Confirm unto the said Philip Dell his heirs and assigns the following Negro Slaves To wit **Primas a man aged forty years black Mary a woman black aged about thirty years and her three children Andrew a boy about Six years old Martha**

girl about Four years Old yellow complexion Paris about four months old black. To have and to hold the above named Slaves unto the said Philip Dell his heirs and assigns forever, And the said Theophilus Williams for himself his heirs Executors and administrators doth Covenant and agree to and with the said Philip Dell his heirs and assigns by these present the title to the Said Slaves above Conveyed forever Provided always Nevertheless that if the said Theophilus Williams his heirs Executors or administrators Shall and do well and truly pay or Cause to be paid unto the said Philip Dell his heirs Executors administrators or assigns the above said sum of twenty Eight hundred & Seventy Seven dollars on the day and time hereinbefore mentioned and appointed for payment thereof with interest thereof from date at Eight Per Cent per annum according to the tenor of the said promissory note without any fraud or further delay and without any deduction defalcation or abatement to be made of any thing for or in respect of any Taxes charges or assessment Whatsoever as well costs charges and expences either in law or Equity as may be incurred in the foreclosure of this mortgage or the Collection of the said sum of money and interest as in the Said promissory note mentioned then & from thenceforth as well this present Indenture and the Slaves hereby Conveyed as the said promissory note shall also determine and become absolutely void and null to all intents and purposes anything herein before Contained to the Contrary in any wise notwithstanding otherwise it is to remain in full force & virtue

March 13, 1860
From Alachua County Ancient Records
Deed Record E
Pages 167-168

Lemuel Wilson indicted for betting at cards; enslaved people were used as part of collateral to ensure he showed up for court: "State of Florida vs Lemuel Wilson - Playing & Betting at Cards - Continued to next term of this Court and the defendant Recognized in the Sum of Five hundred for his appearance at the next term of the Court and acknowledged himself to Stand indebted to the State of Florida in the Sum of Five hundred Dollars to be levied of their respective goods & chattels, Slaves lands & tenements if default be made on the following Condition that is to say if the Said Lemuel Wilson Shall be and appear at the next term of the Court to answer an Indictment for Playing & betting at Cards and Shall not thence depart the Court without leave thereof then this Obligation to be null & void otherwise to remain in full force & virtue"

April 11, 1864
From Alachua County Ancient Records
Judgment Record B page 515

W. B. Wimbly to Sam R. Pyles as collateral for a $500 loan: "This Indenture made this the Twenty Seventh day of March and the year of our Lord one thousand Eight hundred and Sixty Between W B Wimbly of Alachua and State of Florida of the first part and Sam R Pyles of the same place of the Second part Witness that - the Said W B Wimbly for and in consideration of the Sum of five hundred Dollars to him in hand paid by the said Samuel R Pyles as well as for the Securing of the payment of a note bearing after described has granted bargained Sold, delivered transferred and conveyed And by these presents doth grant bargain Sell deliver transfer and convey unto the Said Samuel R Pyles his heirs and assigns **one woman name Pheby her two children Jane and Patsy age of Pheby about Twenty two years old Jane four years old Patsy three years old** to have and to hold the above described Negroes above named to the Said Sam R Pyles his heirs and assigns forever and the Said W B Wimbly will and heirs executors administrators Shall the Said Negroes grant bargain Sell to the Said Sam R Pyles heirs executors and administrators forever Warrant and defend by virtue of these presents and the said W B Wimbly his heirs executors and administrators Shall warrant the Said Negroes to the Said Sam R Pyles his heirs executors and administrators warrant and defend provided nevertheless that if the Said W B Wimbly his heirs executors or administrators Shall pay unto the Said Sam R Pyles his heirs executors administrators or assigns to pay amount of a certain promissory note made by the Said William B Wimbly payable to the Said Sam R Pyles or bearer bearing date with these presents and due January first Eight hundred Sixty one for the sum of five hundred and eighteen Dollars Now if the Said W B Wimbly his heirs Executors administrators Shall pay unto the Said Sam R Pyles his heirs executors administrators or assigns the notes above mentioned and described January first -Eighteen hundred and Sixty one with all expenses incurred by the said Sam R Pyles collecting the Same then as well as this Deed and the above described promissory note to be utterly void otherwise to remain in full force"

March 27, 1860
From Alachua County Ancient Records
Mortgage Record A page 236

John L. Yongue last will and testament: "I, John L. Yongue of Fairfield Dist in the said state being of sound and disposing mind and memory do Testament Hereby revoking all other and former will, at any time by me made

1. I give devise and bequeath to my Grandson, Charles J. Bell and his heirs a tract of land formerly known as the Ross** place containing one hundred and fifty acres, more or less lying in Chester District on

the waters of little River and Rocky Creek and bounded by lands of James Yongue Est of Wm. Robinson Charles J. Bell and others

2. I give to my daughter Nancy L. Whitlock the wife of Franklin Whitlock, in addition to the property I have already given her the following negro slaves **Big Jim and his wife Margaret Dave, Jim, West, William, Nancy, George Jim, Jean McDaniel and her two sons, John and David, together with their future increase** to the sole and separate use of the Said Nancy L. Whitlock for life and at her death such issue born of her subsequent to the date of these presents as may be then living in the proportions prescribed by the Statutes for the distribution of intestates Estates, but if she should die without leaving issue born of her Subsequent to this date, then it is my will that said Slaves and their increase shall revert to my Estate and be divided equaly among my Surviving grandchildren provided however that the issue of my deceased grandchildren should there be any such Shall represent their parent and take the Share to which Such parent would have been entitled if living

3. I give devise and bequeath to my Son Henery W. Yongue his Heirs and assigns a tract of land containing five hundred and Seventy two acres more or less, Situate in Fairfield District on the waters of the Wateree Creek and Little River to include the settlement where he now lives, the line of which land to commence where a white oak corner once Stood immediately on the present bed of the said road running thence a direct line to a spring Known as the Thompson Spring, which said spring is a corner to his land, thence running down the spring branch by a line made by G. H. Miller Deputy Surveyor the 17th day of October 1857 following its different courses until it reaches land belonging to the Estate of David Gillard, thence running South along Gillards line, following all its courses to land belonging to Elizabeth Caldwell, thence running along Said Caldwells line until it reaches Burr Cochrells land, thence along Burr Cochrells land to land belonging to George W. Corder thence along the line of said Corder and Mrs Stirlings following its different courses to the beginning corner to C. S. Phennys land thence along said Phennys line following its different

Courses to the beginning corner - ****** tract of land Known as the Calhoun Land containing one hundred acres more or less situate in Fairfield district on the waters of Dampers Creek bound by lands of G. W. Corder, Robt. G. Cameron Mrs. Stirling and others also the following Negro Slaves, viz **Ann and her three children viz Charlotte, Dick and West, Sam Senr, Lucy Harriet, Henry Jnr. Noah, Joe Jacob Ellison, Snavy Sam & Louisa and her three children Dick, Jacob and Moses**

4. I give and bequeath to my daughter Mary E. Brice the following Negro slaves, **Dick, Adam, Ormond, Leathy, Mariah, Jacob, David, Thomas, Sam Bob Senr. Cinda Sarah, Hariet, Charles, Milly, Sinas, and their future issue** for her sole and seperate use for life, and at her death the said Slaves and their increase I give and bequeath to her issue living at the time of her death to be divided among them in the following way and manner viz to divide them off according to their true value, giving to each one of her Sons three hundred dollars **** more than the daughters

5. I divide and bequeath to the children of my son John C. C. Yongue, he having deceased previous to the Execution of the my last will and testament, viz to Mary my Granddaughter and Margaret her Sister one tract of land containing one Thousand acres more or less Situate in Fairfield District Situate on the waters of Wateree and little River in the district of Fairfield, bounded by land belonging to Mr. Gillard, H. W. Yongue C. L. Phenny Mrs. Polly Robinson Misses Swanns, Samuel Stirling Senr and others also all my Plantation tools of every description, all my Houses hold and Kitchen furniture, except such as may be hereafter bequeathed, all my Stock Neat cattle except four cows and calves to be Selected by my wife Sarah for her own use and all my mules as above the following negro Slaves viz **Isaac and Lina his wife and three children Phillis, Big Harry, Clarisa** (unreadable) which proper I allow to be Kept on the plantation for the sole and Sep use of my said two Granddaughters viz Mary and Margaret to pay the expence of their boarding, cloth and education until one of them Marries or arrives to the age of maturity and then to be equaly divided

between them, but if either of them should die before they Marry or arrive to maturity age, then the share of above named to decend to the surviving one, or the both should die before the arrive to years of ma*** leaving no issue, then their property to revert to my Estate and be equaly divided among the Whole of my Grandchildren

6. previous my marriage with my present wife, I, covenanted to provide for in the event of her Surviving me, an amount of three hundred dollars pr. annum, in accordance with Such contract, I, will and direct my Executors hold as an investment for this purpose a bond ** me be the Estate of David Brice, John L. Ya*** and G. H. Miller, upon which there is now principal and interest about the sum of Eight hundred dollars worth amounting to about four thousand dollars ($4000), now I will and direct that these investments or the proceeds thereof Should the *** paid by the respective ob*****, or if it be deemed pa** by my Executors, or necessary to call them in, be, by my Executors and that from the proceeds there the annual sum of three hundred dollars be paid my wife, surviving me for her life upon her death the Surplus of the investment, and the surplus of in*** to be divided equaly between my Grandsons, *** Charles J. Bell, Yongue Brice, David Brice**** Edmon John L. Yongue, son of my son Henry ** ***** John (unreadable) viz, **June and Eddy and Mariah with her future increase** the two former viz, June and Eddy I bequeath to her for life and the Girl Merah with her future increase I give and bequeath to her absolutely. I further wish it under*** and hereby devise and bequeath to my wife Sarah as her inheritance and possession, otherways than through me especialy if that can be said her portions, Linda included coming from her fathers Estate, I also bequeath to my wife four cows and calves such as she may choose or make choice of, three beds, bedsteads and furniture such ones as she may choose together with the Household furniture pertaining to the room which she and I usualy occupy, also one large Sorrel horse for which I paid one hundred and Sixty five dollars the provision made by marriage contract and herein for my wife is of course in lieu of Dower or other claims by her in or to my Estate or any part thereof.

8. as long as daughter-in-law Mrs. Jane Yongue widow of my Son John remains a widow and her two children remain infants I do not intend that they shall be held responsible for the rent of the tract of land hereby given to her children

9. and as to the Estate real and personal which I own in the State of Florida in Alachua County, I will and direct that my land containing twelve hundred and fifty seven and more, be sold by my executors on a credit of one two and three years equal annual instalments with intrust from the day of sale and to be sold at such time as my executors or a majority of them as may qualify may deem expedient the purchase money being secure in the equal manner, Also that the four lots of land that I hold in town of Gainesville and all my personal Estate not herein before specialy bequeathed and finaly disposed of be (unreadable) as usual and upon the funds so raised by sales ordered in this clause I, charge all the debts due by me at my decease, all expences incured in administering and setteling of my estate of whatsoever Kind and of the proceeds I bequeath to my daughter Nancy L. Whitlock the sum of one Thousand dollars $1000 to my Son Henry W. Yongue the sum of four Thousand Dollars-$4000 to my daughter Mary E. Brice, two Thousand $2000-To my Grandsons viz, J. Yongue Brice, Charles J. Bell, David J. Brice, Edward Brice John L. Yongue Son of my son Henry each the sum of One Thousand dollars, and to each of my Granddaughters, viz, Mary Donnovant, Laura J. Brice, Margaret F. Brice, Elonira M. Brice Harriet Yongue Mary Yongue and Margaret Yongue, Eight hundred dollars and to my wife Sarah Yongue the sum of Eight hundred dollars,

10. all the rest and residue of my Estate I give, devise and bequeath to my Surviving children equaly among them

11. and lastly I nominate, constitute and appoint my Son Henery W. Yongue, George H. Miller and R. Wade Brice to be the Executors of this my last will and testament, and I also invest them with power to make all such sales, and execute such conveyances as may be incident

thereto, or directed by the will or if either Should be dead or refuse to qualify then such as do qualify to have Such power."

December 10, 1860 and in the Eighty fifth year of American Independence
The State of South Carolina
From Alachua County Ancient Records
Will Book B pages 015-020

ACKNOWLEDGEMENTS

Without the efforts of Jim Powell, J. K. "Buddy" Irby, and an army of volunteer transcriptionists making the history of Alachua County more accessible to the public, this book never would have been written.

In 1998 Jim Powell, a genealogist and former construction worker, stumbled across an 1840's record book in Alachua County's ancient records storage area while researching his family tree. Noting that the faded cursive handwriting was very difficult to read, Jim took it upon himself to begin typing up transcriptions of these decaying documents.[3]

Enter J. K. "Buddy" Irby, the Alachua County Clerk of Court, who recognized the importance of what Jim was doing and offered him a job in the ancient records archive to help make it easier for the public to access these historical records. Over more than 20 years, Powell acted as the ancient records coordinator and webmaster, spearheading efforts to digitize these records into an online database. Covering a period dating back to the 1820's through the early 1900's, more than a half million pages of these historical hand-written documents have been scanned into the system. Thanks to the heroic efforts of a host of willing volunteers doing their best to decode the difficult to read cursive handwriting found in the faded original texts, tens of thousands of pages of documents have been transcribed and made searchable online.[4] Although Jim Powell retired in 2023, the Alachua County Ancient Records Project continues. Karen McColl currently heads up the efforts, and volunteer transcriptionists are always welcome.

My deepest thanks to everyone who has ever been involved in the ancient records project. Your efforts are invaluable in preserving history to share with current and future generations.

A huge shout out to Stephanie Chandler, Amberly Finarelli, and the rest of the crew at Authority Publishing for so expertly shepherding me through the publishing process. I honestly don't know where I'd be without you guys guiding me throughout.

Thank you to Karen Kirkman, President and Historian at the Historic Haile Homestead at Kanapaha Plantation for sharing your extensive knowledge of the area and to Chloe Richardson of the Matheson History Museum who was instrumental in guiding me to more writings about Alachua County's history. I'm also thankful for the speakers of the eye-opening lecture series called The Other Book: Black History in Alachua County. In addition to Karen Kirkman, featured speakers included Dr. Rik Stevenson and Dr. Courtney Moore-Taylor from the University of Florida African American Studies Program as well as Dr. Michelle Dunlap, Professor Emeritus of Connecticut College Dept. of Human Development. Although I've learned so much, I know I still have so much more to learn.

I am eternally grateful to my husband, Curt DeGroff, who has always supported my dreams, and to my sons Kyle and Ryan and my daughter in law Alana who are always there to cheer me on. I love you all.

RESOURCES

Alachua County Ancient Records online archives can be found at https://alachuaclerk.org/archive/

Other resources:

Alachua County. "In the Shadow of Plantations - The History of Enslavement in Alachua County (researched, written, and narrated by the late Dr. Patricia Hilliard-Nunn)." February 17, 2021. YouTube video, 30:00. https://youtu.be/dnts2Zwl4Qc?si=RJuw9qXfjafjXlqg

Buchholz, Frederick W. *History of Alachua County Florida: Narrative and Biographical.* The Record Company - Printers, 1929.

Caudle, Everett W., "Settlement Patterns in Alachua County, Florida, 1850-1860," Florida Historical Quarterly Vol. 67 No. 4 (Apr., 1989), pp. 434-437

Chesnut, Mary Boykin Miller. *A Diary From Dixie.* HarperTorch, 2014.

Davis, Jess G. *History of Gainesville, Florida: With Biographical Sketches of Families.* 1966.

Hildreth, Charles H., and Merlin G. Cox. *History of Gainesville Florida 1854-1979.* Alachua County Historical Society, 1981.

Jenkins, Lizzie PRB. *Alachua County Florida (Black America Series)*. Arcadia Publishing, 2007.

Kirkman, Karen and Kevin McCarthy. *The Historic Haile Homestead at Kanapaha Plantation: An Illustrated History*. CreateSpace Independent Publishing, 2014.

Mitchell, Olga Fenton and Magbie, Gloria Fenton. *The Life and Times of Joseph E. Clark: From Slavery to Town Father (Eatonville, Florida)*. CreateSpace Independent Publishing, 2012.

Rivers, Larry Eugene. *Slavery in Florida: Territorial Days to Emancipation*. University Press of Florida, 2009.

Samuel Proctor Oral History Program. "Enslavement in Alachua County (presented by Dr. Courtney Taylor, Ms. Karen Kirkman, Dr. Ron Nutter, and Dr. Rik Stevenson)." February 8, 2025. YouTube video, 1:08:59. https://www.youtube.com/watch?v=sFrqmER1K0U

Smith, Clint. *How the Word is Passed: A Reckoning with the History of Slavery Across America*. Little, Brown and Company, 2021.

Smith, Julia Floyd. *Slavery and Plantation Growth in Antebellum Florida, 1821-1860*. Library Press at UF, 2018.

Stowe, Harriet Beecher. *Dred; a Tale of the Great Dismal Swamp, Together With Anti-Slavery Tales and Papers, and Life in Florida after the War*. Houghton, Mifflin & Co, 1896.

United States Work Projects Administration. *Slave Narratives: A Folk History of Slavery in the United States from Interviews with Former Slaves, Volume III, Florida Narratives*. Legare Street Press, 2022.

Williams, Horace Randall, Editor. *No Man's Yoke on My Shoulders (Real Voices, Real History)*. Blair, 2006

ENDNOTES

1   Everett W. Caudle, "Settlement Patterns in Alachua County, Florida, 1850-1860," Florida Historical Quarterly Vol. 67 No. 4 (Apr., 1989), pp. 428-440

2   From Florida Memory - State Library and Archives of Florida https://www.floridamemory.com/learn/research-tools/guides/civilwarguide/history.php)

3   McKinney, Carl. "Wizard Keeps Watch Over Nearly 200 Years of Alachua County History." Gainesville Sun, April 30, 2013

4   McKinney, "Wizard Keeps Watch Over Nearly 200 Years of Alachua County History"

INDEX

G

H